BARCODE IN BACK

TOURISM AND MOBILITIES

Local–Global Connections

TOURISM AND MOBILITIES

Local–Global Connections

Edited by

Peter M. Burns and Marina Novelli

Centre for Tourism Policy Studies
School of Service Management
University of Brighton
UK

www.cabi.org

CABI is a trading name of CAB International

CABI Head Office
Nosworthy Way
Wallingford
Oxfordshire OX10 8DE
UK

Tel: +44 (0)1491 832111
Fax: +44 (0)1491 833508
E-mail: cabi@cabi.org
Website: www.cabi.org

CABI North American Office
875 Massachusetts Avenue
7th Floor
Cambridge, MA 02139
USA

Tel: +1 617 395 4056
Fax: +1 617 354 6875
E-mail: cabi-nao@cabi.org

A catalogue record for this book is available from the British Library, London, UK.

Library of Congress Cataloging-in-Publication Data

Tourism and mobilities: local–global connections/Edited by Peter Burns & Marina Novelli.
     p. cm.
   ISBN 978-1-84593-404-0 (alk. paper)
1. Tourism. 2. Tourism--Social aspects. I. Burns, Peter (Peter M.) II. Novelli, Marina.

   G155.A1T5893488 2008
   338.4'791--dc22

                                                                        2007044669

ISBN: 978 1 84593 404 0

Typeset by AMA DataSet Ltd, UK.
Printed and bound in the UK by Cromwell Press, Trowbridge.

Contents

Contributors

Editors

Peter M. Burns is Professor of International Tourism and Development and founding Director of the Centre for Tourism Policy Studies (CENTOPS), University of Brighton. Prior to this, he was Head of the Department of Leisure, Hospitality and Tourism at the University of Luton (RAE grade 4).

Peter has two streams of current research. First, the roles and responsibilities throughout the tourism value chain in climate change. The approach thus far has been to identify a series of policy and business paradoxes (cf. http://www.icis. unimaas.nl/eclat/Paris/papers/burns_bibbings_paper.pdf). The findings have prompted the first of a series of online surveys to further investigate attitudes and values among various stakeholder groups.

The second stream, 'A Secret History of Holidays' (funded by the Community University Partnership Programme in cooperation with the Clinical Research Centre for Health Professions and Oxford Brookes University), uses private archive material and interviews to capture experiences and memories of the first generation of post-war tourists. Outputs include a short film, which was presented at the CENTOPS 2007 conference.

Peter is the author of numerous papers on sustainable tourism and of the internationally acclaimed publication, *An Introduction to Tourism and Anthropology*, which has been translated into both Japanese and Portuguese.

Dr Peter M. Burns
Centre for Tourism Policy Studies
School of Service Management
University of Brighton
Darley Road, Eastbourne
East Sussex BN20 7UR
UK

(t) +44 (0)1273 643897
(f) +44 (0)1273 643619
(e) p.m.burns@brighton.ac.uk

Marina Novelli is a senior lecturer in tourism development and management at the Centre for Tourism Policy Studies, School of Service Management, University of Brighton, UK. She is a geographer with a background in rural geography and an interest in development studies applied to tourism. Her most recent research is in the fields of niche tourism, rural tourism, consumptive tourism, responsible and community-based tourism development in sub-Saharan Africa and southern Europe.

Dr Marina Novelli
Centre for Tourism Policy Studies
School of Service Management
University of Brighton
Darley Road, Eastbourne
East Sussex BN20 7UR
UK
(t) +44 (0)1273 643300
(f) +44 (0)1273 643619
(e) mn19@brighton.ac.uk

Authors

Rebecca Jane Bennett researches the conceptualization of the backpacker within popular culture. Using documentaries, blogs, tourist guides and fiction, she investigates how theories of race, nation, class and global injustice are 'managed' by the backpackers.

Rebecca Jane Bennett
School of Media Communication and Culture
Murdoch University
Western Australia
Australia
(e) R.Bennett@curtin.edu.au; rebeccabennett@planetvelocity.net

Tim Coles is Senior Lecturer in Management in the School of Business and Economics at the University of Exeter, UK, where he is also Co-Director of the Centre for Tourism Studies. He was an invited guest editor of the *International Journal of Tourism Research* for its theme issue on Tourism and EU Enlargement in 2005. His research interests include tourism, mobility and transnationalism.

Dr Tim Coles
Centre for Tourism Studies
Department of Management
School of Business and Economics
University of Exeter

Streatham Court, Rennes Drive
Exeter, Devon EX4 4PU
UK
(t) +44 (0)1392 264441
(f) +44 (0)1392 263242
(e) t.e.coles@ex.ac.uk

Sabine Dörry is a research assistant and PhD candidate. Her research interests focus on the economic geography of globalization, spatial firm networks and regional economic development, as well as on tourism geography, on the geography of services and geographic real estate research.

Sabine Dörry
Department of Human Geography
Johann Wolfgang Goethe-University of Frankfurt/Main
Robert-Mayer-Str. 8, 60325 Frankfurt am Main
Germany
(t) +49 (0)69 798 28482
(f) +49 (0)69 798 28173
(e) s.doerry@em.uni-frankfurt.de

David Timothy Duval is Senior Lecturer and Director of International Business at the School of Business, University of Otago, Dunedin, New Zealand. He has written on issues of transnationalism in the context of mobilities. His more recent research interests centre on aviation management. He has published on issues of aeropolitics, alliances, international air service agreements and aviation emissions management.

Dr David Timothy Duval
Department of Tourism
School of Business, University of Otago
4th Floor, Commerce Building, Cnr Clyde & Union Streets
PO Box 56, Dunedin
New Zealand
(t) +64 3 479 5398
(f) +64 3 479 9034
(e) dduval@business.otago.ac.nz

Wael Salah Fahmi was trained as an architect at Cairo University and received his PhD in Planning and Landscape from the University of Manchester, UK (1994). He currently teaches architecture and urban design as an Associate Professor of Urbanism at the Architecture Department, Helwan University in Cairo (since 1996).

On the one hand, as a visiting academic at the University of Manchester he has been working collaboratively (with Keith Sutton at the School of Environment and Development) on Greater Cairo's housing crisis (submitted to the journal *Cities*) and urban growth problems (published in *Cities*). His research focuses on rehabilitation and gentrification of historical Cairo districts for tourism development (journals *Habitat International* and *International Development Planning*

Review); and the impact on the surrounding urban poverty areas and population eviction within cemetery informal settlements (cities of the dead) (journal *Arab World Geographer*) and Zabaleen garbage collectors (journals *Environment and Urbanization* and *Habitat International*). Currently he is working on two research collaborations: Cairo's late 19th-century and early 20th-century European architectural heritage; and Greater Cairo's suburban vacant dwellings.

On the other hand, through his Urban Design Experimental Research Studio (UDERS) he explores deconstructive experimentation within urban space, postmodern spatiality and representation of city imaging employing narratives, digital photo imaging, video stills and architectural diagrams.

Dr Wael Salah Fahmi
Associate Professor of Urbanism
Helwan University
Cairo
Egypt
Principal – UDERS (Urban Design Experimental Research Studio)
34 Abdel Hamid Lotfi Street
Mohandessein, Giza/Cairo
Egypt 12311
(t) +2 02 33370485
(f) +2 02 33351630
(e) uders2004@yahoo.co.uk; uders2003@yahoo.co.uk

Tim Gale is a Senior Lecturer in tourism geography, in the Faculty of the Built Environment at the University of the West of England, Bristol. His research interests include the relationship between late 20th-century processes of economic restructuring and cultural change and the built environment of old water resorts, new forms of tourism production and consumption (e.g. cyber- and ecotourism, urban beaches), and environmental sustainability and tourism development. He is particularly interested in the potential for new knowledge creation, with regard to each of these areas of enquiry, offered by: the so-called 'mobilities turn', integrating leisure and tourism, transport, and migration studies; and critical realism as a philosophy of/for the social sciences.

Dr Tim Gale
Faculty of the Built Environment
University of the West of England
Frenchay Campus, Coldharbour Lane
Bristol, BS16 1QY
UK
(t) +44 (0)117 32 82525
(f) +44 (0)117 32 83002
(e) Tim.Gale@uwe.ac.uk

Frank Go is a professor and holds the Bewetour chair at the Rotterdam School of Management, Erasmus University. His research interests focus on innovation management, particularly how to bridge the gap between information technologies and social interaction to support decision making in organizations, brand identity and image formation for sustainable tourism destination development. He serves on the editorial board of seven international journals and is visiting research professor at the Open University Business School, Catholic University Leuven and Rikkyo University, Tokyo, Japan. Prior to his present post he gained experience in the USA, Canada and Hong Kong.

Dr Frank Go
Rotterdam School of Management
Erasmus University
The Netherlands
(e) fgo@rsm.nl

Stefan Gössling's work focuses on sustainable tourism. He is mostly interested in aspects of energy and transport, and the interrelationship of tourism and climate change. He is also working on the sustainability of tourism-related development processes in islands in the western Indian Ocean.

Stefan Gössling
Department of Service Management
Lund University
Box 882, 251 08 Helsingborg
Sweden
(t) +46 42 35 66 29
(f) +46 42 35 66 60
(e) stefan.gossling@msm.lu.se

C. Michael Hall is a professor of marketing in the College of Business and Economics, University of Canterbury, New Zealand, and Docent in the Department of Geography, University of Oulu, Oulu, Finland. Co-editor of *Current Issues in Tourism*, he has published widely on topics of tourism and human mobility, regional development, environmental history and gastronomy. His current research focuses on issues such as global environmental change, servicescapes, regional development and tourism planning and policy.

Professor C. Michael Hall
Department of Management
College of Business and Economics
University of Canterbury
Private Bag 4800, Christchurch
New Zealand
(t) +64 3 364 2987 ext 8612 or +64 3 364 2606 (secretary)
(f) +64 3 364 2020
(e) michael.hall@canterbury.ac.nz

Michael O'Regan completed a 2-year research Masters of Business Studies at the University of Limerick, Ireland in 1997. He has worked alongside the National Tourism Development Authority of Ireland; Gulliver – Ireland's Information and Reservation Service; and as Marketing Executive for Wicklow County Tourism, Ireland before starting a PhD programme at the School of Service Management, University of Brighton, UK. Michael is a recipient of the MIS Faculty PhD

Studentship, which is jointly supervised by the Centre for Tourism Policy Studies (CENTOPS) and the School of Computing and Information Sciences (CMIS). During 2006, he was awarded a Royal Geographical Society with Institute of British Geographers (IBG) Travel Bursary.

Michael O'Regan
Centre for Tourism Policy Studies
School of Service Management, University of Brighton
PhD Suite, Greynore 2 Bldg
Darley Road, Eastbourne BN20 7UR
UK
(t) +44 (0)1273 643679
(f) +44 (0)1273 643619
(e) M.J.O'Regan@brighton.ac.uk

Paul Peeters studies the relations between tourism transport and the environment, with a focus on climate change. He started his career as an aircraft engineer at Fokker Aircraft, but worked also as a researcher at the Dutch Energy Research Centre on wind energy and took up research on transport and the environment at several Dutch institutes and his own consultancy. Since 2002, he has been a professor teaching and researching sustainable transport for tourism.

Paul Peeters
NHTV Breda University of Applied Sciences
Centre for Sustainable Tourism and Transport
PO Box 3917, 4800 DX Breda
The Netherlands
(t) +31 76 5302203
(f) +31 76 5302775
(e) peeters.p@nhtv.nl

Erik van 't Klooster is a PhD candidate at the Centre for Tourism Management, Department of Marketing Management, Rotterdam School of Management, Erasmus University. His research is on communication and control issues of service delivery in a global international internship network. As a tutor he is involved in bachelor and master marketing courses in the fields of event tourism and hospitality management. In the past years he has guided numerous students during their educational travel experiences such as international internships and international business projects to, among others, Vietnam and Malaysia. He has contributed to various tourism consultancy projects for Maxxton, ANWB (Royal Dutch Touring Club), Hotel School The Hague, Toeristiche Informatie Opleiding (TIO) and Nuffic.

Erik van 't Klooster
Centre for Tourism Management
Department of Marketing Management
Rotterdam School of Management
Erasmus University
Rotterdam

The Netherlands
(e) eklooster@rsm.nl

Jeroen van Wijk is an assistant professor at the Department of Business-Society Management, Rotterdam School of Management, Erasmus University. He studied sociology and political science, and holds a PhD in international relations. His main research interest is business and development, and he uses global value chain analysis and institutional theory to analyse, among other things, the role of tourism multinationals in the economic development of sub-Saharan African countries. Due to his coaching of Rotterdam School of Management (RSM) students during their international internships in non-Western countries, he became interested in studying the learning effects of educational travel.

Dr Jeroen van Wijk
Department of Business-Society Management
Rotterdam School of Management
Erasmus University, Room T7-16
Burg. Oudlaan 50, 3062 PA Rotterdam
The Netherlands
(e) jwijk@rsm.nl

Foreword

This collection of chapters represents a further set of moves that will transform in far-reaching ways the relations between 'tourism' and 'mobilities'. Such a transformed relationship coincides with my own trajectory. I came to mobilities through a long and circuitous pathway that began in Morecambe, a once proud but now run-down seaside resort in north-west England.

Some two decades ago I began to examine, initially in Morecambe, how various places can only be understood as centres for the complex production and consumption of tourist services. Further, such tourist services are not insignificant or simply reflective of broader economic and social processes. They are important or constitutive in their own right. The development of such services is part of a process of structural differentiation, as 'tourist times and spaces' separate themselves off as distinct organized systems with their own rules and dynamics. Part of that differentiation is to generate new professional forms of expertise, including tourism degree programmes.

But as that modern process of structural differentiation gathered pace it came to be countered by what I saw as postmodern de-differentiation. There was the implosion of 'tourism' into a wide range of other systems, of shopping, entertainment, migration, sport, leisure, friendship, business, conferences, sex, family life and so on. There is the end of 'tourism' per se.

Thus our thinking needs to move on. The notion of 'mobilities' seems to provide the basis for examining these multiple overlapping systems of life, which presuppose the corporeal movement of people, as well as complex intersections with the movements of objects, images, ideas and messages. Examining such mobilities is not simply a useful corrective to static notions of social life but is itself transformative of social science. A mobilities turn fundamentally repositions the analyses of tourist times and tourist spaces. They are in a way nowhere and everywhere in societies where there are few limits as yet on what can be turned into zones of pain and pleasure.

To return to Morecambe and two recent mobilities: cockle pickers were transported for a better life from China and around 20 died in the icy waters of Morecambe Bay; and the arrival of urban design company Urban Splash is transforming the wonderful but derelict art deco Midland Hotel into a new icon. These illustrate some of the new mobilities that are examined in rich detail in this book.

Professor John Urry
Centre for Mobilities Research
Lancaster University
Lancaster, UK
2007

Acknowledgements

A number of people have contributed significantly to the realization of this book. First of all, we would like to thank Mercedita (Merz) Hoare for her assistance in the completion of the manuscript, and for her attention to detail and good nature in promptly addressing the editors' demands.

We are particularly grateful to all those colleagues who have refereed the chapters contained in this volume, whose names remain anonymous for the purpose of maintaining integrity.

The photo on the cover was selected from Marina Novelli's (Thailand) personal collection.

Introduction

PETER M. BURNS AND MARINA NOVELLI

> I left Tangier, my birthplace, on Thursday, 2nd Jajab 725 [14th June 1325], being
> at that time twenty-two years of age, with the intention of making the Pilgrimage to
> the Holy House [at Mecca] and the Tomb of the Prophet [in Medina]. I set out
> alone, finding no companion to cheer the way with friendly intercourse, and no
> party of travellers with whom to associate myself. Swayed by an over-mastering
> impulse within me, and a long-cherished desire to visit the glorious sanctuaries, I
> resolved to quit all my friends and tear myself away from my home.

These opening lines from Ibn Battuta's account (Ross and Power, 1929: 43) of
his epic journey around the early Islamic world of Asia and Africa (1325–1354)
emphasize that the deeply rooted desire for travel has been present in humans
for centuries: a rather obvious point, but one that is so embedded that a timely
reminder is not amiss. The difference for citizens of the 21st century is that this
desire for mobility has been heightened: for the very poor often through displacement, climate change and economic migration needs, and for those in
richer countries to help combat ennui resulting from 'having it all' – the idea that
with material benefits in place, all that is left in a spiritually devoid world is travel.
In a time of globalization challenges, mobility and its emerging patterns may help
in making sense of the evolving nature of the relationships between global and
local realities, rich and poor regions of the world, and 'old' and 'new' leisure and
tourism patterns: all perfectly captured by Franklin's notion of 'how tourism
came to be a heterogeneous assemblage "at large" in the world, remaking the
world anew as a touristic world' (2004: 277).

It can be seen then that through the sociology of mobility and Franklin's version of the sociology of 'ordering' the concept of 'tourism' works in a number of
ways: as a description of leisure activity; as global business consumed at a local
level; and as a condition of postmodernism shaping the world we live in. Tourism as a topic for analysis sets out to make theoretical sense of multiple mobile
cultures. Moreover, it can be learnt from MacCannell (1992: 1) that:

Tourism is a primary ground for the production of new cultural forms on a global base. In the name of tourism, capital and modernized peoples have been deployed to the most remote regions of the world, farther than any army was ever sent. Institutions have been established to support this deployment, not just hotels, restaurants, and transportation systems, but restorations of ancient shrines, development of local handcrafts for sale to tourists, and rituals performed for tourists. In short, tourism is not just an aggregate of merely commercial activities; it is also an ideological framing of history, nature, and tradition; a framing that has the power to reshape culture and nature to its own needs.

Given the power that both MacCannell and Franklin attribute to tourism, it becomes obvious that tourism both as business and as a cultural phenomenon extracts value from destinations for the benefit of metropolitan tourism corporations. This extraction is metaphysical as well as financial: given that appropriation of 'Other' in a hypermobile (for one side at least) 'conqueror–native' relationship (Fanon, 1986) is a distinct characteristic of contemporary tourism. The size of global tourism adds weight to the assertion of power relationships dominating the consumption of place, space and Other; we end up with a continuum of mobility with the poles represented by economic need at one end and hyper-mobility at the other. Both ends have one thing in common: desperation. Whatever the definitional ambiguities, tourism is a phenomenon of interlocking networks (Fadeeva, 2005), mobilities (Urry, 2002) and modern mythologies (Selwyn, 1996). Tourism combines not only services, landscapes and culture, but also intangibles such as hospitality, customs and curiosities: a combination of services and enticing images as Lanfant (1980) describes it, but above all an integral part of ephemeral, complex global capitalism and the 'liquid modernity' (Bauman, 1997) of modern life 'in which nothing keeps its shape, and social forms are constantly changing at great speed, radically transforming the experience of being human' (Cummings, 2004).

As Urry is constantly reminding us, the desire for temporary leisure mobility is deeply ingrained in post-industrial cultures. It has changed from an aspirational possibility of discretionary income to the 'expectational will' as we might term it, epitomized by Pine and Gilmore's (1999) suggestion of an emerging 'experience economy' – conceptually not so very far removed from Maslow's work in the 1950s on the desire of humans to seek 'peak experiences', which he described as:

Feelings of limitless horizons opening up to the vision, the feeling of being simultaneously more powerful and also more helpless than one ever was before, the feeling of ecstasy and wonder and awe, the loss of placement in time and space with, finally, the conviction that something extremely important and valuable had happened, so that the subject was to some extent transformed and strengthened even in his daily life by such experiences.

From a research perspective, much of the established, dominant technical oeuvre on how to 'do' tourism has been dismissed on the grounds that 'Middle range theories of motivation, decision modelling, and even destination image . . . do little to bridge fairly substantial gaps in our knowledge of tourism as a representation of contemporary social systems' (Coles *et al.*, 2005). In other words, we are generally aware of the mechanics of the tourism sector and how it works, but have frustratingly little knowledge as to the deeper causes and consequences of mobility, which is a term increasingly used within all sorts of research about tourism.

As the contemporary world that produces tourists becomes increasingly complex, it has been argued that there is no such thing as tourism: only production, consumption and mobility (Urry, 2001; Burns, 2005). That said, over two decades ago, something significant was happening with Fridgen (1984: 33) urging tourism researchers to focus on movement with the following prescient advice: 'Travellers, not laboratory subjects, must be studied in transit, at hotels, in their homes, and on site.' Given the propensity of and predilection for travel experiences in modern society, the study of tourists and tourism comes very close to being a study of *everyday* mobility.

Heritage, arts, architecture, landscapes, places, space and everyday leisure pursuits are commoditized and drawn into a number of diverse businesses that do not see themselves as having any connection with tourism. Yet their activities are supported by sophisticated global structures of a distinctly touristic nature with airlines, reservation systems and product/destination marketing campaigns interconnecting, co-joining, and morphing into new forms and temporary alliances. Urry (2001) captures the spirit of this age with his reference – and passing nod to Bauman – to 'a shift from solid, fixed modernity' to a much more fluid and speeded-up 'liquid modernity'. This speeded-up version of life and culture, characterized by bodies on the move and travelling cultures, does two things. First, it reminds one of Roland Robertson's (1992) early dealings with globalization as the 'compression of the world and intensification of consciousness' – and how useful this is becoming in trying to understand tourism. Secondly, it emphasizes the idea that the flows and 'scapes (Appadurai, 1996) of tourism, being a privileged form of mobility, in the greater sense, cannot be disaggregated from globalization as a complex social phenomenon.

In its most reductive definition, tourism combines destinations, tourists and locals via personal, physical and electronic webs of commercial interconnections and mobilities. However, closer examination reveals not static destinations but fluid 'scapes and places that are imagined, interpreted and engineered; tourists are not the hapless, predictable dupes described in earlier tourism works (e.g. Turner and Ash, 1975; Graburn, 1977; Krippendorf, 1987) but agents in their own travel performances who choose to glance rather than gaze (Chaney, 2002). Locals are not simply victims of impacts and 'Othering' – an idea still being promulgated by the likes of Nowicka (2007) – but differentiated actors negotiating with, contributing to, and taking from the industry as it unfolds in their regions and territories. This corporeal co-presence (Urry, 2002), which is the lifeblood of 'places to play' (Urry and Sheller, 2004), is complex and requires sophisticated analysis – especially if we consider tourism to be a social phenomenon that blurs distinctions between idealized representations, liminalities and the politics of location. If we accept this proposition, then the literature surrounding – and arising from – tourism becomes central to understanding the relationships between global and local cultures, thus 'home' societies and people on the move.

The paradox, however, is that existing literature is bounded by disciplines, notably: anthropology, economics, geography, sociology and business/business history. The multiple narratives from these approaches tend to exacerbate differences rather than create opportunities for osmosis, synthesis and creativity in tourism thinking.

Just by way of a further illustration, Fig. I.1 shows a scenario for the way in which culture, mobility and business might come together to form a new future shape for tourism. It is a schematic elaboration whereby tourism acts as a mediator between cultural heritage and cultural industries coming together as an expression of co-presence and mobilities, which contribute – somewhat tentatively – towards the experience economy (mentioned earlier) as a new shape for tourism. At the juncture of tourism and culture (Fig. I.1, left) constituents blend together to act as a reminder as to the components of cultural heritage. On the right-hand side, a variety of commercial media, events and experiences form the 'cultural industries'– in this case being defined as 'those institutions', profit and non-profit, being 'directly involved in the production of social meaning' (Hesmondhalgh, 2002: 11). Each of these institutions induces mobility of one form or another: both direct and indirect. But, most importantly, the whole picture is drawn together by mobility and a sense of 'people on the move', increased population circulation, and the idea that travel on a daily basis is a right somewhat taken for granted in the rich countries.

Taking the definitions of mobility to be as diverse as 'an actor's competence to realize certain projects and plans while being on the move' (Mayer, no date (ND)) to the broader view of Lancaster University's Centre for Mobilities Research

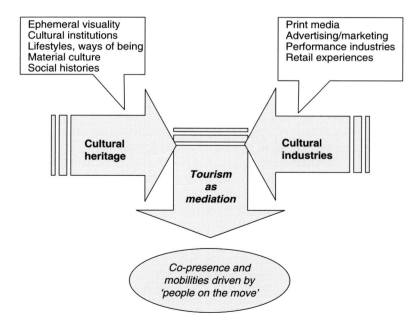

Fig. I.1.   The future shape for tourism?

(CeMoRe) in which 'mobilities encompasses both the large scale movement of people, objects, capital, and information across the world, as well as the more local processes of daily transportation, movement through public space, and the travel of material things within everyday life', our aim is to communicate a series of ideas grounded in the present discussions on how 'mobility studies' can help enrich and enlighten our understanding of tourism. With this contextualizing discussion behind us we now turn to the contents of the present edited volume.

In Chapter 1 Tim Gale picks up the idea of the 'end of tourism' (the theme of the fourth annual symposium on issues in tourism held at Brighton University in summer 2005) and explores the capacity for 'endings' in tourism in the context of wider debates on mobilities, sustainable development and the risk society. He adopts a more literal interpretation of John Urry's ideas on the 'end of tourism', extending his thesis beyond the social construction of leisure travel – which, it is argued, has become less distinct and more ordinary – to encompass a number of issues that problematize existing notions of tourism as an industry and a phenomenon in ascendancy. These include the decline of traditional seaside resorts, the unsustainability of 'old' and 'new' tourism alike, and the potentially deleterious effects of macro environmental and political crises such as climate change and the 'war on terror'.

According to Michael Hall (Chapter 2), notions of mobility have long been circulating in literature on the geography of tourism. Many of these ideas of mobility have been a focal point for research in regional, transport and spatial systems analysis, which, being often highly quantitative, may seem at first glance far away from notions of mobility as currently expressed in sociology, cultural studies and cultural geography. However, they in fact share a common intellectual heritage. His chapter provides a distinctive account of the development of geographical accounts of mobilities and addresses some of the ontological and epistemological issues that they raise, including intersections between the 'old' and 'new' social physics, issues of scale of analysis and method, as well as the sociology of knowledge of tourism mobilities. Also he argues that there is great value in engaging in multiple understandings of mobilities in order to better inform method, theory and debates surrounding human behaviour in space and time, including the issue of whether there are laws of mobility. The chapter concludes by arguing that although notions of grand theory in the social sciences are usually relegated to the position of wishful positivist thinking there are nevertheless certain principles that apply to an improved understanding of accessibility and mobility issues in tourism.

In Chapter 3, Wael Salah Fahmi explores a mobilities connection with urban semiotics within what he calls Moscow's 'post-Soviet' contested Metro(scape) enacting a variety of (re-/de-)constructed local identities within emerging global urban spaces which are subjected to branded global–local ('glocal') landscapes with distinct signs and billboards, representing the corporate identity of postmodern spatiality. As spatial infrastructure and venue for contested social spaces, post-communist Metro(scape)'s spatiality is phenomenologically experienced as 'a series of stages' where individuals – petty traders, commuters, urban youth – assume different identities under space–time compression, and is semiologically represented as a collective collage. The chapter proposes a (de)constructive narrative of a transit journey of dissolved boundaries (within) Moscow's underground Metro, a situational representation of a navigation with the camera's lens inside-out of transit spaces within Moscow's post-Soviet Metro(scape), employing digital pixels and collages.

Tim Coles (Chapter 4) takes an expansive view of tourism and mobility, referring to 'enhanced mobility' as a defining feature of contemporary times. Stereotypical readings of tourism emphasize the wider range of destinations visitors may access and the enhanced scope of activities that tourists may undertake in the temporal bubbles of their vacations. Such a view obscures more important and subtle consequences of changes in mobility, not least those associated with the connections between tourism and other forms of human movement. Contemporary tourism analysts, by and large, continue to ring-fence tourist activities from other types of episodes, when in fact tourism is more routinely and complexly embedded in an individual's temporal and spatial life path. One significant, but often overlooked, strand binding tourism with other forms of human movement is citizenship. This chapter explores how 'tourism', as an activity and as a concept, featured in wider public debates in Britain concerning migration, as a result of the recent 2004 European Union (EU) enlargement from 15 to 25 member states. Media representations of changes in relative mobilities and flows of citizens between the UK and Eastern Europe reveal that multiple interpretations of citizenship and tourism were invoked tactically and flexibly in discussions of the merits and (potential) outcomes of enlargement. On the one hand, tourism was connected as an activity with new conceptualizations of citizenship to highlight the benefits of enlargement for UK residents; on the other, in a more abstract sense, tourism was deliberately connected by means of older, 'traditional' views of citizenship to (im-)migration and used by the government to address, even appease, the concerns of the anti-European lobby. As the case of the emergence of 'benefits tourism' demonstrates, far from being separate from other forms of human movement, tourism is not only intimately linked with them, but also used as a primary means of making sense of them.

Without question, a major consideration within the new literature on (temporary) mobilities has strongly advocated for wider, aggregate conceptualizations of how movement literally and figuratively transforms meanings of place and space. In interrogating this phenomenon, it has been shown how places are transformed, how they are at once as dynamic as they are static, and how shifts in allegiance to places can often be rather subtle. For Chapter 5, however, David Duval wished to lightly revisit social science-based notions of identity and how these might apply to understanding mobilities as an inadvertent, yet conscious, personal exercise in relating person to place. In so doing, the author traces some of his own conceptual thoughts and ruminations, and also introduces data withdrawn (i.e. context-evacuated) from an online discussion forum 'thread' where advice is dispensed on 'how to look less American' while travelling. He attempts a rough discourse analysis and concludes by suggesting that considerations of temporary mobility, of which tourism is most certainly an example, are manifested through the negotiation of tradition, nationalism, citizenship and pleasure.

Students have become increasingly internationally mobile. One of the reasons for their increased mobility is that the ongoing internationalization of business translates into career opportunities, which require students to develop an internationally flexible mindset. Educational travel, the international internship in particular, is important to familiarize students with organizations that employ an international staff and operate in countries with divergent value systems, economic development levels and institutional infrastructures. In Chapter 6, Jeroen van Wijk, Frank Go and Erik van 't Klooster address the impacts of internships on cross-cultural competencies of business students. They report on self-perceived learning effects of internships by 168 Dutch business school alumni. The findings indicate that internships served in countries that required students to cross their cultural and economic 'home zone' resulted in significantly higher learning effects. This was not only in terms of appreciation and understanding of other cultures, but also in a better understanding of international issues and of local stakeholder perceptions.

Our world is one that has few barriers. Aside from having the right to fly where we want (providing our passports are the right kind), when we want, at a price we can afford and the ability to communicate with (almost) anyone anytime (from anywhere), our world today is so networked that strangers no longer exist, but are simply connections waiting to happen. Internet cafés are one of the places where online connections are made. Like business lounges they are regular fixtures in both travel areas and travel lives, often serving as magnets for travellers looking for places to pass time and connect with home. There is increasing interest in understanding how the mobility of communications and information technologies is impacting upon contemporary, connected society, especially in terms of how it may be influencing the way people conceptualize the public and private sectors of their lives and how social relationships, even those conducted offline, are mediated by Internet technology in a networked technospace. In Chapter 7, Michael O'Regan explores how networked technology is made ordinary at an Internet café and how backpackers use the Internet as 'non-places' in the form of Internet cafés, and how this use may be impacting the experience of being an independent traveller.

According to Rebecca Bennett (Chapter 8), touristic popular culture and critical tourist theory is disproportionately focused on the scene of the *self*, especially in relation to the individualized discourse of the independent traveller. Backpacker-inflected popular culture (and its recent emergence as an object of study in tourism) is dominated by material written by tourists for tourists or by theorists about tourist culture. Tourists are not the only identities activated through tourism. Arguing that the individualized, flexible and paradoxical independent travel modality is closely aligned to the late capitalist consumer market, popular and academic backpacker narrations provide critical insights into the complex articulation of power in global leisure mobilities. Demonstrating how backpacking is defined through the absence or subjective presence of *otherness* allows for a more tangible and problematic reading of mobile leisure classes to emerge as a necessary focus for tourism critique. The configuration of otherness is an important facet of critical tourism theory because it exemplifies how the industry maintains and justifies its globalizing power. Orientalist discursive practices persist in individualizing times, and threads of imperial power extend beyond the revival of simplistic political East/West differences. Examples in backpacker theory and popular culture show how late capitalism is generating an obsession with the globally powerful self at the expense of apathy with regard to the tourist's others.

In Chapter 9, Peter Burns and Michael O'Regan look at the growing proliferation of digital information, from place-bound desktops to pocket-sized portable digital technology, which has come to facilitate the mobility of modern society. Mobile technologies, from MP3 music players and mobile phones to PDAs (personal digital assistants), have made their users more networked, more connected, more secure and more mobile, freeing them and digital information from desktops, offices and homes, creating new relationships and meanings, and making information on the go indispensable to their modern existence.

While numerous studies have indicated mobile technologies, particularly mobile phones, are reconfiguring work, leisure and the way social interactions take place, they have tended to ignore, downplay and avoid the importance of movable sound technologies. This chapter explores how budget travellers use a connected, pedestrian, personal and portable mobile sound technology – the iPod, a mobile auditory experience kept close to one's body – in everyday travel life.

The knowledge about climate change in industrialized societies is diffuse. While a substantial share of the population in Europe seems well informed about the very phenomenon of climate change, uncertainty seems to prevail in terms of its seriousness, its consequences for society and action that needs to be taken. More specifically, many people seem to believe that there is no scientific consensus about climate change, and that individual behavioural change is obsolete in the face of uncertainty. Such a 'psychology of denial' seems particularly strong in the context of air travel, the fastest growing transport sector. Since the early 1960s, air travel has turned from a luxury form of mobility for the wealthy few into a contemporary form of hypermobility. This hypermobility is characterized by promises of cheap high-speed travel, as well as by its inclusion of new social groups such as children regularly flying on their own to visit friends and relatives, people commuting to work nationally or transnationally, the health care of elderly people in warmer and drier climates, or the mass movement of long-distance tourists. Obviously, these developments are in conflict with goals to achieve environmental sustainability. Given the environmental harmfulness of air travel and the industry's perspective stressing the high importance of air travel for society and economy, Paul Peeters and Stefan Gössling's Chapter 10 seeks to investigate the narratives and discourses surrounding air travel. A wide variety of discourses are identified and deconstructed and an actor analysis recognizes key players in creating and maintaining existing discourses, showing that these are shaped mostly by the industry, leaving few opportunities for alternative messages to reach the public. Finally, the developments induced by these discourses are evaluated with respect to their short- and long-term consequences for tourism and sustainability.

The change and mobility of images are two of the main forces influencing contemporary tourism. Tourists decide whether to travel to a destination or not on the basis of changing destination images. This is especially true for tourism destinations in the Middle East and North Africa after 9/11. But how do security-related destination images affect the actions of the supply-side agents? While the impact of incidents of violent political unrest and the consequent changes in destination images on tourist behaviour has been subject to wide academic research, there is a lack of similar studies concerning the supply side. The interdependencies and interactions of transnational hotel companies, local agents and tour operators, as well as their specific roles in the destination recovery process, have hardly been researched. Moreover, the influence of travel and changing security-related destination images on the actions of supply-side agents in the tourism industry has not been studied at all.

Flows of tourism from Europe to the Middle East are occasionally threatened by socio-political events such as terrorism. This may cause a sudden drop in tourist arrivals in the affected destination and also influence the relationship between different agents offering package tours. As long as no significant external events happen, the relationship between both is likely to remain stable. In Chapter 11, Sabine Dörry uses the theoretical concept of 'global commodity chains', or more precisely one type – the buyer-driven value chain – to address two important issues. First, the supply chain from source market to the destination is generally governed by a lead firm (an issue of power); and, second, the characteristics of the demand side are not discussed in the concept (an issue of neglect). This is an indication that the tourism value chain (looking at both supply and demand) is not governed by a particular firm, although packaged tourism can be clearly seen as a buyer-driven 'commodity' chain. Dörry then points out that the kind of relationship between the tour operator and the incoming agent changes through a sudden event such as a terror attack and through steadier, predictable changes such as the Internet. These arguments are developed using the case study of German travellers who are culturally and religiously motivated to travel to Jordan.

More often than not, mobility studies have a tendency to focus on movement and transport rather than on the groups that are being mobile. However, the 11 chapters in the present volume will help address this often neglected issue.

References

Appadurai, A. (1996) *Modernity at Large: Cultural Dimensions of Globalization Public Worlds*. Volume 1. University of Minnesota Press, Minneapolis, Minnesota.

Bauman, Z. (1997) Tourists and vagabonds: the heroes and victims of postmodernity. In: *Postmodernity and its Discontents*. Polity Press, London, pp. 83–94.

Burns, P. (2005) The End of Tourism? (Conference announcement). Available at: http://www.brighton.ac.uk/ssm/research/symposia/2005/2005speakers.php?PageId=200 (accessed 27 November 2007).

Chaney, D. (2002) The power of metaphors in tourism theory. In: Coleman, S. and Crang, M. (eds) *Tourism: Between Place and Performance*. Berghahn Books, New York, pp. 193–206.

Coles, T., Hall, C.M. and Duval, D. (2005) Mobilising tourism: a post-disciplinary critique. *Tourism Recreation Research* 30(2), 53–63.

Cummings, D. (2004) *The Trouble With Being Human These Days. Review of Z. Bauman's Identity: Conversations with Benedetto Vecchi (Themes for the 21st Century)*. Polity

Press, Cambridge. Available at: http://www.culturewars.org.uk/2004-02/identity.htm (accessed 1 October 2007).

Fadeeva, Z. (2005) Translation of sustainability ideas in tourism networks: some roles of cross-sectoral networks in change towards sustainable development. *Journal of Cleaner Production* 13(2), 175–189.

Fanon, F. (1986) *Black Skin, White Mask*. Pluto Press, London.

Franklin, A. (2004) Tourism as an ordering towards a new ontology of tourism. *Tourist Studies* 4(3), 277–301.

Fridgen, D. (1984) Environmental psychology and tourism. *Annals of Tourism Research* 11, 19–33.

Graburn, N.H.H. (1977) Tourism: the sacred journey. In: Smith, V. (ed.) *Hosts and Guests: the Anthropology of Tourism*. Pennsylvania Press, Philadelphia, Pennsylvania, pp. 17–3 l.

Hesmondhalgh, D. (2002) *The Cultural Industries*. Sage, London.

Krippendorf, J. (1987) *The Holiday Makers*. Heinemann, Oxford, UK.

Lanfant, M.-F. (1980) Introduction: tourism in the process of internationalization. *International Social Science Journal* 32(1), 14–43.

MacCannell, D. (1992) *Empty Meeting Ground: the Tourist Papers*. Routledge, London.

Maslow, A. (ND) Available at: (1) http://www.themystica.com/mystica/articles/p/peak_experiences.html; and (2) http://psikoloji.fisek.com.tr/maslow/self.htm (both accessed 8 October 2007).

Mayer, P. (ND) The 'Normal' Mobility of Tourism: a Research Outline. Available at: http://www.cosmobilities.net/downloads/Miscellaneous/Mayer_Tourism_and_Mobility.pdf (accessed 12 August 2007).

Nowicka, P. (2007) *The No-Nonsense Guide to Tourism*. New Internationalist, Oxford, UK.

Pine, J. and Gilmore, J. (1999) *The Experience Economy*. Harvard Business School Press, Boston, Massachusetts.

Robertson, R. (1992) *Globalization: Social Theory and Global Culture*. Sage, London.

Ross, E. and Power, E. (eds) (1929) *Ibn Battuta: Travels in Asia and Africa*. George Routledge, London.

Selwyn, T. (1996) *The Tourist Image. Myths and Myth Making in Tourism*. Wiley, Chichester, UK.

Turner, L. and Ash, J. (1975) *The Golden Hordes: International Tourism and the Pleasure Periphery*. Constable, London.

Urry, J. (2001) Globalising the Tourist Gaze. Department of Sociology, Lancaster University. Available at: http://www.comp.lancs.ac.uk/sociology/soc079iu.html (accessed 1 February 2006).

Urry, J. (2002) Mobility and Proximity. Available at: http://www.its.leeds.ac.uk/projects/mobilenetwork/downloads/urry1stpaper.doc (accessed 1 February 2006).

Urry, J. and Sheller, M. (eds) (2004) *Tourism Mobilities: Places to Stay, Places in Play*. Routledge, London.

1 The End of Tourism, or Endings in Tourism?

TIM GALE

Introduction

This chapter considers one of the more intriguing ideas to emerge out of the turn to mobilities in the social sciences, viz. 'the end of tourism'. The phrase in question was coined by Urry (1995) as shorthand for an argument about disorganized capitalism and the de-differentiation of tourism from leisure, culture, retailing, education, sport, hobbies and everyday life in general, to the point where the first of these is no longer perceived to be 'special' vis-à-vis the remainder. However, it is open to various, more literal interpretations and will be employed here as a pretext for exploring the capacity for 'endings' in tourism, in the context of wider discourses on economic restructuring, sustainable development and the risk society. This discussion will be preceded by a brief, but necessary review of the literature on tourism mobilities, paying attention to how others have reported and critiqued Urry's ideas on 'the end of tourism'.

Tourism Mobilities and 'the End of Tourism'

The tendency to view tourism as a form of temporary mobility alongside and analogous to other forms and mobilities, both global *and* local, is in part a response to criticism of the manner in which this particular activity and the people who participate in it are defined. This has been articulated by various scholars in leisure, recreation and tourism studies including Rojek and Urry (1997: 1), who argue that 'tourism is a term waiting to be deconstructed . . . a chaotic conception, including within it too wide a range of disparate phenomena', and Franklin (2003: 65), who considers traditional, or technical, definitions of a tourist as someone who spends at least one night away from home for business or pleasure to be little more than a description of a 'hotel client' (although same-day travel by 'excursionists' is now included in official tourism statistics, as noted by

Hall and Page (2006)). Recent work on the relationships between tourism, leisure and recreation as 'complementary and yet semantically different activities' (Hall and Page, 2006: 226), and tourism, work and migration as hitherto disconnected and contradictory phenomena, has further problematized orthodox ideas about tourism and what it means in showing that the lines of demarcation are blurred, if not porous. Examples include business tourists taking 'time out' between meeting clients or in the course of attending conferences and exhibitions, and backpackers funding their travels through temporary employment at various points in their journey, as suggested by Shaw and Williams (2002), with the caveat that such distinctions are sometimes necessary (e.g. tourism is seen to be driven by commercial imperatives whereas leisure and recreation are rooted in, though not confined to, the public domain). Contributions of note include positioning statements by Bell and Ward (2000), Williams and Hall (2000, 2002), Urry (2001, 2002), Coles *et al.* (2004), Hall *et al.* (2004) and Hall (2005a, b), empirical research by O'Reilly (2003) and Uriely (2001) on British migrants in Spain and touring workers/working tourists in Israel, respectively, and the edited collections of Sheller and Urry (2004) on tourism mobilities, performances and places, Hall and Müller (2004) on tourism and second homes, and Coles and Timothy (2004) on transnationalism, diaspora and tourism. To these we might add parallel publications in sociology (Urry, 2000) and geography (Larsen *et al.*, 2006; Minca and Oakes, 2006), as the two disciplines that are leading the way in 'rediscovering tourism as an area for research, case studies and examples' (Cooper *et al.*, 2005: 14), notwithstanding the claim that the 'mobility turn' weakens such disciplinary distinctions in 'putting into question the fundamental "territorial" and "sedentary" precepts of twentieth-century social science' (Hannam *et al.*, 2006: 2).

The works cited above collectively set down a number of principles for the study of tourism mobilities, which may be summarized as follows. First, whereas conventional tourism research is preoccupied with those factors that push or pull the category of people known as 'tourists' towards the category of places known as 'destinations', which are rendered intelligible by 'middle-range theories of motivation, decision modelling, and even destination image' (Coles *et al.*, 2004: 464), the turn to mobility in the social sciences calls for the decentring of tourism studies so that, rather than being preoccupied with the tourist and travels to distant lands, it recognizes the interconnected mobilities of a variety of *individuals*, including leisure shoppers, second home owners, entrepreneurial migrants, business travellers, 'gap year' students and a whole host of other people voluntarily on the move. The return journeys they undertake may be local, regional, national or international in scale, and last from a few hours to many years in duration (as represented in the two-dimensional models of Bell and Ward (2000) and Hall (2005a)). More profoundly, these movements 'are implicated within complex networks by which "hosts, guests, buildings, objects and machines" are contingently brought together to produce certain performances in certain places at certain times' (Hannam *et al.*, 2006: 13).

Secondly, the concept of mobilities presupposes its opposite, namely *immobilities*. It is easy to be seduced by the idea that everyone (and everything) is on the move but, in practice, the very processes that have enhanced the mobility of some people(s) have merely served to highlight, and sometimes to reinforce, the immobility of others (Hannam *et al.*, 2006). Consideration, acknowledgement even, of the latter is conspicuous by its absence in many studies of tourism, setting aside problems of measurement, and analyses of demand often conflate those who cannot travel with those who do not, under the category of 'no demand' (see Cooper *et al.* (2005: 39), who dismiss this in a mere two lines of text). This is unhelpful at best, fallacious at worst. That said, the emergence of what has been dubbed 'Critical Tourism Studies' has seen the timely recognition of, and more attention afforded to explaining and addressing, variations in access to tourism according to class, age and stage in the family life cycle, race and ethnicity, (dis)ability and, in particular, gender and sexuality (see Ateljevic *et al.*, 2006). However, it will be some time before this body of work is comparable in both volume and efficacy to earlier and ongoing investigations into the comparatively immobile, marginalized and impoverished existence of the host (as opposed to the guest, or would-be guest in this instance).

Thirdly, the emergence of mobilities as an explanatory concept in tourism studies compels us to acknowledge the potential for virtual and imaginative, over and above corporeal (physical), forms of temporary mobility, thanks to new information and communications technologies such as the Internet, the 3G mobile phone, digital television and video-conferencing (Urry, 2001). Their availability and doubts over whether the economic and political stability that accompanied the recent expansion in international tourism can be sustained in the medium to long term (see later) have encouraged tourism researchers to take seriously, and to engage with, the possibilities of 'cyber-tourism' (defined by Prideaux (2005: 5) as 'an electronically simulated travel experience that is a substitute for a physical tourism experience'). By way of example, a number of existing and potential applications of cyber-tourism are identified in a special issue of the journal *Tourism Recreation Research* (Vol. 30, No. 3, 2005), including those that complement leisure and business travel as well as those that might replace it. (Highlights include virtual tours of convention centres for event organizers, the role of technology in the production and reproduction of contrived landscapes such as beach and snow domes, and the use of new communications technologies to repackage an ancient form of Indian medicine as a tourist experience.) However, although it may no longer seem whimsical to talk of travels in cyberspace as a serious alternative to physically moving from one place to another, corporeal mobility still takes precedence over virtual and imaginative mobilities on account of 'the obligations of co-presence' (Boden and Molotch, 1994), including the need to experience first-hand particular places or events, and to spend 'quality time' in the company of friends and relatives. This will continue to be the case until the latter is capable of simulating, at least in part, the pleasures and benefits of the former (Urry, 2002).

Finally, mobilities entail a concern for the by-products of tourism (and human movement in general), notably greenhouse gas emissions from jet aircraft and motor vehicles and threats to biosecurity arising from certain tourist flows, for example avian flu, foot-and-mouth disease (FMD) and SARS (see Hall, 2005a). On first inspection there might seem nothing new about this, for the negative impacts of tourism have been reported in the literature for some time now (Mathieson and Wall's 1982 seminal work being one of the first of numerous points of departure from the notion that tourism is a 'consequence-free' activity). That said, we are talking here not of localized impacts that can be mitigated through appropriate business and resource management interventions, but of the undesirable and unforeseen consequences of living a mobile life that lie outside our control and which, in turn, threaten that very mobility. Putting to one side global environmental change (see later), the perceived risk of being caught up in a terrorist atrocity such as 9/11 or the Bali bombings (which, for many people, outweighs the probabilities involved when determining their choice of destination) is an obvious instance of this, such events being the product of 'illicit mobilities and their attendant security risks' (Hannam *et al.*, 2006: 1). Ironically, the perpetrators of these incidents make use of the very transport and communications infrastructures that connect tourists with the places they visit, and with few exceptions pass unnoticed through the same nodal points (e.g. airports, railway stations). Hence, there is a need for tourism researchers and, for that matter, practitioners to consider the implications of the 'risk society' (after Beck (1992); see also Bauman (2006) on 'liquid fear'), and to pursue programmes for the analysis and assessment of risks and disasters (Hannam *et al.*, 2006).

Underpinning all of the above is globalization (which necessitates this alternative 'way of seeing' tourism). In addition to facilitating the exponential growth over the last few decades in the number of tourists and migrants flowing to and from those countries that comprise the 'pleasure periphery' (after Turner and Ash, 1975), it has also 'stimulated new forms of travel, tourism and migration whose production and consumption are intricately bound together' (Coles and Timothy, 2004: 3). The consequences for tourism *as we know it* are far-reaching. On the one hand, the creation of new and previously inaccessible and undeveloped destinations, and a preference for independent and special interest holidays in non-resort locations, has reduced to a handful the number of places in the world that, by dint of their natural characteristics and remoteness, are yet to be appropriated for tourist consumption. On the other hand, in-migration has brought the remote, the exotic and the 'Other' closer to home (at least from the perspective of those living in the main tourist generating, as opposed to receiving, countries), evidenced by the way in which fashion, architecture and other features of our immediate environment increasingly reflect distant places and ages. These enhanced mobilities, temporary and permanent alike, have contributed to a situation in which 'tourism is everything and everything is tourism' (Munt, 1994: 104), or so it is alleged. More precisely, they have undermined the *agglomeration* and *demarcation processes* in tourism that distinguish 'home' from 'away' (as discussed by Gordon and Goodall (2000) and Rojek (1997), respectively), thus weakening the socio-cultural inversions that are thought to sustain tourist flows (e.g. thrift/self-indulgence, nudity/formal clothing, tranquillity/stress, etc.; see Burns, 1999: 88). We, therefore, see the dissolving of 'tourism's specificity', when tourism ceases to be differentiated from other forms of production and consumption and people *are* for the most part tourists, 'whether they are literally mobile or only experience simulated mobility' (Urry, 1995: 148). This, in essence, is what is meant by 'the end of tourism'.

One does not have to look far in order to find evidence of such de-differentiation, and certainly no further than the increasing number of post-industrial cities

that 'model themselves on tourist resorts and generate a kind of holiday atmosphere all year around' (Franklin, 2003: 79). Here, spectacular and vernacular
architectures combine in inner-city and waterfront areas to create new, vibrant
identities that borrow heavily from the global (e.g. converted warehouses offering loft-style living, and the ubiquitous shopping mall), while reasserting a local
sense of place (e.g. industrial and maritime museums). Distinct recreational
business districts are formed in areas adjacent to retail and financial quarters,
offering 'café culture' by day and 'club culture' by night (becoming, in the process, liminal zones rather like the seaside resorts of old; see Shields, 1991). In
the suburbs, homes and gardens are fashioned into places of escape by
do-it-yourself enthusiasts, the former redecorated with supposedly authentic
paints and fabrics and stocked with souvenirs of previous travels (constituting a
reverse 'demonstration effect' of sorts), and the latter transformed by decking,
aggregates, water features and outside lighting (all materials and devices once
reserved for promenades, parks and other public spaces). Inside, a genera-
tion(s) of 'kidults' surf the 'net and/or play computer games, perhaps visiting
virtual worlds such as Second Life and There that 'provide a more immersive
and satisfying diversion than other forms of entertainment media without
requiring a physical journey to a faraway destination' (Book, 2003: 1). In short,
what this demonstrates is that we can be tourists 'on our own doorstep', and
sometimes without crossing it at all!

Since the publication of *Consuming Places* (Urry, 1995), the tourism
research community has been exposed to Urry's ideas regarding 'the end of
tourism' via several works focusing on tourism consumption and the tourist
experience. Some of these merely summarize the salient points for the benefit
of readers unfamiliar with them (e.g. Shaw *et al.*, 2000; Uriely, 2005), whereas
others are more critical (e.g. Jansson, 2002). One notable objection concerns
the over-arching framework used by Urry to organize these ideas. This suggests
that we have seen a move away from mass, packaged tourism towards
post-Fordist consumption, as indicated by the proliferation of new tourisms
such as cultural/heritage, eco- and adventure tourism, and visiting theme
parks/mega-shopping malls, and increasingly flexible and consumer-focused
forms of supply including short breaks, self-catering holidays and 'seat only'
sales on charter aircraft (see Shaw and Williams, 2004). It is countered by Ritzer
and Liska's (1997) 'McDisneyization' thesis, an elaboration of 'McDonaldization'
(after Ritzer, 1996), in which it is posited that more individualized consumption in tourism has actually been achieved through mass customization and
that the appetite for predictable, efficient, calculable and controlled vacations remains undiminished (this being evocative of Fordism). Meanwhile,
on the issue of virtual and imaginative mobilities and 'the end of tourism',
Jansson (2002: 430) maintains that 'most people uphold the distinction
between simulations and "real experiences" . . . [and that] mediated spatial
phantasmagoria reinforces the desire for "first-hand tourism"'. He rejects
the argument that tourism will ultimately cease to be distinguishable from
everyday life, for it underestimates the ability of the tourist industry to reproduce spaces and products that satisfy the desire for experiences that are out
of the ordinary.

The Beginning of the End (of Tourism)?

From this point onwards, references to the end of tourism are *not* qualified by the use of inverted commas. This marks a shift in emphasis, from a debate concerned for the most part with semantics, albeit an important and interesting one, to serious consideration of the circumstances in which we might actually witness an end to tourism or signs thereof. Also conspicuous by its absence is the suffix 'per se'. Clearly, we are not going to see tourism, or the vast and incredibly diverse industry that sustains it, disappear any time soon (the layman's assumption, if you will, and a ludicrous proposition). However, it is appropriate to anticipate certain 'endings' in tourism, the three particular instances entertained in this chapter being:

- the end of tourism in a given locality;
- an end to the exponential, and arguably unsustainable, growth in international tourism; and
- the end of tourism in a world besieged by risk and uncertainty.

The central message, then, is that it is easy to be complacent about tourism's prospects given the rapid growth in international passenger arrivals over the course of the late 20th century (up from 25 million in 1950 to 808 million in 2005, and forecasted to reach 1 billion by 2010 and 1.6 billion by 2020, World Tourism Organization (WTO), 2004, 2006), but that to do so masks the possibilities for new knowledge creation which, with a little circumspection, could be revealed to us. Indeed, there is no better time to be thinking along these lines; the turn of the millennium brings new challenges for the 'world's biggest industry' (e.g. tourists as a soft target for terrorists, the conduct of holidaymakers in certain mass market destinations and associated negative publicity, consumer dissatisfaction arising from the poor quality of some established tourism products, etc.), which point to a less promising future than the above statistics suggest. Recognizing this, Aramberri and Butler (2005: 293) open their discussion of recent challenges facing tourism, such as SARS, the war in Iraq and Islamic terrorism, with the suggestion that 'for the first time in a history that is only quite recent . . . mass tourism and the industry that caters to it are feeling their vulnerability', and Page (2003: 346) asks 'will tourism stop growing?'. That said, such comments and questions, together with some of the more pessimistic predictions in Hall's (2005a: 280–281) PEST – short for political, economic, social and technological factors – analysis of possible future trends in tourism and its wider environment, are pretty much 'exceptions to the rule' in tourism studies (at least at the time of writing).

Starting with the first of the three 'endings' mentioned above, there are already precedents for the end of tourism at the scale of an individual destination. In the most extreme cases these are associated with natural or man-induced hazards, such as the volcanic eruptions that rendered two-thirds of the Caribbean island of Montserrat uninhabitable in 1995 and the partitioning of Cyprus in the wake of the Turkish 'invasion' of July 1974 (which led to the abandonment of Varósha, a high-rise beach resort not dissimilar to Benidorm on Spain's Costa Blanca and now a ghost town on account of its proximity to the line of

partition that separates the Greek-Cypriot south from the Turkish-Cypriot north).
Even here, tourism has exhibited an uncanny ability to evolve and adapt, albeit
in a diminished form (e.g. the exploitation of the respective areas' 'dark tourism'
potential). More to the point, a number of coastal tourism resorts in Britain and
northern Europe have in the past few decades exhibited symptoms consistent
with the stagnation and post-stagnation, notably decline, phases of Butler's
(1980) tourist area life cycle, precipitated by heightened competition for the
'tourist dollar' and resource depletion linked to disinvestment and the exceeding
of carrying capacities (Gale, 2005, 2007). As a consequence, some places that
would once have been described as resorts are no longer able to attract tourists
in any significant number (e.g. New Brighton in north-west England, Barry
Island in south-east Wales and Severn Beach in the south-west of England), having become dormitory towns and places of recreation for commuters working in
nearby conurbations or, sometimes, for those with no work at all (e.g. retirees
and socially excluded persons of working age).

This loss of 'tourism function' is, to all intents and purposes, an *inevitable*
process. Either the momentum of decline is such that little can be done to arrest it
(see Gale (2005) on the stalled rejuvenation of Rhyl, a one-time mass market
destination on the north Wales coast), or the resort in question cuts its losses and
purposefully exits the holiday industry (Baum, 1998). Brighton's diversification
out of leisure tourism, at least in isolation, and into the high technology and creative industries might well constitute an example of the latter, although this has
come on the back of earlier success in courting the lucrative conference and
exhibition trade (which serves as a reminder that most post-mature resorts, as
peripheral places with monostructured economies and a finite resource base, are
more likely to diversify *within* tourism). Deliberate attempts to restrict supply in
declining markets and attract upscale forms of tourism are not exclusive to
cold-water resorts, either. Indeed, the municipality of Calvià – a district of
Mallorca that contains a number of established 'sun, sea and sand' resorts threatened by the negative environmental impacts of earlier rounds of uncontrolled
development, dependency on a limited number of source markets and a poor
image – is well known for its radical approach to economic restructuring and sustainable development. This approach encompasses the refurbishment or
removal of substandard tourist accommodation, the provision of out-of-season
events and activities, and the promotion of 'agro-tourism' within the interior (see
Knowles and Curtis (1999) for more information and Bramwell (2004) for
further examples of such practices in the Mediterranean region).

Sustainable development in its broadest sense features in the second of the
three aforementioned 'endings' in tourism. This is premised on the idea that it *is*
possible to challenge the capacity of the global tourism system to maintain existing rates of growth, by assuming the 'lose–lose' scenario of either:

- its continued failure, beyond paying lip service, to engage with the tenets of
  sustainability with the result that it eventually collapses under the weight of
  the economic, environmental, social and cultural problems caused by its
  unrestricted development (see Middleton with Hawkins (1998: 76) for a
  comprehensive list of impacts); or

- the realization of genuinely sustainable tourism on a sufficiently consistent and widespread basis, entailing strictures that would surely signal an end to tourism's age of expansion.

The lack of a clear consensus as to what is meant by 'sustainable tourism', apart from embodying the principles of sustainable development laid down by the Brundtland Commission as 'that [which] meets the needs of the present without compromising the ability of future generations to meet their own needs' (World Commission on Environment and Development, 1987: 43), suggests that the former is the more likely outcome *in the long term* (as does the selfishness of much human nature; see Wheeller, 2004). Moreover, the term is *not* value-neutral and different stakeholders can be expected to interpret it to their own ends (whatever these might be), which makes it difficult to afford equal priority to ecological, ethical/equity and economic concerns that, together, comprise the 'triple bottom line' of sustainability (Howie, 2003). However, most would agree that tourism possesses the capacity for self-destruction, notwithstanding the difficulties of disaggregating its impacts from those of other activities, and there is perhaps no better illustration of this than the relationship between tourist transport and climate change.

The use of jet aircraft and motor vehicles as the preferred means of travelling to and within tourist destinations has contributed significantly to emissions of the greenhouse gases carbon dioxide (CO_2), the largest and most enduring contributor to climate change, methane (CH_4) and nitrous oxide (N_2O). With this in mind, Garrod *et al.* (2001) compare CO_2 emissions for different *marine ecotourism* holidays, using a composite measure that takes into account the tourist's point of origin, the mode(s) of transport used, the estimated load factor, the time or distance travelled and the length of stay at the destination. They conclude that the 'least-friendly' tourists are those who fly to long-haul destinations by scheduled carrier or take multiple short-haul holidays using charter flights (which contradicts the notion that ecotourism, as the subject of their study, is somehow more benign than mass tourism). In contrast, domestic tourists using public road or rail transport, backpackers visiting the same long-haul destinations but staying for an extended period of time, and families travelling overseas by private car and ferry, all have a considerably reduced impact. Such findings seem all the more significant when one considers that the tourist industry is, or will become, a *victim* of climate change as well as a perpetrator. Indeed, '[i]n two environments which are vital for tourism activities and where tourism is an equally vital component in regional and local economies – coastal zones and mountain regions – climate change puts tourism at risk' (WTO, 2003: 8). Specific threats to those environments, as discussed by Agnew and Viner (2001) and further explored in Hall and Higham (2005), include erosion and flooding at the coast, loss of snow cover (affecting, in particular, 'first generation' ski resorts developed at lower altitudes), an increased incidence of heat stress (which is particularly problematic, given the ageing populations of many tourist generating countries), the spread of insect-borne diseases such as malaria and yellow fever to areas in which they had disappeared, been eradicated or never existed (necessitating the hassle of preventative medication and injections), and disruption to flora and fauna (e.g. coral bleaching, modified breeding and migration patterns, etc.). Of course, it is likely that such impacts will lead to the displacement of, rather than a net loss in, demand for tourism (perhaps by triggering a renaissance in long holidays at higher, and hitherto colder and wetter, latitudes). Nevertheless, it is certainly conceivable that they will act to limit tourism's growth in the latter part of this century and beyond, in tandem with other destabilizing influences (see below).

Our final 'ending' in tourism concerns the abundance of examples in recent times which remind us that tourism is fraught with risk and vulnerable to a crisis. As an organizing framework, Walker and Page (2003: 222) posit a 'continuum of incidents' ranging from the frequent and trivial, such as minor accidents and the loss of personal effects through carelessness, to the rare but catastrophic, such as morbidity associated with natural disasters or acts of terrorism, and including crimes committed against individual tourists and medical ailments/complaints of varying severity. They note that few of these incidents are media worthy, yet those that are have had a profound impact on tourist flows and (purchasing) behaviour. The two that appear to have captured the imagination of academics and practitioners alike, or at least those located in the English-speaking world, both occurred in 2001. These were the foot-and-mouth outbreak within rural Britain, which in the 12 months to January 2002 resulted in the culling of over 4 million animals together with other measures to prevent contagion such as the closure to the public of large sections of the countryside and the placement of disinfectant mats at various (dis)embarkation points, and the terrorist attacks of 11 September on the World Trade Center in New York and the Pentagon in Washington, DC. For obvious reasons, not least their role in accelerating job losses, downsizing, wage freezes and cuts, and business failure within the industry, each has attracted a sizeable literature within tourism studies, characterized by discussions and evaluations of various responses on the part of principals and public authorities, with an emphasis on contingency planning and crisis management (e.g. Ritchie, 2004).

Suffice to say, there is little that is unprecedented about this. The history of tourism is punctuated with such turbulent phases, as demonstrated by the potent combination of economic recession in Western European economies and political instability in the Mediterranean region that precipitated the spectacular collapse of the Court Line holiday and shipbuilding empire and its tour operating subsidiary Clarksons in August 1974 (see Bray and Raitz, 2001). This explains the body of work on tourism and crisis that predates 'FMD' and '9/11' (e.g. Sönmez *et al.*, 1999). Likewise, tourism's 'parasitic effects' have long been known (e.g. see Pizam and Mansfield's (1996) monograph on tourism and crime). However, these latest hazards and disasters have engaged the West with what Beck (1992) terms the 'Risk Society', which is marked by a fresh set of risks unlike any we have previously faced (including risks that escape perception, risks that are not limited by time, risks that cross national boundaries, risks where no one is accountable for the consequences, and risks where it is impossible to compensate those whose lives are touched by them). Ironically, such risks are born out of overproduction and neo-liberalism, challenging the very conditions that have brought us international tourism. Furthermore, Beck's thesis subjects to critique the idea that they may be anticipated and mitigated (the rationale for the existence of risk brokers, such as the University of Queensland's Centre for Tourism and Risk Management), this belief being predicated on a techno-scientific discourse which fails to recognize that today's risks also exist in terms of the anti- or social-scientific knowledge about them and, thus, cannot be eradicated or even contained by any given 'expert' community (or nation state, for that matter). In such circumstances, the mass media and legal professions come to occupy key socio-political positions, which partly explains the seemingly inverse relationship between the probability and perception of risk in tourism, fuelled by opinion formers and a culture of litigation. This was evident in the negative portrayal of Faliraki, Rhodes in the British popular press, following the murder of an Irish tourist and several arrests related to 'lewd' behaviour in August 2003. Also it is behind the reticence of many major tour operators to subcontract services to the small-scale business sector in developing world destinations, mindful of the European Union (EU) Package Travel Directive and the requirement to provide certain minimum standards of service and security as advertised in their brochures, and appropriate redress where these are not met. As an afterthought, it is worth noting that the elevation of fear over fact has given rise to all manner of contingency measures designed to reassure the public (e.g. more rigorous, protracted and arguably demeaning security checks at airports), which can and do act as an inconvenience to tourists and, almost certainly, a deterrent to travel in their own right.

Conclusions

This chapter essentially flags up some ideas that are already 'out there' in the literature, its original and substantive contribution being to synthesize them in this particular fashion and to demonstrate how they might be indicative of the end of tourism (at least in its present configuration). These ideas are contextualized with reference to a world where people *in general* – together with objects, capital and information – are moving faster, further and more frequently than ever before. In turn, they necessitate new ways of seeing tourism, chiefly as a form of temporary mobility embedded in, not distinct from, our everyday lives (as discussed earlier).

It almost goes without saying that there are limitations to what has been attempted here. Compelling though the notion of 'endings' in tourism may seem, and much as the author would like to be the first to say 'I told you so', it is not difficult to counter each proposed 'ending' with evidence that points to the staying power of tourism. Concerning international tourist arrivals, the World Tourism Organization (WTO) has recently reasserted its projections for 2010 and 2020 (see above), in the belief that the underlying structural trends on which they are based have not changed significantly, despite recent 'irregularities' (WTO, 2004). Of course, it is hardly surprising to find the WTO talking up the prospects of the industry it represents, yet similar messages have been broadcast by academics with no apparent agenda. For instance, Shaw and Williams (2002: 242) speak of 'scope for a social and geographical extension of mass tourism' and of the tendency, when arguing to the contrary, to confuse variations in inbound tourism to individual destinations with generic changes in tourist preferences (e.g. the apparent stagnation of many coastal tourism resorts in the Mediterranean is now understood to be attributable to a combination of contingencies specific to the generating and receiving countries in question, and not a sign of Fordist forms of production and consumption in tourism coming to an end). Meanwhile, it is still too early to predict, with any confidence, the consequences of global environmental change and a perceived lack of political stability and security in source and destination countries alike for future tourism mobilities. Indeed, these threats are open to dispute by virtue of their complex and unpredictable nature, thus lending a rhetorical quality to any discussion of their likely impact on tourist arrivals and tourism receipts that inevitably detracts from it.

Limitations aside, and irrespective of whether or not one agrees with this particular author's interpretation of 'the end of tourism' (after Urry, 1995), the chapter contains an important message for the tourism research community or at least those researchers who have yet to engage with 'the "new mobilities" paradigm' (Sheller and Urry, 2006). In short, it is asserted that, in order to understand the meaning and significance of tourism in the contemporary world, it is sometimes necessary to suspend the various rules that govern how we talk about it (i.e. as something that only tourists do, as the antithesis of everyday life, as a supposedly benign activity and, most importantly, as the world's biggest industry). The 'mobility turn' provides us with an opportunity to do just that, and not before time!

Acknowledgements

The author would like to thank the editors of this volume for their patience while this chapter was being rewritten for publication, and Cara Aitchison for taking the time to comment, most helpfully, on an earlier draft.

References

Agnew, M. and Viner, D. (2001) Potential impacts of climate change on international tourism. *Tourism and Hospitality Research* 3(1), 37–60.

Aramberri, J. and Butler, R. (eds) (2005) *Tourism Development: Issues for a Vulnerable Industry*. Channel View, Clevedon, UK.

Ateljevic, I., Morgan, N. and Pritchard, A. (eds) (2006) *The Critical Turn in Tourism Studies*. Elsevier, Oxford, UK.

Baum, T. (1998) Taking the exit route: extending the tourism area life cycle model. *Current Issues in Tourism* 1, 167–175.

Bauman, Z. (2006) *Liquid Fear*. Polity, Cambridge, UK.

Beck, U. (1992) *Risk Society: Towards a New Modernity*. Sage, London.

Bell, M. and Ward, G. (2000) Comparing temporary mobility with permanent migration. *Tourism Geographies* 2(1), 87–107.

Boden, D. and Molotch, H. (1994) The compulsion to proximity. In: Friedland, R. and Boden, D. (eds) *NowHere: Space, Time and Modernity*. University of California Press, Berkeley, California, pp. 257–286.

Book, B. (2003) Travelling through cyberspace: tourism and photography in virtual worlds. Paper presented at Still Visions – Changing Lives: International Conference on Tourism and Photography, Sheffield (UK), 20–23 July. Available at: http://ssrn.com/abstract=538182 (accessed 26 November 2007).

Bramwell, B. (ed.) (2004) *Coastal Mass Tourism: Diversification and Sustainable Development in Southern Europe*. Channel View, Clevedon, UK.

Bray, R. and Raitz, V. (2001) *Flight to the Sun: the Story of the Holiday Revolution*. Continuum, London.

Burns, P. (1999) *An Introduction to Tourism and Anthropology*. Routledge, London.

Butler, R.W. (1980) The concept of a tourism area cycle of evolution: implications for resources. *Canadian Geographer* 24(1), 5–12.

Coles, T.E. and Timothy, D.J. (eds) (2004) *Tourism, Diasporas and Space*. Routledge, London.

Coles, T., Duval, D. and Hall, C.M. (2004) Tourism mobility and global communities: new approaches to theorising tourism and tourist spaces. In: Theobald, W.F. (ed.) *Global Tourism*, 3rd edn. Butterworth-Heinemann, Oxford, UK, pp. 463–481.

Cooper, C., Fletcher, J., Fyall, A., Gilbert, D. and Wanhill, S. (2005) *Tourism: Principles and Practice*. Pearson, Harlow, UK.

Franklin, A. (2003) *Tourism: an Introduction*. Sage, London.

Gale, T. (2005) Modernism, postmodernism and the decline of British seaside resorts as long holiday destinations: a case study of Rhyl, north Wales. *Tourism Geographies* 7(1), 86–112.

Gale, T. (2007) The problems and dilemmas of northern European post-mature coastal tourism resorts. In: Agarwal, S. and Shaw, G. (eds) *Managing Coastal Tourism Resorts: a Global Perspective*. Channel View, Clevedon, UK, pp. 21–39.

Garrod, B., Wilson, J. and Bruce, D.M. (2001) *Planning for Marine Ecotourism in the EU Atlantic Area: Good Practice Guidance*. University of the West of England, Bristol, UK.

Gordon, I. and Goodall, B. (2000) Localities and tourism. *Tourism Geographies* 2(3), 290–311.

Hall, C.M. (2005a) *Tourism: Rethinking the Social Science of Mobility*. Pearson, Harlow, UK.

Hall, C.M. (2005b) Space-time accessibility and the TALC: the role of geographies of spatial interaction and mobility in contributing to an improved understanding of tourism. In: Butler, R.W. (ed.) *The Tourism Area Life Cycle*, Vol. 2: *Conceptual and Theoretical Issues*. Channel View, Clevedon, UK.

Hall, C.M. and Higham, J. (eds) (2005) *Tourism, Recreation and Climate Change*. Channel View, Clevedon, UK.

Hall, C.M. and Müller, D. (eds) (2004) *Tourism, Mobility and Second Homes: Between Elite Landscape and Common Ground*. Channel View, Clevedon, UK.

Hall, C.M. and Page, S.J. (2006) *The Geography of Tourism and Recreation: Environment, Place and Space*, 3rd edn. Routledge, Abingdon, UK.

Hall, C.M., Williams, A.M. and Lew, A.A. (2004) Tourism: conceptualisations, institutions, and issues. In: Lew, A.A., Hall, C.M. and Williams, A.M. (eds) *A Companion to Tourism*. Blackwell, Oxford, UK, pp. 3–21.

Hannam, K., Sheller, M. and Urry, J. (2006) Mobilities, immobilities and moorings. *Mobilities* 1(1), 1–22.

Howie, F. (2003) *Managing the Tourist Destination*. Continuum, London.

Jansson, A. (2002) Spatial phantasmagoria: the mediatization of tourism experience. *European Journal of Communication* 17(4), 429–443.

Knowles, T. and Curtis, S. (1999) The market viability of European mass tourist destinations. A post-stagnation life-cycle analysis. *International Journal of Tourism Research* 1, 87–96.

Larsen, J., Urry, J. and Axhausen, K. (2006) *Mobilities, Networks, Geographies.* Ashgate, Aldershot, UK.

Mathieson, A. and Wall, G. (1982) *Tourism: Economic, Physical and Social Impacts.* Longman, Harlow, UK.

Middleton, V.T.C. with Hawkins, R. (1998) *Sustainable Tourism: a Marketing Perspective.* Butterworth-Heinemann, Oxford, UK.

Minca, C. and Oakes, T. (eds) (2006) *Travels in Paradox: Remapping Tourism.* Rowman and Littlefield, Lanham, Maryland.

Munt, I. (1994) The 'other' postmodern tourism: culture, travel and the new middle class. *Theory, Culture and Society* 11, 101–123.

O'Reilly, K. (2003) When is a tourist? The articulation of tourism and migration on Spain's Costa del Sol. *Tourist Studies* 3(3), 301–317.

Page, S.J. (2003) *Tourism Management: Managing for Change.* Butterworth-Heinemann, Oxford, UK.

Pizam, A. and Mansfield, Y. (1996) *Tourism, Crime and International Security Issues.* Wiley, Chichester, UK.

Prideaux, B. (2005) Cyber-tourism: a new form of tourism experience. *Tourism Recreation Research* 30(3), 5–6.

Ritchie, B.W. (2004) Chaos, crises and disasters: a strategic approach to crisis management. *Tourism Management* 25, 669–683.

Ritzer, G. (1996) *The McDonaldization of Society*, 2nd edn. Pine Forge Press, Thousand Oaks, California.

Ritzer, G. and Liska, A. (1997) McDisneyization and post-tourism: complementary perspectives on contemporary tourism. In: Rojek, C. and Urry, J. (eds) *Touring Cultures: Modern Transformations in Leisure and Travel.* Routledge, London, pp. 96–109.

Rojek, C. (1997) Indexing, dragging and the social construction of tourist sights. In: Rojek, C. and Urry, J. (eds) *Touring Cultures: Modern Transformations in Leisure and Travel.* Routledge, London, pp. 52–74.

Rojek, C. and Urry, J. (1997) Transformations of travel and theory. In: Rojek, C. and Urry, J. (eds) *Touring Cultures: Modern Transformations in Leisure and Travel.* Routledge, London, pp. 1–19.

Shaw, G. and Williams, A.M. (2002) *Critical Issues in Tourism: a Geographical Perspective*, 2nd edn. Blackwell, Oxford, UK.

Shaw, G. and Williams, A.M. (2004) *Tourism and Tourism Spaces.* Sage, London.

Shaw, G., Agarwal, S. and Bull, P. (2000) Tourism consumption and tourist behaviour: a British perspective. *Tourism Geographies* 2(3), 264–289.

Sheller, M. and Urry, J. (eds) (2004) *Tourism Mobilities: Places to Stay, Places in Play.* Routledge, London.

Sheller, M. and Urry, J. (2006) The new mobilities paradigm. *Environment and Planning A* 38(2), 207–226.

Shields, R. (1991) *Places on the Margin: Alternative Geographies of Modernity.* Routledge, London.

Sönmez, S.F., Apostolopoulos, Y. and Tarlow, P. (1999) Tourism in crisis: managing the effects of terrorism. *Journal of Travel Research* 38(1), 13–18.

Turner, L. and Ash, J. (1975) *The Golden Hordes: International Tourism and the Pleasure Periphery.* Constable, London.

Uriely, N. (2001) Touring workers and working tourists: variations across the interaction between work and tourism. *International Journal of Tourism Research* 3(1), 1–8.

Uriely, N. (2005) The tourist experience: conceptual developments. *Annals of Tourism Research* 32(1), 199–216.

Urry, J. (1995) *Consuming Places*. Routledge, London.

Urry, J. (2000) *Sociology Beyond Societies: Mobilities for the Twenty-First Century*. Routledge, London.

Urry, J. (2001) Transports of delight. *Leisure Studies* 20, 237–245.

Urry, J. (2002) Mobility and proximity. *Sociology* 36(2), 255–274.

Walker, L. and Page, S.J. (2003) Risks, rights and responsibilities in tourist well-being: who should manage visitor well-being at the destination? In: Wilks, J. and Page, S.J. (eds) *Managing Tourist Health and Safety in the New Millennium*. Pergamon, Oxford, UK, pp. 215–235.

Wheeller, B. (2004) The truth? The hole truth. Everything but the truth. Tourism and knowledge: a septic sceptic's perspective. *Current Issues in Tourism* 7(6), 467–477.

Williams, A.M. and Hall, C.M. (2000) Tourism and migration: new relationships between production and consumption. *Tourism Geographies* 2(1), 5–27.

Williams, A.M. and Hall, C.M. (2002) Tourism, migration, circulation and mobility: the contingencies of time and place. In: Hall, C.M. and Williams, A.M. (eds) *Tourism and Migration: New Relationships Between Production and Consumption*. Kluwer Academic Press, Dordrecht, the Netherlands, pp. 1–60.

World Commission on Environment and Development (1987) *Our Common Future*. Oxford University Press, New York.

World Tourism Organization (WTO) (2003) *Climate Change and Tourism*. World Tourism Organization, Madrid.

World Tourism Organization (WTO) (2004) *Long-term Prospects: Tourism 2020 Vision*. Available at: http://www.world-tourism.org/market_research/facts/market_trends.htm (accessed 25 August 2004).

World Tourism Organization (WTO) (2006) *United Nations World Tourism Organization (UNWTO) Tourism Barometer* 4(2) (June). Available at: http://www.unwto.org/facts/eng/pdf/barometer/WTOBarom06_2_en_ex.pdf (accessed 3 November 2006).

2 Of Time and Space and Other Things: Laws of Tourism and the Geographies of Contemporary Mobilities

C. MICHAEL HALL

Introduction: Defining Tourism

Although it may seem a particularly arid pursuit to seek yet again to define tourism, an appropriate conceptualization of tourism is essential to understanding tourist space and mobility and the relative competitiveness of destinations. Tourism has often been portrayed as something existing outside everyday life. For many of the world's population this is undoubtedly true. However, for people in the developed world and the elite of the developing world, travel is an inherent part of their lifestyle. Even if people do not engage in long-distance travel on an annual basis it is still something that is accessible over their lifecourse and which is presented as a probable occurrence in the print and television media as part of contemporary consumptive lifestyles. It is everyday mobility. Nevertheless, while there is considerable lateral theoretical movement to tourism as a domain of study within the social sciences (but perhaps as travellers all social scientists as well as the travelling public now regard themselves as experts on tourism), there is a lack of vertical theoretical integration within broader perspectives of mobility. In order to provide better understanding of tourism phenomena, research agendas in tourism need to interrogate both macro-scale and micro-scale theories of mobilities as opposed to the existing structured, middle-range theories of tourism motivation, decision-modelling, and even destination image that, while useful, do little to bridge fairly substantial gaps in our knowledge of tourism (cf. Hall and Williams, 2002; Coles *et al.*, 2006). In order to undertake this task tourism must be willing to formulate a coherent approach to understanding the meaning behind the range of mobilities undertaken by *individuals*, not tourists. Tourism is therefore presented as a temporary form of mobility, and as such is roughly and conceptually analogous in scope and meaning to other forms of movement (e.g. travel to second homes, return migration, emigration). By extension, a new conceptualization and theoretical approach applied to tourism must consider relationships to other forms of mobility (Coles *et al.*, 2004).

Redefining Tourism: Temporary Mobilities in Time and Space

Tourism is still categorized, and its flows still measured, by raw statistical data. Tourism policy decisions and destination marketing self-congratulations are based almost exclusively on the most recent arrival statistics. Unfortunately, such an approach fails to recognize the position of tourism as one of a number of forms of leisure-oriented mobility. There is often little statistical or intellectual overlap with other fields concerned with mobility such as transport, retailing or migration (Fig. 2.1). Leisure studies tend to focus on leisure in the home or in near-home environments and are often associated with daily leisure behaviours although studies of leisure behaviour on longer trips, i.e. holidays, are also recognized. The field of transport studies is also clearly concerned with human mobility and how people move between A and B: much research is concentrated on the problems arising from daily commuting although long-distance travel is also a significant concern. Tourism studies have historically tended to concentrate on overnight travel behaviour although, as noted above, daytripping is becoming a significant interest while the touristic dimensions of longer-term travel behaviours are also being recognized. Despite their commonalities, tourism and migration research have only recently begun to cross the divide of the supposed 'permanency' of migration mobility and the temporary nature of tourism mobilities and, even then, it is with respect to the relatively restricted intellectual spaces of second homes and retirement migration (e.g. Hall and Williams, 2002; Hall and Müller, 2004). For example, in their otherwise excellent

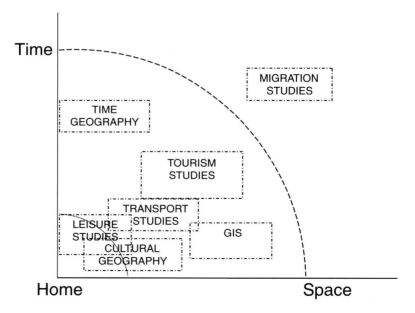

Fig. 2.1. The significance of space–time relationships for disciplinary studies of mobility (Source: Hall, 2003).

introductory text on contemporary migration, Boyle *et al.* (1998: 33) noted that 'the importance of temporary movement . . . cannot be underestimated' but then go on to mention it only once more in the remainder of the book. However, given the increasing rates of mobility of a substantial proportion of the population in developed countries the notion of permanence is itself increasingly contested. Nevertheless, the figure indicates that there are a number of disciplines with clear interests in explaining the patterns and processes of human mobility; to this we may of course add other areas such as sociology, for which mobility has also become a significant issue in recent years (e.g. Urry, 2000; Sheller and Urry, 2004). Yet what is remarkable is the historical relative lack of interplay and cross-fertilization between these fields.

In one sense, the limitations of definitional approaches to tourism have already started to be recognized by the World Tourism Organization (WTO), who have begun to identify the category of daytripping as a form of tourism behaviour. The inclusion of same-day travel 'excursionists' within technical definitions of tourism clearly makes the divisions between what constitutes leisure, recreation and tourism extremely arbitrary, and there is increasing international agreement that 'tourism' refers to all activities of visitors, including both overnight and same-day visitors (United Nations and United Nations World Tourism Organization, 2007). Given innovations in transport technology and networks, international or long-distance same-day travel is also becoming increasingly important at widening spatial scales within the developed world, and is exemplifying space–time compression. This emphasizes the need for those interested in tourism to address the arbitrary boundaries between tourism and leisure, and tourism and migration not only in terms of definition but also in terms of method and modes of analysis. Tourism therefore constitutes just one form of leisure or non-work oriented temporary mobility and is both shaped by and shapes such mobility (Hall *et al.*, 2004).

Figure 2.2 provides a two-dimensional representation of some of the key concepts in tourism in space and time. The figure also illustrates the critical points of time for definitional purposes in that 24 h or overnight stay away from home is usually used to differentiate between daytripping and tourism. Depending on the jurisdiction time is also used to classify migration and tourism, in some countries it is 6 months away from the country of permanent residence, in others it is 12 months. However, tourism has historically been classified as much by space as it is by time. For example, the crossing of a national border separates domestic from international tourism as it does domestic from international migration. Moreover, space is also used as the determinant of regional and local tourism statistics; although these are usually based on political boundaries, other distances may also be used to differentiate between different classifications of mobility. Figure 2.2 also highlights the essential arbitrary nature of delineating tourism from other forms of mobility. For example, although at first glance the location of a political border provides a good basis for determining tourism statistics it does not take into account whether the person being classified lives 20 km or 220 km away from such a border as well as the relative permeability of borders. It also does not take into account how fast people are travelling within a given period of time. Obviously, someone travelling by a very fast train from one

Fig. 2.2. Temporary mobility in space and time (Source: Hall, 2003).

location to another may be able to undertake in less than 24 h what other people may take several days to do. Furthermore, as noted above, such space–time relationships also have implications for the study of human mobility.

Mobilities

As the above discussion indicates, in addition to being defined in relation to the spatial and temporal context of its production and consumption, tourism is increasingly being interpreted as but one, albeit highly significant, dimension of temporary mobility and circulation (Bell and Ward, 2000; Urry, 2000; Williams and Hall, 2000, 2002; Hall and Williams, 2002; Coles *et al.*, 2004; Hall and Müller, 2004). Figure 2.3 presents a model for describing different forms of temporary mobility in terms of three dimensions of space (distance), time and number of trips (Hall, 2003). Figure 2.3 therefore illustrates the decline in the overall number of trips or movements, time and distance away from a central generating point that would often be termed as 'home' or place of permanent residency. Definitions of different types of mobility are clearly related to distance from origin point. However, just as significantly the overall number of movements declines the further one travels in time and space away from the point of origin. The relationship represented in Fig. 2.3 holds whether one is describing the totality of movements of an individual over their lifespan or a specific extended period of time or whether one is describing the total characteristics of a population over a period of time. Such distance decay effects with respect to travel frequency have been well documented (e.g. Smith, 1985; Hall, 2005a). In addition, the figure illustrates the relationship between tourism and other forms of temporary mobility including various forms of what is often regarded as migration (Bell and Ward, 2000; Williams and Hall, 2002; Duval and Hall, 2004). Such activities, which have increasingly come to be discussed in the tourism literature, including travel for work and international experiences (e.g. Mason, 2002), education (e.g. Kalinowski and Weiler, 1992; Kraft *et al.*, 1994; Hsu and Sung, 1996, 1997; Field, 1999), health (e.g. Goodrich and Goodrich, 1987; Becheri, 1989; Goodrich, 1994), as well as travel to second homes (e.g. Coppock, 1977; Müller, 1999; Hall and Müller, 2004), retirement migration (Gustafson, 2002; King, 2002) and return migration and diasporic travel (e.g. Duval, 2002, 2004; Stephenson, 2002; Coles and Timothy, 2004).

Figures 2.2 and 2.3 highlight that there are a number of different components of contemporary travel behaviour which, as noted above, are increasingly studied under the rubric of 'tourism', including travelling for education both in the short and long term, business travel, health tourism, leisure shopping, second home travel, daytrips, the combining of work and travel, and amenity-oriented migration, because of their leisure mobility orientation (Coles *et al.*, 2005, 2006). Arguably, some of these categories could be described as 'partial tourists'

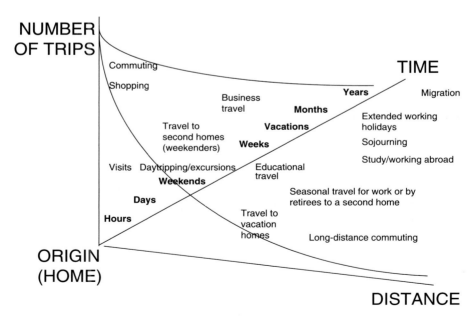

Fig. 2.3. Extent of temporary mobility in space and time (Source: Hall, 2003).

(Cohen, 1974); nevertheless the leisure dimension remains important as a motivating factor in their travel behaviour. It should be noted that migration is often not permanent and individuals may be returning to their original home many years after they left on either a permanent (e.g. for retirement) or temporary basis (e.g. to a second home) (Duval, 2004; Hall and Müller, 2004). Furthermore, for many migrants relationships to the country of origin may be maintained through visits that are invariably described as tourism. Therefore, consideration of leisure mobilities also assists us in relating tourism to the broader consideration in the social sciences of the social relationships and identities that often span multiple localities (e.g. Lee, 2003). In addition, Hall (2005a) has argued that a focus on the space–time dimensions of tourism also necessitates the adoption of a lifecourse perspective that provides for a greater understanding of how one form of mobility behaviour at one point in time will influence later mobility behaviours as well as the constraints on mobility. If such perspectives are adopted this means, as Coles *et al.* (2004) suggest, that the study of tourism must be willing to formulate a coherent approach to understanding the meaning behind the range of mobilities undertaken by *individuals*, not just tourists.

Understanding the Spatial Interactions of Mobility

From a more macro perspective with respect to space–time mobility, tourism mobility is connected to broader empirical research on spatial interaction and diffusion models. Spatial interaction models are used to predict spatial choices reflected in flows of goods or people between origins and destinations, expressing trade-offs between the accessibility of alternative destination opportunities and the perceived intrinsic 'attractiveness' of these opportunities. Such models have been heavily utilized in retail shopping planning and predictive capacities with respect to expenditure patterns and can be generated with rather basic data such as population, travel times (or distances between settlements), and retail floorspace or the number of beds in accommodation providers. Gravity models, with respect to human mobility, have been in development since the 1880s, when they were applied to migration behaviour (Ravenstein, 1885, 1889). The implications of the friction of distance – the decay of interactions such as trips and communication over space and time – are well recognized in the social sciences but have only been lightly touched on in tourism studies (Hall, 2005a, b, 2006). Arguably, this may be because of some of the issues that arise out of the study of distance–decay curves. For example, while such curves may be empirically identified, 'it is not clear to what extent their form depends on the model structures used to replicate them' (Robinson, 1998: 229). Moreover, the nature of the relationships between interaction, mass (population size) and accessibility is inherently complex. Nevertheless, they provide useful macro-level descriptions of mobilities (Tables 2.1 and 2.2) and have a substantial predictive component to them, so much so that Hall (2005a, 2006) argues that such space–time accessibility lies at the heart of understanding destination life cycles and sets out a set of 'laws' that govern tourism behaviour in aggregate form.

Table 2.1. Mobility table for Australia (000s) (Source: see below[a]).

Year	Commuting trips[b]	Daytrips	Domestic travel[c]	Outbound travel Short term[d]	Outbound travel Long term	Departing permanently
1985	–	–	45,250[e]	1,512	51	19
1990	–	–	49,962	2,170	66	30
1991	–	–	48,997	2,099	66	30
1992	–	–	48,235	2,276	67	28
1993	–	–	47,878	2,267	64	28
1994	–	–	48,113	2,355	66	27
1995	–	–	57,898	2,519	69	28
1996	1,495,895	–	63,028	2,732	71	29
1997	–	–	62,780	2,933	77	30
1998	–	153,130	73,811	3,161	81	33
1999	–	170,939	72,981	3,210	84	38
2000	–	161,464	73,771	3,498	88	44
2001	1,627,136	146,008	74,585	3,443	93	48
2002	–	–	75,047	3,461	90	49

[a] Commuting trips: Australian Bureau of Statistics (2002; cited in Hall, 2003); Daytrips: Australian Bureau of Statistics (2002; cited in Hall, 2003); Domestic travel: 1990–1997 – Bureau of Tourism Research (1998; cited in Hall, 2003), 1998–2002 – Department of Industry, Tourism and Resources (2003; cited in Hall, 2003); Outbound travel: Australian Bureau of Statistics (2003; cited in Hall, 2003); Departing permanently: Department of Immigration and Multicultural and Indigenous Affairs (2003; cited in Hall, 2003).
[b] Commuting data estimated from the number of people travelling to work each day multiplied by the number of working days/year.
[c] Measurements for domestic travel changed in 1998, therefore time series data cannot be directly compared.
[d] Short term = less than 12 months.
[e] Estimate from Hall (1995; cited in Hall, 2003).

According to Tobler (1970) the first law of geography is that everything is related to everything else, but near things are more related than distant things. Although this statement has been substantially debated it nevertheless provides an accurate assessment of observed regularity in the spatial relations of human behaviour that can be expressed mathematically (see also Tobler, 2004). The importance of demonstrating the various mathematical expressions of distance decay is not just that it indicates a quantitative basis for understanding tourism and mobility, but also that it demonstrates some key principles with respect to mobility in space and time (Garner, 1967). Accordingly, Hall (2005a, 2007) suggested six laws of tourism although they relate to mobility overall:

1. *The distribution of travel behaviour in space and time reflects an ordered adjustment to the factor of distance.* Distance is basic to accessibility. This means that an understanding of space and time is central to understanding tourism mobility. When we consume space we are also consuming time and vice versa. However, the search for order in travel and human behaviour must be

Table 2.2. Mobility table for the UK (000s) (Source: see below[a]).

Date	Commuting trips[b] (local bus services)	Day-trips	Domestic travel	Outbound	Departing permanently
1995	4,383,000	–	147,790	41,345	236.5
1996	4,350,000	1,200,000	154,220	42,050	263.7
1997	4,330,000	–	162,230	45,957	279.2
1998	4,248,000	1,300,000	148,820	50,872	251.5
1999	4,281,000	–	173,100	53,881	290.8
2000	4,309,000	–	175,400	56,837	320.7
2001	4,434,700	–	163,100	58,281	307.7
2002	–	–	167,300	59,377	–

[a] Commuting trips (local bus services): National Statistics (2001; cited in Hall, 2003); Daytrips: Statistics on Tourism and Research (STAR) (2003a; cited in Hall, 2003); Domestic travel: Statistics on Tourism and Research (STAR) (2003b; cited in Hall, 2003); Outbound: National Statistics (2003a; cited in Hall, 2003); Departing permanently: National Statistics (2003b; cited in Hall, 2003).
[b] Commuting trips – financial year starting for the year shown.

accompanied by flexibility in how we think about distance. Most importantly people behave with respect to relative or non-physical space, which does not possess metric properties of distance rather than the absolute space of Euclidean geometry. In addition, people's behavioural concepts of distance are therefore constructed out of more than a single notion of distance. Therefore types of distance that influence mobility include:

- Euclidean distance, which is the direct physical distance between locations;
- Time distance, which is the time taken to travel between locations;
- Economic distance (cost distance), which is the monetary cost incurred in overcoming physical distance between two locations;
- Gravity distance, a subset of time/economic distance but which reinforces the notion that closer means less effort and is important for a range of behaviours including estimated size of markets for locations and attractions;
- Network distance, which is the distance between locations via intermediate points, as in a transport network or telecommunication network. This can also sometimes be referred to as route or 'Manhattan' distance;
- Cognitive/perceived distance, which is judgements regarding the spatial separation of locations. Cognitive distance is particularly important for example to the ways that actual or potential travellers collect, structure and recall information with respect to locations in physical space and establish mental maps. However, it can also apply at the micro-scale with respect to distance between floors of a building or offices and can be important in design;
- Social distance, which is a distance component associated with differences between social classes (which possess different socio-economic characteristics), which may be expressed in terms of the locational characteristics of class or status;

- Cultural distance, related to the above but which refers more specifically to differences between cultures and how they are expressed in perceptions of distance; and
- Centre–periphery distance, which refers to the economic, social and political differences between metropolitan regions and peripheries and is usually expressed in terms of perceived power and control.

In the above list of different types of distance it should be noted that the first five types of distance are open to substantial quantification, while cognitive distance can also be mapped.

2. *Travel and locational decisions are generally taken in order to minimize the frictional effects of distance.* This concept is otherwise referred to as the 'law of minimum effort' (Lösch, 1954: 184) or the 'principle of least effort' (Zipf, 1949). Zipf's (1949) concept of the 'economy of geography' was essentially based on the interrelationship between the principle of least effort and the effect of distance as a barrier to mobility. The empirically observed regularities in movement patterns that are reflected in the distance–decay relationships described above are ultimately based on the fact that travel decisions generally attempt to overcome this barrier. Therefore, in many situations, minimizing the effort expended in movement is achieved by minimizing the distance travelled. In tourism, exceptions to this rule apply when the trip or transport mode is itself part of the attraction or is the destination, for example cruising or historic train travel. However, even in these situations time and space constraints still apply.

3. *Destinations and locations are variably accessible with some destinations more accessible than others.* Accessibility is a variable quality of any location but basically refers to the ease of getting to a place and is closely related to the concept of movement-minimization, especially when this is measured by the costs involved in overcoming distance.

4. *There is a tendency for human activities to agglomerate to take advantage of scale economies.* Scale economies mean the savings in economic and time distance costs made possible by concentrating activities, such as firm operations, at common locations. However, it can also apply to social relationships as well. Even in the age of the so-called virtual world there are still advantages to be gained through co-location and 'face-to-face' strategies.

5. *The organization of spatial and non-spatial aspects of human activity is essentially hierarchical in nature.* In part this occurs as a result of interrelationships between agglomeration tendencies and accessibility. More accessible locations appear to be the sites of larger agglomerations and vice versa. One of the implications from this is that there exists in an area a *hierarchy* of locations in terms of accessibility. For example, this is something that becomes readily apparent when considering relationships between city population size and airport traffic as well as other transport nodes (Page, 1999) and is also evidenced in the rank–size relationship between countries and international visitor arrivals (Ulubasoglu and Hazari, 2004).

6. *Human activities and occupance are focal in character.* The nodes about which human activity is organized are agglomerations of varying size. Since these are hierarchically arranged it follows that there is a *hierarchy* of different sized focal regions. Again, this becomes evident when considering the order ranking of airports in any given country and the relative size of the regions that they service. Therefore, 'movement-minimization, accessibility, agglomerations and hierarchies are linked together to form a system of human organization in space' (Garner, 1967: 305).

The mobile turn in sociology has been described by Urry (2004) as the 'new social physics'. However, it is important that in developing a new social physics of mobility we do not ignore the old one (Stewart, 1950) that has provided a base for much analysis on regional science, planning and transport (e.g. Stewart and Warntz, 1958). Instead Stewart's (1947) search for empirical mathematical rules concerning the distribution and equilibrium of population, which underlay much of the quantitative revolution in the social sciences in the 1960s, 1970s and beyond, should be extended to mobile populations, and should be seen as complementary to qualitative social science research methods rather than a competitor (Hall, 2005c). Moreover, both quantitative and qualitative methods need to see tourism over the totality of a trip as well as of an individual's life-course and interactions. Without such an approach, for example, we are forever doomed to see tourism's effects only at the destination scale rather than as part of a broader understanding of mobility. Indeed, if the analogy with physics is to be maintained we can argue that macro-level quantitative accounts of patterns of human mobility can be regarded as classical Newtonian physics while micro-level accounts of individual human behaviour can be likened to quantum physics (Hall, 2005c). The task in physics, as it is in examining human mobility, is to unify these understandings into a comprehensible whole. However, also as in physics, students of mobility find it difficult to find consilience between the micro-level mobility behaviours of individual humans, which are reasonably difficult to predict, and the relative predictibility of the mobility behaviours of populations, which are the aggregate of those 'difficult' individuals. The issue then is as much of scale of analysis and connectivities between scales as it is of method.

Beyond the Routine? Developing Time Geographies of Tourism Mobility

Models of spatial interaction and diffusion are an aggregate representation of individual mobilities or time geographies. Time geography examines 'the ways in which the production and reproduction of social life depend upon knowledgeable human subjects tracing out routinized paths over space and through time, fulfilling particular projects whose realizations are bounded by inter-locking capability, coupling and steering constraints' (Gregory, 1985: 297). Based on the work of authors such as Hägerstrand (1967, 1975), Carlstein (Carlstein et al., 1978), Thrift (1977) and Pred (1981a, b) time geography has been influential in seeking to understand individual space–time patterns as well as underlying significant developments in social theory such as Giddens' (1984) notion of structuration.

According to Giddens (1984: 116), 'Time-geography is concerned with the constraints that shape the routines of day-to-day life and shares with structuration theory an emphasis upon the significance of the practical character of daily activities, in circumstances of co-presence, for the constitution of social conduct', while also stressing 'the routine character of daily life' connected with features of the human body, its means of mobility and communication, and its path through the 'life cycle' (1984: 111). Significantly, however, time geographies were not related to tourism, which was seen as being an occurrence outside that of the routine, a perspective that continues to the present day in much tourism writing. For example, Aronsson (2000: 57) argues, '[W]e are prisoners in the present-day time-space structure that we have created for our lives, we often use the free time we have in the evenings, at week ends and during our holidays to change this state of affairs through, for instance, a change of environment or, if you will, a change of time-space'. Similarly, Wang (2000: vii) observes that tourism is 'a kind of social action which distances the paramount reality' both in time and geography and in terms of culture. Yet such perspectives fail to acknowledge the extent to which space–time compression has led to fundamental changes to individual's space–time paths in recent years. The routinized space–time paths of those living in the developed world in the present day are clearly not the same as those of people in 1984 when Giddens was writing or even more so in the 1960s when Hägerstrand was examining daily space–time trajectories. Instead, because of advances in transport and communication technology, for a substantial proportion of the population being able to travel long distances to engage in leisure behaviour (what one would usually describe as tourism) is now a part of their routine activities (Hall, 2005a, b), while the possibilities to be able to engage in such travel, as suggested via the media, Internet and contemporary lifestyles, have also become more routine.

People's travel time budgets have not changed substantially, but the ability to travel further at a lower per unit cost within a given time budget (Schafer, 2000) has led to a new series of social encounters, interactions and patterns of production and reproduction as well as consumption. The locales in which this occurs are sometimes termed destinations, and are part of the socio-economic path space of a particular type of lifestyle mobility that, when it occurs away from the home environment, is usually termed 'tourism' (Hall, 2005a). Just as significantly, space–time distancing through both tourism and changes in communication technology has provided for the development of often dense sets of social, cultural and economic networks stretching between the two ends of the mobility spectrum from daily leisure mobility through to migration and which also promote the development of transnational communities in which movement is the norm. Such shifts are highly significant for a destination seeking to reinvent itself. For example, the distance decay effects of travel are substantial in terms of seeking new markets. In general, the long-distance trip making (e.g. journeys to destinations beyond 100 km from home or current base) usually associated with tourism constitutes a very small share of all journeys (about 0.5%), but represents a much larger share of the total kilometres or miles travelled (about 20%) and therefore of the commercial and environmental impacts of travel (Axhausen, 2001). However, because we are aware that human mobility generates further human mobility – because co-presence is still important in most cultures to maintain social relations over space and time – then focusing on transnational network maintenance or generation becomes a key activity for destinations seeking to increase visitor numbers.

A further dimension of such space–time approaches to tourism mobility is that tourism does not occur randomly in space. The time/distance sensitivity of tourist related travel leads to specific spatial patterns related to distance from origin. Space–time constraints exist for a range of accessibility relations between a point of origin and a destination. The space–time framework recognizes that participation in activities, such as leisure, has both spatial and temporal dimensions, i.e. activities occur at specific locations for finite temporal durations. In addition, the transportation system dictates the velocities at which individuals can travel and therefore the time available for activity participation at dispersed locations (destinations) (Miller, 1999). Individuals and households, possessing knowledge of the distance costs, select a tourism destination that maximizes their utility subject to their time/distance constraints. However, a uniform plane clearly does not occur in the real world and travel distances are highly affected by transport networks as well as the distribution of amenity locations. Such a constraint is accounted for by Miller's (1991) notion of potential path space (PPS) defined in terms of the space–time prism that delimits all locations in space–time that can be reached by an individual based on the locations and duration of mandatory activities (e.g. home, work) and the travel velocities allowed by the transportation system (Fig. 2.4). Assume an individual located at time t1 at the point of origin (X_0, Y_0). Again assume that at time t2 the individual has to be back at the origin. Then the available time for all activities is given by:

(1) $t = t2 - t1$

The projection of PPS on to two-dimensional XY-space represents the potential path area that an individual can move within, given the available time budget. For example, according to Hall and Müller (2004) the location of second homes

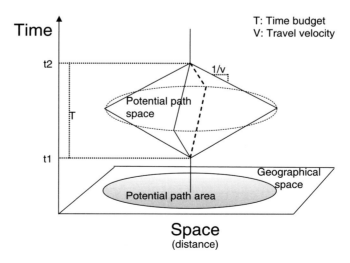

Fig. 2.4. Mobility space–time prism.

is substantially explainable in terms of space–time relationships between the location of the second home and the primary residence. In the case of Sweden, Müller (2004) reported that 25% of all owners have their second homes within 8 km from their permanent residence, 50% within 32 km and 75% within 93 km (the average value was 87 km), with distance explaining more than 97% of the variations in volume of second homes ($r^2 = 0.9789$) (Fig. 2.5). These empirical results clearly reinforce the validity of the first three laws of tourism mobility.

Nevertheless, space–time relations between locations do change as a result of changes in transport technology (e.g. a shift between or within technologies) or transport infrastructure (e.g. improvement in road quality allowing for faster travel or direct network access as a result of new airline routes) and, to a much lesser extent, perceptual distance as a result of place marketing. Although not discussed here it should also be noted that population growth and urbanization processes will also encourage such changes in the location of daytripping,

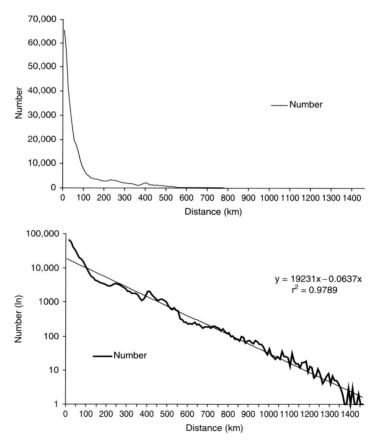

Fig. 2.5. Relationship between number of second homes and distance between second home and permanent residence in Sweden (untransformed data and log form) (Source: Müller, 2004).

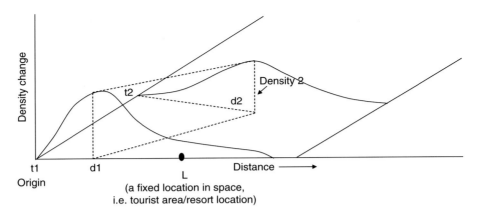

Fig. 2.6. Wave analogue (Source: Hall, 2003).

overnight stays and second homes. These changes can also be represented as a wave analogue in which changes in time/distance from a central point of origin will lead to different densities d of overnight stay at a specific location L over times t1, t2, . . . in relation to the overall distribution of overnight stays as a function of distance from origin (Fig. 2.6). This has been argued elsewhere (Hall, 2005a, 2006) as representing an analogue to the tourism area life cycle that because of its grounding in accessibility provides an empirical basis by which to predict future visitor numbers through the application of market area models. Nevertheless, such an example only touches the surface of the value of space–time approaches to tourism mobilities, with advances in communications technology that can be spatially analysed, such as mobile phones and Global Positioning System (GPS), offering a potential means to strongly connect the mathematical approach to aggregate mobility behaviour to the behavioural dimensions of individuals' paths in space–time.

Conclusions

This chapter has focused on concepts of mobility and space and time as being central to understanding tourism mobilities and how destinations see themselves in tourist space. It has taken an aggregate geographical perspective of mobility as opposed to the individual perspective typically utilized within sociological approaches to mobility. Yet both approaches fit into the rubric of social physics (Urry, 2004; Hall, 2005c). Such approaches are not in opposition to one another. Instead, they are complementary because they are operating at different scales of analysis though findings at one scale can inform the other. Significantly both approaches are utilizing time-geographic methods as a way of better understanding human mobility in both qualitative and quantitative forms (Baerenholdt *et al.*, 2004; Hall, 2005a, b). Nevertheless, a significant barrier to their adoption is the need for students of tourism to be sufficiently grounded in method so as to be able to appreciate their complementarity. In doing so it remains important that basic geographic concepts such as space, time and accessibility become core components in our understanding of tourism mobilities.

Acknowledgements

Earlier versions of this chapter were presented to the Fourth International Symposium, Centre for Tourism Policy Studies, Eastbourne, UK, 23–24 June 2005; to a meeting on reinventing destinations on the Canary Islands in 2004; and to graduate symposia in Sweden and Finland in 2004 and 2005, respectively.

The author would like to acknowledge the feedback provided by those meetings and particularly the contributions of Tim Coles, David Duval, Stefan Gössling, Dieter Müller and Jarkko Saarinen.

References

Aronsson, L. (2000) *The Development of Sustainable Tourism*. Continuum, London.

Axhausen, K.W. (2001) Methodological research for a European survey of long-distance travel. In: *Personal Travel: the Long and Short of It. Conference Proceedings June 28–July 1, 1999 Washington, DC*. Transportation Research Board (TRB) Transportation Research Circular E-C026. TRB, Washington, DC, pp. 321–342.

Baerenholdt, J.O., Haldrup, M., Larsen, J. and Urry, J. (2004) *Performing Tourist Places*. Ashgate, Aldershot, UK.

Becheri, E. (1989) From thermalism to health tourism. *Revue de Tourisme* 44(4), 15–19.

Bell, M. and Ward, G. (2000) Comparing temporary mobility with permanent migration. *Tourism Geographies: International Journal of Place, Space and the Environment* 2(3), 87–107.

Boyle, P., Halfacree, K. and Robinson, V. (1998) *Exploring Contemporary Migration*. Longman, Harlow, UK.

Carlstein, T., Parkes, D.N. and Thrift, N.J. (eds) (1978) *Timing Space and Spacing Time*. Edward Arnold, London.

Cohen, E. (1974) Who is a tourist? A conceptual clarification. *Sociological Review* 22, 527–555.

Coles, T.E. and Timothy, D.J. (eds) (2004) *Tourism, Diasporas and Space*. Routledge, London.

Coles, T., Duval, D. and Hall, C.M. (2004) Tourism, mobility and global communities: new approaches to theorising tourism and tourist spaces. In: Theobold, W. (ed.) *Global Tourism*, 3rd edn. Heinemann, Oxford, UK, pp. 463–481.

Coles, T., Hall, C.M. and Duval, D. (2005) Mobilising tourism: a post-disciplinary critique. *Tourism Recreation Research* 30(2), 31–41.

Coles, T., Hall, C.M. and Duval, D. (2006) Tourism and postdisciplinarity in the social sciences. *Current Issues in Tourism* 9, 293–319.

Coppock, J.T. (ed.) (1977) *Second Homes: Curse or Blessing?* Pergamon, Oxford, UK.

Duval, D.T. (2002) The return visit – return migration connection. In: Hall, C.M. and Williams, A. (eds) *Tourism and Migration: New Relationships Between Production and Consumption*. Kluwer, Dordrecht, the Netherlands, pp. 257–276.

Duval, D.T. (2004) Conceptualising return visits: a transnational perspective. In: Coles, T.E. and Timothy, D.J. (eds) *Tourism, Diasporas and Space: Travels to Promised Lands*. Routledge, London, pp. 50–61.

Duval, D.T. and Hall, C.M. (2004) Linking diasporas and tourism: transnational mobilities of Pacific Islanders resident in New Zealand. In: Coles, T.E. and Timothy, D.J. (eds) *Tourism, Diasporas and Space*. Routledge, London, pp. 78–94.

Field, A.M. (1999) The college student market segment: a comparative study of travel behaviors of international and domestic students at a southeastern university. *Journal of Travel Research* 37, 375–381.

Garner, B. (1967) Models of urban geography and settlement location. In: Chorley, R.J. and Haggett, P. (eds) *Models in Geography*. Methuen, London, pp. 303–360.

Giddens, A. (1984) *The Constitution of Society: Outline of the Theory of Structuration*. University of California Press, Berkeley, California.

Goodrich, J.N. (1994) Health tourism: a new positioning strategy for tourist destinations. *Journal of International Consumer Marketing* 6(3/4), 227–237.

Goodrich, J.N. and Goodrich, G.E. (1987) Health-care tourism – an exploratory study. *Tourism Management* 8, 217–222.

Gregory, D. (1985) Suspended animation: the status of diffusion theory. In: Gregory, D. and Urry, J. (eds) *Social Relations and Spatial Structures*. Macmillan, London, pp. 296–336.

Gustafson, P. (2002) Tourism and seasonal retirement migration. *Annals of Tourism Research* 29(4), 899–918.

Hägerstrand, T. (1967) *Innovation Diffusion as a Spatial Process*. (Translated by A. Pred). University of Chicago Press, Chicago, Illinois.

Hägerstrand, T. (1975) Space, time and human conditions. In: Karlqvist, A., Lundqvist, L. and Snickars, F. (eds) *Dynamic Allocation of Urban Space*. Saxon House/Lexington: Lexington Books, Farnborough, UK, pp. 3–14.

Hall, C.M. (2003) Tourism and temporary mobility: circulation, diaspora, migration, nomadism, sojourning, travel, transport and home. Paper presented at International Academy for the Study of Tourism Conference, 30 June–5 July, Savonlinna, Finland.

Hall, C.M. (2005a) *Tourism: Rethinking the Social Science of Mobility*. Prentice-Hall, Harlow, UK.

Hall, C.M. (2005b) Reconsidering the geography of tourism and contemporary mobility. *Geographical Research* 43(2), 125–139.

Hall, C.M. (2005c) Time, space, tourism and social physics. *Tourism Recreation Research* 30(1), 93–98.

Hall, C.M. (2006) Space–time accessibility and the tourist area cycle of evolution: the role of geographies of spatial interaction and mobility in contributing to an improved understanding of tourism. In: Butler, R. (ed.) *The Tourism Life Cycle: Conceptual and Theoretical Issues*. Channel View Publications, Clevedon, UK, pp. 83–100.

Hall, C.M. (2007) *Introduction to Tourism in Australia*, 5th edn. Pearson Education/Hospitality Press, Melbourne.

Hall, C.M. and Müller, D. (eds) (2004) *Tourism, Mobility and Second Homes: Between Elite Landscape and Common Ground*. Channel View Publications, Clevedon, UK.

Hall, C.M. and Williams, A.M. (eds) (2002) *Tourism and Migration: New Relationships Between Consumption and Production*. Kluwer, Dordrecht, the Netherlands.

Hall, C.M., Williams, A.M. and Lew, A. (2004) Tourism: conceptualisations, institutions and issues. In: Lew, A., Hall, C.M. and Williams, A.M. (eds) *Companion to Tourism*. Blackwells, Oxford, UK, pp. 1–21.

Hsu, C.H.C. and Sung, S. (1996) International students' travel characteristics: an exploratory study. *Journal of Travel and Tourism Marketing* 5(Winter), 277–283.

Hsu, C.H.C. and Sung, S. (1997) Travel behaviors of international students at a Midwestern university. *Journal of Travel Research* 36, 59–65.

Kalinowski, K.M. and Weiler, B. (1992) Educational travel. In: Weiler, B. and Hall, C.M. (eds) *Special Interest Tourism*. Belhaven Press, London, pp. 15–26.

King, R. (2002) Towards a new map of European migration. *International Journal of Population Geography* 8, 89–106.

Kraft, R.M., Ballatine, J. and Garvey, D.E. (1994) Study abroad or international travel? The case of semester at sea. *Phi Beta Delta International Review* 4, 23–61.

Lee, H.M. (2003) *Tongans Overseas: Between Two Shores*. University of Hawai'i Press, Honolulu, Hawaii.

Lösch, A. (1954) *The Economics of Location*. Yale University Press, New Haven, Connecticut.

Mason, P. (2002) The 'Big OE': New Zealanders overseas experiences in Britain. In: Hall, C.M. and Williams, A.M. (eds) *Tourism and Migration: New Relationships between Production and Consumption*. Kluwer, Dordrecht, the Netherlands, pp. 87–102.

Miller, H.J. (1991) Modeling accessibility using space–time prism concepts within Geographical Information Systems. *International Journal of Geographical Information Systems* 5, 287–301.

Miller, H.J. (1999) Measuring space–time accessibility benefits within transportation networks: basic theory and computational methods. *Geographical Analysis* 31, 187–212.

Müller, D.K. (1999) *German Second Home Owners in the Swedish Countryside: On the Internationalization of the Leisure Space*. European Tourism Research Institute, Östersund, Sweden.

Müller, D.K. (2004) The attractiveness of second homes areas in Sweden: a quantitative analysis. Paper presented at the 30th Congress of the International Geographical Union, 15–20 August, Glasgow.

Page, S.J. (1999) *Transport and Tourism*, 2nd edn. Addison-Wesley Longman, London.

Pred, A.R. (1981a) Social reproduction and the time-geography of everyday life. *Geografiska Annaler* 63B, 5–22.

Pred, A.R. (1981b) Production, family, and free-time projects: a time-geographic perspective on the individual and societal change in 19th century US cities. *Journal of Historical Geography* 7, 3–6.

Ravenstein, E.G. (1885) The laws of migration. *Journal of the Royal Statistical Society* 48, 167–235.

Ravenstein, E.G. (1889) The laws of migration. *Journal of the Royal Statistical Society* 52, 214–301.

Robinson, G.M. (1998) *Methods and Techniques in Human Geography*. Wiley, Chichester, UK.

Schafer, A. (2000) Regularities in travel demand: an international perspective. *Journal of Transportation and Statistics* 3(3), 1–31.

Sheller, M. and Urry, J. (2004) Mobile transformations of 'public' and 'private' life. *Theory, Culture and Society* 20(3), 107–125.

Smith, S.L.J. (1985) US vacation travel patterns: correlates of distance decay and the willingness to travel. *Leisure Sciences* 7(2), 151–174.

Stephenson, M. (2002) Travelling to the ancestral homelands: the aspirations and experiences of a UK Caribbean community. *Current Issues in Tourism* 5(5), 378–425.

Stewart, J.Q. (1947) Empirical mathematical rules concerning the distribution and equilibrium of population. *Geographical Review* 37, 467–485.

Stewart, J.Q. (1950) The development of social physics. *American Journal of Physics* 18, 239–253.

Stewart, J.Q. and Warntz, W. (1958) Physics of population distribution. *Journal of Regional Science* 1, 99–123.

Thrift, N.J. (1977) Time and theory in human geography, part 2. *Progress in Human Geography* 1, 23–57.

Tobler, W.R. (1970) A computer movie. *Economic Geography* 46, 234–240.

Tobler, W.R. (2004) On the first law of geography: a reply. *Annals of the Association of American Geographers* 94(2), 304–310.

Ulubasoglu, M.A. and Hazari, B.R. (2004) Zipf's Law strikes again: the case of tourism. *Journal of Economic Geography* 4, 459–472.

United Nations and United Nations World Tourism Organization (2007) *International Recommendations on Tourism Statistics (IRTS)*. Provisional Draft. United Nations and United Nations World Tourism Organization, New York.

Urry, J. (2000) *Sociology Beyond Societies: Mobilities for the Twenty-First Century*. Routledge, London.

Urry, J. (2004) Small worlds and the new 'social physics'. *Global Networks* 4(2), 109–130.

Wang, N. (2000) *Tourism and Modernity: a Sociological Analysis*. Elsevier Science/ Pergamon, Oxford, UK.

Williams, A.M. and Hall, C.M. (2000) Tourism and migration: new relationships between production and consumption. *Tourism Geographies* 2(1), 5–27.

Williams, A.M. and Hall, C.M. (2002) Tourism, migration, circulation and mobility: the contingencies of time and place. In: Hall, C.M. and Williams, A.M. (eds) *Tourism and Migration: New Relationships between Production and Consumption*. Kluwer, Dordrecht, the Netherlands, pp. 1–52.

Zipf, G.K. (1949) *Human Behaviour and the Principle of Least Effort*. Prentice-Hall, Reading, UK.

3 'Glocal' Heterotopias: Neo-flâneur's Transit Narratives

WAEL SALAH FAHMI

Theoretical Background

Globalization and mobility

With increased mobility and telecommunications and with the rise of new media and cyberspace, the experience of time, space and place identity has changed. Contemporary technologies are expanding cities horizontally through new systems of digital and physical infrastructure. The emerging modes of communication, embedded within the very means of mobility, have promoted new types of spatial experiences that are increasingly more fluid, complex, surreal and a-geographical than in the past. Beckmann (1998) argues that globalized liquid 'soft architectures' of digital media flow over, under and through the local concrete and 'hard architectures' of our contemporary cities, creating an indeterminate, 'floating' environment, an interface between public and private, collective and subjective, provincial and planetary. Places do not disappear, but their logic and their meaning become absorbed in the network, enabling the flexibilization of people's paths through space–time, while transforming the requirements and characteristics of co-presence (Sheller and Urry, 2000).

Heterotopias of mobile communications have formed supermodern spatiality (Augé, 1995), while being influenced by forces of global capitalism. Functioning as signs rather than places, bland shopping malls, indistinguishable airports, transit and informational spaces, gated communities and theme parks have become eloquent geographical media and expressions of a new global cultural economy of space. Terkenli's (2002) study negotiates the processes whereby 'replicated co-presence', produced by mobile computers, palmtops, computer connections on trains and aircraft as 'portals' to the Internet, imprint on tourist landscapes and newly emerging cultural reorganization of space. This is substantiated in terms of landscape seduction and the desire to travel, and constructed through complex bodily, emotional and cognitive interrelationships between the tourist and the visited landscape.

Although cultures can no longer be thought of as exclusively territorial in their scope as a result of travel and mobility entailed in globalization, locality and place attachment are still significant in people's lives (Nederveen-Pieterse, 1995; Rapport and Dawson, 1998; Tomlinson, 1999). This global–local hybridity involves the dialectical relationship between culture as an inward-looking fixed localized process defined by territory, and as an outward-looking mobile global process, with both processes not being mutually exclusive (Nederveen-Pieterse, 1995: 61). This appears to be the case of tourism as the fixed local culture combines with transient tourism to create a hybrid touristic culture, with a need to specify which particular elements are 'authentically' local, and which are 'authentically' transnational (Nederveen-Pieterse, 1995, 2001; Urry, 2002; Meethan, 2003).

Urban images and the tourist gaze

Past decades have seen the rise of 'a new society of the image' based on 'consumption by the eyes' (Jameson, 1991). As postmodern society becomes increasingly fragmented, with community groups being less clearly defined, global companies – through sales and branding – have developed a new niche of 'fluxus' community based on image consumption. It is not simply that urban life has become more superficial, more image- and consumption-based under conditions of late capitalism, but rather that the city in itself has become 'soft' (Raban, 1974), with the border between the 'self' and city becoming fluid (Fahmi, 2001).

'Cities, unlike villages and small towns, are plastic by nature. We mould them in our images: they, in their turn, shape us by the resistance they offer when we try to impose a personal form on them' (Raban, 1974: 10). 'The city as we might imagine it, the soft city of illusion, myth, aspiration, nightmare, is as real, maybe more real, than the hard city one can locate in maps and statistics, in monographs on urban sociology and demography and architecture' (Raban, 1974: 10).

However, Lefebvre (1991) distinguishes between 'representations of space' engaged in by planners and cartographers, and symbolic 'representational spaces' in cities, drawing on shared experiences and interpretations of people's everyday 'spatial practices', where making space is very much a way of making meaning. Postmodern urbanism is conscious of the power of discursive production of urban representational spaces where 'people not only live their space through its associated images and symbols' (Lefebvre, 1991: 39), they actively construct its meaning through cognitive and hermeneutical processes. Discourses express human ontology (beliefs, fantasies, values and desires about how the world is) and epistemology (how better understandings of the world might be achieved).

Nevertheless, multimedia technologies intervene in processes of representation, performance and exchange as they operate simultaneously as vehicles for production and distribution of signs, and as signs themselves. Barthes' (1976) semiotic approach is concerned with the how of representation, with how language produces meaning in terms of a system of signs. This is related to the view of tourist attractions being regarded as semiotic or textual meaning structures connected reciprocally to larger cultural discourses such as heritage sites, literary landscapes and theme parks (Rojek, 1993: 136–137). These postmodern categories have a place-bound history and meanings that are produced both locally and globally through the movement of capital and the process of space–time compression. The idea of a tourist attraction as a semiotic structure and a sign is related to MacCannell's (1976) interpretation of the relationship between the tourist and sight. Through the interaction of symbolic markers, the tourist attraction is interpreted as a dynamic socio-spatial structure and as a cultural landscape subject to continual transformation and (re)production.

While the visual reproduction of tourist attractions involves the creation of travelogues, brochures, postcards and souvenirs, the social dimension is concerned with local groups, communities, cities and regions. Santos and da Paula (2003) present tourist place as mediated through images in terms of various representational systems: the officialdom gaze (as portrayed in the official tourism information); the individual tourist gaze (tourists' photographs); the commodity gaze (illustrated postcards); and the inhabitants' gaze (local inhabitants' photographs of their place). Furthermore, Urry's (1990) tourist gazer metaphor has been applied to the experience of mobility as related to how tourists view and consume the visual nature of the tourism, with a distinction being made between individual and collective tourist gazes. These gazes are dependant upon a variety of social discourses and practices, while being discursively organized by professionals, including photographers, writers of travel books and guides, travel agents, hotel owners and designers, tour operators, TV travel programmes and tourism development officers. In one sense we do live in a society of spectacle in which most environments have been transformed into diverse and collectable spectacles (Debord, 1994).

In Western thought 'knowing' has been closely associated with 'seeing', a stance that bears on photography, constituting it as a powerful form of knowledge of the world in the present-day highly image-mediated postmodernity. Simultaneously, the visual is being criticized within discourses surrounding travel, as mere sightseers are regarded to be superficial in their appreciation of environments, peoples and places (Urry, 2003). The criticism of the sightseeing tourist is further tackled in the analysis of the 'hyper-real', those simulated designed places which have the appearance of being more 'real' than the original (Baudrillard, 1981; Eco, 1986), where the sense of vision is reduced to a limited array of visual features.

Post-tourism and photography

Tourist activities occur within sites firmly rooted in the contingent circumstances of a locality, regarded as the natural relationship between traditional cultures, local environment and face-to-face community interaction. As transient outsiders, tourists can hardly acquire the crucial knowledge and understanding, or 'habitus' that local communities possess. The 'post-tourist' sensibility is developing in a context in which commodification of tourism remains the most obvious fact about the experience of travel for pleasure (Rojek and Urry, 1997).

Postmodern leisure theory has heralded the arrival of the 'post-tourist' defined as having a 'playful, ironic, and sometimes formally individualized attitude to sight-seeing' (Rojek, 1997: 62), while appreciating the performance and exhibiting a non-exploitative manner of utilizing the site. Post-tourism can be seen as an indicator of postmodernism in terms of consumption and the 'proliferation of images and signs presented as spectacles' (Bryman, 1995: 176).

> The following are relevant to understanding the changing sociology of the tourist gaze: the social tone of different places; the globalisation and the universalisation of the tourist gaze; the processes of consuming tourist services; tourist meanings and signs; modernism and postmodernism; history, heritage and the vernacular; and post-tourism and play.
>
> (Urry, 1990: 135)

Zhao and Chen (2006) unpack the tourist experiences by drawing from recent social cultural consumption theories of performance, gazing and encounter by tourists (Urry, 1990; Hall, 1994; Crouch, 1999; Edensor, 2000), while emphasizing differences between packaged and non-packaged post-tourists. Lee (2001) suggests that, as post-tourism emerges, the 'tourist gaze', the systematic ways in which tourists are seeing, experiencing and consuming signs, symbols and places when they are travelling, has increasingly been universalized. Post-tourist experience does not merely combine the imagery of tourist promotion with an exploitative posture, but depends on self-rediscovery using individuals' knowledge and skills to engage space, environment and cultures through their own encounters with cultural signifiers and various staged performances.

Santos and da Paula (2003) highlight the need to move into a broader approach to tourist experience within a place, one that requires the consideration of both a semiotics approach and a discursive social practice perspective. Sternberg (1997) and Garlick (2002) discuss the role of photography in determining the nature and meaning of post-tourist experience through an array of representations, images, cognitive understandings and emotional responses. Yeh (2003) suggests that research on photography and post-tourism regards both as devices for consuming visual images and as aspects of the analysis of cultural encounters. In particular, there is a desire to project imagery that represents an authentic identity of place, where photography deploys particular aesthetics that excludes as much as it includes. There is a need to offer sufficient evidence for explaining what the tourist gazes upon through photographic practices, introducing broader questions of identity, social interaction and representation by focusing on the role of the camera in staging tourist performance, while embodying practices of sociability (Sontag, 2002).

Authenticity and aesthetic reflexivity

The perceived significance of tourist cultural spaces has promoted themes of aestheticization in today's postmodern society, reflecting the increasing role of image consumption. Thus, apart from the component of knowledge or information intensity, sign value and aesthetic image become significant in urban production and consumption, triggered by economic boosterism and disappearance of traditional local meaning. What this tends to generate is a cocoon-like existence, predicated upon aesthetic gratification (Leach, 2001). And it is this cocoon, this isolated state of being cosseted from reality and locked into some dream world, that can be expanded and developed to offer a representational system for postmodern contemporary life.

In postmodern societies people are increasingly able to distinguish and evaluate 'style and taste' images and symbols operating at the level of cognition. With the heterogeneity and complexity of spatiality and everyday consumption, people reflect upon their social conditions, with such reflexivity becoming aesthetic, opening up possibilities for recasting meaning in work and in leisure. Aesthetic reflexivity can be seen in terms of the increased choice element of consumption which involves a set of identity-choices: an aesthetic-expressive dimension of the (post)modern self (Lash and Urry, 1994). Understanding aesthetic reflexivity about the value of different physical and social environments is connected to the increasing transnational mobility of people (Lash and Urry, 1994).

Lash and Urry (1994) state that postmodernity produces 'semiotic' rather than industrial goods. The mobility of these objects or goods in flows changes their nature – they are progressively emptied out of both symbolic and material content and thus of their traditional local meaning. What increasingly is being produced are no longer material objects but signs as goods often take on the properties of sign value through the process of branding, in which marketers and advertisers attach images to goods (Lash and Urry, 1994). This reflexivity is partly based on aesthetic judgements and stems from the proliferation of many forms of real and simulated mobility.

While sociologists maintain that postmodern society is becoming increasingly fragmented as community groups become less clearly defined, global companies, through sales and branding, have developed a new analysis of community based on tourist consumption. Society's dependence on image and the perceived value of goods has created unprecedented control over people's choices. Accordingly themes of aestheticization in today's postmodern society reflect the increasing role of tourist consumption as an art form (Ritzer and Liska, 1997). With the emergence of a new consumer type – the 'fluxus' consumer – multiple selection and a combination of products allow a unique spatial experience, the architecture of the postmodern commercial take-away.

With commodification of postmodern place, fragmentation of spatial experience and globalization of local culture, commercial interests are keen to stage authenticity to represent desirable tourist experiences as convenient commodities for consumption. This involves the invention of nostalgic representation of the past and replication of history for contemporary 'leisure and tourism' consumption, leading to tourists' immersion in hyper-reality and simulation, where the distinction between reality and its representation is easily blurred (Baudrillard, 1993). Authenticity is not only a social construction but a performed achievement where each post-tourist pieces together his or her own unique 'rite of passage' (Shaffer, 2004), rather than the experience of packaged tourism in terms of mere sightseeing and a brief superficial introduction to a destination's history, landmarks and culture.

Conceptual Framework and Methodology

Transit spaces and heterotopias

In a territory where non-place (Augé, 1995) and space of flow (Castells, 1996) prevail, more and more people belong to temporary inhabitants who commute, in high-speed vehicles. Accordingly, there is a new category of landscapes 'in transit' which 'users on the move' experience as they cross these 'in-between' landscapes by train, by bus or by plane (Fahmi, 2003b). They do not fully engage their senses in the landscape experience but reduce the physical interaction to a remote gaze. While Urry's (1990) notion of the 'tourist gaze' has become paradigmatic in explaining touristic vision, trains and cars provide a radically different viewing position and visual experience than the static photographic gaze: the travel glance. The mobile travel glance provides a visual 'cinematic' experience of moving landscape images to the travelling yet corporally immobile 'armchair' spectator.

Larsen (2001) seeks to bring a cultural analysis of experiences of motorized mobility (train and car) into tourism studies. In their early years, the train and the car, regarded as simultaneous vision machines, were perceived as shocking speed machines that radically changed people's experiences of distance, movement, time and landscape and became discursively associated with various 'tourists bodily movements'. De Certeau (1984) refers to a heterotopian state as 'traveling incarceration, immobile inside the train, seeing immobile things slip by'. A train is an extraordinary bundle of relations 'because it is something through which one goes, it is also something by means of which one can go from one point to another, and then it is also something that goes by' (Foucault, 1986).

According to Foucault (1986), heteropology is a sort of simultaneously mythic and real contestation of the space in which we live. Heterotopia, like utopia, was conceived by Foucault (1986) as 'a site which had the curious property of being in relation with all the other sites, but in such a way as to suspect, neutralise, or invert the set of relations that they happen to designate, mirror or reflect' (Warschauer, 1995). But, whereas utopias exist only in the imagination, heterotopias are actual places formed in the very founding of social life, with these curious sites being socially constructed, simultaneously recreating and revealing the meaning of social being (Soja, 1995). These heterotopias juxtapose in a single real place several spaces and sites that are in themselves incompatible, always presupposing a system of opening and closing (Foucault, 1986: 26).

Heterotopian urbanism supports a new type of public space, characterized by peripheral landscapes, such as service areas and landscapes adjacent to railway lines or airports, interconnecting transport means, and entry or exit zones between the city and countryside (Fahmi, 2003b, 2004). These have become the new social places of a mobile society, with distinction between spaces of transit and city boundaries becoming more blurred. Rather than separate spaces that correspond to rationally defined roles, transit stations (trains, metro subways, buses, airports) have become an extension of the space of commercial transactions (Shuffield, 1999).

If the sealed-off traveller is the inhabitant of temporary landscapes, then fast trains, which blur one's vision by compressing physical distance to the limits, result in the distortion of the idea of physical landscape itself (Virilio, 1997). The railway passenger can usefully be read as a reinvention of the flâneur, as Ward (2005) explores the potential of the (literary) imagination within technologically driven historical processes and the rationalizing networks of modernity. Larsen (2001) argues that a contemporary pleasure of leisurely automobility is related to the vehicle's flexibility and the imagined freedom that set in motion the motorized flânerie (neo-flânerie). The neo-flâneur is therefore subjected to a changing visual experience of mobility which imposes a specific viewing position and, hence, way of seeing with respect to touristic vision and landscape.

The flânerie

Gillespie (2005) points to Benjamin's (1973) analysis of the flâneur with respect to drawing together a configuration of historically distinct experiences and forms of representation. Its first incarnation is the Balzacian flâneur, who emphasizes the need for composure and proper conduct in urban space. The second flâneur, embodied by Baudelaire, is deracinated and economically alienated. The two embodiments of the flâneur differ most starkly in their self-representation with the Baudelairen flâneur being defined by his/her 'incognito' and narratives, while relying on a fetishistic identification with the camera's lens. According to Benjamin (1973), the Baudelairean flâneur is a figure/object (for interpretation) that embodies ambivalence: one who always borders on leisure, joy, melancholy, alienation and familiarity, resulting from the fragmentary nature of city life.

'The flâneur is still on the threshold, of the city as of the bourgeois class. He seeks refuge in the crowd. No matter how protective the crowd can be, the flâneur is still a loner, someone abandoned in the crowd' (Benjamin, 1973: 55).

The sensual pleasure the flâneur derives from the 'phantasmagoria', the dazzling urban spectacle, is both momentary and exciting. What he sees is montage, one snapshot after another with the dream world of urban spectacle offering the flâneur no complete narrative. He has to make sense of the fragments by himself.

> The importance of the figure of the flâneur lies in its utopian presentation of a carefree individual in the midst of the urban maelstrom. To be precise, the flâneur is an 'urban native', whose discernment of the subtle pleasures of urban life and detection of the truth of the street indicate a form of pedestrian connoisseurship and consumption of the urban environment.
>
> (Shields, 1994: 61)

In this sense, Huang (2000) retains the quintessential attribute of the classical flâneur's detachment from the urban spectacle, while strolling through the city's diorama. The gaze of the flâneur can be compassionate, invested and inquiring and at the same time detached, alienated and passive. By walking in a city dominated by space–time compression with conspicuous global landmarks and representation of local consumption patterns, the flâneur experiences spaces of encounter and interpersonal relationships.

Clarke (1997) traces the development of the modern city in terms of the imposition of law and its transgression, and in terms of cognitive space and the 'spectral presence' of the stranger. The significance of the postmodern is theorized in relation to the systemic appropriation of an aesthetic space initially traced out by the flâneur. The existence of the flâneur is translated into the general condition of a society oriented around consumption, implying a new form of cybernetic control, governed by the play of the code, rather than the direct surveillance characteristic of the modern city (Clarke, 1997). The flâneur as an alternative vision and an image of movement through the urban spectacle of modernity is the 'botanist of the asphalt' who walks through the city while exploring shifting social space. Simultaneously, urban space has undergone a transition, which we might begin to address in terms of a 'posturban hyperspace'.

Urban graphics

Sinclair's literary narratives (1997, 2002) have arrived from the experience of walking London's nocturnal streets and perceiving the city's flows of energy (Moshenska, 2005; Wolfreys, 2005). The graphic condition of Sinclair's phantom-graphic interventions disturbs the boundaries and ontologies of genre and aesthetic ideology. Neither simply narrative nor image, the city is marked symbolically, and graphically, with its immediate citation of film, topography, myth and architecture (Wolfreys, 2005). According to Seale (2005), the spectral figure of the flâneur signifies a spatio-temporal representation in Sinclair's non-fictional accounts of London (1997, 1999, 2002). The flâneur metamorphoses, 'multilayered palimpsest'-like, into contemporary incarnations, stalker, photographer – by adding and/or erasing urban layers (Jenks, 1995). It is important to distinguish the flâneur from any official apparatus of visual surveillance, or what Foucault identifies as 'panopticism'.

Eye-swiping

Sinclair (2002) introduces the notion of 'eye-swiping' – scanning the urban landscape for creative material. The term eye-swiping evokes the avidity of the flâneur's eye sweeping up material for literary or artistic reinscription (Seale, 2005). Simultaneously, eye-swiping suggests the act of appropriation, saturating the text with proliferation of information. The precise recall of place is enabled by Sinclair's methodology, which he states is 'walks, photographs then at some later date, a book' (Sinclair, 2002), while referring to the camera to eye-swipe the detail, to log the sights which will later be translated into words (Seale, 2005). Sinclair's eye-swiper reads the photograph as a machine-like reproducer of real images. It is the type of filter that Baudelaire stressed was essential to the flâneur's depiction of urban life. Photography presents itself as the ideal technology for eye-swiping, with the insatiability of the camera's eye being commensurate with the insatiability of the flâneur's *eye*. Baudelaire (1995) speaks of the flâneur as if he were a type of camera in 'The painter of modern life'.

Narratives

Narratives and story telling have formulated architectural fiction while being instrumental to the communication of meaning and urban images. The term 'to narrate' means the binding together of myths and fantasies through constructing a story in motion-narratives based on movement that weave in and out from a building to a street, motorway to river, fact to fiction, past to present (Silver, 2005).

> Walking is the best way to explore and exploit the city; the changes; shifts, breaks in the cloud helmet, movement of light on water. Drifting purposefully is the recommended mode, trampling asphalted earth in alert reverie, allowing the fiction of an underlying plot to reveal itself.
>
> (Sinclair, 1997: 4)

> I suppose that's the nature of London. Endlessly intersecting narratives. Tale-tellers interrupting tale-tellers. Lives that fade into other lives. Cardboard boxes stuffed full of photographs. Manuscripts with merciless annotations. Maps with fictional journeys superimposed. Films that diverge from the purity of the original intention. Mistranscribed recordings. We had what we had, now it was time to assemble the images, to improvise.
>
> (Sinclair, 1999: 44)

> London is whatever can be reached in a one-hour walk. The rest is fictional.
>
> (Atkins and Sinclair, 1999: 40)

The (neo-)flâneur

The fate of the flâneur constantly invites us to consider whether or not the era of globalization allows the kind of walking space that might liberate the contemporary (neo-)flâneur from traditionally defined social space and relations. Such a neo-flâneur is a type that is out to take its artistic or aesthetical distance from its consumerist urban surroundings. In the city that Benjamin inhabits, the flâneur is an endangered species, marginalized by the social and technological conditions of modernity: the hegemony of the vehicular transport; the dominant power of social space by consumer culture; the bureaucratization of the everyday; and the standardization of time.

While the 19th-century cityscape seduces the flâneur with the illusion of infinite spatial freedom, the Baudelairean flâneur might not feel at home in the global postmodern city. The current chapter conceptualizes the 19th-century figure of the Baudelairean flâneur as a (neo-)flâneur or post-tourist, and as being engulfed in the signs and stimuli of global flows, while witnessing the fetishism of commodification and aestheticization of image consumption in a postmodern metropolis (Benjamin, 1973). It is essential to examine the way the (neo-)flâneur's gaze mediates the walker's experience and multi-layered narratives within transit spaces, while becoming an absorbent recipient of postmodern imageries. This will enable us to achieve a reflexive (and cognitive) understanding of epistemologies, with such reflexivity being regarded as the act of making oneself the object of one's own observation. This will attempt to bring to the fore the assumptions embedded in our perspectives and descriptions of the world, while emphasizing the subject-centred nature of human–human encounters which are often a feature of tourism research (Feighery, 2006).

The methodology adopted in the current study proposes a (de)constructive narrative of a journey (within) Moscow's underground Metro (October 2003), engendering frameworks of place and memory and space–time compression (Fahmi, 2001, 2002). This is a situational representation of a navigation with the camera's lens inside-out of transit spaces within Moscow's post-Soviet Metro (scape), employing digital pixels and collages to reaffirm hybrid immersion and spatial flow. As photography presents itself as the ideal technology for Sinclair's notion of eye-swiping (Seale, 2005), the camera's lens is commensurate with the neo-flâneur's urban gaze, presenting a sequence of deconstructive hybrid interfaces of digital images, signs and simulacra. The digital imageries and textual narratives of the journey through transit spaces reflect the hybrid architecture of post-Soviet Metro(scape) and Moscow's postmodern urban scenery, visually fluctuating between the retrospective, projected grandeur of the Stalinist past and the neo-realist quotidian cityscapes of the present. The neo-flâneur's imageries generate a constant reworking of the urban present via memory and experience, in a way suggestive of Lefebvre's (1996) interest in the process of perception and interpretation. Lefebvre (1996) experiences the city not as a static spectacle but as a series of intersecting narratives and patterns of collective movement in the street.

The neo-flâneur attempts to establish a new definition of what may be a subjective Metro space, one that transcends, or even encompasses, existing depictions of Moscow's Metro myths, suggesting a new methodology for constructing and representing urban spaces. Mapping Moscow's Metro(scape) with the camera and assuming the identity of the walker on the street, we take on the characteristic of a Baudelairean flâneur approaching the reality of the vast terrain of Moscow's post-Soviet urban spaces with his interested and investigative gaze. There is an attempt to recuperate and reassemble from the fragments a different picture of post-Soviet Metro(scape)'s spatiality, through the flow and distribution of images (Benjamin, 1985).

The Study Context

Ditchev (2005) explores the Eastern European utopian project of the communist period, tracing their effort to create an urban form that erased the spatial contradictions of human settlements, and promote a way of living in line with socialistic values. Ditchev (2005) uncovers two competing visions for the ideal socialist territoriality, based on either an ameliorated form of concentration or a decentralization of population to erase the division between core and periphery. Yet, as Ditchev illustrates, the daily reality of living under communist spatial organization of population was far from the utopia envisioned by their theoreticians, where 'mobility and urbanisation did not become a tool of liberation, but one of tightening control over the population'. The stringent internal restrictions on travel and settlement shaped complex geometries of citizenship, where the privilege of mobility contributed to definitions of status, appropriate individual behaviour and quality of life, as will be noted in the case of Moscow's Metro(scape).

A spatio-temporal journey through Metro's history

The 1931 monograph 'Socialist Reconstruction of Moscow and other Cities in the USSR' by Kaganovich, who organized the building of the Moscow Metro, described the need for comprehensive city planning as an integral part of the building process of the new 'proletarian' socialist capital (Alden *et al.*, 1998). Stalinist 'socialist realism' planning approaches involved the construction of wide boulevards and large blocks of flats serviced by an underground Metro transit system, which were later adopted in other communist Eastern European cities (Appendix 1).

The Moscow Metro has 11 radial lines, with a 20-km circular connection line, comprising 171 stations, covering over 200 km of track and serving 9 million people each day. There are 70 deep-level stations, 87 shallow stations, with ten ground-level stations and four above ground. Two of the stations exist as double halls, with two having three tracks, and five having side platforms. From 1935 until 1955, the Metro was named after Lazar Kaganovich, an instrumental figure in the construction of the Metro, but the system was later renamed the V.I. Lenin Moscow Metropolitan Railway. Similarly Okhotnyi Ryad Metro station was renamed Imeni Kaganovicha in honour of Lazar Kaganovich between 1955 and 1957, but then was changed in 1961 to Prospekt Marksa (the station still contains a mosaic portrait of Karl Marx) with its original name being re-established in 1990 (Graeme, 2005).

The stations of Moscow's Metro system have often been called 'the people's underground palaces', for their lavish profuse use of marble, mosaics, chandeliers and stucco-covered ceilings, with popular art deco-style compositions merged with socialist realist design and artwork commemorating historic events (Fig. 3.1). As a system of public transportation and a work of urban infrastructure, the Metro, part of the Moscow reconstruction plan as an urban, high-density metropolis, represented the most grandiose architectural phenomenon of the Stalinist era. Such a vast system not only mapped the huge ambitions of the Soviet state under Stalin, but recorded the ideological and artistic shifts that characterize the Stalinist post-war period. From the vast forces marshalled for its construction to the shelter it provided for Muscovites during the Second World War, the Metro had evolved from a monumental public works project and a place of rapid mass transit, with aesthetic media, architecture, sculpture, painting and decorative arts, to a hybrid of palace, basilica and fortress.

The political and ideological proletarian course of the Soviet Union during the Stalinist period is reflected in the vision of public social space with distinct aesthetic styles of four principal lines and 40 stations constructed from 1932 to 1954:

- The First Line, built in the early 1930s, possesses an invigorating modernism representative of the Soviet avant-garde.
- With the Second Line, built in the late 1930s, a programme of monumental sculpture and art was introduced that signalled Stalin's stranglehold on the ideological goals of the Soviet state.

Mosaics regarded as urban semiotics which depict symbols of Soviet production, monuments to Russian soldiers, during the Second World War, the Great Patriotic War, and other scenes from everyday life represent more than just a glimpse back into the life of the Soviet Union.

Fig. 3.1. Mosaics within Metro stations (semiotics).

- The Third Line, built during the 'Great Patriotic War' from 1939 to 1944, became a symbol of Soviet tenacity and ultimately a memorial to the people's resistance during this period.
- The Fourth Line, completed in 1954 shortly after the death of Stalin, is perhaps the most flamboyantly ideological and represents the epitome of the leader's vision for the Metro. With the demise of Stalin, the expression of the system reverted to its rationalist origins.

The natural-stone materials used for the Moscow's Metro stations (about three-quarters of the total wall area and more than half of the floor area) contribute to Russian architectural expressionism. The use of different natural-stone materials, including semi-precious stones, makes Moscow's Metro one of the most interesting tourist destinations. The most ancient decorative material used in the 'Underground Palaces of Moscow' is a coarse-grained pink marble from the southern shore of Baikal Lake, while white marble was brought from the deposits of the Ural Mountains, Altay, Middle Asia and the Caucasus (Appendix 2).

Particularly notable stations are: Komsomolskaya (1952), Kievskaya (1954), Mayakovskaya (1938–1939), Novoslobodskaya (1950) and Ploshchad Revolutsii (1939). Built during Stalin's rule, these Metro stations were supposed to display the best of Soviet architecture and design and show the privileged lifestyle of Russian people. Along the Gorkovsk–Zamoskvoretskaya Line, the Dushkin-designed Mayakovskaya Metro station, opened in 1938, is considered the main architectural masterpiece of Moscow's Metro. The station features glistening chrome columns and vaulting of the central hall adorned with 33 mosaic panels depicting designs by the Russian artist Alexander Deineka. The theme of all mosaics is called 'One Day of Soviet Skies' or 'A Day in the Land of Soviets', showing happy Soviet workers rising with the dawn, combining happily in the fields and toiling in the factories before returning to their beds as the sun sets in the last panel (Fig. 3.1).

Station Kropotkinskaya (known until 1957 as 'Palace of Soviets') stands on the First Line to have been inaugurated in 1935 and was spectacularly designed and decorated by the architect Dushkin. Built to serve visitors to the proposed new Palace of Soviets, the station's columns are carved into five pointed Soviet stars, with walls decorated with marble from the demolished Cathedral of Christ the Saviour (site of the planned new Palace). The Dushkin-designed Ploschad Revolutsii station, opened on 13 March 1938, abounds with bronze statutes of the creators of the new socialist order, engraved into niches between the station's broad columns. The sculptor Manizer created a total of 76 statues of soldiers, workers and collective farm workers, as well as a heroic sculpture of soldiers and sailors who defended the Young Soviet order, placed at the top of the station escalator.

During the Second World War, Moscow's Metro stations were used as air-raid shelters and many of the larger stations were used for important political and tactical meetings. Kirovskaya station and Chistiye Prudy station were used as the nerve centre for Supreme Command Headquarters and the Soviet Army General Staff. Mayakovskaya was used as a command post for the city's anti-aircraft batteries and on 6 November 1941 hosted an underground ceremony to celebrate the 24th anniversary of the October Revolution (Appendix 3).

During the late 1950s, the architectural extravagance of new Metro stations was significantly toned down, and decorations at some stations, like VDNKh and Alekseevskaya, were greatly simplified compared with original plans. This was done on the orders of Nikita Khrushchev, who favoured a more basic decoration scheme. A typical layout (known as 'Sorokonozhka') was developed for all new stations, which were built to look almost identical, differing from each other only in colours of marble and ceramic tiles. It was not until the mid-1970s that architectural extravagance was restored, and original designs once again became popular.

One characteristic of post-communism was the creation of a new symbolic culture in terms of renaming of street and place names (Graeme, 2005). Of the 11 Metro stations whose names were changed, one was named after Karl Marx (previously Marksa: renamed Okhotnyi Riad) and another the institution of the collective farm (Kolkhoznaia: Sukharevskaia). Two stations with Lenin's name were changed (Lenino: Tsaritsyno; Leninskie gory: Vorob'evye gory), with all of the renamed stations acquiring local geographical place names. A number of Metro stations retained the names of Lenin (Biblioteka im. Lenina, Leninskii Prospekt and Ploschad' Il'icha) and Marx (Marksistskaia), together with those commemorating the October Revolution (Oktiabr'skaia and Oktiabr'skoe pole) and May Day (Pervomaiskaia). A significant number of stations have retained names resonant of the Soviet era, representing a number of institutions: VDNKh (the exhibition of economic achievements) and Red Guards; the revolutionary heritage: the 1905 Revolution (Ulitsa 1905 goda) and Revolution Square; and the labour ethos: Proletarian and Trade Unions.

At the beginning of the 1990s the Metro received no money from the federal budget, with part of the Serpukhovskaya Line from Savelovskaya to Altufievo stations being launched only at the expense of the money earned by leasing Metro buildings. After a decade of decline in Metro construction in the 1990s, the situation with funding in Moscow has relatively stabilized in recent years. While Moscow's Metro stations have always reflected the tough persona of the city, the introduction of new train cars within recently upgraded stations contributed to the feeling of an airport terminal train rather than Metro subway. Although the recently adopted 15-year programme for network expansion has not been accomplished, in May 2002 the Moscow government approved the programme of Metro construction until 2010 which planned the building of new stations and parts of the Metro lines (Appendix 4).

The Study Discussion

Over the last decade the post-communist city has been at the centre of dramatic changes while increasingly seeking to redefine and re-imagine itself through place marketing along a different set of global dynamics. Light (2000) considers 'communist heritage' tourism (the consumption of sites and sights associated with the former communist regimes) in contemporary Central and Eastern Europe as an illustration of the ever-diversifying tourist gaze. However, such tourism also raises wider issues concerning the relationship between tourism and the politics of identity in the region. While the former communist countries of Central and Eastern Europe are seeking to construct new, post-communist identities (a process in which tourism can play a significant part), this project is frustrated by tourists' interest in the 'heritage of communism'. Through consideration of three case studies of communist heritage tourism (the Berlin Wall, Budapest's Statue-park and Bucharest's 'House of the People'), Light (2000) examines the strategies which different countries (Germany, Hungary and Romania) have adopted to negotiate and accommodate such tourism without compromising post-communist identities.

Rátz (2005) focuses on Hungary as one of the few Eastern European countries that have decided to capitalize on their socialist past in the process of tourism development. The creation of heritage attractions such as the Park of Socialist Statues has been necessary in order to preserve the socialist era's political heritage for younger generations, and to provide an opportunity for tourists to get a glimpse of the country's socialist past. According to Coles (2002) tourism has assumed great significance in the space-economy and space-society of the new German Länder since unification, in relation to job and wealth creation, the regeneration of urban fabric, and the progressive elimination of inequalities between West and East. He provides subtle readings of tourism in the process of post-socialist transformation, focusing on the relationship between tourism, place promotion and economic restructuring, which is teased apart for the city of Leipzig, referred to as 'boomtown east'. In this study, the tourism sector produces and reinforces the messages of local place promotion campaigns through its deployment of heritage narratives, 'flagship' projects and infrastructure delivery to support business. Its models of economic development and urban governance have been widely consulted and copied in the new Länder.

Neo-flâneur's narratives within 'post-Soviet' Metro(scape)

As consumption and mobility frame everyday life, under regimes of global capitalism, the post-Soviet Metro(scape) is explored in the context of re-defined West–East transitional identities while globally restructuring Moscow's global urban images. In the post-Soviet era, Moscow's Metro(scape) is subjected to branded global–local ('glocal') landscapes with distinct signs and images, while representing the corporate identity of postmodern spatiality. A series of post-Soviet scenarios are constructed within Moscow's Metro(scape) as they are re-inserted into 'capitalist' urbanization. Socio-economic restructuring impacted land use development and local community with respect to transformation of 'post-Soviet' urban spaces by new cultural practices, influencing the expression of identity and spatiality (Andrusz, 1996).

Spaces of transition

As spatial infrastructure and venue vie for contested social spaces, post-Soviet Metro(scape)'s spatiality is phenomenologically experienced as 'a series of stages' where individuals (petty traders, commuters, urban youth) assume different identities under space–time compression, and is semiologically represented as a collective collage, a 'theatre of memory'. Moscow's Metro(scape), as a hetero-topian setting in contesting ontologies of a society in 'transition' (Foucault, 1986), is experienced as hybrid transit spaces at the frontier of post-communist transfor-mation, involving a critical examination of symbols of 'Stalinist' spatial monu-mentality, alternately standing for social, economic and political dialectics. This is a situational representation of a navigation with the camera's lens inside-out of transit spaces within Moscow's post-Soviet Metro(scape), employing digital pixels and collages to reaffirm hybrid immersion and spatial flow and to intensify individuals' emotions, sensations and perceptions (Deleuze, 1997) (Figs 3.2, 3.3 and 3.4).

Narratives made about Metro transit spaces are related to general political and social concerns related to movement and people after regime shift. Metro stations are fundamentally intermediary spaces, maintaining a transit system which keeps people moving through subways with the minimum level of conges-tion. Among the characteristics that define the Metro experience is a strong sense of enclosure, keeping passengers in close proximity for extended periods of time, with minimal and often complete lack of personal space. The Metro walls not only respond to the physical need for enclosure, but give very subtle direction to a continuous movement along their sinuous surface (Shuffield, 1999). In con-trast to urban streets, Metro stations limit the line of sight to short distances (Shuffield, 1999), while forming anchor points for spatial conceptualization,

Fig. 3.2.   Collages of Metro's transit spaces (circulation spaces).

Fig. 3.3. Neo-flâneur's navigation within Metro's transit spaces (corridors and halls).

(b)

(a)

Fig. 3.4. Neo-flâneur's navigation between Metro's transit spaces: (a) platforms and (b) trains.

with a concentration of people and commercial activities, giving such transit nodes a broader cultural centrality as they provide entry and exit to specific urban places.

With a lack of visual references within Metro stations, Moscow's urban experience is identified along Metro lines, as spatial cognition compresses the space–time experience, and simultaneously distorts the physical experience within the Metro(scape).

> It is no longer possible today to found an urban restructuring principally on architecture. This is not only because of the lack of space and financial means, but also because it is the circulation paths, the planning of networks, of connections, of nodes, that direct, since the end of the 60s, urban organization.
>
> (Grout, 1995: 17)

The experience of hybrid transit spaces within Moscow's Metro stations involves a critical examination of Metro(scape), as contested social spaces, at the frontier of post-Soviet transformation. Metro stations are regarded as intermediary transit spaces between train routes and city streets and anchor points for exit and entry access areas, compressing space–time experience and altering the spatial cognition of Moscow's urban experience. These stations have become places where 'transition' was most visible to the inhabitants of Moscow, with the Metro being considered both a background to local narratives about social order, and a place-setting in contesting ontologies of society in 'transition' as related to the emergence of a new consumer type – the 'fluxus' consumer (Lemon, 2000).

Recently, Moscow's post-Soviet Metro(scape) has experienced major spatial changes which affected the monumentality and rituals associated with Soviet urban spaces. Alongside images/symbols of the Soviet era, commercial activities became highly visible around Metro stations, with hawkers and street musicians (violin players) filling transfer tunnels and underground crosswalks, and with Metro pedestrians combining shopping and commuting without making detours.

Spaces of marginalization

As the presence of petty traders was regarded as unlawful and inappropriate as they were considered as 'people out of place', movement restrictions (propiska system) requiring the registration of residence with municipal authorities were called for. Document checks take place in the context of administrative regulations that specify that even Russian citizens must have documentation showing registration of their place of residence if they have lived at that residence for over 90 days. Anecdotal evidence suggests that police in Moscow are using ethnic profiling in their law enforcement and policing of the Metro stations. Ethnicity may be a primary criterion for police document checks, with people from the Caucasus and Central Asians being the primary targets; they are commonly described in the media as being the cause of crime and economic problems.

Much of the literature on social exclusion ignores its spatial and mobility related aspects. Cass *et al.* (2005) seek to rectify this by examining the mobile processes and infrastructures of travel and transport that engender and reinforce social exclusion in contemporary societies. Claims about access and socio-spatial exclusion routinely make assumptions about what it is to participate effectively in society and how mobilities of different forms would constitute societal values and sets of relations which may become significant for social inclusion.

Nevertheless, the persistence of institutional and cultural discrimination within Moscow's Metro stations characteristic of the Soviet era, where order was imposed through state-controlled population mobility (the propiska registration system), has forced poor migrants to adapt to the new urban environment by creating informal spaces of their own. Because of institutionally based exclusion from the post-Soviet urban system, the urban poor have been obliged to locate to the outside periphery of the Metro. Non-state kiosks were set up at subway entrances, with vendors' trading being conducted on folding tables, stalls or cardboard boxes, with more permanent structures recently coming closer to the Metro proper. This is in contrast to the historical socialist realism aestheticization further down the Metro platforms and halls and through tunnels and cavernous stations (Lemon, 2000). Spatial variations ranging from suburban Metro stations and Central Moscow's gentrified stations reflect the scene of the sharpest contest between traditional street markets and the exigencies of the changing high commercial development. Therefore, viewing the transit experience and its spatial practices reflects aspects of inclusion and exclusion within Moscow's cityscape and its Metro heterotopias.

In addition to ticket attendants (*babushka*) in charge of entrances and exits, Metro stations have recently been characterized by the installation of closed circuit television (CCTV) cameras. With the need to maintain order and stability, new surveillance measures were introduced to enhance security within the Metro stations. Security measures and CCTV reinforce the imperative to prevent passengers from loitering, marking stations as surveillance spaces and defensive areas rather than as places for civic involvement and social exchanges, thus becoming an articulation of an 'aesthetic cocoon' – a heavily serviced space of scrutiny.

Moscow's Metro lines are represented by symbolic language, for orienting passengers, in the form of signs and symbols (semiotics), with some stations having distinctive exterior designs (pavilions) that allow them to function as visual landmarks. New works of art, as well as fragments of 'Stalinist' spatial monumentality and the historical socialist realism aestheticization further down the Metro platforms, reflect the postmodern rejection of a unified public sphere. This exemplifies the contest that occurs when Metro stations are commodified and imagineered into spaces of marketable characteristics (shopping malls) while being devoid of their socio-cultural contexts (Deutsche, 1996).

Spaces of globalization

Amid Moscow's promotional tourism strategy to establish a new place image and foster a new reinvented identity, the postmodern landscape of contested East–West transformation is observed. This is in terms of experiencing a metropolis under intense revision, exploring the discourse on the future of post-Soviet Moscow and recounting the erasure of its 'Stalinist' past from its historical narratives. This was noted in 1990, when Moscow's Mayor Luzhkov embarked on a major development programme to reverse many Stalinist deprivations. The capital has seen a remarkable programme of reconstruction and restoration of historic structures such as the Victory Memorial, the Gostinny Dvor (guests' court), Kazanskiy Cathedral and Resurrection Gates at Red Square to name a few (Glushkova, 1998; Vinogradov, 1998; both cited in Lang, 2004). In addition, new monuments were constructed, notably a controversial statue of Peter the Great.

While Moscow's Kremlin and Red Square were designated as UNESCO World Heritage sites in 1990, a wider programme of historic preservation and revitalization was launched including museums and nine railway stations dating from Tsarist times (Luzkov, 1998; cited in Lang, 2004). New strategic plans for Moscow have been drawn up coupled with the growth in active citizen participation and street protests regarding road plans and historic preservation issues (Colton, 1995). There was the downtown development of large, new postmodern hotels and office and apartment buildings, often funded by foreign consortiums. These have impinged on such historic areas as the Arbat, a major tourist area near the Kremlin.

The 'bazaarization' of Moscow was the main agent of structural change during the first phase of post-Soviet transformation with spontaneous proliferation of small business structures belonging to the retail and service sectors (Rudolph and Brade, 2005). Shrines of market places appeared together with bazaars, street petty trading and informal exchange of goods (Andrusz, 1996), with the commodification of post-Soviet urban spaces near the Red Square: Tverskaya Ulitsa and Vozdvizhenkaya Ulitsa commercial streets, GUM (Gosudarstvennyj Universalnyj Magazin, State Universal Store) shopping mall and Manezh commercial store.

Conforming to the modern notion of a unified and independent public sphere, Metro stations, as intermediary public spaces and as civic projects, have historically been removed from retail systems while being established in autonomous locations within the public right-of-way. Nevertheless, commercial uses have recently been located within the boundaries of some Metro stations, and were thus regarded as an extension to the commercial street fabric. The insertion of such global (commercial) spaces into the urban fabric (post-Soviet Metro stations) was accompanied by aestheticization of urban consumption linking Metro stations to 'gentrified' post-Soviet public spaces: Okhtny Ryad Metro station to Tverskaya Ulitsa street and Red Square; Ploshchad Revolyutsii Metro station to GUM shopping mall; and Biblioteka im Lenina and Arbatskaya Metro stations to Vozdvizhenkaya Ulitsa street. Therefore, the distinction between the Metro's transit spaces and Moscow's urban commercial surroundings is becoming more blurred, similar to Tokyo metro stations which were founded by department store companies as a way of funnelling customers to their stores.

With postmodern transformation challenging the modernist notion of public space, and with the separation between various central Metro stations and commercial spaces diminishing, the recognition of these Metro stations as public spaces has declined. As Deutsche (1996) points out, the prevalence of commerce as a public function, reinforcing the role and dominance of consumption spaces, has led to the privatization of public space, with the introduction of shopping activities aspiring to the gentrification of Metro transit spaces. Rather than separate/demarcated spaces that correspond to rationally defined roles, transit Metro stations have recently become an extension of the space of commercial transactions and part of the shopping experience.

Open-air and covered markets, stalls and kiosks were located on major transportation routes and especially at Metro stations. On large expanses of open space within large, high-rise residential areas of Moscow's periphery, huge kiosk markets and open-air markets selling groceries and other goods appeared. Market trading has become a primary means for the accumulation of capital and the way towards consumption-oriented tertiarization. At the end of the 1990s, the following types of large-scale retail locations dominated the Moscow landscape:

- open-air and kiosk markets with much of the activity in these markets being classified as part of the informal sector, and often controlled by different ethnic groups;
- covered markets with stands in converted buildings (production sheds and sports centres), often closely linked to nearby open-air markets;
- specialist trade centres (Torgovye Centry) in purpose-built facilities that often started as kiosk markets, the owners of which gradually began to construct premises, in which they leased shops;
- new arcades with individual and mainly high-status outlets;
- large-scale Western-style retail complexes (supermarkets, shopping malls and car showrooms).

During the 20th century, Moscow acquired a limited number of downtown shopping centre spaces, mostly in the form of high-profile fashion galleries such as the 35,000-m^2 Manezh Square near the Kremlin, the 63,000-m^2 Smolensky Passage and the 10,000-m^2 Petrovsky Passage. A symbolic sign of the times was the conversion of the famous state department store GUM, a Moscow shopping tradition since 1887, which is now a 30,000-m^2 mall arcade with 185 speciality retailers, including many Western brands.

Manezhnaya Square
At the turn of the 20th century Manezhnaya Square was characterized by the History Museum, which was built in 1883, and the City Hall Duma-edifice, in 1892, with the Moscow Hotel being established later on. One part of the current Manezhnaya Square serves as a link between Tverskaya Ulitsa street and the History Museum and the nearby Manege (the square of Arts). One of the most notable new projects within Manezhnaya Square has been the five-level joint venture underground shopping centre at Manezhnaya Plochad near the Kremlin's walls, which is covered by a park, fountains and statues.

In the late 1990s Manezhnaya Square was reconstructed, with the installation of 'the Clock of the World' in the form of a dome with a northern hemisphere map painted on its outside vault and a figure of George the Victorious, the patron saint of Moscow. The Clock of the World, which makes a full turn over 24 h showing the exact time in the largest cities of the hemisphere, also serves as a cover for the underground atrium of the Okhotny Ryad (Hunters' Row) shopping complex. Manezhnaya Square has become part of Moscow's landscape due to a combination of modern design and preservation of the historical architectural scenery of the city centre. The square has been turned into a recreation area with fountains, greenery, sculptures and decorative street lanterns, supplemented with a replica of the Neglinka riverbed that was reconstructed in the historic place of the real river.

GUM State Universal Store

Gosudarstvennyj Universalnyj Magazin (GUM) is a common name for the main department store in many cities of the Soviet Union and some post-Soviet states. The ornate neo-Russian façade of GUM, Moscow's state department store, takes up almost the entire eastern side of Red Square. Prior to the 1920s the place was known as the Upper Trading Rows (Appendix 5).

At the end of the Soviet era, GUM was partially and then fully privatized, and passed through a number of owners. It ended up in the hands of the super-market chain Perekryostok. As a private shopping mall, it was renamed in such a fashion that it could maintain its old abbreviation and still be called GUM. The first word 'Gosudarstvennyj' has been replaced with 'Glavnyj main', so that GUM is now an abbreviation for 'Main Universal Store'. The GUM is a popular tourist destination, which locals refer to as the 'exhibitions of prices' as no one can afford to buy the high-fashion brand names and items on display (Fig. 3.5). Another similar historic department store, rivalling GUM in size, elegance and opulent architecture, is called the Central Universal Store (Tsentralniy Universalniy Magazin, abbreviated to TsUM) and sprawls just east of the Bolshoi Theatre.

Moscow's post-Soviet spaces of consumption are an inevitable outcome of pursuing commodity-oriented city development, while attempting to create new forms of place marketing through territorial post-Soviet restructuring dynamics. Globalization brings a new imperative to post-Soviet Moscow, with

Fig. 3.5. Moscow's post-Soviet urban spaces: GUM State Universal Store and Kazanskiy Cathedral.

its transformation into the 'entrepreneurial city'. The new imperative invokes the legitimacy of place remaking, even through substantial public investment. The townscape of merchant stalls in the early years of post-Soviet transition is gradually fading into one of supermarkets, chain stores, shopping centres and malls. Newly built suburban shopping outlets are competing with inner-city retail centres. Indeed, the emergence of consumption spaces is driven by the changing urban experience: from a place to work and live to a source of leisure and amenity.

Conclusion

Transit narratives

Walking through Moscow's gentrified urban spaces and post-Soviet Metro-(scape) dominated by space–time compression, the neo-flâneur is engulfed by signs of global flows within the GUM mall (near the Red Square in Moscow) (the aesthetic cocoon, Leach, 2001), witnessing the fetishism of commodification and aestheticization of postmodern consumption. The neo-flâneur's experience through Moscow's gentrified urban spaces and post-Soviet Metro(scape) represents a heterotopian gateway and exchange place linking global and transitional economies, exploring narratives about local identities within the city's fragments.

In the current study, the representation of post-socialist Moscow's Metro (scape) provides a sequence of narratives as metaphors of 'space' and 'being' in the journey along the West–East transition. The experience of navigating a metropolis under transition attempts at weaving anecdotal observations, encounters and reflections oriented by metaphors of shifting images, recalling dialectics in post-socialist contexts. By means of narratives (Fahmi, 2003a), the postmodern representation of 'heterotopian' urbanism reflects a 'glocal' sense of place identity within Moscow's gentrified urban spaces and post-Soviet underground Metro (Fahmi, 2003a,b). This is in relation to:

- epistemological reading of 'post-socialist' urban spaces (images and signs), with the semiotic matrix (of Tverskaya Ulitsa and Vozdvizhenkaya Ulitsa streets in central Moscow) 'at night' forming a text of transit trajectories and aesthetic representation while creating a hybrid identity for its inhabitants (Fig. 3.6);
- phenomenological engagement within post-Soviet Metro(scape) as an ontological experience of spatial practices (Figs 3.2, 3.3 and 3.4).

Transit narratives reflect the post-socialist situation under the transnational flow of cultures brought on by global travel, while re-interpreting local identities and belongings, exhibiting new types of hybrid spatial experiences. Such experiences are substantiated through the interrelationships between the post-tourist (neo-flâneur) and the city landscape (Terkenli, 2002; Causey, 2004).

Fig. 3.6. Semiotic matrix within Moscow's nocturnal spaces: Tverskaya Ulitsa and Vozdvizhenkaya Ulitsa streets.

Collective memory within post-Soviet Metro(scape)

Meaning is being (re)constructed within Moscow's post-Soviet Metro(scape), with issues of collective memory and erasure of historical Soviet symbols being reflected upon imageries of contested urban spaces (between historical 'Soviet' elements of the city and recent 'postmodern' architectural development). The juxtaposition of historical traces of communism and postmodern urban spaces has promoted themes of aestheticization while reflecting the increasing role of image consumption (Lash and Urry, 1994). Consequently, the definition of Metro stations' public role is beginning to reflect the gaining dominance of postmodernism, with the introduction of shopping facilities, gentrification and commodification of 'touristic' urban spaces, while challenging symbols of 'Stalinist' spatial monumentality within Moscow's post-Soviet Metro transit spaces.

Leach (2002) emphasizes the waning of historical sensibility that is often associated with the 'postmodern condition', with perceptions of history being reduced to a collection of images of the past. In a culture of simulation, a hyper-real world of images detached from their original cultural referents, we progressively lose the potential to grasp the ontological reality of the past. In dealing with urban monuments, collective memory and historical erasure, Leach (2002) identifies two strategies: first, the physical eradication of monuments – 'Berlin Wall syndrome'; and secondly the symbolic re-appropriation and re-use of monuments – 'Bucharest syndrome' (in relation to Nicolai Ceauşescu's People's House redeployed as the House of the Parliament and as a conference centre).

While many of Moscow's Metro mosaics are regarded as urban semiotics which depict symbols of historical Soviet production, monuments to Russian soldiers during the Second World War and the Great Partriotic War, such questions are posed:

- Will the artwork change with time or will it remain as a representation of the past? Also, as time passes how will people perceive the mosaics that will fade further and further into Russia's past?
- Will new stations reflect the life of modern times, with modern depictions of Russian life?
- How is one to deal with the architectural fabric of Moscow's Metro which bears witness to the traces of a former communist regime?

Various factors emerge to play a crucial role in determining the political content of spatial forms within Moscow's Metro(scape). One is the Metro's historical context in terms of both time and place, with its 'social ground' lending it meaning. The Metro assumes a socio-political status through a mechanism of semantic associations, either individually, through its particular politics of use as a space of transition, or collectively, through its stylistic affinities with Stalinist monumentality associated with its use as a space of memory.

Function therefore becomes a crucial factor in determining the meaning of the Metro(scape), while conforming relatively to the model of language posited by Wittgenstein (1961; cited in Leach, 2002), in which meaning is determined by use. This is in accordance with Roland Barthes' (1997) claim that 'use never does anything but shelter and generate meaning'. Accordingly we find that the Metro's meaning is defined by its actual function as a transit infrastructure and its symbolic meaning as a tourist Soviet monument of Stalinist Moscow. Political content is therefore a question of allegorical content, depending upon a memory of what a particular form is supposed to mean, and, as that memory fades, so the meaning is erased. The shift from communism remains a profoundly ambiguous process, one to which parts of the population remain resistant and others distinctly ambivalent. This ambiguity has been reflected not only in the policy sphere but in the symbolic one as well, as noted in the pattern of name changes of Metro stations, which reflects one aspect of the nature of post-Soviet Russian experience (Graeme, 2005).

Appendices

Appendix 1

Under Stalin (1879–1953), Moscow saw the destruction of many of its oldest buildings, in violation of Lenin's pronouncement calling for the protection of all ancient buildings. In the Red Square, the ancient Kazan Cathedral was demolished, as was the Resurrection Gate. The monuments of modern Russia were added: Lenin's massive tomb, the graves of John Reed and other selected heroes of the Revolution and the Second World War. Much of the destruction in the Red Square was designed to facilitate the massive display of military might during Labour Day parades that became emblematic of the Soviet state. Most symbolic of Stalin's new Moscow was the demolition in 1931 of the huge

Cathedral of Christ the Saviour, near the Red Square. It was removed to make room for a monumental Palace of the Soviets, which was to be the centrepiece of the Soviet capital. The Palace was never built due to site problems and a municipal swimming pool replaced what was regarded as the world's largest building set within the world's largest plaza (Colton, 1995).

Monumental boulevards were another Stalinist initiative. Soviet planners straightened and widened many of the radial streets leading to the Kremlin. Architectural historians decried the fate of classical Moscow, much of which was lost by road widening and housing developments that affected ancient streets such as Tverskaya (Gorgii) in the 1930s and the new Kalinin Prospect that cut through the old Arbat district in the 1960s. These boulevards constitute an unwavering commitment to monumental style planning traditions.

Whole sections of Moscow were rebuilt according to Stalin's notions of civic design, as boulevards were lined by large apartment blocks which created a monumental panorama en route towards the Kremlin. The imposing and commodious apartment blocks were designed in a neoclassical style, built around large, open communal courtyards, often referred to as a 'superblock' (French, 1995; Lang, 2001). In addition, Stalin worked to rid Moscow of its vestiges of the 'large village', demolishing many of the one-storey wooden houses near the city centre. The Communist Party played a strong role in imposing its 'socialist realism' approach to urban design. Many existing squares were enlarged and lined with new civic buildings, large statues and monuments of revolutionary heroes, literary and artistic figures. In addition to the towering design for Moscow State University, the most visible symbols of the Stalin era were the seven monumental skyscrapers built after the Second World War, housing several government ministries, hotels and apartments (Colton, 1995). Later, during the Khrushchev era, a large modern glass and steel office building, the Palace of Congresses (1961), was constructed within the Kremlin for Communist Party conferences.

Appendix 2

Interior decorations of Moscow's Metro stations.

Type of decorations	Source	Metro stations
Deep-red marble	Georgia	Krasnye Vorota
Black marble	Urals, Armenia and Georgia	Byelorusskaya, Aeroport, Elektrozavodskaya and Ploshchad Revolutsii
Grey landscape marble	Ural Mountains	Lubyanka, Sokolniki, Paveletskaya and Chystye Prudy
Velvet-pink marble	Russian Far East	Byelorusskaya and Aeroport
Spotted marble-type limestone	Crimea	Park Kultury and Alexandrovsky Sad
Quartzite (grains of quartz)	Kareliya	Baumanskaya
Semi-precious stones of marble onyx	Armenia	Dinamo, Byelorusskaya and Kievskaya

Appendix 3

The beginning of the Cold War led to the construction of a deep part of the Arbatskiy Line, where the upper tracks between Ploshchad Revolutsii and Kievskaya were closed and later reopened in 1958 as a part of the Filyovskaya Line. Some studies mention a purported deeper secret underground Metro system, Moscow Metro 2, which parallels the public Moscow Metro, supposedly built in the time of Stalin.

Appendix 4

New stations and Metro lines:
2004 – South Butovo/Kievskaya–Moscow City
2008 – Tchkalovskaya–Marina Rosha/Marino–Zyablikovo/Krasnogvardeiskaya–Brateevo
2009 – Victory Park–Kuntsevskaya/Krylatskoe–Strogino/Strogino–Mitino/Novogireevo–Gorodetskaya/Vykhino–Pronskaya (Zulebino)

Appendix 5

The GUM was built between 1890 and 1893 by Alexander Pomerantsev, featuring an interesting combination of elements of Russian medieval ecclesiastical architecture and an elegant steel framework and glass roof, reminiscent of the great turn of the century railway stations of Paris and London. This modern three-storey arcade is the largest shopping complex in Moscow and was built to replace the old hall of the Upper Trading Rows, which existed earlier on the same site but burnt down in 1825. The original hall contained some 1200 separate shops and stalls and was one of Moscow's liveliest markets. After the 1917 Revolution the arcade was nationalized and renamed GUM. Commercial activity continued there until 1928 when the committee in charge of Stalin's First Five-Year Plan took over the building to use it as office space.

Acknowledgement

The study visit to Moscow was funded by a grant from the Bauhaus-Dessau Foundation in Germany as part of the Bauhaus Kolleg V – Transit Spaces Programme 2003–2004.

References

Alden, J., Crow, S. and Beigulenko, Y. (1998) Moscow planning for a world capital city towards 2000. *Cities* 15(5), 361–374.

Andrusz, G. (1996) Structural change and boundary instability. In: Andrusz, G., Harloe, M. and Szelenyi, I. (eds) *Cities After Socialism.* Blackwell, Oxford, UK, pp. 30–69.

Atkins, M. and Sinclair, I. (1999) *Liquid City.* Reaktion Books Ltd, London.

Augé, M. (1995) *Non-Places – Introduction to an Anthropology of Supermodernity.* (Translated by J. Howe). Verso, New York.

Barthes, R. (1976) *The Pleasure of the Text.* (Translated by R. Milter). Hill and Wang, New York.

Barthes, R. (1997) The Eiffel Tower. In: Leach, N. (ed.) *Rethinking Architecture, a Reader in Cultural Theory.* Routledge, London, pp. 172–181.

Baudelaire, C. (1995) The painter of modern life. In: Mayne, J. (ed.) *The Painter of Modern Life and Other Essays.* Phaidon, London, pp. 9–10.

Baudrillard, J. (1981) *For a Critique of the Economy of the Sign.* Telos Press, St Louis, Missouri.

Baudrillard, J. (1993) Hyperreal America. (Translated by D. Macey). *Economy and Society* 11(1), 243–252.

Beckmann, J. (ed.) (1998) *The Virtual Dimension: Architecture, Representation and Crash Culture.* Princeton Architectural Press, New York, pp. 145–155.

Benjamin, W. (1973) 'The Flâneur' *Charles Baudelaire: a Lyric Poet in the Era of High Capitalism.* (Translated by H. Zohn). New Left Books, London.

Benjamin, W. (1985) *One Way Street and Other Writings.* Verso, London.

Bryman, A. (1995) *Disney and His Worlds.* Routledge, London.

Cass, N., Shove, E. and Urry, J. (2005) Social exclusion, mobility and access. *The Sociological Review* 53(3), 539–555.

Castells, M. (1996) *The Information Age: Economy, Society and Culture:* Volume 1: *The Rise of the Network Society.* Blackwell, Oxford, UK.

Causey, A. (2004) Belonging and belongings: creating identities and souvenirs on Samosir Island. In: *Post-Tourism Times. Proceedings of Fifth International Conference Crossroads in Cultural Studies.* University of Illinois at Urbana-Champaign, 25–28 June. University of Illinois at Urbana-Champaign, Illinois, pp. 105–106.

Clarke, D. (1997) Consumption and the city, modern and postmodern. *International Journal of Urban and Regional Research* 21(2), 218–237.

Coles, T. (2002) Urban tourism, place promotion and economic restructuring: the case of post-Socialist Leipzig. *Tourism Geographies* 5(2), 190–219.

Colton, T. (1995) *Moscow: Governing the Socialist Metropolis.* The Belknap Press of Harvard University Press, Cambridge, Massachusetts.

Crouch, D. (1999) The intimacy and expansion of space. In: Crouch, D. (ed.) *Leisure/ Tourism Geographies: Practices and Geographical Knowledge (Critical Geographies).* Routledge, London, pp. 257–276.

Debord, G. (1994) *Society of the Spectacle.* Zone Books, New York.

De Certeau, M. (1984) *The Practice of Everyday Life.* (Translated by S. Rendall). University of California Press, Berkeley, California.

Deleuze, G. (1997) *Essays: Critical and Clinical.* University of Minnesota Press, Minneapolis, Minnesota.

Deutsche, R. (1996) *Evictions: Art and Spatial Politics.* MIT Press, Cambridge, Massachusetts.

Ditchev, I. (2005) Communist urbanization and conditional citizenship. *City: Analysis of Urban Trends, Culture, Theory, Policy, Action* 9(3), 341–354.

Eco, U. (1986) *Travels in Hyper-Reality.* Picador, London.

Edensor, T. (2000) Staging tourism, tourists as performers. *Annals of Tourism Research* 27(2), 322–344.

Fahmi, W. (2001) Reading of postmodern public spaces as layers of virtual images and real events. In: *'Honey, I Shrunk the Space' Planning in the Information Age.*

Proceedings of 37th ISoCaRP International Planning Congress. Utrecht, 16–20 September. (CD-Rom).

Fahmi, W. (2002) Re-conceiving the urban experience: deconstructive experimentation with cognitive imaging in postmodern cities. In: *The City of Tomorrow. Proceedings of the 10th International Planning History Conference IPHS 2002.* London and Letchworth. 10–13 July. (CD-Rom).

Fahmi, W. (2003a) City inside out(side): postmodern (re)presentation – city narratives and urban imageries. In: *Proceedings of the Planning Research Conference PRC2003.* Oxford, 8–10 April. Oxford Brookes University, Oxford, UK. Available at: http://www.brookes.ac.uk/schools/planning/conference/papers%20pdf/fahmi.PDF! (accessed 2 November 2005).

Fahmi, W. (2003b) Transit landscapes and shifting place-identities: a spatio-temporal narrative of transit spaces and post-socialist urbanism (Berlin and Moscow). In: *Transit Spaces – Bauhaus Kolleg V Documentation of the First Trimester.* The Bauhaus Dessau Foundation, Dessau, Germany, pp. 46–58.

Fahmi, W. (2004) Postmodern spatialities of glocalisation: conceptualising heterotopian urbansim. In: *Planning Models and the Culture of Cities. Proceedings of 11th International Planning History Conference IPHS 2004.* Barcelona, 14–17 July. (CD-Rom). Available at: http://www.etsav.upc.es/personals/iphs2004/pdf/055_p.pdf (accessed 18 August 2006).

Feighery, W. (2006) Reflexivity and tourism research: telling an(other) story. *Current Issues in Tourism* 9(3), 269–282.

Foucault, M. (1986) Of other spaces. *Diacritics* 16(1), 22–27.

French, R.A. (1995) *Plans, Pragmatism and People: the Legacy of Soviet Planning for Today's Cities.* University of Pittsburgh Press, Pittsburgh, Pennsylvania.

Garlick, S. (2002) Revealing the unseen: tourism, art and photography. *Cultural Studies* 16(2), 289–305.

Gillespie, C. (2005) Vigo incognito: fetishism and the identity of the flâneur. Paper presented at Visualising the City Symposium. Organized by the Centre for Screen Studies, the School of Arts, Histories and Cultures and the School of Languages, Linguistics and Cultures, University of Manchester, Manchester, 26–28 June.

Graeme, G. (2005) Changing symbols: the renovation of Moscow place names. *The Russian Review* 64(3), 480–503.

Grout, C. (1995) *Le Tramway de Strasbourg.* Editions du Regard, Paris.

Hall, C.M. (1994) *Tourism and Politics: Policy, Power and Place.* Wiley, Chichester, UK.

Huang, T. (2000) Hong Kong blue: flânerie with the camera's eye in a phantasmagoric global city. *Journal of Narrative Theory* 30(3), 385–402.

Jameson, F. (1991) *Postmodernism or the Cultural Logic of Late Capitalism.* Duke University Press, Durham, North Carolina.

Jenks, C. (1995) Watching your step: the history and practice of the flâneur. In: Jenks, C. (ed.) *Visual Culture.* Routledge, London, pp. 142–160.

Lang, M.H. (2001) Town planning and radicalism in the progressive era; the legacy of F.L. Ackerman. *Planning Perspectives* 16(2), 143–167.

Lang, M.H. (2004) Red Moscow: capital of the revolution or a revolution in capitals. In: *Planning Models and the Culture of Cities. Proceedings of 11th International Planning History Conference IPHS 2004.* Barcelona, 14–17 July. (CD-Rom). Available at: http://www.etsav.upc.es/personals/iphs2004/pdf/109_p.pdf (accessed 18 July 2006).

Larsen, J. (2001) Tourism mobilities and the travel glance: experiences of being on the move. *Scandinavian Journal of Hospitality and Tourism* 1(2), 80–98.

Lash, S. and Urry, J. (1994) *Economies of Signs and Space.* Sage, London.

Leach, N. (2001) The aesthetic cocoon. *OASE* 54, 105–121.

Leach, N. (2002) Erasing the traces: the 'denazification' of post-revolutionary Berlin and Bucharest. In: Leach, N. (ed.) *The Hieroglyphics of Space: Reading and Experiencing the Modern Metropolis.* Routledge, London, pp. 80–100.

Lee, Y.-S. (2001) Tourist gaze: universal concept. *Tourism, Culture and Communication* 3(2), 93–99.

Lefebvre, H. (1991) *The Production of Space.* Blackwell, Oxford, UK.

Lefebvre, H. (1996) *Writings on Cities.* (Translated by E. Kofman and E. Lebas). Blackwell, Oxford, UK.

Lemon, A. (2000) Talking transit and spectating transition: the Moscow Metro. In: Berdahl, D., Bunzl, M. and Lampland, M. (eds) *Altering States: Ethnographies of Transition in Eastern Europe and the Former Soviet Union.* University of Michigan Press, Ann Arbor, Michigan, pp. 14–39.

Light, D. (2000) Gazing on communism: heritage tourism and post-Communist identities in Germany, Hungary and Romania. *Tourism Geographies* 2(2), 157–176.

MacCannell, D. (1976) *The Tourist. A New Theory of the Leisure Class.* Schoken Books, New York.

Meethan, K. (2003) Mobile cultures? Hybridity, tourism and cultural change. *Tourism and Cultural Change* 1(1), 11–28.

Moshenska, J. (2005) The energy of the walker, the absorption of the passenger. *The Literary London Journal* 3(2). Available at: http://www.literarylondon.org/london-journal/september2005/joe.html (accessed 25 October 2006).

Nederveen-Pieterse, J. (1995) Globalization as hybridization. In: Featherstone, M. and Lash, S. (eds) *Spaces of Culture: City, Nation, World.* Sage, London, pp. 45–68.

Nederveen-Pieterse, J. (2001) Hybridity, so what? The anti-hybridity backlash and the riddles of recognition. *Theory, Culture and Society* 18(2–3), 219–245.

Raban, J. (1974) *Soft City.* Hamish Hamilton, London.

Rapport, N. and Dawson, A. (1998) Home and movement: a polemic. In: Rapport, N. and Dawson, A. (eds) *Migrants of Identity: Perceptions of Home in a World of Movement.* Berg, Oxford, UK, pp. 19–38.

Rátz, T. (2005) Socialist heritage in Hungarian tourism – innovation, interpretation and identity. Association for Tourism and Leisure Education (ATLAS) Annual Conference. Catalonia, Spain, 2–4 November.

Ritzer, G. and Liska, A. (1997) McDisneyization and post tourism: complementary perspectives on contemporary tourism. In: Rojek, C. and Urry, J. (eds) *Touring Cultures: Transformations of Travel and Theory.* Routledge, London, pp. 96–109.

Rojek, C. (1993) *Ways of Escape. Modern Transformations in Leisure and Travel.* Macmillan, London.

Rojek, C. (1997) Indexing, dragging, and the social construction of tourists sights. In: Rojek, C. and Urry, J. (eds) *Touring Cultures: Transformations of Travel and Theory.* Routledge, London, pp. 52–74.

Rojek, C. and Urry, J. (1997) Transformations of travel and theory. In: Rojek, C. and Urry, J. (eds) *Touring Cultures: Transformations of Travel and Theory.* Routledge, London, pp. 1–23.

Rudolph, R. and Brade, I. (2005) Moscow: processes of restructuring in the post-Soviet metropolitan periphery. *Cities* 22(2), 135–150.

Santos, M. and da Paula, J. (2003) Tourist experimentation of place in Porto's old city. Tourism and Photography Conference. Sheffield: Center for Tourism and Cultural Change, International Festivals Events Association (IFEA), 20–23 July.

Seale, K. (2005) Eye-swiping London: Iain Sinclair, photography and the flâneur. *The Literary London Journal* 3(2). Available at: http://www.literarylondon.org/london-journal/september2005/julian.html (accessed 25 October 2006).

Shaffer, T.S. (2004) Performing backpacking: constructing 'authenticity' every step of the way. *Text and Performance Quarterly* 24(2), 139–160.

Sheller, M. and Urry, J. (2000) The city and the car. *International Journal of Urban and Regional Research* 24, 737–757.

Shields, R. (1994) Fancy footwork: Walter Benjamin's notes on flânerie. In: Tester, K. (ed.) *The Flâneur*. Routledge, New York, pp. 61–80.

Shuffield, J. (1999) *The Subway as Intermediary Public Space*. Working paper. Available at: http://www. urbanresidue.com/theory/subway.html#7 (accessed 30 May 2006).

Silver, R. (2005) Telling tales about architects. *The Literary London Journal* 3(2). Available at: http://www.literarylondon.org/london-journal/september2005/silver.html (accessed 25 October 2006).

Sinclair, I. (1997) *Lights Out for the Territory*. Granta Publications, London.

Sinclair, I. (1999) *Dark Lanthorns, Rodinsky's A to Z*. Goldmark, Uppingham, UK.

Sinclair, I. (2002) *London Orbital: a Walk Around the M25*. Granta Publications, London.

Soja, E. (1995) Heterotopologies: a remembrance of other spaces in the citadel-LA. In: Watson, S. and Gibson, K. (eds) *Postmodern Cities and Spaces*. Blackwell, Oxford, UK, pp. 13–34.

Sontag, S. (2002) *On Photography*. Penguin Classics Series. (Reprint of 1977 original edition). Penguin, London.

Sternberg, E. (1997) The iconography of the tourism experience. *Annals of Tourism Research* 24(4), 951–969.

Terkenli, T.S. (2002) Landscapes of tourism: towards a global cultural economy of space? *Tourism Geographies* 4(3), 227–254.

Tomlinson, J. (1999) *Globalization and Culture*. Polity Press, Cambridge, UK.

Urry, J. (1990) *The Tourist Gaze: Leisure and Travel in Contemporary Societies*. Sage, London.

Urry, J. (2002) Mobility and proximity. *Sociology* 36(2), 255–274.

Urry, J. (2003) *Mobile Cultures*. The Department of Sociology, Lancaster University, Lancaster. Available at: http://www.comp.lancs.ac.uk/sociology/papers/Urry-Mobile-Cultures.pdf (accessed 1 November 2006).

Virilio, P. (1997) *The Open Sky*. (Translated by J. Rose). Verso, London, pp. 1–45.

Ward, S. (2005) The passenger as flâneur? Railway networks in German-language fiction since 1945. *The Modern Language Review* 100(2), 412–428.

Warschauer, M. (1995) Heterotopias, panopticons, and Internet discourse. *University of Hawaii Working Papers in ESL* 14(1), 91–121.

Wolfreys, J. (2005) Londonography: Iain Sinclair's urban graphic. *The Literary London Journal* 3(2). Available at: http://www.literarylondon.org/london-journal/september2005/seale.html (accessed 25 October 2006).

Yeh, J. (2003) Embodiment of sociability through the tourist camera. Tourism and Photography Conference. Sheffield: Center for Tourism and Cultural Change, International Festivals Events Association (IFEA), 20–23 July.

Zhao, H. and Chen, W. (2006) Touristic experiences in city open spaces – implications for policy-making, with special reference to Shanghai. Tourism in Asia: New Trends, New Perspectives. Conference co-hosted by the Department of East Asian Studies, University of Leeds, and the Tourism, Hospitality and Events School of Leeds Metropolitan University, Leeds, 10–12 June.

4

Telling Tales of Tourism: Mobility, Media and Citizenship in the 2004 EU Enlargement

Tim Coles

Introduction: a New 'Europe of the Citizens'?

The European Union (EU) has become an established feature of the regulatory landscape over the previous half century. As the EU has evolved, the ethos of stability and prosperity through harmonization and cooperation culminated in an association of 15 member states in 2004 committed to the free movement of labour and capital within their collective frontier (Coles and Hall, 2005). This group of states covered most of western, southern and northern Europe, but stopped at the former Iron Curtain frontier with the old Eastern Bloc states in the Soviet sphere of influence (Fig. 4.1).

Two sets of motives underpinned EU Enlargement on 1 May 2004. Expansion was portrayed as a chance to secure even greater political stability by expanding the membership to include former Cold War enemies. As Romano Prodi, then Head of the European Commission, decreed, 'five decades after our great project of European integration began, the divisions of the world war are gone, once and for all, and we now live in a united Europe' (in Woods, 2004: 1). EU leaders also recognized its limitations in the geopolitics of global trade. When the ten Accession Countries (AC10) – Cyprus, Czech Republic, Estonia, Hungary, Latvia, Lithuania, Malta, Poland, Slovenia and Slovakia – joined, the EU population swelled at a stroke by 75 million people. The total population became 430 million and the GDP €850 billion (£565 billion) which for the first time made the EU market roughly the same size as the USA (Islam, 2004).

In theory, all 430 million citizens should share the same rights of freedom and work within the EU's collective frontier (Parker, 2004). Where once there had been restrictions of travel to and from (some) AC10 states, Enlargement raised the prospect of restructured visitor flows and investment patterns (Coles and Hall, 2005). United Nations World Tourism Organization (WTO) Secretary General Francesco Frangialli predicted that 'we may expect an increase in

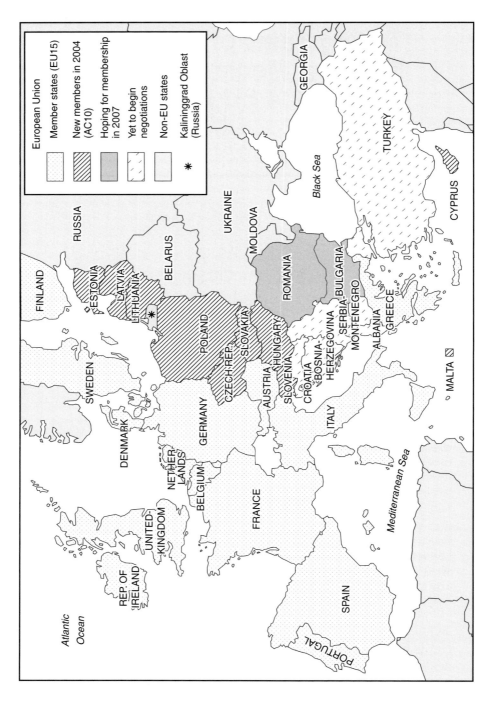

Fig. 4.1. Europe at the time of EU Enlargement in 2004.

East–Western European flows and vice versa . . . The new countries are not just destinations, but tourism-generating markets as well' (WTO, 2004). This chapter examines how tourism was portrayed and tactically used in the British print-media in the run-up to and shortly after EU Enlargement in 2004. It contrasts how the tourism potentials of EU Enlargement for British citizens were presented positively; indeed, in many respects tourism represents the epitome of the EU ideal of freedom of movement. Conversely, stereotypical constructs of tourism were used to underscore more negative discourses of the anticipated short-term mobilities of Eastern Europeans to the UK. Here I argue that citizenship is a key, but routinely overlooked unifying conceptual framework in studies of tourism and mobility, and perhaps as importantly immobility. It is all well and good to be offered the right to travel but this is meaningless if the right of entry is restricted (Coles, 2008).

Tourism, Citizenship and Mobility: Some Conceptual Links

Like so many concepts in the social sciences, citizenship is a highly contested term that lacks clear and irrefutable definition. According to Turner (1993: 2), 'Citizenship may be defined as that set of practices (juridical, political, economic and cultural) which define a person as a competent member of society, and which as a consequence shape the flow of resources to persons and social groups'. For Delanty (2000: 9) citizenship 'involves a set of relationships between rights, duties, participation and identity' which serve to establish the terms of reference and nature of social group membership. Several commentators, not least Turner (1993: 2), have noted that it is important to stress the social practices of citizenship or become embroiled in legal, state-based discussions that centre exclusively (and hence erroneously in this context) on rights and obligations. Thus, citizenship concerns the membership of a social group, not necessarily one aligned to a state (Clarence, 1999) or a national group. It incorporates issues of participation in the group and access to resources, while simultaneously affiliation to the group is manifested in the form of responsibilities as well as a series of entitlements. A further duality exists as van Steenbergen (1994) has noticed, in so far as a citizen may simultaneously be one who governs and who is governed. In this respect, an essential feature is the qualification process for citizenship. All of these features point towards, as Turner (1993: 3) has noted, citizenship as a key sociological concern whereby a series of social arrangements advantage and penalize different sectors of society in behaviour and access to resources.

There have been a number of historical forms of citizenship from the Ancient Greeks and Romans through the Republican models in Revolutionary France and America to the present day (Heater, 2004). Historiographies of citizenship almost always consider the seminal, but now highly contested views of T.H. Marshall (1950), who identified three forms of citizenship and their historical appearance. Civil citizenship emerged in the 18th century and established basic rights to individual freedom such as property ownership, personal liberty and justice; political citizenship was a product of the 19th century and resulted in the right to participate in elections to institutions that exercise power; and social citizenship was seen as first an essentially 20th-century phenomenon which involved rights to economic welfare, security, social heritage and a socially acceptable way of life. These forms of citizenship materialized sequentially and Marshall evidenced the third form of citizenship in the rise of the welfare state in Britain.

Marshall's approach has been heavily criticized in recent times. Not only is it highly situated, based on the British experience and some of the historical datings are suspect, but also, according to feminist critique, it lacks sensitivity to inequalities of gender and sexuality and differential levels of participation in society through other processes of inclusion and exclusion (Urry, 2000). For others, its relevance is questionable in light of the transformation of society, economy and polity in the last half century. Isin and Wood (1999: 4) argue that legal, political and social rights are no longer conferred solely by states. For instance, the position of the welfare state in many advanced democracies would challenge whether social citizenship should be the final and crowning stage. Rather they view citizenship as an 'articulating principle' for other forms of group rights defined by membership such as diasporic and aboriginal, sexual, cosmopolitan, cultural and radical citizenships. These reflect the cultural fragmentation of contemporary global society, and the membership of individuals in new groups that seek to establish new rights or sustain existing ones.

Pearson (2002) notes that in Marshall's view nation and state were mutually implicated, while ethnic or national identity were taken for granted. Murphy and Harty (2003) point out that citizenship rights may exist at the sub-state level, in particular for national groups denied state representation. For Tambini (2001), the rise of globalization has functioned to challenge and erode the role of national citizenship. Instead, rights associated with social group membership can in fact exist across state boundaries; that is, citizenship beyond the state, or 'post-sovereign citizenship' because it is no longer institutions with sovereignty over a territory that exclusively ascribe rights and responsibilities. Urry (2000: 172) has identified the rise of what he terms 'global citizenship' the scope of whose 'socio-spatial practices highlight, or secure or threaten various rights and duties'.

Still, Marshall's (1950) approach is one of the first to suggest that individuals participate in multiple forms of citizenship. As Isin and Wood (1999: 20) have pointed out, studies of citizenship are marked by an important paradox. Although much of the discussion implies whole group membership, there are no empirical cases where citizenship has been expanded to all members of a polity. Others have used different terms to describe similar multiple belongings such as 'expanded citizenship' (van Steenbergen, 1994: 6), 'multicultural citizenship' (Kymlicka, 1995) or even 'civic cosmopolitanism' (Delanty, 2000: 5). Individuals participate in a number of citizenships simultaneously, and these arrangements may be either complementary or difficult to reconcile with one another.

As Kofman (1995, 2005) has demonstrated, dual citizenship has continued to trouble individuals living in EU states. They have rights and responsibilities not only with respect to the states in which they reside, but also granted by a union in which they are also members simply by virtue of domicile or birth. The EU offers additional rights of freedom of movement, justice, trade and defence beyond those provided by state but the state – in reasserting its own power, legitimacy and sovereignty over a supranational body – has the ultimate control over whether an individual has access to or must relinquish those rights. Bellamy and Warleigh (2001) note the long-standing difficulties in determining citizenship priorities in this configuration, not least because of the competing vested interests among the national governments and EU politicians and institutions. Dunkerley *et al.* (2002: 20) suggest that the 1997 Treaty of Amsterdam has gone some way to resolving the matter in a legal if not political sense. It articulates a principle of subsidiarity so that EU citizenship is intended to complement not replace national citizenship and in so doing creates two groups of EU citizens. For instance, with respect to tourism and mobility, through residence it creates beneficiaries of freedom of movement and those who are excluded (because other states opt out from deregulation).

In the context of tourism and mobility, this truncated review points to two pivotal features. The first is that travel can be a major expression of citizenship. Several types of Urry's (2000) global citizenships are mediated directly through the movement of individuals. In the EU, freedom of movement is seen as a fundamental right and hence travel is one of the more obvious ways in which many citizens experience the union and its benefits (Verstraete, 2002). Travel restrictions, such as those related to the Schengen Zone, can have a similar but opposite effect. Nevertheless, citizenship clearly presents a series of possibilities for travel which contribute to the increasingly wide-held view that understanding mobilities is vital to our understanding of current times (Hannam *et al.*, 2006). Whether it is possible to talk of a 'mobilities paradigm' (Sheller and Urry, 2006) is clearly an altogether different matter; however, advocates of this approach stress the greater motion and opportunities for the movement of labour, capital, goods, objects, information, images, plants, animals and organisms (Sheller and Urry, 2004: 1). As a second key observation, it is useful to sound a note of caution. Rather than focus solely and exclusively on mobilities, it is just as important to switch the emphasis and consider movement from the opposite perspective; that an increasing number of immobilities, relative or absolute, warrant our attention (Coles, 2008). As discussed below, the ways in which nation-state and EU citizenships collide for individuals living in different parts of the union have a considerable influence on the degree to which they are mobile or not and the types of short-term movement they exhibit. Moreover, tourism is used as a metaphor for conveying aspects of citizenship to public audiences and, in turn, has become a mechanism by which to regulate further short-term movements.

Telling Tales: Tourism in the Media at the Time of Enlargement

The empirical research reported here started in late 2003 and 2004 as Enlargement loomed large on the political horizon. Stories about the mobility, migration and movement of people to and from AC10 states featured in television programmes, radio broadcasts and newspaper and magazine articles. Two sets of connected discourses became increasingly prevalent. 'Discourses of pleasure and play' concerned the new tourism potentials of once closed destinations that were about to be opened for business. 'Discourses of denial' surrounded the issues faced by the UK government in managing the size, uncertainty and impacts of visitor flows to 'destination Britain' after 1 May 2004. Tourism was used in these discourses as a metaphor to help the public and politicians conceptualize and comprehend the likely impacts of movement as new AC10 citizens exerted their rights. Journeys to Britain were routinely depicted as temporary and short term (even of less than a year duration) and hence come under the direct purview of standard definitions of tourism. Moreover, the connection between the newly mobile citizen and the UK was equated to that of the stereotypical (mass) tourist and the destination.

An ad hoc archive of press articles about tourism, mobility and EU Enlargement was assembled at the time and this was supplemented some months later by an extensive search of the *LexisNexis Business and News* (now *Nexis UK*, www.lexisnexis.com/) online database. One of its strengths is the range of titles it includes and their spatial coverage. It includes stories filed by wire services as well as (former) 'broadsheets', 'tabloids' and regional and local newspapers. These are helpful because they reveal provincial interpretations of stories that emanate in the major national, even metropolitan presses.

Various approaches have been advocated as the means to structure the analysis of media content in tourism studies (Hall, 2002; Jaworski *et al.*, 2003). Discourse analysis was adopted here as a means to reflect the strength and tone of the positions articulated within the published accounts and the deliberate choices of language made by the commentators. Here highly indicative accounts and texts are used as evidence.

Discourses of Denial

The first and larger body of debate focused on a series of denials made by the government concerning its position on EU Enlargement, and specifically how to manage the new mobilities catalysed by Enlargement. These narratives first appeared intermittently in late summer 2003, were most frequently debated in the first quarter of 2004, and then largely faded from view in July 2004. They featured mainly in the news, home, politics and European affairs sections of the newspapers, and they were also articulated in editorials, commentaries and letters to the editors. While the initial tone of the argument was reflective and balanced, towards the end of the period it was more aggressive and accusational as mobility became a party-political issue.

The 'discourses of denial' developed in five mutually reinforcing and overlapping steps. Initially there were general denials from the government that there would be problems in granting AC10 citizens free movement around the EU. These were a response to stories that rehearsed speculation in other EU15 states that income and standard of living differentials between the old and new member states may lead to widespread migrations from East to the West. AC10 citizens would seek out opportunities in EU15 labour markets and, wherever possible, take advantage of their generous welfare systems. Enlargement effectively would open the EU15 to 75 million people, many of whom had incomes much lower than the EU average (Browne, 2004). As a result, several states had taken pre-emptive action to restrict entry rights to future AC10 citizens, which, according to the Treaty of Accession, was their prerogative until 2011 (Parker, 2004).

The second denial was, effectively, an extension of the first. As the public debate gathered speed, the government refuted the need to regulate further new mobilities of AC10 citizens to the UK. In January 2004, several articles appeared in which the spectre of short-term migrants and their social costs was openly discussed (*Guardian*, 2004). In the context of East–West mobilities, it was claimed that the UK may suffer badly because its economy was performing more strongly than other EU15 states; it had a relatively open system of welfare benefits; and unlike other countries it had yet to introduce restrictions (Browne, 2004; Johnston, 2004; Walker, 2004). These fears were compounded by anxieties over the internal openness of borders, a lack of checks over cross-border movements in the Schengen Zone, and the permeability of the EU's new border to the east (Fig. 4.1). Instead of stopping at the Oder River in Germany, the EU now bordered the Ukraine and Byelorussia in the 'wild, wild, east' of Poland (Vulliamy, 2004). Succinctly put, the government's position was that appropriate systems were in place that would be able to deal with the migratory, employment and welfare consequences of the new mobilities. Besides, it was absurd to contemplate that AC10 citizens would travel to Britain simply to work in the black market or just to collect welfare benefits (Johnston, 2004; Parker, 2004).

Gradually, the government acknowledged that AC10 citizens may not understand or respect the formal operations of the UK employment and welfare systems, in which one has to work to qualify for welfare, and they may come anyhow. Early attempts to forecast the scale of the perceived problem were marked by a paradox. According to Beverley Hughes, a Home Office Minister, no research had been 'able to the predict the exact numbers expected from specific countries or ethnic groups to the UK' (in Johnston 2004: 12); however, that had not prevented the publication of alarmist estimates. These first focused on the Roma populations of Central and Eastern Europe (Sparks and Hellen, 2004). The *Sunday Times* reported that 'at least 100,000 gypsies [were] expected to arrive from Eastern Europe' (Sparks and Hellen, 2004: 14). Early Home Office prognoses in January 2004 were based on a report by University College London in July 2003. Between 5000 and 13,000 migrants/year were anticipated from new member states (*Guardian*, 2004: 25). Migrationwatch UK claimed that more than 20,000 people from these countries tried to enter Britain in 2001 (Sparks and Hellen, 2004: 14); actually, it estimated that 40,000 migrants/year would enter Britain from the post-socialist countries (Johnston, 2004: 12), apparently based on a scaling factor of three (*Guardian*, 2004: 25). Further fantastic estimates were published, including the *Express*'s claim that '1.6 million Roma were ready to "flood in"' (*Guardian*, 2004: 25).

New terms were coined to describe to readers the strategies and tactics new EU citizens were likely to use and these have now become established terms in contemporary English usage (Box 4.1). Their movements were likely to be temporary – interestingly, there is usually no direct suggestion of their being permanent – and they were motivated by the citizen's desire to profit as far as possible from benefits and work before returning home. 'Benefit tourism'

> **Box 4.1.**   The world according to Wikipedia: 'benefit tourism' (Source: Wikipedia, 2008).
>
> **Benefit tourism** is the name given to the perceived threat that after 1 May 2004 huge masses of citizens from the European Union's ten new member countries would move to the previous 15 member states to benefit from their generous social welfare systems rather than to work. This threat was used as a motivation for some (initial, temporary) restrictions on the free movement of labour within the EU. However, evidence since May 2004 does not suggest that a large number of people from Eastern Europe are claiming benefits in Western Europe.

(*Express*, 2004; Parker, 2004) and 'welfare shopping' (Sparks and Hellen, 2004) entered the lexicon of public debate and accepted working definitions emerged (see Box 4.1) alongside academic and legal interpretations (Hunt and Wallace, 2004). Welfare shopping implied more cynical practices whereby an individual would move from country to country comparing and contrasting the rules, regulations and likely proceeds of the local welfare system and labour market. On the basis of a cost–benefit analysis, the individual would decide whether to stay put and take advantage of the current system or move on to where benefits were perceived to be greater. Thus, a migrant might live in a number of states for short periods of time before settling on Britain as the optimal choice.

By February 2004, the emphasis had shifted once again in the third stage of denial. While it was acknowledged that it could not be certain how many people would enter the UK, the government objected to charges that it had not acted quickly enough or with due diligence to protect the interests of UK citizens. The defining moment appears to have been the apparent failure of the Prime Minister to answer adequately questions on the matter from Michael Howard, then Leader of the Opposition, in Parliament on 4 February 2004. Immigration policy is a traditional strength for the Conservative Party (Adams, 2004; Hinsliff, 2004). The provisionality of Blair's answers gave the impression that the government was weak on immigration, that it had been caught off-guard on 'benefits tourism', and that it was being forced into a knee-jerk response (Bowcott, 2004).

Gone was the preference for unregulated movement in keeping with the EU ethos (Wagstyl, 2004). In its place, within the Ministries of State a more coordinated legislative response was being devised (Dougherty, 2004; O'Flynn, 2004). In part, this was intended to address the criticism that the issue of benefit tourism had emerged as a result of conflicting positions within government (Bowcott, 2004; White, 2004). The government's new harder line was epitomized by Andrew Smith, Work and Pensions Secretary:

> Our position is clear: people won't be allowed to come here for benefits tourism, to get benefits they are not entitled to.
>
> The whole purpose . . . is to ensure that our labour market, our economy, benefits from the skills and contribution which people have to make from other countries. But I emphasise, not to allow them to take advantage of our benefits system.
>
> (in Deane, 2004)

Later in the month, more detail of the government's solution started to emerge. The agenda was now dominated by the need to address fears of whole-sale mobilities rather than the economic benefits AC10 citizens would be able to deliver (McRae, 2004). The government was to apply strict tests to limit new arrivals' entry, their rights to work and hence access to the welfare system. These were based on the so-called 'habitual residence test' (*Guardian*, 2004; White, 2004): an EU citizen had to demonstrate a genuine intention to work and spend a particular period of time in the UK before being considered for income support or housing benefit (two main social benefits) (Johnston, 2004). This approach reflected the continuing desire of the government to maintain rights of entry while making it more difficult to qualify for benefits, not least through contribut-ing taxation to the state (Baldwin, 2004a; Chapman, 2004a).

For the Conservatives, this represented a humiliating U-turn in government policy. By concentrating on a test, the government attempted to defuse the situa-tion by steering debate into more mundane areas of definition. By mid-February, Hinsliff and Bright (2004: 13) were defining benefit tourists as those 'arriving for seasonal work and then claiming benefits once the job is over' (cf. Baldwin, 2004b). Moreover, a test and its implementation were prudent because practi-cally every other EU15 state had applied restrictions (Baldwin, 2004a; Browne, 2004: 2). Still, critics pointed out that mismanagement of mobility had the potential to impact significantly on the rights of UK citizens and returned to the theme that local authorities (and hence taxpayers) would have to pay for benefit tourism (cf. Lyons, 2004). Some of the commentary was pretty blunt, reaction-ary and arguably in bad taste. Sinister problems were noted such as the big increase in Aids sufferers in seven of the Eastern European accession countries, with particularly stark rates of increase in Latvia and Estonia (Chapman, 2004b; Jones and Brogan, 2004). James Chapman (2004b: 8) warned:

> There is growing concern that looking after asylum-seekers, refugees and so-called 'health tourists' is costing the NHS [National Health Service] billions of pounds a year. An HIV-positive patient typically costs the NHS £15,000 a year. If full-blown AIDS develops, the bill soars to around £40,000.

In fact, when the regulations arrived, they were tougher than many had expected (see Mason *et al.*, 2004; Treneman, 2004; White and Travis, 2004). Of AC10 citizens wanting to enter the UK, David Blunkett, then Home Secretary, pronounced: 'They cannot draw down on benefits without contributing themselves to the rights and entitlements which should go hand in hand with the responsibilities and duties' (in Mason *et al.*, 2004). Ann Treneman (2004: 2), in a parliamentary sketch, reflected on his performance and the muddle the government had got itself into, with the acerbic observation that benefit tourism:

> is the kind of thing that everyone agrees on as no one likes it when those people come over here (and wearing those awful Bermuda shorts, too) and go round taking photographs of all our best-looking benefits. There will be no more of that.

Thus, first in February 2004 and continuing right until Enlargement, a fourth set of denials was evident: the government refuted (Conservative) claims that it was reacting too late and too little, and, despite its rhetoric, the problem continued to prove difficult to solve (Baldwin, 2004a; Jones and Brogan, 2004; Lyons, 2004). Amid complaints from the opposition parties of its almost literally 11th-hour tactics, the government's benefit tourism legislation was passed on 30 April 2004, just 3 h before Parliament concluded its business for the week and the AC10 joined the EU (Hardie, 2004; Wintour, 2004). The final denial was that there had been a problem in the first place. Early estimates of mobility from the AC10 into the UK were argued to be contested and unrepresentative of future trends (Doughty, 2004).

Discourses of Pleasure and Play

The travel (and less commonly business) sections of the newspapers extolled the new possibilities for travel, tourism and second home ownership. The coverage was by and large highly concentrated in a window of publication just prior to and immediately after Enlargement. The 'discourses of pleasure and play' were far less voluminous and the tone was much more playful and ironic, not least because many new destinations had not been at the top of most people's holiday 'wish list' in the past (Table 4.1).

Important geographical dimensions were evident. Cyprus and Malta tended to be overlooked (Table 4.1). As established tourism destinations, they were presented as offering fewer new opportunities to the reader. However, it should be

Table 4.1. Things you never knew you could do in places you didn't know existed (Sources: adapted from Bridge, 2004; Calder, 2004b).

Country	Nation in a nutshell	'Must do' attraction
Cyprus	Once Britain's toe-hold in the eastern Med, now Europe's last divided territory	The Berlin Wall revisited
Czech Republic	Castles, countryside and the world's best beer	Breweries of Bohemia
Estonia	The smallest former Soviet republic, already making a big impression in the new Europe	The floating sauna
Hungary	A chunk of central Europe colonized by Asian hordes a millennium ago	Drive a steam train
Latvia	A piece of Prussia that has endured a century of conflict and emerged flourishing	A night at the opera
Lithuania	Once the core of an empire that covered half of Europe, now rediscovering its somewhat diminished identity	Loop-the-loop (aerobatics)
Malta	Two-and-a-bit islands in the sun, close to Tunisia	Ollie Reed's (screen actor) last pub
Poland	The biggest new arrival, and a destination as yet undiscovered by most Brits	Visit a salt mine
Slovakia	A green, pleasant and welcoming land	Find Andy Warhol
Slovenia	A pocket-sized version of Austria	Ride a Lippizaner horse

noted that some attention was afforded to the Turkish Republic of Northern Cyprus. As the less developed part of the island, it was singled out because rejection of a UN plan for reunification of the island had generated some sympathy for its underdeveloped, undervisited nature and its unspoiled charm (Bowes, 2004; Patrickson, 2004).

The eight post-socialist states formed the main focus. Their potentials were identified in two principal respects. First, they were identified as 'Europe's new playground' (Behr *et al.*, 2004: 9); that is, new alternatives to previously visited destinations (Bridge, 2004; Calder, 2004a; Hodson, 2004). Tallinn, Riga and Vilnius were presented as substitutes for the more popular, much busier and well-established European city-break destinations such as Barcelona, Paris and Rome. Among the Baltic state capitals Riga was identified as an alternative to the long-standing city destinations of Prague and Budapest (Hodson, 2004). Bratislava, the capital of Slovakia, was portrayed as a low-cost alternative to nearby Vienna and an alternative gateway from Budapest and Prague from which to discover the heritage of the Austro-Hungarian Empire. In brief, much of the discussion centred on the degree to which established marketing formulas as well as popular and original attractions could be found in hitherto undiscovered destinations. Although they had been difficult to reach in former times, access had improved (by low-cost airlines mainly), they were comparatively cheap, comfortable and served by acceptably high levels of amenities (Calder, 2004a, b).

A second overlapping form of portrayal focused on the opportunities arising from partially developed tourism industries. For some, their naivety and lack of regulation presented new possibilities for hedonistic consumption. Cities like Tallinn, Riga, Prague and Vilnius were noted for their abilities to support the serious party-goer but without the cost or congestion of established destinations such as Dublin and Amsterdam (Behr *et al.*, 2004). Eastern Europe was also identified as a new source of affordable and available second homes (Allen, 2003; Collinson, 2004). Traditional regions for British second home owners such as western France, southern Spain and the Algarve had become more densely populated with expatriates, prices had risen and demand was outstripping supply. AC10 states would become popular because they 'should offer excellent value for money. On the whole, membership is expected to spur growth in the joining countries, which should ultimately mean rising property prices' (Allen, 2003: 20). New member states were portrayed as lands of opportunity, spaces for capital accumulation and places of consumption. Britons could take advantage of the market for skilled labour (if they required employment) or relatively depressed wages (if they required work done). As older EU citizens, they could avail themselves of facilities and services – such as excellent clinics, public transport systems and infrastructure – provided they demonstrated patience and understanding of the alien system (Crichton, 2004).

Discussion: Citizenship as a Double-edged Sword

The purpose of this chapter is not to pontificate over the merits of or justifications for the discourses, but rather to point to their existence and the pivotal role of citizenship in engineering or frustrating new mobilities. Whether or not there have been unacceptably high levels of mobility to Britain since 2004 remains highly contested (George *et al.*, 2005). Notwithstanding, the government learned from its bumpy ride in 2004. Ahead of the 2007 accession of Bulgaria and Romania, it announced in late October 2006 major restrictions on the mobility of new citizens from those countries to the UK in the form of a quota system (BBC, 2006).

Nevertheless, a major double standard is evident in the two sets of discourses and for that matter in the emergent situation with the two Balkan states. The print media was happy to propagate and endorse the view that the AC10 states were lands of tourism opportunity for British citizens. Simultaneously, it communicated, and in some cases precipitated, debate over the tightening of legislation in order to deny AC10 citizens full and unfettered rights to make movements, perhaps even short term and/or temporary in nature, to the UK.

Tourism as mobility was presented as an inalienable right for UK citizens and because of their status as full members of the 'EU club' they had the right to benefit from the enhanced opportunities on offer in the new member states. Very little reference was made to their responsibilities in terms of their impacts on local communities. Where once Amsterdam and Dublin were the exclusive haunts of lairy stags and hens, in comparative terms copy was conspicuously lacking on the fate about to befall Tallinn and others. Across the globe, second homes have been the source of much controversy (Hall and Müller, 2004) and in the UK one newspaper has claimed they are the 'next fox hunting' (Taylor, 2005: 16); that is, they are perceived as a major anti-social practice by virtue of their potential to inflate property prices beyond the means of local people. Be this as it may and the debate continues in the UK, once more there was little coverage of the consequences of properties 'going for a song' in the Czech Republic, Slovakia or Slovenia. UK citizens may be able to make a 'fast buck' or a long-term 'killing' on their second homes, but at what cost of escalating levels of deprivation and destitution in AC10 as prices spiral well beyond the local populations' willingness and ability to pay?

If the discourses of pleasure and play emphasize rights over responsibilities, then the opposite applies in the discourses of denial. Rights of movement were contested because AC10 citizens were painted as far more interested in obviating responsibility; that is, they wanted to exercise their rights of movement without a care for their responsibilities to contribute towards the upkeep of the services they sought to exploit. Treneman's metaphor may be somewhat absurd because who – apart from perhaps the most obsessive tourist – would be motivated to visit the 'lowlights' of British public services? Moreover, it evokes images of the stereotypical American visitor abroad in the 1960s and 1970s and clearly this is an extremely dated view of how tourists behave and appear. When teased out further, though, the image implies a blissful ignorance and disregard towards impacts. It reminds readers that typically visitors arrive in a destination; they are there to enjoy themselves and to take advantage of the facilities on offer; and they return after a short time with little thought for or commitment to the destination communities and the environment they have visited. It plays on long-held prejudice against (mass) tourists (Mowforth and Munt, 1998: 92), and it is sharply at odds with other more recent conceptualizations of the tourist, including the ideal of the responsible tourist. Perhaps most strikingly, the use of tourism to help restrict mobility is almost diametrically opposed to the fact that tourism is one of the principal modes by which citizens experience the EU at first hand through freedom of movement (Verstraete, 2002).

Conclusion: on the Importance of Citizenship in (Im)mobilities

Despite the rhetoric of harmonization and integration, there remain a series of significant de facto differences in the rights afforded and exercised by members of the AC10 and their allegedly 'fellow citizens' in the EU15. Recently, Rigo (2005) has argued that the situation with respect to the Eastern European states is reminiscent of the post-colonial condition. AC10 citizens are subject to a form of colonial history, where rules and regulations from the centre have been progressively imposed on them, yet they resist and contest the 'place' assigned to them in the new order of political and legal boundaries (Rigo, 2005: 5). There are, therefore, limits to which we can talk of a universal rights-based model of citizenship, and to which tourism mobilities are orchestrated by such a model. Instead, it is important to recognize that there are 'multiple citizenships' that trigger and shape short-term mobilities in the EU. These citizenships include full or partial membership status within the EU and citizenship rights afforded by the member state of domicile or birth.

These observations challenge some of the dominating rhetoric of the emerging mobilities paradigm. Talk of 'hypermobility' and 'fluid modernity' may be fashionable and the emergence of these concepts reflects the enhanced potentials for movement that we enjoy as part of the global condition in the early 21st century. On first inspection, the tone of the discourse is suggestive of unrestricted movement, of potential and possibility, of coverage and the ephemerality of flow. Of course, liquids flow based on the topography of the surface they flow over. Features of citizenship are just as capable of blocking or inhibiting flows of people as facilitating the freedom of their movement. Urry (2000) prefers the metaphor of the human circulatory system to conceptualize mobilities. Blood courses throughout the body by flowing through a series of arteries, organs and vessels back to the heart. People move from their home to and from their destinations through a series of links and nodes in transport systems. The location of hubs and their connectivity determine the major characteristics of the geographies of movement. However, circulation systems often suffer blockages and failures, and in some cases bypasses and grafts are necessary. Rather than get carried away purely with the potentials of mobility, a closer integration of citizenship would suggest that we should also map out more rigorously the routine and frequent restrictions to movement. Fortress Europe may have been opened up to citizens of the AC10, its outer walls even expanded in their direction, but access to the central citadel remains heavily protected. As George Parker (2004: 8) wrote in the *Financial Times*, 'the EU's expansion is a sullen affair marred by mistrust, barely concealed xenophobia and a failure by European leaders to explain its benefits'. With respect to tourism and other short-term mobilities, it is difficult to disagree with this view. It can only be hoped that the situation improves in forthcoming rounds of Enlargement, but sadly early evidence would suggest a case of *plus ça change, plus c'est la même chose*!

References

Adams, C. (2004) Tough line signalled on immigration from Eastern Europe. *Financial Times* 5 February, p. 4.

Allen, L. (2003) Going for a song in the Eastern Block. *Observer* 7 September, p. 20 (Cash).

Baldwin, T. (2004a) Curb on benefits for new EU migrants. *The Times* 18 February, p. 2.

Baldwin, T. (2004b) Migrants will have to sign work register. *The Times* 21 February, p. 15.

Behr, R., Bird, L., Bowes, G., Eilers, R. and Wilkinson, C. (2004) Europe's big playground. *Observer* 2 May, pp. 9–12 (Escape).

Bellamy, R. and Warleigh, A. (2001) Introduction: the puzzle of EU citizenship. In: Bellamy, R. and Warleigh, A. (eds) *Citizenship and Governance in the European Union*. Continuum, London, pp. 1–18.

Bowcott, O. (2004) EU expansion: is this the *Daily Mail* effect? Why Blair will look again at the risk of influx from Europe. *Guardian* 4 February, p. 4.

Bowes, G. (2004) Cyprus: direct flights to North? *Observer* 2 May, p. 4 (Escape).

Bridge, A. (2004) The buzz of new Europe. *Daily Telegraph* 1 May, pp. 1–3 (Travel).

British Broadcasting Corporation (BBC) (2006) Reid Outlines New EU Work Curbs. Online document. Available at: http://news.bbc.co.uk/1/hi/uk_politics/6076410.stm (accessed 2 November 2006).

Browne, A. (2004) How Europe closed door on migrants from new countries. *The Times* 5 February, p. 2.

Calder, S. (2004a) The field of Euro dreams. *Independent* 1 May, pp. 8–9 (Explorer).

Calder, S. (2004b) New Europe in your hands. *Independent* 1 May, pp. 15–16 (Explorer).

Chapman, J. (2004a) Blair plans U-turn on EU's new migrants. *Daily Mail* 17 February, p. 22.

Chapman, J. (2004b) Britain is warned over the migrants with HIV. *Daily Mail* 18 February, p. 8.

Clarence, E. (1999) Citizenship and identity: the case of Australia. In: Roseneil, S. and Seymour, J. (eds) *Practising Identities. Power and Resistance*. Macmillan, Basingstoke, UK.

Coles, T.E. (2008) Citizenship and the state: hidden features in the internationalisation of tourism. In: Coles, T.E. and Hall, C.M. (eds) *International Business and Tourism: Global Issues, Contemporary Interactions*. Routledge, London, pp. 55–69.

Coles, T.E. and Hall, D.R. (2005) Tourism and EU enlargement. Plus ça change? *International Journal of Tourism Research* 7(2), 51–62.

Collinson, P. (2004) Next stop for the property boom. *Guardian* 1 May, p. 5 (Jobs and Money).

Crichton, T. (2004) Europe: the heart beat of history. *Sunday Herald* 2 May, p. 16.

Deane, J. (2004) 'Benefit tourists' will not be welcome, insists Minister. *Press Association* 12 February.

Delanty, G. (2000) *Citizenship in a Global Age. Society, Culture, Politics*. Open University Press, Buckingham, UK.

Dougherty, H. (2004) Ministers move to block new influx of migrants. *Evening Standard* 11 February, p. 4.

Doughty, S. (2004) How East Europe migrants overshot Labour estimates. *Daily Mail* 8 July, p. 15.

Dunkerley, D., Hodgson, L., Konopacki, S., Spybey, T. and Thompson, A. (2002) *Changing Europe. Identities, Nations and Citizens*. Routledge, London.

Express (2004) Alert over new EU migrants. *Express* 20 January, p. 5.

George, N., Mulligan, M., Parker, G. and Williamson, H. (2005) Invasion of benefit tourists from EU's east fails to materialise. *Financial Times* 28 April. Online edition. Available at: www.ft.com (accessed 1 October 2006).

Guardian (2004) Gypsies, false figures. *Guardian* 21 January, p. 25.

Hall, C.M. (2002) Travel safety, terrorism and the media: the significance of the issue-attention cycle. *Current Issues in Tourism* 5(5), 458–466.

Hall, C.M. and Müller, D.K. (2004) *Tourism, Mobility and Second Homes. Between Elite Landscape and Common Ground*. Channel View, Clevedon, UK.

Hannam, K., Sheller, M. and Urry, J. (2006) Editorial: mobilities, immobilities and moorings. *Mobilities* 1(1), 1–22.

Hardie, A. (2004) EU benefit rules rushed through Commons. *Scotsman* 1 May, p. 8.

Heater, D. (2004) *A Brief History of Citizenship*. Edinburgh University Press, Edinburgh.

Hinsliff, G. (2004) Tories come to defence of immigrants: Howard accused of hypocrisy over party rebranding. *Observer* 29 February, p. 4.

Hinsliff, G. and Bright, M. (2004) Blair warned over migrant xenophobia. *Guardian* 15 February, p. 13.

Hodson, M. (2004) Hot shots: if you want style in your city break, go Baltic. *Sunday Times* 2 May, pp. 6–7 (Travel).

Hunt, J. and Wallace, C.J. (2004) The high water point of free movement of persons: ending benefit tourism and rescuing welfare. *Journal of Social Welfare and Family Law* 24(2), 211–222.

Isin, E.F. and Wood, P.K. (1999) *Citizenship and Identity*. Sage, London.

Islam, F. (2004) May Day or mayday for the EU? *Observer* 25 April, p. 4 (Business).

Jaworski, A., Ylanne-McEwen, V., Thurlow, C. and Lawson, S. (2003) Social roles and negotiation of status in host-tourist interaction: a view from British television holiday programmes. *Journal of Sociolinguistics* 7(2), 135–163.

Johnston, P. (2004) Will benefit tourists flood Britain? *Daily Telegraph* 4 February, p. 12.

Jones, G. and Brogan, B. (2004) Blair bid to avoid immigrant rush. *Daily Telegraph* 18 February, p. 2.

Kofman, E. (1995) Citizenship for some but not for others: spaces of citizenship in contemporary Europe. *Political Geography* 14(2), 121–137.

Kofman, E. (2005) Citizenship, migration and the reassertion of national identity. *Citizenship Studies* 9(5), 453–467.

Kymlicka, W. (1995) *Multicultural Citizenship. A Liberal Theory of Minority Rights*. Clarendon Press, Oxford, UK.

Lyons, J. (2004) Blair moves to stop 'benefit shoppers'. *Western Morning News* 18 February, p. 22

Marshall, T.H. (1950) *Citizenship and Social Class*. Cambridge University Press, Cambridge. (Available as a revised edition: Marshall, T.H. and Bottomore, T. (1992) *Citizenship and Social Class*, revised edn. Pluto Press, London.)

Mason, T., Moncrieff, C. and Sheringham, S. (2004) EU migrants will have to register for jobs. *Press Association* 23 February.

McRae, H. (2004) Flood of migrants may bring growth with them. *Independent*, 19 February, p. 41 (Business).

Mowforth, M. and Munt, I. (1998) *Tourism and Sustainability. New Tourism in the Third World*. Routledge, London.

Murphy, M. and Harty, S. (2003) Post-sovereign citizenship. *Citizenship Studies* 7(2), 181–197.

O'Flynn, P. (2004) Summit on the migrant muddle. *Express* 13 February, p. 8.

Parker, G. (2004) EU nationals harden their hearts against club's new members. *Financial Times* 4 February, p. 8 (International Economy and Europe).

Patrickson, S. (2004) A new place in the sun. *Sunday Times* 2 May, p. 5 (Travel).

Pearson, D. (2002) Theorizing citizenship in British settler societies. *Ethnic and Racial Studies* 25(6), 989–1012.

Rigo, E. (2005) Citizenship at Europe's borders: some reflections on the post-colonial condition of Europe in the context of EU Enlargement. *Citizenship Studies* 9(1), 3–22.

Sheller, M. and Urry, J. (2004) Places to play, places in play. In: Sheller, M. and Urry, J. (eds) *Tourism Mobilities. Places to Play, Places in Play*. Routledge, London, pp. 1–10.

Sheller, M. and Urry, J. (2006) The new mobilities paradigm. *Environment and Planning A* 38, 207–226.

Sparks, J. and Hellen, N. (2004) Britain faces influx of Europe's gypsies. *Sunday Times* 18 January, p. 14.

Tambini, D. (2001) Post-national citizenship. *Ethnic and Racial Studies* 24(2), 195–217.

Taylor, C. (2005) Second homes are the new fox-hunting. *Sunday Business* 26 June, p. 16.

Treneman, A. (2004) Panic? There's no need to frighten the horses. *The Times* 24 February, p. 2.

Turner, B. (1993) Contemporary problems in the theory of citizenship. In: Turner, B. (ed.) *Citizenship and Social Theory*. Sage, London, pp. 1–18.

Urry, J. (2000) *Sociology beyond Societies. Mobilities for the Twenty-first Century*. Routledge, London.

van Steenbergen, B. (1994) The condition of citizenship: an introduction. In: van Steenbergen, B. (ed.) *The Condition of Citizenship*. Sage, London, pp. 1–9.

Verstraete, G. (2002) Tourism and the global itinerary of an idea. *Thamyris/Intersecting* 9, 33–52.

Vulliamy, E. (2004) Europe's frontier pushes Poland close to the edge. *Observer* 18 April, pp. 20–21.

Wagstyl, S. (2004) Restrictions contradict the ideals of unity. *Financial Times* 9 February, p. 13 (Comment and Analysis).

Walker, K. (2004) UK asylum crackdown as Holland takes action; finally Blair faces the EU gypsy crisis. *Express* 18 February, p. 2.

White, M. (2004) Migrants: Blair acts on benefits: restrictions likely to include employers' work permits and tighter residence test. *Guardian* 18 February, p. 1.

White, M. and Travis, A. (2004) Benefits clampdown for new EU citizens. *Guardian* 24 February, p. 1.

Wikipedia (2008) Benefit Tourism. Online document. Available at: http://en.wikipedia.org/wiki/Benefit_tourism (accessed on 5 December 2007).

Wintour, P. (2004) EU enlargement: payouts to migrants restricted: immigration Home Office rushes through benefit rules. *Guardian* 1 May, p. 4.

Woods, R. (2004) Our extended family comes knocking. *Sunday Times* 2 May, p. 1.

World Tourism Organization (WTO) (2004) WTO welcomes EU enlargement as a stimulus for tourism. Online document. Available at: http://www.world-tourism.org/newsroom/Releases/2004/march/eu.htm (accessed 26 April 2004).

5 'Claim You Are From Canada, Eh': Travelling Citizenship Within Global Space

DAVID TIMOTHY DUVAL

Introduction

The academic literature on citizenship, while rich in theoretical and conceptual annotation, can be said to be proportionately weak on the fluid nature of polity and identity as a result of modern electronic tools for communication (cf. Pajnik, 2005). The implications for identity and co-presence in an age of 'instant' communication and vociferous mapping of ideas and constructs by users have resulted in new networks of identities being formed (Urry, 2003). The subsequent implications for mobilities are immediately apparent: identities as negotiated variables may be acknowledged in the context of more permanent movement such as migration or return migration, yet how identities are streamed and moulded en route through a course of mobility (however depicted, and of course varying in time and space) is an important consideration in how such temporary mobility is manifested.

The purpose of this chapter is to present, using netnographic methods, a series of represented nationalist identities as captured on an international online discussion forum in 2003. The original 'poster' to a discussion 'thread' within the forum expressed a desire to learn from fellow 'netizens' how to appear 'more European' and thus 'less American' while travelling. The majority of the responses were intended to be humorous, but several illustrate clearly a mix of identity politics, intentional configuration of how identities and citizenship are manifested and the permeability of identity construction. The intent of this chapter is not to evaluate the efficiency of identities as prescribed in an online community as this has been addressed in the literature (e.g. Holeton, 1998; Riva and Galimberti, 1998; McKenna and Bargh, 1999; Wallace, 1999; Berman and Bruckman, 2001; Bargh *et al.*, 2002). Rather, the intent is to locate how identities are constructed in a social and political online environment and to demonstrate the fluid expressions of citizenship by travellers. This achieves an alternative exposé of identity constructions in anonymous contexts where personal identities are masked but expressions of nationalism are unconstrained.

Netnographic Methods

The data featured in this chapter were culled and analysed using principles of netnography (Kozinets, 2002), a method by which online discussions and inter-actions are treated in an ethnographic manner, thus following Hine's (2000) notion of virtual ethnography. Netnographic methods have grown from recog-nized sociological and anthropological methods for processing data from online environments (e.g. Hine, 2000; Ruhleder, 2000; Wittel, 2000; Sade-Beck, 2004). Originally devised by Kozinets (2002) as a means of providing new marketing insights into customer perceptions, netnographic methods are useful for under-standing temporary mobility for two reasons. First, online portals have captured a significant share of the distribution channels associated with tourism. Second, the Internet itself, and more specifically online discussion forums, gives a voice to travellers and would-be travellers. Many forums offer travel advice, hints and tips and destination profiles. In essence, they provide a platform through which par-ticipants can contribute to discussions, argue/debate and help others in need.

To some extent, netnographic methods can be manipulated and altered to have a stronger correlation with textual or content analysis. Indeed, Kozinets (2002: 64) notes that 'Netnography is based primarily on the observation of textual discourse, an important difference from the balancing of discourse and observed behaviour that occurs during in-person ethnography'. For the purposes of this chapter, textual discourse takes centre stage, as opposed to traditional ethnography, which tends to insert the researcher in the fieldwork. (Indeed, some of the central tenets of netnographic methods speak to the insertion, in an ethnographic sense, of the researcher into online communities.) As online discussion forums generally allow for direct responses to previous posts, on occasion a method of post/response reporting is adopted here. As well, it is important to point out that, dur-ing the virtual fieldwork, a conscious effort was made not to participate in the online discussion itself, even though there are variables of nationality and reflex-ivity at work here, given that the author is Canadian (a fact that was partially responsible for becoming aware of the particular discussion under scrutiny). Importantly, the anonymity of the posters has been preserved throughout, and the forum at which this discussion takes place has not been revealed.

Identities in Flux: Online Discussion Boards

The original message to the bulletin board, initiated by an individual known in these circumstances as the original poster (OP), began with the title 'How to look European or at least less American'. The text of the post indicated that the OP was about to spend 3 months in Europe and thought it might be 'wise' to 'blend in', given the political and military tensions worldwide. Importantly, the OP sug-gested that such a topic might be 'fun' to discuss, but after quite some time (almost 3 months) the responses to the OP (and the responses to the responses) highlighted that the identities are, in fact, in flux, such that the resulting discussion hinged around several broad themes. These included: (i) the perceptions of 'Americans' (intentionally written in inverted quotation marks to highlight the problematic nature of identifying a typical American or US identity); (ii) the rejection of the alteration of one's overt and/or malleable phenotypic appearance that would, in effect, negate nationalist identities; and (iii) general humour which addresses common stereotypes associated with specific nationalist identities. Here, focus is directed at how nationalist identities are seen to be represented by a community of travellers (given that the discussion board itself is directed at frequent travellers). Within these three themes, the advice and answers to the OP floated around several issues that showcase how identities may be constructed during periods of temporary mobility.

Banal indicators of identity: dress and mannerisms

First among these signposted issues of how identity can be altered is one of dress and mannerism. Several posters highlighted common attributes and stereotypes designed to highlight the banal nature of identity reaction (as opposed to construction) on the part of American travellers:

> 'One tip is not to wear sneakers all the time. Especially white ones.'
> 'Or wear white sneakers with a white suit. People will think you are a South-American dictator.'
> 'Not every American wears jeans and white sneakers – just those west of the Hudson.'
> 'I just returned from Mexico City – while waiting for the Metro my brother-in-law said to me, "Look, there are some of your compatriots from the USA." I looked over to see a half-dozen people dressed in shorts, t-shirts, and white sneakers carrying cameras and guidebooks. Talk about advertising the fact that you are a tourist!'
> 'No Disneyland, Planet Hollywood, or "I am with stupid" shirts.'
> '1) No white sneakers with black socks; 2) No Aloha shirt; 3) No SLR Camera with 500 mm lens.'

This sample of postings to the discussion revolve around how 'Americans' (as nationalist-constructed identities) can be perceived on the basis of overt indicators. For the most part, it could be argued that many of these posts have an element of humour built into their purpose, yet they do highlight how dress and appearance form elements of identity and recognition. Indeed, in this case, 'Americans' are typified by white sneakers (or 'trainers' as they are colloquially known) and shirts which bear some degree of nationalist corporate monikers (excluding the fact that EuroDisney in Paris exists and that Planet Hollywood can be found in several countries around the world). With respect to actual performance in the form of mannerism, several posts highlighted how a typical 'American' acts, and thus offer specific advice to the OP on how to act 'less American':

> 'Don't read USA Today or the Herald Tribune. Try a local newspaper instead.'

'Keep your voice down. By comparison to many nationalities, Americans tend to speak very loudly.'

'If you can't read the local language, try the Economist. You might be mistaken for British or Irish.'

– *Response*: 'I read The Economist so that people mistake me for being smart.'

– *Response*: 'No risk of that with me. Even with an Economist in hand, I look [as] thick as two short planks.'

'Try to be a little less "cowboyish" or manly. Perhaps more feminine is the word, as men over there [Europe] do look a lot better in terms of appearance than the US, with all the Gucci clothes and what not.'

'Depends on where you are going, but if you shave your head and wear a rugby shirt in the correct colors (somebody else will have to help you out there) you'll fit right in. You will also realize that it's not the clothing you wear that tells people where you are from, it's you manner [sic] and all the rest, and will realized [sic] that you shaved your head for nothing.'

'On the tube in London last Fall my husband and I were sitting apart. 2 men we [sic] grinning and talking about the man down the way. They confided in me that they were playing spot the Yank. I admitted the "Yank" was my husband. They were delighted. I was told I looked very cosmopolitan. Unlike my hubby who wore his white tennis shoes, North Face wind breaker and Raiders baseball cap. We laughed and chatted about the states [sic]. They were introduced to my husband when we got off at the same stop and we all enjoyed the interchange.'

Many of the comments relating to mannerism tended to centre around how 'Americans' were typified in terms of actions and activities. What is interesting is that, with respect to mannerism, these posters feel that there are discernable differences between how 'Americans' act and how they represent themselves. In some instances, posters would suggest that nationalities may be hidden by travellers.

Hidden identities/mobilities?

While aspects of mannerism, behaviour and dress coalesce around stereotypical beliefs about how 'Americans' should and do act while on holiday, there is room to consider the posts of some participants who suggest that it might be better to distance one's 'Americanness' by attempting to portray oneself as from a different country:

'Claim you are from Canada, eh.'

'If someone asks where you are from, just say Canada, as everybody likes Canadians.'

'If in any doubt, claim to be Canadian. It excuses any North-American dress/accent without drawing criticism of the American political regime.'

'If you are truly paranoid, brush up on your Canadian geography and become a "temporary" resident of Toronto or Montreal.'

'I always wondered why the American love to make joke about Canada, and rub in the fact mercilessly, when a whole lot of them pretend to be us overseas. Bloody hell, I say.'

'If you speak English with a neutral American accent as do people from metro New York and San Francisco, you should easily be able to pass for Canadian as most Europeans couldn't tell you apart. I know people who wear Canadian flag lapel pins, or even t-shirts.'

Interestingly, these kinds of posts which encouraged the OP to appear to be Canadian rather than 'American' were met with consternation from several other posters:

> 'I have to weigh in on the whole "Just say you are Canadian" thing, which most people think nothing of. It is a very sore point for most Canadians because we don't understand why the citizens of the USA, which are ordinarily a quite patriotic and proud bunch (and there is nothing wrong with that), should feel that they have to lie about their citizenship in order to be accepted. Quite paradoxical if you ask me, and maybe something to think about. Us Canadians are usually not very patriotic, don't have a large sense of nationhood and are generally quite insecure when it comes to our big brother to the south but . . . nothing will p*ss off a Canadian more than someone walking around with a Maple Leaf on their pack, or saying they are Canadian when they are not. It is one of the only topics that ALL Canadians will agree with. If you are so uncomfortable with being American, why don't you come join us in the Great White North!'

That the comparison between Canada and the USA arose in the discussion is not surprising, given that these kinds of comparisons are made in popular culture, politics and the media.

Indignation and nationalism

The issue of whether to claim citizenship, which is often perceived to bring with it specific mannerisms and behaviours, of another country resulted in several posters expressing indignation at the thought of misrepresenting one's nationality and/or citizenship. To a large extent, this was collapsed into misrepresenting one's *identity*:

> 'What a topic?! Why on hearth [sic] would you feel the need to change your appearance to look less American? This is simply wrong!'
> 'Do not apologize for being an American. It is a rare priveledge [sic].'
> 'If you are an American, it is something to be proud of. (If you are an ignorant, discourteous American, it's not!) There is no need to pretend to be Canadian.'

These responses encouraged their own kind of response, including the following:

> 'BTW [By the way], I don't think there's anything wrong with trying to be "less American" when traveling abroad. It's not a matter of lack of American pride – it's about trying to respect the local cultures/peoples and to try to learn how others live by doing. For example, when I travel, I try to learn the local language, if only a few phrases (or if I'm in the UK, I'll say, for example, "return ticket" instead of "roundtrip"). I'll try to observe local customs (e.g. soap up outside the tub and take off my shoes indoors in Japan), eat local cuisine in the local manner (e.g. use spoon and fork in Thailand and chopsticks in China), and wear appropriate dress.'

Interestingly, the original poster offered a response to this line in the discussion:

> 'I personally cannot relate with a fellow American who would choose to market themselves as Canadian. I am looking for subtlety and clothing ideas not substitute citizenship.'

In one instance, another poster reflected on reverse mobilities and whether identity politics were at work:

> 'I hate to turn this thread on its head, but do Europeans work at not looking European when traveling to the U.S.? When I encounter Europeans in the U.S. it never dawned on me to assume that they would materially change to be more American – and I've seen no evidence that they do. Is it really that important to blend in anywhere? I understand about respecting other cultures and practice same, but I don't really get the chameleon thing that others are suggesting here. The discusion [sic] here and elsewhere seems very one sided – so any feedback on how foreigners should look in the USA?'

This post met with an interesting reply:

> 'well, not sure about physical changes i.e. outfits.. etc..but it is pretty clear that many Europeans, particular the younger male ones trying to meet attractive females when traveling in the US will do the exact opposite regarding their accents, meaning they will in fact take extra care to sound european [sic] when speaking. Think Hugh Grant..etc..'

Other examples of indignation at the thought of expressing non-nationalist identities met with some consternation:

> 'I've been lurking on this site for a long time and have resisted the urge to post – until I read this thread. Frankly, I think this is the most preposterous idea I've ever read. Apparently there are at least some Americans out there who are A) ashamed of their heritage or B) unnecessarily paranoid about it. Do you think there are scads of Europeans out there who freak out about how to look "more American" when they go to the U.S. on holiday? I'm probably not as worldly as some others on this site, but I've been to almost 20 countries on four continents. I have never pretended to be anything I'm not, which is a typical American. I don't forget to say "please" and "thank you," and I do try to at least say a few things in the language of wherever I'm at. I'm conservative politically and don't bring up politics in overseas discussions (I think it's rude), but I answer honestly when asked. And you know what? In *every* country but one, I've never had any problems. In fact, I've had overwhelmingly positive experiences everywhere I've been. (The only exception, oddly? Canada. Of course, if you know anything about the Canadian national psyche, you'll know this isn't a surprise.) Americans are far, far from holding a monopoly on boorish behavior overseas. The notion that there should be a sea change in how Yanks behave in other countries, or that they should pose as somebody else, is ridiculous. And those who are ashamed of being American should seriously consider finding a place to live or a nationality that better conforms to their world view, whatever that might be.'

Situation-specific identities – 'Where are you from?'

In many ways, the hybridized nature of identities was captured in the online discussion. Many individuals wrote about how difficult it can be to ascribe mono-nationalist identities to individuals:

> 'If anyone (a stranger) ever asks if I am American, I deflect the question, but might say, I am Irish, but I live in America for work.'

'Being Taiwanese-Canadian, Europeans usually mistake me for Japanese, if anything.'

'Despite growing up in the USA, very few people would identify me as American – which is mostly down to the fact that I've lived abroad for quite a long time. On the other hand, in London at least, I can spot most American tourists at 100 yards – without ever hearing them speak.'

'I lived in Provence for two years and never had a thought about how my clothes might project my nationality.'

'As an Asian-American, I read this discussion so far with conflicting views. Just coming back from an [sic] European trip. I had to agree with my Asian-American friends who said that "Europe is the place where we can feel truely like American." Whenever I travel within U.S., a usual response after I told people that I am from San Francisco is "WHERE are you REALLY from." And it's pretty common, even for the 4th-5th generation Asian-Americans. When traveling in Asia, locals usually looking down [sic] on Asian-Americans who stress their American identity too much. But Europeans seems to take my claim to be American at face value.'

'I am at a point now, if I feel the question was not asked sincerely, I tell people that I am 0.1% Dutch. Which is true and absurd at same time. But then, many issues about races are absurd to begin with.'

'Some Europeans don't seem to regard "American" as a nationality or ethnic group, only as citizenship, and behave as if you are missing the point when you respond so.'

'If anyone is so rude as to ask, "Where are you really from?", just respond with a question of your own, such as, "That's an interesting question. Why do you want to know?" or "Where do you think I'm from?" Turn the attention back on them. Works for me!'

'Have you ever met a German or a Frenchman pretending to be Swiss? If so, would you respect them for that? It is our responsibility as travellers to represent the best of our culture. Much of the worst of our culture is improperly exported to the rest of the world, be it fast food, bad TV, or hostile media.'

These indicate that there is recognition of the influence mobility has on ascriptions of home and nationality. There is also a strong sense of nationalist identity 'protection' for the purposes of reifying patriotism. The work of Pascual-de-Sans (2004) can be used to situate patriotic tendencies in expressions of identity. Pascual-de-Sans (2004) forwarded the concepts of idiotopy and idiotope to explain and rationalize geographical identification and place identification, respectively. Idiotopes are manifested traits such that multiple places can often be attached to individuals. As such, they are a useful concept for understanding the centrality of place recognition and allegiance. While some of the comments from forum participants would suggest that an idiotopic notion is strong (hence the resistance to portray themselves as anything but American), other instances (where the emphasis is to look anything but American) would suggest that idiotopes are malleable themselves and entirely situation-specific.

Assessment: (re)configured identities through virtual space

The impact of globalization on citizenship has generated significant discussion in the academic literature (e.g. Falk, 2000; Brodie, 2004). For the most part, these studies have focused on the regulatory environment in which citizenship and national identities permeate geopolitical borders, and the consequential thinning of nationalist ties. Desforges *et al.* (2005) point to the importance that space has in formulations of citizenship, noting particularly that other conceptual terms such as mobility, scale and landscape offer an equally important window into which citizenship can be formulated. The preceding discussion has been consciously designed to fit with what Sheller and Urry (2006: 209) have termed the 'new mobilities paradigm', where 'places are tied into at least thin networks of connections that stretch beyond each such place'. Consideration can also be given to these discussions as examples of nation-building texts (e.g. Thornley, 2004) in the sense that genocidal events need not be at work in order to define and delineate national status. As Whitaker (2005: 585) points out, in examining Edensor's (2002) work, 'National identity is robust even where no one is dying in its name'.

Whereas Wang (2004) argues that passports and visas are, in essence, manifestations of citizenship, it is perhaps more appropriate to explore the *corporeal* manifestation of citizenship and allegiance and, more importantly, how the corporeal is influenced by the social. To this end, it has been argued here that the Internet presents the fulcra for such identity negotiation, supporting the suggestion by Hill and Wilson (2002: 3) that 'The Internet will undoubtedly come to serve as an even more prominent locus for constructing and negotiating social identities in the 21st century'. The Internet, then, provides a conduit through which identities are negotiated and traversed. Identities, if fluid and ultimately situation specific, are malleable, and thus perhaps Dolby and Cornbleth (2001: 293) are correct in their argument that 'it would be more appropriate to speak of social identification processes than of social identities, in order to emphasize their ongoing, interactive, mobilized, in-use nature'.

Indeed, Dolby and Cornbleth (2001) follow on from Kearney's (2004) challenge that the cultural group as a traditional anthropological unit of assessment is giving way to the focus on identities as deterritorialized representations. Many social scientists have long held that identities were rooted in nation states, and the multitude of groups (the mosaic of the human enterprise) would allow for convenient comparisons to be made between and among groups. The problem that we face now, however, is that some people (although Tomlinson (1999) says not all) are not necessarily tied to one place; in other words, gone is the idea that expressions of identity are foremost concentrated in the nation which gave birth to that identity. We have, instead, the mobile elite traversing the globe (often virtually, as demonstrated in this chapter). Exactly how these manifestations of pseudo-nation hybrids are to be interpreted, however, remains problematic.

Goffman's (1963) work on stigma provides at least one lens through which the meeting(s) of the corporeal and the social meet, and may provide some insight into how social identification processes described by Dolby and Cornbleth (2001) can be conceptualized. In fact, Goffman's concept can be applied on two levels in the case of the above discussion: (i) the discrepancies between virtual and actual identities (Goffman, 1963: 31) are amplified due to the anonymous nature of online interactions and discussion; and (ii) while mobile, tourists as actors manage self-ascribed traits (Goffman's 'tribal' traits) in the social stage that results from travel. The latter is of key importance, as Goffman outlines differences in discredited groups, where traits are not hidden, and the discreditable, where traits can be concealed. The above example blends a curious mix of the two: where some individuals offered suggestions to the OP regarding the concealment of traits that would lead others to conclude the OP was an American, others would suggest that to conceal these traits belies the social foundation upon which they are/were constructed. In other words, the stigma of identity while on holiday applies to those who wish to alter social and/or physical traits as well as those who do not. Identity and stigma, then, are co-present and co-dependent (managed for the purposes of how much 'we' reveal about 'ourselves') and specific to none but universally addressed by most.

Conclusions: Identities in Global Space

As an alternative to investigating tourist behaviour while on holiday, this chapter has utilized a rough form of netnographic methods to illuminate perceptions and meanings of traveller behaviour and identities. From a methodological perspective, online discussion forums present unique opportunities to observe and catalogue overt expressions of those identities. As such, given that new forms of communication and information acquisition/sharing have expanded exponentially in most Western countries, future netnographic work might find a useful home within social scientists' toolkits.

As the chapters in this volume attest, mobilities has become a significant conceptual framework (perhaps even a paradigm (Sheller and Urry, 2006)) through which the human condition is observed and modelled. As Urry (2003) argued, mobilities at once encompass scapes, flows, objects, people, places and information, thus operationalizing some of the previous work stemming from transnationalism (e.g. Faist, 2000) in the social sciences. Mobilities, as a manifestation of transnational social capital, focus on meaning behind movement and the potential for movement. Of importance in this chapter is how identity is reflected in mobilities. Sheller (2004: 50) noted that social interaction presents new forms of identities:

> The structure of social interaction is metamorphosing not so much because increasing numbers of social actors join a 'network' (for example, adding more telephone lines to a fixed-line system, or more hubs to a transportation network), but because new 'persons' and 'places' are constantly emerging out of the social gel itself, bubbling up as it were from nowhere. The challenge before us, then, is to begin to devise empirical research that will reveal the dynamics of the communicative processes that animate these unstable fluid structures.

Netnographic methods provide some insight into dissecting the structures that Sheller speaks of, and the added bonus that is provided is a window into which identity constructions emerge and, equally important, are debated. This chapter has interrogated a snapshot of the manifestations of a social network of travellers in relation to the identities conceived and overtly presented. As shown, actors within the network have clear ideas as to how appearance and mannerisms should be extolled, largely in an effort to secure comfortable positions within other social situations. The sphere of interactivity that is the electronic forums through which these actors have debated cultural and social representations has contributed to the transnational characteristics that embed modern mobilities.

Intriguingly, the online discourse presented above is a window into which the construction of transnational identities can be witnessed as they develop. Such discourse presents an example of the hyper-reality of modern mobility systems (Hannam *et al.*, 2006). In many respects, future research might be able to monitor variances in identity constructs as presented online, and marry these with actual practice to form a more complete picture of representations of identity.

Acknowledgements

Many thanks to Jennie Germann Molz and John Urry for comments on some of the issues presented herein. Thanks also to participants at the Fourth International Symposium on Aspects of Tourism (Brighton, UK) in 2005 for comments on the conference paper from which this chapter grew, and to the anonymous referee for useful feedback on an earlier draft. Special thanks to the forum owner/administrator from which the online discussions were observed/analysed. Errors and omissions are solely the responsibility of the author.

References

Bargh, J., McKenna, K. and Fitzsimons, G. (2002) Can you see the real me? Activation and expression of the 'true self' on the internet. *Journal of Social Issues* 58, 33–48.

Berman, J. and Bruckman, A. (2001) The Turing game: exploring identity in an online environment. *Convergence* 7, 83–102.

Brodie, J. (2004) Introduction: globalisation and citizenship beyond the national state. *Citizenship Studies* 8, 323–332.

Desforges, L., Jones, R. and Woods, M. (2005) New geographies of citizenship. *Citizenship Studies* 9, 439–451.

Dolby, N. and Cornbleth, C. (2001) Introduction: social identities in transnational times. *Discourse: Studies in the Cultural Politics of Education* 22, 293–296.

Edensor, T. (2002) *National Identity: Popular Culture and Everyday Life*. Berg, Oxford, UK.

Faist, T. (2000) Transnationalization in international migration: implications for the study of citizenship and culture. *Ethnic and Racial Studies* 23, 189–222.

Falk, R. (2000) The decline of citizenship in an era of globalisation. *Citizenship Studies* 4, 5–17.

Goffman, I. (1963) *Stigma: Notes on the Management of Spoiled Identity*. Prentice-Hall, Englewood Cliffs, New Jersey.

Hannam, K., Sheller, M. and Urry, J. (2006) Editorial: mobilities, immobilities and moorings. *Mobilities* 1, 1–22.

Hill, J.D. and Wilson, T.M. (2002) New identities. *Identities: Global Studies in Culture and Power* 9, 1–6.

Hine, C. (2000) *Virtual Ethnography*. Sage Publications, London.

Holeton, R. (1998) *Composing Cyberspace: Identity, Community, and Knowledge in the Electronic Age*. McGraw-Hill, Boston, Massachusetts.

Kearney, M. (2004) *Changing Fields of Anthropology: from Local to Global*. Rowman and Littlefield Publishers Inc., Lanham, Maryland.

Kozinets, R.V. (2002) The field behind the screen: using netnography for marketing research in online communities. *Journal of Marketing Research* 39, 61–72.

McKenna, K. and Bargh, J. (1999) Causes and consequences of social interaction on the internet: a conceptual framework. *Media Psychology* 1, 249–269.

Pajnik, M. (2005) Citizenship and mediated society. *Citizenship Studies* 9, 349–367.

Pascual-de-Sans, A. (2004) Sense of place and migration histories: idiotopy and idiotope. *Area* 36, 348–357.

Riva, G. and Galimberti, C. (1998) Computer-mediated communication: identity and social interaction in an electronic environment. *Genetic, Social and General Psychology Monographs* 124, 434–463.

Ruhleder, K. (2000) The virtual ethnographer: fieldwork in distributed electronic environments. *Field Methods* 12, 3–17.

Sade-Beck, L. (2004) Internet ethnography: online and offline. *International Journal of Qualitative Methods* 3(2), Article 4. Available at: http://www.ualberta.ca/~iiqm/backissues/3_2/ pdf/sadebeck.pdf (accessed 14 February 2006).

Sheller, M. (2004) Mobile publics: beyond the network perspective. *Environment and Planning D* 22, 39–52.

Sheller, M. and Urry, J. (2006) The new mobilities paradigm. *Environment and Planning A* 38, 207–226.

Thornley, D. (2004) Breaking with English: the nation as ethnoscape. *National Identities* 6, 61–76.

Tomlinson, J. (1999) *Globalization and Culture*. University of Chicago Press, Chicago, Illinois.

Urry, J. (2003) Social networks, travel and talk. *British Journal of Sociology* 54, 155–175.

Wallace, P. (1999) *The Psychology of the Internet*. Cambridge University Press, Cambridge, UK.

Wang, H.-L. (2004) Regulating transnational flows of people: an institutional analysis of passports and visas as a regime of mobility. *Identities: Global Studies in Culture and Power* 11, 351–376.

Whitaker, R. (2005) Questions of national identity. *Identities: Global Studies in Culture and Power* 12, 585–606.

Wittel, A. (2000, January) Ethnography on the move: from field to net to Internet. *Forum Qualitative Sozialforschung/Forum: Qualitative Social Research* [Online journal] 1(1). Available at: http://qualitative-research.net/fqs (accessed 11 July 2006).

6 International Student Mobility: Cross-cultural Learning from International Internships

JEROEN VAN WIJK, FRANK GO AND ERIK VAN 'T KLOOSTER

Introduction

Students have always been on the move. Foreign travel used to be a part of the education of wealthy young aristocrats by which they might become civilized by exposure to European art, architecture and manners. This concept of undertaking a period to journey abroad to get to know other ways of living, working and learning, different governance systems, another language – personally enriching experiences, which the sojourner could integrate for application back home – was known as the Grand Tour in the 17th and the 18th centuries. In fact, the term 'journey' in Middle English means progress and conveys the significant effects which international travel can have on the sojourner's self-perceived personal development and cross-cultural awareness and understanding.

The significance of international student mobility in terms of its possibilities for participation and contribution to appreciate and understand other cultures and international issues has not escaped the European Commission (EC). In 1987 it began to support a mobility programme designed to facilitate university students' mobility among European universities. The programme was named after the cosmopolitan scholar Erasmus and became very popular among European students. In 1987 the Erasmus programme was incorporated under Europe's education programme entitled 'Socrates', involving 30 European countries.

> Its main objective is to build up a Europe of knowledge and thus provide a response to the major challenges of this new century: to promote lifelong learning, encourage access to education for everybody, and help people acquire recognized qualifications and skills. In more specific terms, Socrates seeks to promote language learning, and to encourage mobility and innovation.
>
> (European Commission, 2002)

In October 2002 the 'Erasmus week' was launched across European Union (EU)-member states. The EC and its academic networks celebrated the event that a million students had participated in the Erasmus programme (European Commission, 2002). Overall, international student mobility has doubled over the past decades, up to over 1.5 million students that were studying abroad in 2003 (UNESCO, 2004). Most of these students travel to the Organization for Economic Co-operation and Development (OECD) area, which received 85% of the world's foreign students in 1999 (see Fig. 6.1) (Larsen and Vincent-Lancrin, 2002).

International student mobility results from political rationales behind policies to internationalize higher education, but increasingly has business motives as well. Student mobility represents an important source of export revenue in some OECD countries, amounting to an estimated US$30 billion in 1999. Students incur large expenditures for their travel expenses, education costs and living expenses (Larsen and Vincent-Lancrin, 2002). The great value involved in the education market has been one of the reasons for the liberalization of trade in higher education services under the World Trade Organization (WTO). During the next decades the world's student population is expected to become ever more mobile, and universities will continue to reach beyond borders to tap the international flow of students in order to survive in the increasingly competitive world of higher education.[1]

Among the beneficiaries of the growing educational travel market will be businesses involved in transport, hospitality and intermediary service organizations. However, the tourist industry appears to be still 'unaware of the true size of this market segment' (Ritchie *et al.*, 2003: 1). The sub-segment of international internships is as yet serviced by mainly non-profit mediating organizations, such as Internship International, Projects Abroad, Dublin Internships, Go Abroad and AIESEC International, and international offices of academic institutions.

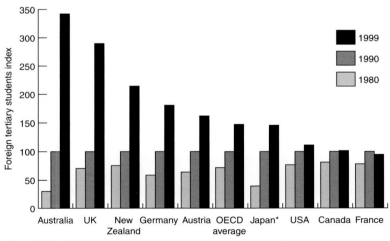

Source: 1980 and 1990, UNESCO (*except Japan: Education Ministry); 1999: OECD Education Database

Fig. 6.1. Studying abroad – increase of foreign tertiary students in OECD countries 1980–1999 (1990 = 100) (Source: Larsen and Vincent-Lancrin, 2002).

Increased international student mobility must be placed in the context of the process of globalization, which involves the 'extensivity of global networks, the intensity of global interconnectedness, the velocity of global flows and the impact propensity of global interconnectedness' (Held *et al.*, 1999: 21). The world has been witnessing an acceleration in human activity in a globalizing world in terms of flows of people (tourists, business people, migrants, refugees), capital, information, political ideas and values within particular ethnoscapes, finanscapes, technoscapes and ideoscapes (Appadurai, 1990). Clearly, within this framework, these characteristic features of the 21st-century landscape are central to understanding the theme of mobility, particularly its cultural, ecological and economic impacts.

The flow of people is regulated, steered and restricted by various technical, juridical and economic factors. On the other hand, the current boom of mobile technology enables humans to move and connect with almost everything, everywhere. Largely due to the increased volume of mobility, bound to concepts of time and space and rooted in the material world in which we live – a tangible world of places, territorial landscapes, artefacts, urban areas – the way in which we work is changing rapidly; for instance, through outsourcing certain tasks to low wage countries (Go and van Fenema, 2006).

Multinational organizations operate in world markets and have had a major influence on the restructuring of the international labour market. The advent of modern computing, and bridging technologies such as telecommunications and affordable air transport due to liberalization, has altered socio-political frames of reference, and the trend towards business processes and work distributed across the globe has gained considerable momentum. Some companies have been successful in evolving new structures and patterns of working in a globally distributed environment. But many others, through a perception of risks and problems, have been deterred or frustrated in their attempts to do so.

As corporations are increasingly dependent on a complex network of outsourcing relationships with stakeholders, who are often located in remote locations, managers must constantly assess these relationships and the intentions and reactions of their counterparts, who often represent an 'other' culture. In a knowledge-based economy the recognition gains momentum that value is distributed and resides in individuals in the context of the primacy of individual space (Zuboff and Maxmin, 2003). This perspective on distributed value necessitates distributed structures to support the building blocks of relationships with and among individuals. In the transnational context, it implies the necessity to foster research expertise and provide clarity regarding which research priorities should be included when setting the globally distributed work research agenda for decision making and action (Kumar and Krishna, 2005). Within an international business environment it would include, according to the University of Michigan Business School (2005), the following set of variables:

1. Diversity, i.e. variations in conditions, patterns and processes across countries, regions, cultures and economic/social and political systems.
2. Border crossing, i.e. physical, financial, human, informational and other flows across national borders, which differentiate international from domestic business.

3. Change, i.e. dynamic trends and alterations in external conditions that restructure the product, capital/labour markets, organization, regulation, management and strategies of multinational corporations.
4. Interdependence, i.e. reciprocal effects of networks of causal relations among business environments arising via multiple channels involving multiple actors and multiple issues.
5. Responsibility, i.e. consistent with the emergent distinctive competence to advance economic globalization with ethics, equity, inclusion, human security, sustainability and genuine development.

The nature and development of particular transnational networks of people and places entails research on intercultural processes and their consequences. This involves an understanding of the significance of the emergence of a globalizing culture characterized by a continuous flow of ideas and knowledge mediated through mobile individuals. The flow is increasingly digital in nature, in the form of e-commerce in the shape of value constellations with temporary role participants, leading experts or unique artists (Edvinsson, 2000: 13). Developments in information and communication technologies, with their direct influences on the mass media and on education have also served to push this globalization process forward. However, the internal contradictions of this process are becoming all too clear.

Within the framework of a globalizing society, we argue that educational travel deserves a high priority to enable youth to experience the 'other'. However, the reality is that universities around the world are faced with many programmatic demands, under the constraint of shrinking resources. Against this backdrop, international internships can be applied as an effective educational mechanism to contribute to cross-cultural learning. An internship is a student's closely monitored, paid or unpaid work experience at a corporation or nonprofit organization. Such an experience offers students opportunities for socializing into the management profession and tackling 'real world' challenges faced by organizations. International internships enable students to live and work side-by-side with people of the host country, and to get to know values, customs and world views in other regions of the world. Student mobility for internship purposes tends to be more beneficial than most other educational travel forms, as the latter tend to be characterized by organized group travel for leisure motives. In contrast, interns typically operate on an independent basis and face demands from their employer and the mental confusion that often results from differences in cultural values and ecology between their home and host environment.

The main question addressed in this chapter is whether the international internship serves as an effective educational mechanism to facilitate the learning of required cross-cultural skills. Below, we first explore briefly the magnitude of study travel and its related emerging educational travel industry. Secondly, we discuss the literature on cross-cultural competency development, and then present the findings of a survey on the learning effects of international internships among alumni of the Rotterdam School of Management (RSM). We conclude with a discussion.

Learning Cross-cultural Skills from Educational Travel

One important question that needs to be answered is whether educational travel fosters the development of dynamic cross-cultural competencies, and enables students to bridge the obstacles which they may encounter during their stay in a novel environment. Studies on learning effects of educational travel indicate that study tours and student exchange programmes are effective mechanisms for enhancing cross-cultural understanding. In a study concerning 70 American students who had participated in a 3-month study programme in Nepal, participants stated that the programme particularly impacted on their understanding and appreciation of Nepal, other cultures, international issues and human differences. They also indicated that they became deeply aware of social issues (such as poverty and health) in developing countries (Farrell and Suvedi, 2003). Carlson and Widaman (1988) found that studying and living lead to heightened levels of international understanding, that is 'the knowledge of and awareness about issues and events of national and international significance, as well as general attitudes that reflect heightened sensibility to international issues, people, and culture'. Their research involved over 800 American college students of which 300 studied abroad at a European university during their junior year, while 500 remained on the campus. The study-abroad group showed higher levels of international political concern, cross-cultural interest and cultural cosmopolitanism than those who did not.

In another study, cross-cultural interaction was found to be important particularly for personal growth. Gmelch (1997) followed 51 American students who travelled through Europe in 1993, and found little impact on their cognitive development (i.e. the acquisition of knowledge about European cultures). The main impact of the (extensive) travelling was on the student's personal development. Students themselves, as well as their parents, indicated that the travels had increased students' self-confidence and maturity, and their ability to cope with unusual and unpredictable situations. Gmelch explains this development of the self in psychological terms: periods of discontinuity and displacement trigger individual change and maturation. The independent travelling in unusual environments confronted the students continuously with problems they had to solve themselves (where to go, how to go there, where to stay, what areas of the city to avoid, etc.), required a certain level of organization (keeping track of their passport, money, train pass, etc.), and forced them to cope with the unpredictable (missing train connection, train strike, no available accommodation).

Social networks enhance students' cross-cultural learning. In one study it was found that feelings of loneliness and cultural distance were important determinants for the psychological well-being of 155 sojourners (tertiary students from 42 countries) in New Zealand (Ward and Searle, 1991). According to Ward *et al.* (2001) various types of social networks can offer the support that students can use to adjust to a novel environment. Network linkages with host nationals are important for instrumental reasons, such as to facilitate contact with the local bureaucracy, language problems, *etc.* Networks of non-compatriot foreign students are used for recreational purposes and for mutual support based on their shared 'foreignness'. However, the main supportive network for students abroad is that of fellow compatriots, who are important for companionship and emotional support.

Empirical research on the cross-cultural adjustment of international interns is limited. One major study was carried out by the American Institute for the International Education of Students (IES). The IES conducted a survey among 3700 study-abroad alumni who had studied abroad between 1950 and 1999. It found that alumni who had participated in internships and field placements on IES programmes were more likely to say that such experience allowed them to better understand their own cultural values and biases, that they had influenced their perspective on how they view the world, and influenced their interaction with people from different cultural backgrounds. Around a third of respondents remained in contact with host country friends (Gillespie and Slawson, 2003). Similarly, Stronkhorst (2005) confirmed that international internships produced better learning outcomes than study exchanges and national internships in terms of foreign language skills (reading and writing), multicultural personality (cultural empathy and open-mindedness), self-efficacy and intercultural competencies, but reliability of these results is low due to small sample size (33 international internship students).

Another study on the skills and competences that students had developed during their internship was carried out by AIESEC International in 1998 and involved approximately 1000 alumni. The respondents indicated that their international experience had enhanced their skills in cross-cultural communication (82%), their open-mindedness (76%) and tolerance (63%), 'created awareness on global issues and trends' (72%), and enriched and developed their 'values in life' (70%) (AIESEC International, 2001).

Cross-cultural Skills Development

The assumption that travel results in more cross-cultural understanding is rooted in social contact theory. In studying inter-racial relations, social psychologists found that inter-group contacts (i.e. face-to-face interaction between members of clearly different groups) reduce prejudices, although not under all conditions (see e.g. Pettigrew, 1998). Tourism researchers have applied social contact theory to guest–host interaction, but have reported widely different effects of tourist contact on intercultural understanding and stereotypes (Litvin, 2000, 2003). The conditions under which tourist contact takes place seem vital. For instance, a typical escorted bus tour resembles as it were a 'cultural bubble' and therefore would contribute little to change the passengers' negative attitudes towards the host population of hostile or unfriendly nations. However, opinions and attitudes may change positively from a tourist experience under specific conditions, such as careful preparations for the trip, guidance during the exposure to and encounters with the host population, and post-trip contemplation and discussion (Pizam, 1996).

The latter conclusion is relevant to educational travel. Studying abroad and particularly internships abroad are forms of educational travel that involve conditions which are more conducive for generating an understanding of the 'other' than most forms of leisure travel. Internships in particular offer students the opportunity to bridge cultural barriers.

Interns typically serve individually in a foreign country and organization, in a formal position, over a prolonged period of time (3–6 months). They operate without a supporting network of compatriots. Fellow student interns may be present in larger organizations, but in far smaller numbers than in study exchange programmes. The intern relies basically on the coaching and networks of host-national colleagues. Internships thus offer students the opportunity to cross the barriers that normally separate exchange or touring students from host population: the bus, recreational enclaves, tourist guides or the group of fellow students who create a sense of safety when travelling abroad. The intern's success depends on his or her mental, cognitive and relationship competencies, which would translate into effective collaboration and interaction with the population in the host country.

Where people from different regions meet, cultural differences often confuse social interaction. When travellers cross cultural borders, they meet people who have been taught different assumptions and understandings, and this may result in a state of mental disorientation: the culture shock. Knowledge of tacit rules of behaviour is no longer effective. In the new environment, the expressions, gestures, customs and norms that the traveller is used to tend to have a different meaning.

It has been argued that the concept of culture shock is too narrowly defined, because not only foreign social rules and assumptions may be upsetting. The sudden and close encounter with extremely poor, sick or disabled people in public spaces may cause a 'life shock', especially to travellers from Western societies who are normally shielded from direct exposure to the less desirable facts of human life by social security and state institutions (Hottola, 2004). Political attitudes of the host population may also be very different from those in one's home country. Especially in emerging markets and other developing countries, sojourners may come across unfamiliar perceptions of wealth distribution, international distribution of power and regulation, multinationals or advanced technology. Finally, ecological differences may also require time to cope with. Going abroad often implies exposure to significant differences in temperature, humidity, height and degree of pollution. The encounter of unfamiliar small creatures, including bugs, may cause distress as well. Crossing borders therefore often involves what we might call a 'foreign experience shock', which is the mental confusion resulting from differences in values, behaviour, political perceptions and ecology.

People normally slowly adjust to their foreign experience. This adjustment process is visualized in the literature as an 'acculturation curve'. The curve represents the dynamics in feelings one may have in respect of the new cultural environment. Initial euphoria is followed by negative feelings (the shock), after which acculturation sets in when the visitor slowly learns to adapt to the new conditions. The curve may be U or W shaped. The feelings towards the foreign society may be either positive or negative, but at least they become more or less constant (Hofstede, 1991: 210).

The U-curve theory (UCT) is often used in research, but empirical evidence fails to give a good reason to either accept or reject the UCT (Black and

Mendenhall, 1991). Moreover, the UCT is a description of phases of adjustment rather than a theoretical framework that explains how and why individuals move from one stage to the next. The increasing ability to cope with and adjust to the new environment is the result of a learning process in which the foreign individual develops cross-cultural competency (i.e. the ability to effectively perform a task).

Three competencies have been distinguished that are normally considered to be necessary to effectively operate abroad. *Self-maintenance* refers to the capability to substitute sources of reinforcement in order to manage stress and to deal with obstacles, and the readiness and confidence for such self-management. *Cross-cultural relationship competency* involves the willingness and capability to foster and maintain interpersonal relationships with members of a host culture, and to effectively deal with diverse communication styles, social customs and the feelings of another person. Finally, the *perceptual competency* concerns the mental capacity to interpret and understand the behaviour of culturally different others (Black and Mendenhall, 1990; Leiba-O'Sullivan, 1999). A further distinction can be made between stable and dynamic competencies. A *stable competency* relates to a person's personality, which is a stable pattern of behaviour across time and situations and therefore relatively fixed. Knowledge and skills are *dynamic competencies*, because they may be acquired through training (Leiba-O'Sullivan, 1999).

The development of dynamic cross-cultural competencies depends on preparation and on the individual stable competencies, but also on the degree of cultural, economic and ecological difference that the traveller encounters. A 'robust finding' in the culture contact literature is that the processes of adjustment and coping with difficulties of sojourners increase with the distance between their home and host cultures (Ward *et al.*, 2001: 169). Cultural distance is a concept that has been widely researched in the business literature, based on the work of various cultural dimensionalists, such as Hofstede (1991) and Inglehart and Baker (2000). These authors developed meaningful sets of ultimate dimensions to compare cultures of different countries, and to explain international differences in beliefs, attitudes and world views. It has been pointed out that the measurement of cultural variation on cultural dimensions in combination with the metaphor of distance involves conceptual and methodological problems (Shenkar, 2001).[2] Moreover, most of the literature focuses on culture per se, and tends to omit economic and ecological differences.

An exception may be the contribution of Inglehart and Baker (2000), who relate cultural shifts to economic development. Their main argument is: (i) that the cultural values of societies shift from traditional to secular when their economy develops from an agrarian into an industrial society; and (ii) that values shift from survival to self-expression when the economy develops from industrial to post-industrial. The cultural variation between the zones indicates that more cross-cultural adjustment difficulties for travellers can be assumed when they cross cultural zones. Western travellers are used to an individualistic, horizontal society with high levels of security, and tend to embrace values such as trust, tolerance, subjective well-being, political activism and gender equality. When they cross over to other zones it is highly likely that they will encounter collectivistic, more vertical societies, often with (far) lower levels of economic development. The highest degree of economic and cultural difference will be encountered in developing countries, which are often agrarian societies that are associated with strong family ties, male dominance and informal governing structures. Given the fact that the developing countries are often located in tropical climate zones, ecological differences tend to be perceived by Western travellers as significant obstacles in the course of carrying out their assigned duties.

Methodology

In order to complement the knowledge of cross-cultural learning from international internships a survey was carried out among alumni from the RSM, Erasmus University Rotterdam, The Netherlands, who had served as an intern. The aim was to examine how the alumni perceived the value of internships for their personal cognitive development, career development and cross-cultural understanding. The study had two working hypotheses:

1. Alumni who served their internship abroad will report higher learning effects than their counterparts who interned in The Netherlands.
2. Alumni who served their internship in a region which is culturally and economically different from The Netherlands will report higher learning effects, than alumni who served as interns in a cultural environment that is similar to their home country.

The regions were split up, according to the work of Hofstede (1991) and Inglehart and Baker (2000). Hofstede's individualism/power distance matrix was used as those dimensions are also identified by other dimensionalists such as Triandis (1995) and widely applied by cross-cultural psychologists (Chirkov *et al.*, 2005: 470). The bottom left quadrant (Hofstede, 1991) almost perfectly matches the Protestant Europe and English speaking zones of Inglehart and Baker (2000: 29), which we label as zone 1 or the 'home zone'. Zone 2 comprises the remaining regions, including the European 'historically Catholic and communist' zones, Asia and Africa.

In October 2004, a survey was conducted among RSM alumni to generate knowledge about alumni's perceptions of the importance and learning effects of international internships. The survey was included in the October 2004 issue of the electronic RSM *Alumni Nieuwsbrief* (newsletter) that was distributed among 2300 alumni, who account for around 30% of the total alumni population. Eventually, responses were received from 168 alumni. Their internships took place somewhere in the period ranging from 1971 to 2004, with the majority of internships (over 70%) taking place in the 1990s.[3] The average time respondents spent on their internships was 4.8 months. Around half of the alumni (81) indicated their internships had taken place abroad. A majority of these alumni (45) worked in eight different countries in zone 1. The other alumni (33) had interned in zone 2, including 27 different countries spread over the world.

Findings

Overall perceived impact of internships

While they served their internships (many) years ago, the respondents are, overall, very enthusiastic about their internship experiences. As is shown in Table 6.1, the alumni perceive their internships as an element in their curriculum that has had a big positive influence on their career (mean score = 4.2). The statements about the positive impact of the internship on management and social skills, knowledge of the future profession, and knowledge of the role of companies in society are modestly supported. The mean scores on these items are between 3.5 and 3.9. Most alumni (76%) strongly agree with the statement that the internship is an indispensable element in the BA curriculum (mean = 4.6).

Table 6.1 shows that the foreign experience has an effect on the perceived value of the alumni. The positive effect of the internship on career and social skills is significantly higher for internships abroad. With respect to the other items, the geographical location of the internship generates no significant differences.

Personal development

Table 6.2 shows that the alumni are moderately positive about their foreign internships in respect of 'management skills' they learned, the 'political awareness' that was raised by the internship, or the effect of the internship on 'their first job' choice. They highly appreciated the impact of the foreign internship on their 'language skills', a perception that should be placed into the context of the limited Dutch language area. Dutch students abroad almost always have to communicate in a foreign language. Remarkable are the high mean scores for 'learning about oneself' and particularly 'personal development'. The alumni clearly look back on their foreign internship experiences as a period in their life which contributed importantly to their personal growth. The variable of cultural and economic zones is not relevant for any of the personal development statements.

Cross-cultural understanding

The hypothesis on the positive effect of internships on alumni's 'appreciation of other cultures' and on alumni's 'awareness of prejudices towards other cultures' can be said to be modestly confirmed. The highest mean scores were for those statements regarding the effects on the alumni's 'understanding of other cultures' and 'manners of other cultures'. It should be noted that the alumni's appreciation of the native Dutch culture did not increase due to the internship.

Internships abroad tend to result in a moderate perceived effect on alumni's understanding of international societal relations, either between countries or between governments, business and civil society. Also, in the perception of

Table 6.1. Value of internships according to RSM alumni.

	Mean scale 1–5	Location[a]	n	Mean scale 1–5	Std dev.[b]	Std error mean[c]	t[d]	Sig. (2-tailed)[e]
In my view internships are an indispensable element of the BA curriculum	4.6	A	80	4.6	0.82	0.0916	0.350	0.727
		NL	87	4.6	0.98	0.1056		
The internship has had a big positive influence on my career	4.2	A	80	4.4	0.83	0.0933	2.975	0.003**
		NL	86	3.9	1.11	0.1202		
The internship improved my social skills	3.9	A	79	4.1	0.93	0.1046	2.943	0.004**
		NL	85	3.7	1.10	0.1188		
The internship substantially improved my personal management skills	3.7	A	81	3.9	1.13	0.1259	1.913	0.057
		NL	85	3.5	1.20	0.1303		
The internship gave me a better understanding of the societal role of companies	3.7	A	79	3.7	1.13	0.1270	0.236	0.813
		NL	84	3.6	1.03	0.1121		
The internship taught me much about my future profession	3.5	A	76	3.4	1.31	0.1503	−1.034	0.303
		NL	86	3.6	1.22	0.1310		

[a] (A) internship abroad; and (NL) internship in The Netherlands.

[b] Std dev. = standard deviation.

[c] Std error mean = standard error of the mean.

[d] t = statistic derived in Student t-test.

[e] Sig. = significance; ** = difference significant at 1% level.

Table 6.2. Impact of international internships.

	Mean scale 1–5[a]	Zone[b]	n	Mean scale 1–5	Std dev.[c]	Std error mean[d]	t[e]	Sig. (2-tailed)[f]
Personal development								
The internship was beneficial to my personal development	4.7	1	43	4.7	0.57	0.086	−0.839	0.404
		2	35	4.8	0.43	0.072		
The internship improved my foreign language skills	4.3	1	42	4.3	0.95	0.147	0.345	0.731
		2	35	4.3	0.98	0.166		
Due to the internship I learned more about myself	4.1	1	42	4.0	0.94	0.144	−0.933	0.354
		2	35	4.2	1.12	0.190		
The internship taught me management skills I still use	3.9	1	43	4.0	0.83	0.127	0.298	0.767
		2	34	3.9	1.08	0.186		
The internship influenced the choice of my first job	3.7	1	39	3.8	1.37	0.220	0.620	0.537
		2	33	3.6	1.56	0.272		
The internship raised my political awareness	3.4	1	42	3.1	1.34	0.206	−1.915	0.059
		2	32	3.7	1.28	0.223		
Cross-cultural understanding								
Due to my internship, I have developed a better understanding of other cultures	4.3	1	42	4.1	0.73	0.112	−3.434	0.001**
		2	32	4.6	0.55	0.098		
Due to my internship, I have developed a much better understanding of manners in other cultures	4.2	1	43	4.1	0.76	0.116	−1.344	0.183
		2	34	4.4	0.77	0.133		
My internship has deeply influenced my appreciation of other cultures	3.9	1	42	3.7	0.879	0.137	−2.221	0.029*
		2	32	4.2	0.68	0.120		
My internship enhanced my awareness of my prejudices towards other cultures	3.7	1	43	3.6	0.98	0.149	−0.380	0.705
		2	32	3.7	1.08	0.192		

(Continued)

Table 6.2. *continued*

	Mean scale 1–5[a]	Zone[b]	n	Mean scale 1–5	Std dev.[c]	Std error mean[d]	t[e]	Sig. (2-tailed)[f]
My internship abroad has increased my understanding of international societal relations, such as between countries, and between governments, companies, and civil society	3.4	1	41	3.1	1.45	0.226	−2.312	0.024*
		2	34	3.8	1.08	0.188		
My internship has left me with lasting friendships	3.3	1	43	3.3	1.59	0.238	−0.320	0.750
		2	33	3.4	1.50	0.261		
Due to my internship abroad I have a better understanding of local stakeholders' perceptions of my host organization	3.3	1	38	3.0	1.17	0.190	−2.260	0.027*
		2	34	3.7	1.15	0.198		
Later, I have visited the region of my internship at least twice	3.2	1	42	3.0	1.87	0.288	−1.257	0.213
		2	34	3.5	1.73	0.296		
Due to my internship, I have developed more appreciation for the Dutch culture	3.2	1	43	3.3	0.97	0.148	1.379	0.172
		2	34	3.0	1.29	0.231		
My internship abroad has increased my understanding of international issues, such as malnutrition, contagious diseases, poverty, corruption and war	2.6	1	41	2.2	1.51	0.236	−2.471	0.016*
		2	33	3.1	1.51	0.262		

[a] 1 = strongly disagree; 5 = strongly agree.
[b] Zone 1: Switzerland, Germany, Sweden (European historically Protestant), the UK, Ireland, the USA, Australia, Canada (English-speaking historically Protestant), Austria, Liechtenstein, Luxembourg. Zone 2: Belgium, France, Spain, Greece, Italy (European historically Catholic), Czech Republic, Uzbekistan, Poland (historically communist), Costa Rica, Curaçao, Honduras, Ecuador, Colombia (Latin America), Indonesia, Vietnam, Thailand, Taiwan, Japan, Sri Lanka, Papua New Guinea (Asia), and Turkey, Dubai, South Africa, Sri Lanka and Hong Kong.
[c] Std dev. = standard deviation.
[d] Std error mean = standard error of the mean.
[e] t = statistic derived in Student t-test.
[f] Sig. = significance; * difference significant at 5% level; ** difference significant at 1% level.

alumni, the internship had only a modest effect on the understanding of local stakeholder perceptions of their host organization. The statement that the internship increased their understanding of international issues, such as malnutrition, poverty, corruption, etc., received a mean score of 2.6, which indicates that alumni did not confirm the aforementioned. Remarkable, however, is the effect of cultural and economic zones. Internships in other than the home zone resulted in a significantly higher support for the five statements.

Conclusion and Discussion

This chapter addressed the central issue of whether the international internship serves as an effective educational mechanism to facilitate the learning of cross-cultural competencies, which is relevant due to the rise in international business, and in view of an emerging educational travel industry. If one were to place internship travel on a typology of educational travel it would probably tip the balance as one of the most uncertain educational travel types. Whereas most other educational travel forms tend to be of a more leisurely variant and/or characterized by organized group travel, interns are typically operating on an independent basis and are expected by their employer to perform in a 'satisfactory' manner. Therefore, they need to possess the competencies to manage the mental confusion that often results from differences in cultural values, behaviour, political perceptions and ecology between their home and host environment. Furthermore, interns must be able to effectively operate abroad, particularly to manage stress, foster and maintain interpersonal relationships within a host culture, and to interpret and understand the behaviour of culturally different others.

Throughout this chapter theoretical support has been presented with regard to the significance of internships. Empirical research among the alumni of the RSM showed that they view the internship as an indispensable element in the BA curriculum. In particular, internships abroad have an advantage over internships at home in that they are especially important for career development and personal development. Also, the value of international internships is rated higher with regard to the learning about oneself, the development of language and management skills, and the development of cross-cultural understanding and appreciation of other cultures.

Of all segments of educational travel, the internship is potentially characterized by the steepest learning curve, especially for those students who must cross a significant cultural distance. In order to explain such insight this chapter built on Hofstede (1991) and Inglehart and Baker (2000). The latter developed meaningful sets of ultimate economic and cultural dimensions to compare the dominant values of different countries, and particularly explain international differences in beliefs, attitudes and world views. Although the present research only distinguishes between two regional zones, it underscores that learning effects bear a direct relationship to cultural differences.

This finding is significant because it implies that interns who are required to cross cultural and economic gaps tend to experience significantly higher learning effects as a result of the efforts they must make to understand and appreciate the 'other'. Moreover, the findings indicate that such a process also raises the comprehension of international issues.

Both experience and literature on expatriates and educational travel suggest that the learning effects with international student mobility could benefit from decision support systems that students can use in a dynamic manner, that is before, during and after their journey. Such a support system should contribute towards cultivating an environment of trustworthy relations, which gives the student confidence in handling stress resulting from the crossing of economic and cultural zones. In particular, trust and confidence seem to be created through various interactions (virtual and physical) between students and supporting networks of intermediary internship organizations, fellow interns, colleagues, the local host community and academic coaches.

The support system should be flexible, as different interns will have different needs, depending on for example their personality ('stable competencies') and the cultural gap that they need to bridge. The systems should also integrate converging communication technologies, including e-mail, mobile phones, wireless PDAs and the maintenance of 'travelblogs', which will increasingly support the decision making of students who seek to work abroad.

Research is required to show how such a flexible and trustworthy dispersed decision support tool can be created. Theoretically, such a study will integrate studies in the field of learning, cross-cultural adjustment, sociology, information and communications technology (ICT), marketing and mobility. Practically, such research has the potential to benefit academic international offices, public/private internship intermediaries, business units dealing with expatriates and other organizations involved in educational tourism. Key is the facilitation of the international internship, by incorporating it in international chains, represented by means of an electronic marketplace.

Acknowledgements

The authors would like to thank Marianne Aalders, Quintra Rijnders and Arthur van de Kamp for their valuable support in collecting data.

Notes

[1]For example, the 1999 Bologna agreement introduced the bachelor–master system and a uniform transfer credit system in all EU countries to enable students to move between institutions. It is estimated that 12,000 European master programmes will compete to attract 2.4 million students once the EU-wide reorganization is completed in 2010 (Bradshaw, 2005).

[2]For example, the distance metaphor creates illusions of symmetry and of stability, which are difficult to defend. It is unlikely that a German firm investing in China faces the same cultural distance as a Chinese firm investing in Germany, because investor culture and the role of the host culture have proven to be important factors too. Cultural distance stability

is also difficult to uphold taking into account that cultures change and individuals learn to adjust to other cultures (Shenkar, 2001).

[3]Retrospective analysis entails potential research problems of 'misremembering' (Carlson and Widaman, 1988). Respondents, particularly those for whom the internship experience is two or even three decades ago, may disremember the attitudes they had in the past, resulting in biased results. On the other hand, because most of the respondents are senior professionals now, with (long) working experience, they can judge very well the role that the internship has played in their own careers. Retrospective analysis in this case may thus also be an advantage.

References

AIESEC International (2001) *Global Annual Report 2000–2001*. AIESEC International, Rotterdam, the Netherlands.

Appadurai, A. (1990) Disjuncture and difference in the global culture economy. *Theory, Culture and Society* 7, 295–310.

Black, S.J. and Mendenhall, M. (1990) Cross-cultural training effectiveness: a review and a theoretical framework for future research. *Academy of Management Review* 15(1), 113–136.

Black, S.J. and Mendenhall, M. (1991) The U-curve adjustment hypothesis revisited: a review and theoretical framework. *Journal of International Business Studies* 2, 225–247.

Bradshaw, D. (2005) Bologna: the future: massive change is on the way. *Financial Times* 24 January, p. 7.

Carlson, J.S. and Widaman, K.F. (1988) The effects of study abroad during college on attitudes toward other cultures. *International Journal of Intercultural Relations* 12(1), 1–17.

Chirkov, V., Lynch, M. and Niwa, S. (2005) Application of the scenario questionnaire of horizontal and vertical individualism and collectivism to the assessment of cultural distance and cultural fit. *International Journal of Intercultural Relations* 29, 469–490.

Edvinsson, L. (2000) Some perspectives on intangibles and intellectual capital 2000. *Journal of Intellectual Capital* 1(1), 12–16.

European Commission (2002) One Million Erasmus Students: a European Success Story. Website of the European Commission. Available at: http://ec.europa.eu/education/archive/million/million_en.html (accessed 5 September 2006).

Farrell, P. and Suvedi, M. (2003) Studying abroad in Nepal: assessing impact. *Frontiers: The Interdisciplinary Journal of Study Abroad* IX (Fall), 175–188.

Gillespie, J. and Slawson, C. (2003) IES Outcomes Assessment Project. American Institute for the International Education of Students (IES) NASFA: Association of International Educators 2003, Salt Lake City. Retrieved from the homepage of IES. Available at: http://www.iesabroad.org/info/AlumniOutcomes.pdf (accessed 20 August 2004).

Gmelch, G. (1997) Crossing cultures: student travel and personal development. *The International Journal of Intercultural Relations* 21(4), 475–489.

Go, F. and van Fenema, P.C. (2006) Moving bodies and connecting minds in space: a matter of mind over matter. In: Clegg, S.R. and Kornberger, M. (eds) *Space, Organizations and Management Theory*. Liber and Copenhagen Business School Press, Malmo, Sweden, pp. 64–79.

Held, D., McGrew, A., Goldblatt, D. and Perraton, J. (1999) *Global Transformations. Politics, Economics and Culture*. Stanford University Press, Palo Alto, California.

Hofstede, G. (1991) *Cultures and Organizations. Intercultural Cooperation and Its Importance for Survival. Software of the Mind*. Profile Books, London.

Hottola, P. (2004) Culture confusion. Intercultural adaptation in tourism. *Annals of Tourism Research* 31(2), 447–466.

Inglehart, R. and Baker, W.E. (2000) Modernization, cultural change, and the persistence of traditional values. *American Sociological Review* 65 (February), 19–51.

Kumar, K. and Krishna, S. (2005) Editorial preface. In: *GDW and Asia – Opportunities, Strategies and Challenges. Proceedings of the First International Conference on Management of Globally Distributed Work (GDW)*. Indian Institute of Management, Bangalore, India, 28–30 December.

Larsen, K. and Vincent-Lancrin, S. (2002) The learning business. Can trade in international education work? *OECD Observer* 252 (December), 26–29.

Leiba-O'Sullivan, S. (1999) The distinction between stable and dynamic cross-cultural competencies: implications for expatriate trainability. *Journal of International Business Studies* 39(4), 709–725.

Litvin, S.W. (2000) Revisiting tourism and understanding. *Annals of Tourism Research* 27(2), 526–529.

Litvin, S.W. (2003) Tourism and understanding. The MBA study mission. *Annals of Tourism Research* 30(1), 77–93.

Pettigrew, T.F. (1998) Intergroup contact theory. *Annual Review of Psychology* 40(1), 65–85.

Pizam, A. (1996) Does tourism promote peace and understanding between unfriendly nations? In: Pizam, A. and Mansfield, Y. (eds) *Tourism, Crime, and International Security Issues*. Wiley, Chichester, UK.

Ritchie, B.W. with Carr, N. and Cooper, C. (2003) *Managing Educational Tourism*. Aspects of Tourism 10. Channel View Publications, Clevedon, UK.

Shenkar, O. (2001) Cultural distance revisited: towards a more rigorous conceptualization and measurement of cultural differences. *Journal of International Business Studies* 32(2), 519–535.

Stronkhorst, R. (2005) Learning outcomes of international mobility at two Dutch institutions of higher education. *Journal of Studies in International Education* 9(4), 292–315.

Triandis, H. (1995) *Individualism and Collectivism*. Westview Press, Boulder, Colorado.

United Nations Educational, Scientific and Cultural Organization (UNESCO) (2004) Globalization and Higher Education: Implications for North-South Dialogue. UNESCO website. Available at: www.unesco.org/education/studyingabroad/highlights/global_forum/gf_oslo_may03.shtml (accessed 17 August 2004).

University of Michigan Business School (2005) Global MBA. Available at: www.bus.umich.edu (accessed 15 February 2005).

Ward, C. and Searle, W. (1991) The impact of value discrepancies and cultural identity on psychological and sociocultural adjustment of sojourners. *Journal of Intercultural Relations* 15, 209–225.

Ward, C., Bochner, S. and Furnham, A. (2001) *The Psychology of Culture Shock*, 2nd edn. Routledge, Guildford, UK.

Zuboff, S. and Maxmin, J. (2003) *The Support Economy: Why Corporations Are Failing Individuals and the Next Episode of Capitalism*. Viking Penguin, London.

7 Hypermobility in Backpacker Lifestyles: the Emergence of the Internet Café

MICHAEL O'REGAN

Introduction

Mobility, an inherent quality of globalization, is characterized by movement and is arguably an integral part of modern travel. A particular category of mobility can be associated with the travel lives of budget travellers (backpackers, vagabonds, gap year travellers), falling within the realm of extreme mobility as they move from location to location. Internet cafés play a vital function in traveller mobility networks and are a symbol of their mobility. While all tourist places are mobility places, Internet cafés are a particular and growing type of tourist activity place – a place of hypermobility, where travellers can manage and facilitate their multiple mobilities, fully embracing a hypermobile lifestyle. This chapter will argue that Internet cafés materialize by necessity (market forces) in specific places like traveller enclaves and within hostels but are not fully embedded in the place. A café then isn't just defined by its fixity and physically bounded location but also by the multiple mobilities of today's travellers; not just from their increased numbers and diversity but also from the technology they bring and use. By using mobility studies as a conceptual base for this chapter, we can learn something about what it means to live and consume in the age of globalization and ask how globalization processes such as hypermobility (and how travellers have to manage and facilitate it) mesh with countercultures like backpacking.

Mobility

A degree of mobility is central to everyday, routine society as it enables people to go about their everyday lives whether it is travelling to work or visiting family. It is embedded into modern society and is fundamental for modern society to work. Mobility is a word that has become ordinary in common vocabulary, politics and the social sciences as it has become associated with modernity and globalization

(Urry, 2000a, b). It is now seen as an essential part of modern society and of achieving a modern lifestyle. Thomsen *et al.* (2005: 1) believe we need to 'recognize mobility as a precondition for modern social life as well as a derived product of it'.

> [T]he interconnection between mobility and modernity arises from the idea that late modernity is closely connected to and dependent on mobility when they encourage each other in a reciprocal process because modernity both demands and facilitates mobility. Living a late modern life demands a certain level of mobility.
>
> (Freudendal-Pedersen, 2005: 36)

Tourism and tourist places are manifestations of this mobility (Urry, 2002), with their own character and meaning. According to Clifford (1997: 1) travel is arguably an integral part of the postmodern 'new world order of mobility, of rootless histories'. It is important therefore to understand and examine mobilities to 'consider circuits, not a single place' (Clifford, 1997: 37), meaning local places and even local culture should be examined in terms of the global flows of which they are part. Urry, in his book *Sociology Beyond Societies*, argues that the focus of analysis should turn away from individual societies – the 'social as society'– and towards 'global mobilities' – the 'social as mobility' (2000a: 2). He argues that analysis should move away from the study of the societies of fixed sites and categories (nation states, societies, regions) to the connections that flow within and beyond territories, which are nowadays bound up in global flows and mobilities such as imaginative travel, movements of images and information, virtuality and physical movement. Urry also seeks to 'develop . . . a sociology which focuses upon movement, mobility and contingent ordering, rather than upon stasis, structure and social order' (2000a: 18), while other researchers believe this movement has implications for the experiences of time and space, travelling and dwelling, and citizenship (Clarke, 2004b).

Backpackers enact through mobility for a specific period of time a lifestyle that is characterized by a high degree of movement and environment change. They move from geographic location to geographic location with a constant high rate of change in their local environment highlighted by budget travel, an eagerness for interaction and freedom of movement, many travelling from anywhere from 3 weeks to 24 months, staying in locations for short periods. This mobility is acted upon as a type of performance to varying levels of intensity. While some backpackers actively choose to reject certain aspects of their potential for hypermobility, by taking, for example, slower public transport over direct point-to-point backpacker transport, it is generally acknowledged that backpacking as a genre is becoming increasingly commercialized and institutional as a growing number of contemporary tourists identify and travel within this genre, for shorter but intense periods during breaks from work and careers. Many of these travellers exhibit an extreme mobility – hypermobility – which defines and characterizes the places they transiently inhabit. To a bigger or smaller degree, all travellers and tourists will have the potential to exhibit this type of mobility for periods during their travels.

To characterize the extreme of this mobility performance, travellers can now manage multiple lifestyles (travel, work, home) while on the move – a type of traveller that couldn't exist 20 years ago, in the age before Internet cafés, mid-career breaks, mobile phones, work and family obligations and backpacker infra-structure. They have constructed 'notions of mobility in their everyday lives and practice' (Thomsen *et al.*, 2005: 2) which Thomsen *et al.* believe actively contrib-ute to justifying and maintaining specific patterns of travel choice and behaviour. These travellers are part of the new elite, defined by their relationships to technol-ogy, financial capital and information. For Zygmunt Bauman (1998) what sepa-rates elites and non-elites is their relationship to space and time. Elites (such as business people and budget travellers) tend to be globally mobile; they are not tied to place. They can traverse national borders with ease. You can see them through-out the travelscape, from airport lounges, hostels, hotel lobbies to tour buses, utiliz-ing an array of technology. These new travellers are always networked, able to log on from virtually anywhere (Wi-Fi, mobile Internet, the Internet café) and to con-nect to anyone (by e-mail, texting, instant messaging), to update their travel blog with digital pictures and to spend an increasing amount of time on a web–phone synchronized travel life. They are equipped with the technologies of mobility (laptops, cell phones, credit cards and wireless connections to the global informa-tional system) and a nomadic institutional structure has developed to support them (like the airline industry, credit cards, hostels and hotels, travel agents and thousands of websites). These diverse mobilities can ideally help a traveller search for the traditional, authentic or exotic, leading to a competition for uniqueness (Cohen, 2004). Therefore for many 'there is an underlying drive for something not ordinary, a drive for mobility as an extraordinary experience' (D'Andrea, 2006: 106). Therefore, travellers are not just characterized by being hypermobile in a geographical sense but are actively managing a range of mobilities – becoming hypermobile mentally as well as corporeally.

Much of their mobility, driven by the search for unique experiences, is driven by guidebooks and word of mouth between travellers. These mobility net-works span the globe and lead to the creation of a traveller support infrastructure along these mobility routes and eventually at a number of popular traveller points enclaves emerge (Gogia, 2006: 366). These local properties are devel-oped for the global transient travellers and 'represent neither arrival nor depar-ture but the "pause", consecrated to circulation and movement and demolishing particular senses of place and locale' (Urry, 2003). While the search for the expe-riences is idealized by travellers, culture plays a part as travellers seek out those places and people with whom they share similar frames of reference, values, principles, norms and beliefs during these pause periods, helping to create an identity and sense of belonging to an 'imagined community' of fellow travellers. Van Houtum and Van Naerssen (2002: 131) believe '[i]t leads to the packing and clustering together of the same kind of people in pre-structured, standard-ized enclaves of fashion'. In many ways it is an institutional life, one that is con-fined in large part to the facilities provided in the traveller enclaves such as the Khao San Road (Bangkok), Pham Ngu Lao Street (Ho Chi Minh City), Kuta in Bali (Indonesia), St Kilda's in Sydney (Australia) and Yangshuo in China as outlined by Murphy (2001), Spreitzhofer (2003), Allon (2004), Binder (2004) and others. Spreitzhofer (2003) believes enclaves are places where large numbers congregate to experience home comforts including a mass of Internet cafés with good connections, familiar foods and the company of other travellers. When we think of the life of a budget traveller we normally don't see these more mundane realities – 'mundane mobilities' of the day-to-day life: the airport lounges, the railway termini and Internet cafés – while travelling on identifiable circuits following similar routes as they go. This extreme mobility and connectedness have produced 'landscapes of mobility', 'non-places', 'the fleeting', the 'temporary' and 'ephemeral' (Augé, 1995: 44). Allon (2004), utilizing the work of Augé, believes:

> one of the most visible manifestations of increasing global interconnectedness has been the appearance of spaces shaped by and supporting various technologies of mobility (transport, commerce, communication), which, defined more by movement than by stasis, have been specifically designed to be moved through rather than lived in.

In particular, places where mobility flows interconnect, such as hostels, hotels, airports (Gottdiener, 2004), railway stations and motorway service areas, facilitate and have the potential to facilitate traveller mobility as well as granting the virtual and human contacts that are still essential for travellers. These 'networks of mobility' therefore have spatial consequences that can reshape the connections between the local and the global. Travellers are fully equipped to enter these places or what Marc Augé (1995) would describe as 'non-places' of supermodernity.

> The hypothesis advanced here is that supermodernity produces non-places, meaning spaces which are not themselves anthropological places and which, unlike Baudelairean modernity, do not integrate the earlier places: instead these are listed, classified, promoted to the status of 'places of memory', and assigned to a circumscribed and specific position.
>
> (Augé, 1995: 74)

> Clearly the word 'non-place' designates two complementary but distinct realities: spaces formed in relation to certain ends (transport, transit, commerce, leisure), and the relations that individuals have with these spaces . . . For non-places mediate a whole mass of relations, with the self and with others, which are only indirectly connected with their purposes. As anthropological places create the organically social, so non-places create solitary contractuality.
>
> (Augé, 1995: 94)

While cafés share some characteristics of the 'non-places' of supermodernity described by Augé (1995), they are not fully non-places as travellers are figures through which 'non-places' regain their status of 'places', but they share many of their characteristics, as hypermobile places are embedded in both the global and local, as this chapter will illustrate. One needs to judge places such as Internet cafés by how much they are present in the global and how much they are placed in the local.

Hypermobility, Technology and Internet Cafés

Globalization facilitates mobility – the mobility of money, the global reach of corporations, the tidal flows of people, mobile workers and tourists. For the hypermobile, the world is one that has few barriers. Aside from having the right to travel where they want, when they want, at a price they can afford and the ability to communicate with (almost) anyone, anytime (from anywhere), the world today is so networked that strangers no longer exist, but are simply connections waiting to happen. Living an extremely mobile lifestyle requires travellers to rest heavily on things: passports, visas, airlines, credit cards, telephones, the Internet, cameras, travel guides (Clarke, 2004a). Their repeated patterns of movement create larger cultural structures, and those same structures then serve to make sense of particular mobilities (Anderson and De Paula, 2006: 84). These global flows of extremely mobile travellers require infrastructure to support them, including communication systems and facilities which connect the extremely mobile with the world. Traveller mobility (and globalization in general) according to Wilk might lead to the 'spread of a common set of structures that mediate between cultures and through which notions of cultural differences are refracted' (Wilk, 1995; cited in Phipps and Jack, 2003: 287). This global mobility and the subsequent infrastructure that comes to support it, identified by Wilk (1995; cited in Phipps and Jack, 2003), spread along clearly identifiable mobility trails – the 'beaten track' of popular budget traveller itineraries.

Together with traveller hostels, bars and restaurants along the traveller transnational trails are Internet cafés where online connections are made and fulfil some kind of deep desire for virtual connections with information and networks. The partial unbundling of the local, if not the neutralization of place, is produced through the practices of these global nomads, which in turn produce their own specific spatialities. According to Bull (2004):

> [t]he continuum represents new developments in the search for public privacy and a discounting of the 'public' realm, while the transformation lies in citizens' increasing ability and desire to make the 'public' spaces conform to their notion of the 'domestic' or the 'intimate', either literally or conceptually.

While newer forms of connection are emerging in Western society such as Internet-capable smartphones and laptops, computing and the control that it gives its users is something still primarily in the travelscape (much budget travel is within developing countries, due to the low cost of travel) linked to particular places like hostels and particularly the Internet café.

Access to the Internet as well as Internet applications have developed quickly since the mid-1990s when simple web-based e-mail accounts like Hotmail for communication were the main applications used by travellers. As well as simply using the Internet as a cheap communication tool, travellers have embraced the potential of networked computing to let them seek, share and discuss information and participate with others online. Mintel (2006) found 95% of 18- to 24-year-old travellers said that a camera was important on the road, followed by Internet cafés. A survey by Yahoo (Taylor, 2004) found that 69% of young British travellers claim they used e-mail regularly to touch base with people back home, 42% set up a new Internet e-mail account before leaving and over one in eight (13%) took a laptop away with them. It also found that a fifth of younger travellers sent an e-mail within a day of arriving in a new town. Richards and Wilson (2003) found e-mail and the Internet were the main communication channels used by budget travellers during their trip (with 68% of respondents having used them at some point), especially from long-haul destinations. According to Richards and Wilson (2004: 37) there was a strong reaction against the suggestion that travellers '[d]on't use the Internet to contact home'. The Internet is becoming increasingly central to the experience of long-term travel (Dobers and Strannegård, 2002).

Internet Cafés

Internet cafés (also known as cybercafés or Net cafés) are businesses that provide Internet access to the public on a fee for service basis. They offer services like web browsing, e-mail, File Transfer Protocol (FTP), Internet telephony (VOIP), Instant Messaging (IM) and multiplayer (Local Area Network (LAN)/online) gaming, in addition to basic computing services such as word processing and printing. They may or may not serve as a regular café as well, with food and drinks being served. The majority of Internet cafés operating along traveller routes, within enclaves and hostels, are small independents targeting a distinct clientele – affluent Western travellers.

There is very little academic literature published on the topic of Internet cafés. Many of the articles were published in the middle to the late 1990s when first generation Internet cafés first appeared in the UK. Research has centred on themes like digital divide/digital inclusion (Ferlander, 2003; Haseloff, 2005), the sociology of individual cafés in advanced economies, community access, site location but rarely user type. Liff et al. (1998) conducted a survey of Internet cafés in the UK (cited in Middleton, 2003) which found that many respondents already had work access to the Internet or had the means to go online, but that at least half of respondents were unfamiliar with personal computers (PCs) and the Internet. Lee (1999) offered insights into user behaviours in a single Internet café in Brighton, UK and found almost a third of respondents had Internet access at home (Middleton, 2003). Lee (1999: 346) noted that, despite the social nature of the café setting, users' 'attention remain[ed] fixed on terminals making public Internet use an atomized and profoundly uncollective experience so that consumption of technology in this context remains an individuated and discrete act' (Middleton, 2003). Lee's paper found that, although the café is a public space, people's uses of the Internet within that public space are highly individuated and people's public uses of the Internet are very integrated with their personal and work routines (Johnson, 2004). Stewart (2000) focused on local use and believed cafés were not transitory phenomena but evolved out of the ancient institution of café culture. Other papers that deal specifically with Internet cafés include that from Wakeford (2003), who believed patterns of migration and local demographics are found to be just as important as the layout of the space or the technological infrastructure. Middleton (2003) asked why Internet cafés were used in Toronto, where affordable residential Internet access was widely available and what people did with this access, while Laegran and Stewart (2003) found that cafés are neither footloose spaces nor locally embedded, based on empirical studies in Scotland and Norway. Liff and Steward's (2003) paper theorized Internet cafés in terms of social networks and Foucault's concept of heterotopia and found that the juxtaposition of the real and virtual creates opportunities for Internet participation and e-access. Boase *et al.* (2002) focused on public uses and local users of public Internet terminals in a worldwide survey, while Salvador *et al.* (2005) offered design perspectives based on a reflection of Internet cafés as 'third places'. More recent work has focused on the effect of Wi-Fi within cafés and other spaces (Gupta, 2004; Johnson, 2004), censorship (Hong and Huang, 2005) and LAN gaming (Szablewicz, 2004; Beavis *et al.*, 2005).

According to Liff and Laegran (2003), Murfett (2004) and Duffy (2004) the world's first Internet café was called Cyberia, and opened in London's Tottenham Court Road during September 1994. According to Duffy (2004) customers had to pass the time with coffee, and there was plenty of time to pass with download speeds some 50 times slower than today's broadband connection. While some early commentators (Nunes, 1999) believed Internet cafés were points of democratic access and social exchange, Duffy (2004) believes many of today's Internet cafés in the travelscape are impersonal and functional and are used primarily by travellers who previously relied on an erratic combination of phone calls and poste restante for communication. Due to the mobility of travellers from enclave to enclave, Internet cafés within these enclaves appear to offer very similar capabilities, facilities and services. While there are some variations in facilities and service, for example connection speed, printers, scanners, Internet telephony, they are remarkably similar. Few Internet cafés (especially in developing countries) offer conscious styling and atmosphere to permit face-to-face and verbal interaction, but rather it is the centrality of technology which marks it as a 'technospace' for passing travellers – that is, a space which is defined by and given meaning by technology (Laegran, 2002) rather than a 'technosocial place' (Laegran and Stewart, 2003: 360). The Internet café functions much like a public telephone, in which the location of the service meets their individual needs rather than defining them. They are familiar by virtue of their generic technospace (rather than their technosocial) nature; they discourage any type of attachment.

> Those temporal realms where technology meets human practice. Significantly, technospaces are lived, embodied fluctuations in human/machine interaction. At the momentary intersection of the human being and the machine there is spatial praxis: there is technospace.
>
> (Munt, 2001: 11)

This linkage between technology and the social–spatial is immediate in an Internet café, where a visitor encounters the physical artefacts of desktop computing – computers, monitors, chairs, webcams, headsets and keyboards. Logging into virtual applications or sites enables the virtual mobility of the traveller, reaching out in search of information or connection with family, friends, home, routines and multiple lifestyles. What motivates Western travellers to visit an Internet café varies: it may be out of a routine, out of necessity (online banking, waiting for a response to an e-mail), reporting on their offline existence or simply boredom when a 'real' place does not fulfil their expectations. Goffman (1963), who wrote in the era before cell phones and Internet cafés, might have judged their use as a 'subordinate activity' (Rosen, 2004), a way to pass the time such as reading or doodling that could and should be set aside when the dominant activity resumes. Internet cafés allow travellers to connect to a larger world where they can broadcast their transient attachment to a hypermobile elite. As a badge of identity, the majority of travellers maintain e-mail accounts (many setting up new accounts for the trip). There has also been a growing trend towards documenting one's trip via travel blogs (Germann Molz, 2005). Lash refers to this relationship between technology and humans as an 'interface' (Lash, 2002: 15; cited in Aas, 2005: 1–2) and argues that we are obliged to interact with technology because 'we make sense of the world through technological systems'. Indeed, Lash suggests, the only way of coping with a social life that is now lived 'so normally and chronically at-a-distance' is through technological devices that span the distance. Amin and Thrift believe 'humans are defined by their use of tools: they are technical from their very origins as a species' (Amin and Thrift, 2002: 78; cited in Clarke, 2004b: 417). Unconnectedness and immobility do not appear a realistic option in a seemingly permanently changing world (Dobers and Strannegård, 2002).

The use of computers within an Internet café is primarily a solitary activity (Nunes, 1999). Edwards (2004: 14) believes '[i]f our time in trajectory is eliminated, what happens to the strange companionship', the 'collective loneliness' that Alain de Botton (2002: 46–47) describes finding among fellow travellers in a motorway service station? One, then, may suggest that, rather than serving as places of gathering or as a point of exchange, Internet cafés function as 'spaces of elsewhere' in which the potential for displacement becomes a mode of membership. What they share is their nomadism. Rather than serving as a kind of gathering point, the café takes part in a space that is already globally dispersed, what Manuel Castells calls a 'space of flows'. This space of flows 'dominates the historically constructed space of places, as the logic of dominant organizations detaches itself from the social constraints of cultural identities and local societies through the powerful medium of information technologies' (Castells, 1989: 6).

Internet cafés located in or near to traveller enclaves have the potential to be interpreted as global diasporic places. Many café names are in English, pricing is in English (sometimes in Hebrew in Israeli-dominated space) and facilities and services are geared towards travellers. For example, VOIP, memory card reading, scanning and the transfer and burning of digital camera pictures are advertised. Their computer homepages are usually set to the English language versions of Yahoo or Hotmail and many cafés in Asia add Western toilets and air fans. The local buildings for travellers on the move have to adapt and upgrade to facilitate their mobility. While Internet cafés are not generic, coming in a wide range of styles, they do reflect their location, main clientele and the business/social agenda of the owner. The presence of a critical mass of transient travellers with extremely high profit-making capabilities contributes to a build-up of Internet cafés in concentrated traveller areas, increasing the prices of commercial space and Internet access, and the exclusion of local users. The cafés provide a home away from home, but unlike diasporic cafés or local cafés (Laegran and

Stewart, 2003; Powell, 2004); independent travellers are transient as new travellers move into the enclaves every day as others move out. A café catering for traveller needs can be successful despite not attracting the same users back. While Powell's study looks at community cafés, one can suggest that Internet cafés are merely sites of placeless cosmopolitanism unconnected to a specific and unique place. This promotes social distance and minimizes communication (Urry, 2006: 363), whereby café users carefully ignore each other; a type of behaviour Goffman would call 'civil inattention' (Goffman, 1963: 139), which provides the illusion of anonymity and is key to maintaining individual distance in public social situations. Marc Augé talks about this kind of experience as 'collectivity without festival and solitude without isolation' (Augé, 2002: 7; cited in Anderson and De Paula, 2006: 82). For example, glancing at other people's screens can be perceived by other people in the café as indicative of an intrusion (Powell, 2004). The focus on one's computer screen also excludes the immediate environment, something that Jonathan Crary believes has grown since late modernity and has individuals defining and shaping themselves in terms of 'paying attention', that is 'for an engagement from a broader field of attraction, whether visual or auditory, for the sake of isolating or focusing on a reduced number of stimuli' (Crary, 1999: 1). This civil inattention, demand for privacy and exclusion of other stimuli except what's happening on the computer, enables users to view and use content that might be inappropriate (pornography) as well as facilitating more mundane private or personal activities like people writing e-mails. Internet cafés are not places where you can randomly begin to talk to strangers. The risks are that it may be seen as disrespectful and an invasion of someone's privacy, like at airports, where 'people are expected to keep to themselves' (Gottdiener, 2004: 187).

Hypermobile Characteristics of an Internet Café

The Internet café as a global site of refuge

Dobers and Strannegård (2002) believe it is important to be able to disconnect from the outside world, to provide peace and a feeling of being at home even away from home. As Internet cafés are to a great extent indifferent to contexts, it becomes possible to disconnect amid the rush and panic, creating a strictly personal space. Internet cafés allow travellers to detach from the local place in order to go elsewhere. Germann Molz (2004: 104) believes 'travellers often depict Internet cafés as places outside of place; quiet, climate-controlled havens where they can escape from the noise and heat or the rain and cold of the local place'. As long as they are staring at the screen there are no substantial differences between different cafés. Their home country, private work and travel habits, whether it be instant messaging a friend, a check on banking details or an e-mail to their parents, can remain the same. Augé (1995: 106) believes '[a] paradox of non-place: a foreigner lost in a country he does not know (a "passing stranger") can feel at home there only in the anonymity of motorways, service stations, big stores or hotel chains'. Many travellers feel for the sense of security that hyper-mobile places and devices like the mobile phone can give, as lack of access to a communicative network in the travelscape may make travellers feel unsafe or at greater risk. These places are in the words of Van Houtum and Van Naerssen (2002) transnational places of refuge where the clustering may represent welcome familiarity and recognition in light of their multiple mobilities. They offer a respite, a temporary rootedness in a familiar anonymous place.

Much technology is aimed at bringing distinct but familiar individuals like friends and family closer, at making experiences more uniform, making people feel 'always at home' but this is in conflict with budget travellers' supposed inquisitiveness and their yearning to see, feel, touch and experience something new. Travellers within cafés are protected from the world outside by tilted windows, disconnected from life outside and connected with the networked computer. They are undergoing 'interpersonal disenfranchisement' – disconnecting from one another (Carducci, 2000). Increasingly, travellers deal with the hyper-culture cacophony by cocooning – commuting virtually towards home while working on their computer (Carducci, 2000). They go from the traveller enclave to the hostel, to the café, maintaining strong ties with only a small circle of friends and family via the Internet. As other travellers become just e-mail addresses, locals become faceless voices at the other end of electronic transactions. This isn't to say that the virtual world and travel will replace offline travel, as connectivity can help stimulate and facilitate traveller mobility by allowing them to plan activities, book airline tickets or request electronic visas (i.e. Australia), but also increasingly mediate local interactions (and places) as well, whether it be booking a plane ticket or transferring funds, becoming less dependent on local infrastructure to facilitate physical movement. This virtual mobility is 'a shorthand term for the process of accessing activities that traditionally require physical mobility, but which can now be undertaken without recourse to physical travel by the individual undertaking the activity' (Kenyon et al., 2002). While some online activity may lead to offline proximity with locals, having a hypermobile lifestyle does not allow the time for long-term relationships to become established locally. To be hypermobile means existing within multiple mobilities – physical travel, physical movement of objects, imaginative travel, virtual travel and communicative travel (Larsen et al., 2006: 263) – and requires travellers to acknowledge these multiple mobilities, facilitate and manage them.

Indeed they are so busy managing these multiple mobilities while in an Internet café that they have neither time nor need to seek to communicate with others in the café. There are very few 'exposed positions' (Goffman, 1963; Powell, 2004) – that is, when a physical, verbal or technological anomaly opens up the possibility for a social interaction, travellers are physically separated from other co-present users by cubicle divisions and bulky desktops. Compared to reading a book or writing a postcard in a real café, Internet cafés do not encourage interruption and draw people out of social space to interact with co-present others. Internet cafés are not 'third places', a term coined by Ray Oldenburg (1989), the sociologist, to describe places beyond first place (home) and second place (work) that are essential to our well-being. Oldenburg said a good third place draws a mix of generations, unites neighbourhoods and may be independently owned (Hevrdejs, 2004). Such places according to McGuire (2003) are 'cafés, coffee shops, bookstores, bars, hair salons and other public hangouts' that Oldenburg believes constitute the heart of vibrant communities. Oldenburg also observes that a successful third place is on neutral ground where everyone can feel comfortable. It is a leveller; rank and status are unimportant and it is open to the general public without requiring any form of membership. Individuals can go there at almost any time and be sure that friends will be there. The mood is playful and regular visitors give the place character. It is a comfortable, congenial environment. Above all, third places are characterized by lively, engrossing and inclusive conversation. Certainly, Internet cafés along traveller routes do not meet any of these requirements.

Leaving your local identity at the door

Sarman (2002: 11) believes non-places assign shared identities to their participants, which are determined only on entering and leaving through security checkpoints. Individuals entering the place are relieved of their usual determinants. Individuals become no more than what they do or experience in the role of customer or passenger. Non-places welcome *every* day more and more individuals who leave behind their identity at the entrance barrier (Aubert-Gamet and Cova, 1999: 40).

In Internet cafés you normally get assigned a computer on entry. The administrator allowing access may activate your computer. Payment depends upon the times you check in and out of the Internet café, not on your identity as a person. At the EasyInternet Café group (easyinternetcafé.com), a large Internet chain in Europe, you enter money into a self-service machine to get a number. You type the number on your ticket into a box on your computer's display and choose a password – which identifies you (Barron, 2004). This is exactly the same as other hypermobile places, which use self-service check-ins like many airlines in airports all over the world and chain hotels such as the Sheraton, Marriott and Hilton Groups (Elliott, 2005). In places that don't use self-service kiosks, instructions are normally reduced to gestures.

> [H]e obeys the same code as others, receives the same messages [and] [s]ince non-places are there to be passed through, they are measured in used time . . . by a screen giving minute-to-minute updates. . . [and] the user of a non-place is in contractual relations with it (or with the powers that govern it). He is reminded, when necessary, that the contract exists.
>
> (Augé, 1995: 101–104)

Non-place (non-local) feelings

Internet cafés like the majority of hypermobile places serve mobility, commerce and entertainment and one may spend a full day 'without feeling a need to visit the real actual world' (Sarman, 2002: 13). Cafés are not designed with local co-present communication in mind and are designed purely as a conduit for commerce. Some places such as hostels offer free computer access to attract travellers to pay and stay in their properties and so remain within the 'regime of commerce'. Time is usually limited to 10–15 min per individual to allow for multiple users on a queue basis.

> A person entering the space of non-place is relieved of his usual determinants. He becomes no more than what he does or experiences in the role of passenger, customer or driver. Perhaps he's still weighed down by the previous day's worries, the next day's concerns; but he is distanced from them temporarily by the environment of the moment.
>
> (Augé, 1995: 103)

Internet cafés are filled with travellers from all parts of the globe communicating online with others in their native languages and not the language of the country in which they travel. Due to their extreme mobility travellers rarely learn the local language, making verbal face-to-face communication difficult, reducing it to gestures and wordless expressions as they try to comprehend the rules of entry (prices, services, passwords) or engage with the gatekeeper's directions on where to sit and how to access the World Wide Web. But like other non-places you 'go where they (you) are told' (Augé, 1995: 101).

The Internet's geographically uneven distribution

Non-places are filled with numerous technologies of representation (Sarman, 2002: 11). Urry (2000c) terms it 'banal globalism'. Global symbols exist in many Internet cafés from advertising about the global, the use of the globe to represent access to the World Wide Web to the widespread use of international gaming posters. These familiar logos reassure the hypermobile the same as 'an oil company logo is a reassuring landmark; among the supermarket shelves he falls with relief on sanitary, household or food products validated by multinational brand names' (Augé, 1995: 106).

Germann Molz (2004: 105) believes that, when travellers log on to the Internet, they do so in locally specific places because keyboards differ from country to country and there are differences in hardware, computer interfaces reminding travellers that they are not just anywhere, but that they are in a particular place with its own local materialities. One can argue that these differences are eliminated for those who use their own laptops within cafés and at Internet cafés in traveller areas as they serve a particular clientele. Although there are a large number of different keyboard layouts used with different languages written in roman script, most of these layouts are quite similar, no more than the differences between a Macintosh keyboard and one produced by IBM. The majority of Internet cafés use café management software on each computer to manage access, security and time (CYBERCAFÉPRO, CAFÉSUITE, CAFÉTIME), which supports a choice of multiple languages once the user logs in. Also there is the ever-present familiarity of the operating system and the computers themselves, the logos of, for example, Dell, Microsoft Windows and IBM homogenizing the physical aspects of access.

In terms of uniformity, Microsoft, for example, currently has around a 90% share of the client operating system market with Windows (Legard, 2004). Internet

Explorer has held more than 95% of the browser market since 2004 (McMillan, 2004). Logos and symbols like those for Internet Explorer, Outlook and Windows are uniform throughout the world just as exit and emergency signs are in hotels, railways and airports. Many travellers often bring USB flash drives to use within cafés loaded with their preferred Internet browser, e-mail client, IM client and FTP client, all preconfigured with the travellers' personal preferences. What may start as local changes its orientation from the local to the global because traveller mobility requires hypermobile places – such as the Internet café – which need to have computers, computer power, keyboards and monitors. While these technologies are all partly place-bound artefacts, they are usually sourced globally and link their traveller users directly to the global. What begins as local gets rescaled at the global level. It is actually a hypermobile microenvironment with global span insofar as it is configured for transient travellers.

Regulation (and over-regulation)

Does the local reassert itself through regulation and poor connectivity or does traveller mobility lead to mobility exclusion for locals wishing to go online? Internet cafés in traveller destination areas are more numerous and far cheaper in relation to their income for Western travellers than in their home countries, even though the proportional cost to locals may be high (Anon., 2006: 53). According to a United Nations Conference on Trade and Development report (2006: 8) the cost of Internet access for locals in a low-income country, which encompasses 37% of the world's population, even if it has numerous Internet cafés, is 150 times the cost of a comparable service in a high-income country. This may lead to high prices in cafés, which may have to upgrade equipment to facilitate traveller mobility. High prices in traveller areas for Internet access in developing countries do not naturally lead to mixed use. Locals may feel excluded because of Western racial dominance (especially within enclaves), lack of local flavour, lack of sociality or over-commercialization – their mobility moving at a slower pace. Does the 'local' reassert itself by poor connectivity or equipment? Many traveller cafés install broadband through digital subscriber lines or satellite (if local infrastructure doesn't exist) to meet the demands of Western travellers as well as services and facilities like CD/DVD burning, webcams, headphones, digital camera picture downloading and photo manipulation software, even if local demand does not exist. Even if there is a slow Internet connection within a café, few travellers would exit. Taking a reference from other hypermobile places such as hotels, motorways or airports, you are not going to leave a queue, not even a slow-moving one, on the way to check-in or while in a traffic jam on a motorway. This was established by Wakeford (2003), who found in her study of Internet cafés in London that technological infrastructure (specifications or speed of machines) was not in itself a reliable guide to the way place representation took place as 'customers did not ask about the speed of connections, or the specifications of the machines' (p. 382).

According to Germann Molz (2004: 106), the local can also impinge on the Internet café in cultural ways such as thwarted access due to censorship. In countries with censoring regimes such as Saudi Arabia, China or Singapore (Schwarz, 2005) Internet cafés are closely controlled. Yet one can argue that this censorship is not local but global (Kahn, 2006). British Telecom and most other Western telecoms are already blocking an unknown number of sites in a crackdown on pornography online (Bright, 2004). Censorship is a global concern and takes place in all budget traveller-producing countries to some degree, including Australia, the UK, Brazil, France and Germany, as it does in popular traveller destination counties like Vietnam, India, China and Singapore. (More details can be found online at: the Electronic Frontier Foundation, http://www.elf.org; the Open Net Initiative, http://www.opennet.net/index.php; and Reporters Without Borders, http://www.rsf.org/.) In most cases national censorship impinges on locally based websites and certain types of sites (pornography, gambling) and not on sites that Western budget travellers would normally visit. This discussion does not include the many controls that café owners, particularly those in developed countries, themselves put on user freedom. For example these include administrator controls to stop downloading and filters to stop users viewing certain categories of sites. While Internet cafés situated in places like libraries and certain countries such as China, Italy and India (Campbell, 2003) require forms of identification, these restrictions usually do not apply to affluent and transient travellers primarily from Western society. They can surf the web anonymously (unless spyware which could collect personal information about users is installed without the users' informed consent). Additionally, if the Internet is used within hostels or with Wi-Fi, anonymity is assured. The transient nature of cafés can make them popular among criminals and those involved with terror, as raids on cafés connected with terror plots in the UK have shown regularly in 2006 and 2007.

Are hypermobile places tourist attractions?

One budget traveller questioned by Germann Molz (2004: 102) believed Internet cafés to be 'tourist attractions' and a place for authentic experiences because smoking was allowed and travellers shared in the smoking experience. It reminds one of MacCannell (1976), who writes of the increasingly futile search for authenticity, and of an essay by Barron (2004) about when she used the Internet at an EasyInternet Café franchise at a McDonald's in London. While she typed away at a keyboard, she found it was sticky with someone else's burger grease. Does this experience make it an authentic site, a shared eating experience with Londoners? Other travellers have noted the experience of playing LAN gaming with locals, even though it is an experience played out on an individual's screen. If you are playing LAN or online games with locals, you cannot join in conversation onscreen, verbally or face to face – only gestures. Caesar (2005) believes the closest to a real experience one can have when abroad is during the search for the Internet café you need to find (and most local cafés outside enclaves do not make it on to traveller guidebooks). Fortunately, hypermobile places (airports, service stations) are easily recognizable and familiar by what goes on there (technospaces). Travellers see only the use they can make of the cafés (as they would view a public telephone box) – as a technospace – and not by the local experiences they can have there, the co-present locals they can meet there or the specific names of the cafés they have passed through.

Do external events cause the local to reassert itself?

Can the local impinge on the Internet cafés and cause place to have local meaning? The answer to this is yes, to an extent, as recent terrorist events have shown. Hypermobile places can gain renewed importance and symbolic stature by attacks, because they are seen as places that Westerners frequent. According to Augé (1995: 111) it is the very fact that they are places where the mobile elite gather that makes them attractive places for terrorist attack. He says 'they are the particular target of all those whose passion for retaining or conquering territory drives them to terrorism' and '[a]irports and aircraft, big stores and railway stations have always been a favourite target for attacks (to say nothing of car bombs); doubtless for reasons of efficiency, if that is the right word'.

For example, attacks on Rome and Vienna airports on 27 December 1985 killed 16 people and wounded 80, while on 7 October 2004 Taba's Hilton hotel in Egypt was hit by a bomb that killed 34 people. There have been numerous attacks on hypermobile places associated with Westerners such as attacks on the Marriott hotel in Islamabad, Pakistan in October 2004 and again in January 2007, an attack on the Marriott in Jakarta, Indonesia in August 2003, and attacks on international hotels in Amman during November 2005. Tragedies like hostel fires such as the 'Down Under Hostel' fire in Sydney's Kings Cross in 1989, when six people died; the Palace Backpackers Hostel fire in 2000, which claimed the lives of 15 tourists in the small town of Childes, Australia; and the 13 tourists killed in a hostel fire in Punta Arenas at the southern tip of Chile in February 2007, all make international headlines. These terrible events make hypermobile places (with non-place characteristics) – for a moment – very local places. The fact the hypermobile elite may have been victims makes international headlines. They may be frequented by many transient tourists but in reality many locals working in these places are casualties. The US State Department routinely warns American citizens to keep a low profile and avoid places where foreigners gather such as Internet cafés. A specific warning was given for Afghanistan in August 2005 (Constable, 2005) and not long before in May 2005 a blast at the Park Net Café in Kabul's upscale Shahr-e-Naw district café killed three, including a United Nations worker. Like all hypermobile places of transit and transience, identity checks and surveillance like the use of closed circuit television (CCTV) and security are increasing (Adey, 2004). EasyInternet Cafés, for example, banned baseball hats at their branches in the UK because wearers were difficult to identify on CCTV (Horne, 2005).

The Future

How many Internet cafés will still be there in 2014, 20 years after their introduction? Middleton (2003: 3) cites Forrester Research from 1995, which predicted, 'at best, these new venues [Internet cafés] will be a two-to-three year phenomenon that exists only while PC users without Internet connections exist', while Taylor (2004) believes Internet cafés are a product of the pre-mobile Internet era. Who needs to download their e-mail on an ageing PC when they can take their own smartphone or Blackberry or log into a high-speed wireless zone (Wi-Fi) using a laptop? According to Kakihara and Sørensen (2001) a large part of the facilities and tools at home and in the office will be reduced enough in size to be carried, making people geographically independent. People who use such mobile technologies, it is claimed, will be 'free to live where they want and travel as much as they want' and thus they will be forced to consider whether they are settlers or true 'global nomads' (Kakihara and Sørensen, 2001). Although the mobile phone has become the dominant personal mobile device over the past decade, e-mail and Internet access on phones is in its infancy, although mobility is getting built into phones (music capabilities, a pedometer, unlimited storage, Global Positioning System (GPS), Internet access). They will not replace the Internet café as the spatial metaphor for travellers' connectivity for many years due to device cost, lack of Wi-Fi/3G in developing countries and cost of roaming and data transfer. Internet cafés will remain tethered to hostels, airports, cruise ships, railway stations, enclaves, tourist attractions and urban areas reinforcing travellers' semi-fixed networks of mobility. Internet cafés are also somewhat more than just virtual connections. These places have become havens for the stressed-out extremely mobile hypermobile travellers and the cost for these havens to Western travellers, especially in developing countries, is relatively low.

The cafés have also undergone a quiet evolution over the past few years; far from dying out they remain a focal point for independent travellers in maintaining their hypermobile lifestyle. This is especially true for travellers who need desktop computers to fully utilize and web sync with the increasing mobility of objects in the travelscape, like the digital camera, the Walkman, the credit card, the Discman, laptops, mobile phones and MP3 players such as the iPod. These may include the need to download music on to an iPod, to download podcasts, upload digital pictures, run a video conference, pay credit card bills, utilize VOIP or to access the increasing amount of destination specific information available online. It can be argued that these mobile technologies are as important to their users as corporeal mobility in the way travellers grasp, feel, make sense of and discover new countries, towns, landscapes and the places that they encounter. These devices are in constant use and as part of the café experience they are extensions of identity, worn on their bodies or kept in day packs. Everything from a traveller's total music collection, favourite web applications and digital pictures becomes portable, including memories. Travellers can use VOIP, play music or answer a phone call without a second thought within these cafés, as there is no expectation in a technospace that they are intrusive. These mobile technologies extend the footprint of their homes and help them to manage their multiple mobilities.

Conclusion

This chapter argues that Internet cafés as hypermobile places are not aimed at encouraging digital inclusion and at enhancing social contacts between locals and travellers or any sense of community. It argues that cafés are used by travellers as part of their hypermobile lifestyle, and that many cafés are embedded within enclaves and hostels and are not fully embedded in place. Internet cafés can have two meanings. First, they can be social and contribute to the making of a place – like the 'third places' that Oldenburg (1989) describes – in local neighbourhoods, but only to locals, staff and long-term residents. Secondly, they may be hybrids where travellers and locals use the same space but for different purposes. Locals may use the café socially but travellers with extreme mobility use the space once and may never enter there again. Neither are they a lost diasporic group from one nationality hoping to generate group solidarity, although Israelis may be an exception as they travel in large groups utilizing certain enclaves/ spaces en masse (Noy and Cohen, 2005). While the local can act locally in such situations, the new global nomads of backpacking are members of a cross-border culture, an 'imagined community' (Anderson, 1991), and are in many ways continuously embedded while travelling in a global network of 'hypermobile' places like Internet cafés, railway stations, airports and hostels. It affirms Virilio's vision that 'speed undoes place' (Healy, 1999) as the café becomes a place where the fixed and mobile meet, both an escape and a home away from home – a place of hypermobility – 'a place of strategic installation, a place of lodgement in which different times co-exist' (Healy, 1999).

Local and traveller use of cafés never completely erases each other as '[p]laces and non-places intertwine and tangle together' (Augé, 1995: 106). Paraphrasing Frances Cairncross (1997), the death of distance loosens the grip of geography but does not destroy it. For travellers, Internet cafés are a transient place where they can reach out globally for information and communication to places and servers thousands of miles away. Internet cafés and other hypermobile places erode the sense of place, bringing travellers to a uniform space that has all the distinctiveness of any other Internet café experienced over a journey that may last up to 24 months. 'It gives us a premonition of the world that globalization might eventually create – one in which, no matter where you happen to go, you've never really left' (Moorehead and Christie, 2002: 3). A new world to be experienced by the new hypermobile cosmopolitan elites – a space made up of uniform international hostels, enclaves, round-the-world tickets, credit cards, iPods and popular traveller spots linked together by 'backpacker transport' and firms selling 'backpacker experiences' so that the local and off-the-beaten tracks never get known as budget travel – becomes 'increasingly institutionalized especially along the beaten tracks' (Shaw and Williams, 2004: 154). Budget independent travellers' supposed interest in the new, the novel, freedom and flexibility are bound by the infrastructure built for their mobility. The ability to contact family or friends from anywhere, to retrieve information about the destination, to make decisions about what to do and where to travel to next has changed the mobility of travellers. They can transmit between worlds and lifestyles so that the 'local' place is only one adventure. Various virtual adventures can be accessed via the 'imagined' community of backpackers, online via virtual tribes like those found on MySpace or through connecting with memories and home by listening to an iPod.

Internet cafés created to serve travellers have changed those same travellers, transforming expectation and altering the very rhythm of their travel days, the use of travel time, perhaps undermining the systems in place that provided expertise, the middlemen/women and locals. Cafés and backpacker hostels which increasingly offer Internet access facilitating this hypermobility have become 'centres of gravity' for travellers, where they have come to expect connectivity and connectedness. The need for passports, CCTV, identity checks, body searches – like entering an exclusive business lounge – are becoming a reality for many hypermobile places. It becomes a selling point for hostels and cafés to offer connectivity and (online and offline) security. According to Harvey '[a] world of individuality and freedom on the surface conceals a world of conformity and coercion underneath' (Harvey, 1978: 102; cited in Clarke, 2004a: 502). Aubert-Gamet and Cova (1999: 40) believe people are not necessarily unhappy in these circumstances but they are alone. As Augé (1995: 101) says, '[n]o doubt the relative anonymity that goes with this temporary identity can even be felt as liberation'. But what next, as the uses for the Internet have yet to reach their full potential? Travellers are spending more and more of their time online and in Internet cafés as the effectiveness and efficiency of VOIP, streaming media, travel information, photo manipulation and real-time communication become more efficient. According to Pitts Jr (2005) technology is almost always sold to us as a means of making life less hectic, but nature abhors a vacuum.

Disconnecting from their hypermobile lifestyle and technology is not an option for the extremely mobile; they will increasingly use Internet cafés and networked portable technology to manage multiple lives. Internet access has become as commonplace as the telephone or television, and is increasingly considered a necessity for the smooth functioning of networked contemporary life (Powell, 2004), following travellers into the travelscape. According to Holmes (2001: 8) individuals need to be 'plugged' into a network and to be denied the virtual world of e-mail and information in the travelscape, to deny mobility to the hypermobile 'separated from the networks' they are accustomed to, may lead to distress. The question remains as to whether travellers come to terms with and appropriately navigate the social and public spaces in their use of technology. It would be a terrible irony if 'being connected' required or encouraged a disconnection from travel life – from the middlemen/women, from other travellers, from locals, from the destination, from off-the-beaten-track areas where no Internet access exists, from the spontaneous encounters and everyday occurrences that make travelling such a fantastic activity and experience. Also it would be ironic to see budget travelling, which is characterized by its search for authenticity (even if it is an intellectual cul-de-sac), fall entirely into predictability and a mainstream hypermobile lifestyle while the respect for the local and the appreciation for 'real' local people and local places around them decline. Adams (2004: 412–413) believes '[h]ypermobile societies are anonymous societies, and anonymity breeds crime, fear and paranoia'. It is unlikely that these hypermobile places will become 'smarter' in the short term – becoming places where locals and transient travellers can spend quality time and enjoy experiences together; places where the virtual, the digital and physical local environments come together in on- and offline conversations, interactions, entertainment and play so that cafés' local and global characteristics can fuse together in a meaningful way.

While the advantages of travel and mobility are routinely espoused, the disadvantages of hypermobility get less interest. Therefore the distinction between the global and the local needs to be rethought, notably the impact of not only traveller corporeal mobility on the travelscape but also the effect of mobility of objects like mobile phones and iPods and the virtual mobility which travellers play out on computer monitors. The effect of increased traveller mobility on traveller infrastructure, like hostels, and on travellers themselves also need to be investigated as the globalization processes 'interfere with countercultures, taken as an analytical site that potentially anticipates new forms of subjectivity and identity' (D'Andrea, 2006: 97). By analysing these changes using mobility studies as a conceptual base we can investigate budget traveller identity, cultural mobilities, travellers' 'imagined community', authenticity and social norms, and discuss mobility exclusion (against locals), traveller motivation and diversity.

Acknowledgements

The author would like to acknowledge the comments and suggestions given by participants at the Fourth International Symposium on Aspects of Tourism Conference – Mobility and Local–Global Connections, which took place with the support of the Centre for Tourism Policy Studies (CENTOPS), University of Brighton, Eastbourne, UK, as well as the support of his supervisors, Professor Peter Burns and Dr Lyn Pemberton (School of Computing, Mathematical and Information Sciences).

References

Aas, K.F. (2005) *Sentencing in the Age of Information; from Faust to Macintosh*. Glasshouse Press, London.

Adams, J. (2004) A letter from the future. In: Graham, S. (ed.) *The Cybercities Reader*. Routledge, London, pp. 411–414.

Adey, P. (2004) Secured and sorted mobilities: examples from the airport. *Surveillance and Society* 1(4), 500–519.

Allon, F. (2004) Backpacker heaven: the consumption and construction of tourist spaces and landscapes in Sydney. *Space and Culture* 7(1), 49–63.

Anderson, B. (1991) *Imagined Communities: Reflections on the Origin and Spread of Nationalism*. Verso, New York.

Anderson, K. and De Paula, R. (2006) We we we all the way home: the 'we' affect in transitional spaces. The Second Ethnographic Praxis in Industry Conference (EPIC). Intel Corporation Conference Center, Portland, Oregon, 24–26 September.

Anon. (2006) The cost of staying connected: Internet cafe prices are all over the map. *Wired Magazine* May issue, p. 53.

Aubert-Gamet, V. and Cova, B. (1999) Servicescapes: from modern non-places to postmodern common places. *Journal of Business Research* 44, 37–45.

Augé, M. (1995) *Non-Places: Introduction to Anthropology of Supermodernity*. Verso, London.

Barron, C. (2004) No lonely avenue in cyberspace. *Financial Times* 25 September, p. 4.

Bauman, Z. (1998) *Globalization*. Columbia University Press, New York.

Beavis, C., Nixon, H. and Atkinson, S. (2005) LAN cafés: cafés, places of gathering or sites of informal teaching and learning? *Education, Communication and Information* 5(1) (Special issue: New Media, Production Practices, Learning Spaces), 41–60.

Binder, J. (2004) The whole point of backpacking: anthropological perspectives on the characteristics of backpacking. In: Wilson, J. and Richards, G. (eds) *The Global Nomad: Backpacker Travel in Theory and Practice*. Channel View Publications, Clevedon, UK, pp. 92–108.

Boase, J., Chen, W., Wellman, B. and Prijatelj, M. (2002) Is there a place in cyberspace? The uses and users of public internet terminals. *Géographie et Cultures* 46 (Été), 5–20.

Bright, M. (2004) BT puts block on child porn sites. *Observer* 6 June. Available at: http://www.guardian.co.uk/online/news/0,12597,1232506,00.html (accessed 10 November 2006).

Bull, M. (2004) The intimate sounds of urban experience: an auditory epistemology of everyday mobility. Paper presented at The Global and the Local in Mobile Communication: Places, Images, People, Connections. Hungarian Academy of Sciences, Budapest, Hungary, 10–12 June.

Caesar, T. (2005) E-mail: connections, contexts, and another space. *Fast Capitalism* 1.1. Available from: http://www.uta.edu/huma/agger/fastcapitalism/1_1/caesar.html (accessed 10 November 2007).

Cairncross, F. (1997) *The Death of Distance: How the Communications Revolution will Change our Lives*. Orion Business Books, London.

Campbell, D. (2003) Virtual shoot-outs turn into reality at LA cybercafés. *Guardian* 2 January. Available at: http://www.guardian.co.uk/international/story/0,,867342,00.html (accessed 10 November 2006).

Carducci, B. (2000) Shyness: the new solution. *Psychology Today* Jan/Feb. Available at: http://cms.psychologytoday.com/articles/index.php?term = PTO-20000101-200032 (accessed 10 November 2006).

Castells, M. (1989) *The Informational City*. Basil Blackwell, Oxford, UK.

Clarke, N. (2004a) Free independent travellers? British working holiday makers in Australia. *Transactions of the Institute of British Geographers* 29(4), 499–509.

Clarke, N. (2004b) Mobility, Fixity, Agency: Australia's Working Holiday Programme. *Population, Space and Place* 10, 411–420.

Clifford, J. (1997) *Routes: Travel and Translation in the Late Twentieth Century*. Harvard University Press, Cambridge, Massachusetts.

Cohen, E. (2004) Backpacking: diversity and change. In: Wilson, J. and Richards, G. (eds) *The Global Nomad. Backpacker Travel in Theory and Practice*. Channel View Publications, Clevedon, UK, pp. 43–59.

Constable, P. (2005) US warns citizens in Afghanistan – Americans told to avoid high profile locations after bombing. *Washington Post* 30 August. Available at: http://www.washingtonpost.com/wp-dyn/articles/A46818- 2004Aug30.html (accessed 11 November 2006).

Crary, J. (1999) *Suspensions of Perception: Attention, Spectacle, and Modern Culture*. MIT Press, London.

D'Andrea, A. (2006) Neo-nomadism: a theory of post-identitarian mobility in the global age. *Mobilities* 1(1), 95–119.

de Botton, A. (2002) *The Art of Travel*. Pantheon, New York.

Dobers, P. and Strannegård, L. (2002) Head home. In: Schwartz-Clauss, M. and von Vegesack, A. (eds) *Living in Motion – Design and Architecture for Flexible Dwelling*. Vitra Design Museum, Weil am Rhein, Germany, pp. 238–245.

Duffy, J. (2004) Will Internet cafés survive 10 more years? *BBC News Online* 2 September. Available at: http://news.bbc.co.uk/go/pr/fr/-/1/hi/magazine/3618068.stm (accessed 10 November 2006).

Edwards, C. (2004) Ghost phenomena: user experiences of place and non-place in cyberspace. Paper presented at Critical Themes in Media Studies: Fourth Annual Graduate Conference. Available at: http://beard.dialnsa.edu/~treis/pdf/Ghost%20 Phenomena.pdf (accessed 10 November 2006).

Elliott, C. (2005) Is the check-in kiosk in the lobby for real? *New York Times* 31 May. Available at: http://www.nytimes.com/2005/05/31/business/31soff.html (accessed 14 November 2006).

Ferlander, S. (2003) The Internet, social capital and local community. PhD thesis, Department of Psychology, University of Stirling, UK.

Freudendal-Pedersen, M. (2005) Structural stories, mobility and (un)freedom. In: Thomsen, T.U., Nielsen, L.D. and Gudmundsson, H. (eds) *Social Perspectives on Mobility*. Ashgate, Aldershot, UK, pp. 29–46.

Germann Molz, J. (2004) Destination world: technology, mobility and global belonging in round-the-world travel websites. PhD thesis, Department of Sociology, Lancaster University, UK.

Germann Molz, J. (2005) Getting a 'flexible eye': round-the-world travel and scales of cosmopolitan citizenship. *Citizenship Studies* 9(5), 517–531.

Goffman, E. (1963) *Behaviour in Public Places*. The Free Press, New York.

Gogia, N. (2006) Unpacking corporeal mobilities: the global voyages of labour and leisure. *Environment and Planning* 38(2), 359–375.

Gottdiener, M. (2004) Life in the air: surviving the new culture of air travel. In: Graham, S. (ed.) *The Cybercities Reader*. Routledge, London, pp. 185–188.

Gupta, N. (2004) Grande Wi-Fi: understanding what Wi-Fi users are doing in coffee-shops. Masters dissertation, Massachusetts Institute of Technology, Massachusetts.

Haseloff, A.M. (2005) Cybercafes and their potential as community development tools in India. *The Journal of Community Informatics* 1(3). Available at: http://www.ci-journal. net/index.php/ciej/article/view/226/181 (accessed 10 November 2006).

Healy, C. (1999) White feet and black trails: travelling cultures at the Lurujarri Trail. *Postcolonial Studies: Culture, Politics, Economy* 2(1), 55–73.

Hevrdejs, J. (2004) Reality beats technology. *Chicago Tribune* 12 August. Available at: http://www.psychlinks.ca/forum/showthread.php?p=1177 (accessed 10 November 2006).

Holmes, D. (2001) *Virtual Globalization: Virtual Spaces/Tourist Spaces*. Routledge, London.

Hong, J. and Huang, L. (2005) A split and swaying approach to building information society: the case of Internet cafes in China. *Telematics and Informatics* 22(4), 377–393.

Horne, M. (2005) Stelios puts ban on baseball caps. *Sunday Times* 18 December. Available at: http://www.timesonline.co.uk/article/0,,2087- 1938253,00.html (accessed 10 November 2006).

Johnson, C. (2004) How are college students using the Internet in Wi-Fi enabled cafes? Institute for Communications Research. Available at: http://www.inquiry.uiuc. edu/ bin/unit_update.cgi?command=select&xmlfile=u13899.xml (accessed 10 November 2006).

Kahn, J. (2006) In rare briefing, China defends Internet controls. *New York Times* 14 February. Available at: http://www.nytimes.com (accessed 10 November 2006).

Kakihara, M. and Sørensen, C. (2001) *Mobility Reconsidered: Topological Aspects of Interaction*. *IRIS 24*, University of Bergen, Ulvik, Norway.

Kenyon, S., Lyons, G. and Rafferty, J. (2002) Transport and social exclusion: investigating the possibility of promoting inclusion through virtual mobility. *Journal of Transport Geography* 10(3), 207–219.

Laegran, A.S. (2002) The petrol station and the Internet cafe: rural technospaces for youth. *The Journal of Rural Studies* 18(2), 157–168.

Laegran, A.S. and Stewart, J. (2003) Nerdy, trendy or healthy? Configuring the Internet café. *New Media and Society* 5(3), 357–377.

Larsen, J., Urry, J. and Axhausen, K. (2006) Geographies of social networks: meetings, travel and communications. *Mobilities* 1(2), 261–283.

Lee, S. (1999) Private uses in public spaces: a study of an Internet café. *New Media and Society* 1(3), 331–350.

Legard, D. (2004) Why windows won't always dominate. *IDG News Service* 23 April. Available at: http://www.pcworld.com/news/article/0,aid,115823,00.asp (accessed 10 November 2006).

Liff, S. and Laegran, S. (2003) Cybercafés: debating the meaning and significance of Internet access in a café environment. *New Media and Society* 5(3), 307–312.

Liff, S. and Steward, F. (2003) Shaping e-access in the cybercafé: networks, boundaries and meteretopian innovation. *New Media and Society* 5(3), 313–334.

Liff, S., Steward, F. and Watts, P. (1998) Cybercafés and Telecottages: Increasing Public Access to Computers and the Internet, Survey Report, Virtual Society? Programme, Economic and Social Research Council, UK, 1998. Available at: http://virtualsociety.sbs.ox.ac.uk/text/reports/access.htm (accessed 10 November 2006).

MacCannell, D. (1976) *The Tourist: a New Theory of the Leisure Class*. Macmillan, London.

McGuire, M. (2003) PlayStation 2: selling the third place. In: *Proceedings of DAC03* [the Digital Arts and Culture Conference]. Royal Melbourne Institute of Technology, Digital Arts and Culture Conference, Melbourne, 19–23 May.

McMillan, R. (2004) Mozilla gains on IE. *IDG News Service* 9 July. Available at: http://www.pcworld.com/news/article/0,aid,116848,00.asp (accessed 10 November 2006).

Middleton, C.A. (2003) Broadband Internet usage outside the home: insights from a study of Toronto Internet cafes. In: *Proceedings of the International Telecommunications Society Asia–Australasian Regional Conference*. Perth, Australia, 22–24 June. Available at: http://www.ryerson.ca/~cmiddlet/pubs/cafes.pdf (accessed 10 September 2006).

Mintel (2006) Round the World Travel/Backpacking – UK. Mintel International Group Ltd 1 May, 71 pp. Available at: http://reports.mintel.com (accessed 18 November 2006).

Moorehead, C. and Christie, I. (2002) Motorway culture and its discontents. *Open Democracy* 23 May. Available at: www.opendemocracy.net/content/articles/PDF/466.pdf (accessed 10 November 2006).

Munt, S.R. (2001) Technospaces: inside the new media. In: Munt, S.R. (ed.) *Technospaces*. Continuum, London.

Murfett, A. (2004) Cyber on the side. *The Age Newspaper* 30 September. Available at: http://www.theage.com.au/articles/2004/09/29/1096401633085.html?from = storylhs (accessed 10 November 2006).

Murphy, L. (2001) Exploring social interactions of backpackers. *Annals of Tourism Research* 28(1), 50–67.

Noy, C. and Cohen, E. (2005) *Israeli Backpackers: from Tourism to Rite of Passage*. State University of New York Press, Albany, New York.

Nunes, M. (1999) The realities and virtualities of cybercafes. Paper presented at the 1999 Popular Culture Association Conference. San Diego Marriott Hotel and Marina, San Diego, California, 30 March–4 April.

Oldenburg, R. (1989) *The Great Good Place: Cafés, Coffee Shops, Community Centers, Beauty Parlors, General Stores, Bars, Hangouts and How they get you through the Day.* Paragon House, New York.

Phipps, A. and Jack, G. (2003) On the uses of travel guides in the context of German tourism to Scotland. *Tourist Studies* 3(3), 281–300.

Pitts Jr, L. (2005) Even North Pole no escape from technology. *Aberdeen News* 11 May. Available at: http://www.aberdeennews.com/mld/americannews/ 2005/05/11/news/ opinion/11617876.htm (accessed 10 November 2006).

Powell, A. (2004) Space, place, reality and virtuality in urban Internet cafés. In: *Proceedings of the Second Annual Canadian Association of Cultural Studies Conference*, February 2004. Available at: http://www.culturalstudies.ca/proceedings04/proceedings.html# powell (accessed 10 November 2006).

Richards, G. and Wilson, J. (2003) A report for the International Student Travel Confederation (ISTC) and the Association of Tourism and Leisure Education (ATLAS). Available at: http://www.atlas-euro.org/pages/pdf/FINAL_Industry_Report.pdf (accessed 10 November 2006).

Richards, G. and Wilson, J. (2004) The global nomad: motivations and behaviour of independent travellers worldwide. In: Wilson, J. and Richards, G. (eds) *The Global Nomad: Backpacker Travel in Theory and Practice.* Channel View Publications, Clevedon, UK, pp. 14–42.

Rosen, C. (2004) Our cell phones, ourselves. *The New Atlantis* 6 (Summer), 26–45.

Salvador, T., Sherry, J.W. and Urrutia, A. (2005) Less cyber, more café: enhancing existing small businesses across the digital divide. *Information Technology for Development* 11(1), 77–95.

Sarman, N. (2002) Public Space, Mediated Environment, Public Participation: an Inquiry into the Transformation of Public Space and its Effect on Public Opinion. The New School, New York City. Available at: http://www.newschool.edu/mediastudies/ conf/pdf/hatice_naz_sarman.pdf (accessed 2 November 2006).

Schwarz, R. (2005) Avoiding bugs and bots at internet cafes. *The Dominion Post* 27 June. Available at: http://www.stuff.co.nz/stuff/0,2106,3325994a11275,00.html (accessed 10 November 2006).

Shaw, G. and Williams, A.M. (2004) *Tourism and Tourism Spaces.* Sage, London.

Spreitzhofer, G. (2003) Low-budget backpacking in Southeast Asia. The golden goal of local development? *Pacific News* 20 (July/August). Available at: http://www.geogr. uni-goettingen.de/kus/apsa/pn/pn20/pn20-spreitzhofer.pdf (accessed 2 November 2006).

Stewart, J. (2000) Cafematics: the cybercafe and the community. In: Gurstein, M. (ed.) *Community Informatics: Enabling Communities with Information and Communications Technologies.* Idea Group Publishing, London.

Szablewicz, M.T. (2004) A space to be your (virtual) self – an introduction to the world of Internet gaming in the urban Chinese Wangba. Masters dissertation, Duke University, Durham, North Carolina, USA. Available at: http://www.duke.edu/APSI/pdf/ MarcySzablewicz.pdf (accessed 19 November 2006).

Taylor, R. (2004) Internet cafes around the world. *Guardian* 1 May. Available at: http://travel.guardian.co.uk/travelsites/story/0,7631,1207247,00.html (accessed 10 November 2006).

Thomsen, T.U., Nielsen, L.D. and Gudmundsson, H. (eds) (2005) *Social Perspectives on Mobility.* Ashgate, Aldershot, UK.

United Nations Conference on Trade and Development (2006) The digital divide report: ICT Diffusion Index. In: Report on the United Nations Conference on Trade and Development 2005. Available at: http://www.unctad.org/en/docs/iteipc20065_en.pdf (accessed 22 November 2006).

Urry, J. (2000a) *Sociology Beyond Societies: Mobilities for the Twenty-First Century.* Routledge, New York.

Urry, J. (2000b) Mobile sociology. *British Journal of Sociology* 51(1), 185–203.

Urry, J. (2000c) The Global Media and Cosmopolitanism. Published by the Department of Sociology, Lancaster University, UK. Available at: http://www.comp.lancs.ac.uk/sociology/soc056ju.html (accessed 10 November 2006).

Urry, J. (2002) *The Tourist Gaze (Theory, Culture and Society Series)*, 2nd edn. Sage, London.

Urry, J. (2003) Inhabiting the Car. Published by the Department of Sociology, Lancaster University, UK. Available at: http://www.comp.lancs.ac.uk/sociology/papers/Urry-Inhabiting-the-Car.pdf (accessed 10 November 2006).

Urry, J. (2006) Travelling times. *European Journal of Communication* 21(3), 357–372.

Van Houtum, H. and Van Naerssen, T. (2002) Bordering, ordering and othering. *Tijdschrift voor Economische en Sociale Geografie* 93(2), 125–136.

Wakeford, N. (2003) The embedding of local culture in global communication: independent Internet cafés in London. *New Media and Society* 5(3), 379–399.

8 Entering the Global Margin: Setting the 'Other' Scene in Independent Travel

REBECCA JANE BENNETT

Here, the 'other scene' would mean that crucial determinants of our own action remain invisible in the very forms of (tele) visibility, whereas we urgently require them to assess the conjuncture or 'take sides' in conflicts where it is possible neither simply to attribute the labels of justice and injustice, nor to 'rise above the fray' in the name of some superior determination of history.

(Balibar, 2002: xii–xiii)

Many of the ideological, economic and cultural impacts of global tourism remain unseen in backpacker media and praxis. This absence allows tourism to present itself as a mutually exclusive pleasure industry absolved of political responsibility and class bias. Backpacker discourse requires the input of usually unseen and unheard perspectives if it is to self-reflexively challenge and change its globally unbalanced power structure. Mobile pleasure seekers are rarely shown the full impact of their touring actions through the narrow focus of tourist information readily available to them. If missing critical, non-tourist, poor, immobile and local perspectives are not realized in popular backpacker discourse and theory, travelling leisure seekers are not shown how their choices potentially have the power to instigate necessary and important global political and economic change. Tourism theories need to focus on the configuration of otherness in a myriad of tourist texts, rather than continuing the increasingly redundant project of determining how mobile leisure seekers choose to define themselves. A critical investigation into backpacker media's rendering of otherness reveals underlying bias and powers that reinscribe colonial and imperialist attitudes into the global everyday.

Since the bombing of the World Trade Center in New York on 11 September 2001, the visibility of a terrorism that targets global citizens has increased. Terror attacks aimed at transit and tourist areas dominate news headlines worldwide, while the tourism industry continues to grow in popularity, size and strength. Smith (2005: 78–79) tracks this trend stating that:

> Since 1994 . . . trade in tourism services has played a significant role in the progressive
> liberalization of markets through the reduction and removal of barriers to international
> trade. Over 120 countries have made commitments to the World Trade Organization
> to liberalize trade in tourism services, more countries than for any other trade
> sector.

Widely accepted as a 'sure-fire' way to economic prosperity, nations are trading
in tourism to an unprecedented degree. Tourism has allowed globalization to
continue its multinational market dominance unfettered and unfazed by emergent dangerous political and ideological opponents. The transnational trend of
market liberalization for tourism purposes has made the 'trade of people' for leisure
one of economic globalization's widespread earners. It is ironically fitting that the
smaller institution that once shared the World Trade Organization's initials (the
United Nations World *Tourism* Organization) is becoming one of the World
Trade Organization's largest benefactors.

This chapter searches for 'alternative' information about backpacking by
critiquing narratives that suggest globalization (and by implication global tourism)
is changing the world for the better. Tourism is not a neutral leisure institution
that should be absolved from serious political debate and critique. Orientalism
has survived, relatively unchallenged, in contemporary tourism discourse. Demonstrating how backpacking is defined through the absence or subjective presence
of otherness in a variety of tourism texts allows for a tangible and problematic
reading of mobile leisure classes to emerge as a necessary focus for tourism
critique. Tourist media encourages binary oppositions between pleasure and
politics and subsequently tourism and terrorism that arbitrarily politicize and
neuter the tourist experience in a global economic setting. A critical enquiry into
a tourist-centric bias in backpacker discourse is justified through tourism's
metonymic relationship with economic globalization.

Politics can be infused into tourist practice when it is remembered that tourism *is* globalization, not a mutually exclusive mobility. Tourism plays an active
part in the maintenance of global hegemony. As Richards and Wilson (2004b: 4)
realize:

> Globalisation not only increases the speed at which cultures are marginalised, but
> also increases the speed with which the tourist can travel. The presence of tourists
> around the globe is not only a sign of the progress of globalisation; it is also an
> integral part of the globalisation process.

Subsequently, if globalization results in the marginalization of particular voices,
economic classes, religions, stasis and movements, then tourism is implicated in
the marginalization process. This chapter focuses on how backpacker media and
theory contribute to the systematic silencing of one half of the tourist equation:
the 'non-tourist' half. It implicates backpacker tourism in the re-emergence of a
popular Orientalism that infuses tourist movement with surface politics, while
simultaneously silencing oppositional or critical narratives about the future of
late capitalist globalization.

Similar – if not synonymous with Bhabha's 'colonial margins' – backpacker
discourse is taken to its limits; to the moments when it defines its self by describing or
denying the agency and appearance of its others. Entering the global/colonial

margin unmasks the paradoxical power and exclusiveness in tourist mobility and agency. Bhabha's (1990: 71) theory articulates that:

> It is there in the colonial [and global] margin that the culture of the west reveals its difference, its limit-text, as its practice of authority displays an ambivalence that is one of the most significant discursive and physical strategies of discriminatory power – whether racist or sexist, peripheral or metropolitan.

Given that tourist readings of difference are informed by a powerful legacy of imperialism and colonialism, discussions about cultural difference cannot avoid retracing Orientalist ideologies and writing subaltern positions. This should not, however, deter academics from continuing difficult discussions about tourist others. To reveal the authority underpinning ambivalence is a necessary step towards social and economic change. The complexity of the subject of otherness, and the politically dangerous consequences of speaking for or about other people, is why it should be a primary focus for backpacker study. Non-tourists are frequently discussed and appropriated in tourist discourses, but they rarely speak. Although a West/East distinction is increasingly redundant in globalization, Sardar's (1999: 63) Orientalist observation rings true if the West/East content changes to global/local. He states that 'Western culture was bound up with moral values as much as with a certain fundamental aspiration. Both of these, however, have managed to change their content while protecting their overall purpose.' A defining feature of backpacker popular memory is absence of other voices in the first person. Tourist others are not necessarily 'Oriental'; they simply do not have the choice, agency or income to become global tourists. Global Orientalism superimposes a mobile/immobile binary on to a structure formerly labelled 'West/East'. Locals and non-tourist voices are repeatedly absent in backpacker media. Travelling from Richards and Wilson's (2004a) recent backpacker study, through Olsen's (1997) 'backpacker' interviewees to cultural studies academic turned travel writer Berger (2004, 2005), to a reconfiguration of the dangerous other in the Lonely Planet's latest recommendation of places to go, is a consistent narration about the tourist self that manifests its others to justify, empower and promote tourist mobility. When the language used to describe or overwrite otherness in global backpacker discourse is examined with Orientalist discursive practices in mind, the contested and political global terrain that supports tourist mobility is visualized as something that may be benefited by structural and ideological change.

Backpacker Research: Reading a Self-ish Scene

Multiple perspectives of independent travel presented in fiction and theory, travel journal and game show, conversation and newspaper article, conflate to form a large and cohesive discourse that reconstitutes historically familiar exclusive patterns. Backpacker images and sites are multiple, conflicting and dynamic and thus they easily align with fluid capitalist global 'scapes marked by individualized post-Fordist consumer desire. Backpacker travel modalities and symbols such as backpacks, youth hostels, camping equipment, flexible itineraries and unusual and/or developing destination choices, are pervasive and familiar in global travel popular culture and popular memory texts. They have not, however, been so easy to locate in the academy until very recently. Cohen (2004: 43) argues that critical tourism research barely scratches the surface of the accelerated global industry that forms its subject matter. Not only is tourism a relatively under-developed critical study, but backpacking theory has barely begun. He states that:

> While research on tourism generally lagged behind the rapidly expanding industry, research on backpacking was particularly tardy to pick up with the growing phenomenon – perhaps since it lacked the support of the tourism industry, which had little interest in its exploration.

Backpacking's assumed 'budget' focus and individually customized structure contradicted the uniformity and economic standardized demands of 'old' Fordist capitalism. Backpacker tourist modalities have become more prevalent in the post-Fordist era because they easily adapt to suit mobile, flexible and customized consumer demand. Keeping theory in pace with the independent tourist market is a challenging task in accelerating times because backpacking does not have a long history of institutional support. Lagging behind in an already underdevel-oped field of critical tourism studies, backpackers (and tourists in general) are rarely placed under the kind of critical scrutiny their pervasiveness in globaliza-tion networks demands.

The increasing popularity of tourism across the globe has encouraged an exponential development of a critical consciousness about leisure travel modali-ties. Backpacking has thus recently infiltrated a small niche in the tourist studies academy. An international team of researchers called the Backpacker Research Group (BRG) have released a publication that validates independent travel as a site worthy of critical attention. Richards and Wilson's (2004a) edited text titled *The Global Nomad: Backpacker Travel in Theory and Practice* collects and analy-ses data from over 2000 'backpacker' respondents from eight countries. They emphasize that an 'important question regarding the identity of the young travel-lers was the extent to which they considered themselves to be "travellers" as opposed to "backpackers" or "tourists"' (Richards and Wilson, 2004c: 16).

Analysing the ways in which tourists contest and choose to label themselves and their mobility is vital in tourism studies; however, it is also important to investigate the way tourists define their others. This BRG study shows little inves-tigation into how backpacker tourists consider and label local people, cultures and landscapes they interact with. Desiring to take tourism theory a step away from postmodern consumer identity politics and self-labelling, this encounter with focused backpacking theory finds a useful 'primary source' to catalyse a more thorough global critique.

Richards and Wilson (2004c: 17) articulate questions that offer a detailed description of backpacker discourse – as defined by a cross-section of backpack-ers, limited by Internet access, student status and relative 'youth'. They state that:

> By allowing the respondents to the global nomad survey to define their own travel style, it was hoped that more light could be shed on the relationship between previous definitions and the actual experience of travellers themselves.
>
> Richards and Wilson (2004c: 16)

This narrow focus on self-definition does not allow space for thorough critique. No room is left for the 'actual' experience of locals, tourism workers and other non-tourists touched by backpacking industries and practice. The BRG survey approach does not contextualize independent travel from a holistic perspective. Backpacking is a melange of tourists, travellers, workers, locals, landscapes, technologies, religions, classes and economies. Non-backpacker perspectives are essential in attempts to assess, define or describe the form in a transparent manner with a view to change for the global better.

Instead of reflexively questioning themselves and the global class that allows their research and mobility, Richards and Wilson avoid silences and omissions in the backpacker responses as they gather and regurgitate the vocal and familiar narrations of mobile classes. A tourist-centric academic focus is evident in the four questions they present as their main points of discussion. These questions are as follows:

1. Why do people become backpackers?
2. What do they experience on their travels?
3. How has backpacking experience changed over time?
4. What impact does backpacking have on later life?

(Richards and Wilson, 2004b: 7)

Backpacker self-definition is a questionable focus for tourism theory because it authenticates tourist-centric narrations in popular travel media that forget a vital half of the pleasure travel experience. Hollinshead (2004: 30) warns against repetition that encourages a singular way of approaching tourism. He states that:

> tourism undoubtedly comprises the collaborative-consciousness industry for many places, today, and constitutes a mechanism of arbitrary and repetitive authentication which frequently freezes places within particular but limited visions of being and self-celebration.

The BRG investigation of the backpacker self is consistent with the tourist-centric world view espoused in popular travel publications. Olsen (1997: 22) suggests that tourists have more authority over destinations than the people who live there when he emphasizes in bold font that '**the best travel advice comes from other travellers who have been there** [sic]'. Tourism discourse is too often written for tourists by tourists. Non-tourists are spoken 'about' and evaluated in tourist texts, but rarely are they given the agency or opportunity to speak for themselves about where they live, how they feel and what they know.

The blurb on the back cover of Kuhne's (2000) Lonely Planet edited collection titled: *On the Edge: Adventurous Escapades from Around the World* reads, 'travel is the basis of true adventure, and a thirst for adventure lies at the heart of the most memorable travel'. Here, travel is discursively removed from the macro-political global economic environment. It is presented as being an exclusive entity in and of itself. Studies of self-definition in isolation create a neutered and de-politicized critical space. Naming, labelling, data collection and seemingly 'objective' accounts of backpacker's opinions and trends do not challenge dominant images of the backpacker. The collation of large amounts of backpacker data allows 'backpacker discourse' to enter the academy as unproblematic, empirical evidence. Decontextualized and absolved of political responsibility, independent travel is misleadingly isolated as a mutually exclusive space for tourists *about* themselves.

The Global Nomad (Richards and Wilson, 2004a) is both motivating and concerning in its presentation of backpacker tourist culture in a global context. It is motivating as a launching pad for critical and reflexive investigations into backpacking's contributions and challenges to the global status quo. The publication is also concerning because the survey focus and data suggest that inward-looking, self-defining aspects of backpacker discourse are superseding the desire to know, understand and communicate with disparate others. A hyper-individualized focus on backpacker praxis comes at the expense of immobile parties in tourist interactions who stand to lose more of an already tenuous hold on the discourse, industry and praxis.

Silenced and Celebrated: the Other in Popular Travel Pedagogy

People not 'on tour' are as vital as backpackers in the global industrial matrix that keeps tourist practice and discourse thriving and justified. Unfortunately *The Global Nomad* (Richards and Wilson, 2004a) is guilty of a familiar bias because it does not track the power structures that work beneath the shiny market surface of backpacker travel. I heed Balibar's (2002: 100) statement as a warning for tourism scholars that 'we are always narcissistically in search of images of ourselves, when it is structures that we should be looking for'. Introducing backpacker discourse into the academy as a neutral and exclusive object of study validates subjective, arbitrary and loaded truths about tourist interactions with 'difference'. Tourism promotion and pedagogy necessitate further discussion and negotiation between tourists and locals. Backpacker practice and theory are enhanced by recognition of the silencing of the tourist-other's voice. Searching for Orientalist structures that encourage self-imaging through interactions with otherness expands the BRG research pool.

Backpacker discourse presents subjective interpretation as universal 'truth' by utilizing the popular persuasion that travel is education. Pedagogic connotations intrinsic to tourism discourse provide incentives and justifications for backpacking. The assumption appears to be that having been a tourist is the sole prerequisite to becoming a tourism teacher. The positive aspects and benefits of tourism for tourists are popular knowledge with promises of 'experiences of a lifetime', 'finding yourself' and 'getting away from it all' being familiar tourist clichés. The effects of tourism on non-tourists are less publicized, and the negative impacts of contemporary forms of tourism on tourists and locals alike are written out of backpacker popular memory. Backpacker 'Rachel' (Olsen 1997: 9) writes that travel is 'Learning customs, people, history, and education. Smiles. Body Language, exotic tongues and ways of communication. Religions; Buddhist, Christian, Hindu, Jewish, Muslim . . . the oneness (om) of them all [sic].' Despite her eccentric English grammar, Rachel's travel 'wisdom' is published for 'global' consumption in Olsen's travel guide, along with similar claims of universalism, equality and spirituality made by nine other 'world travellers' from the USA, the UK, Germany and Ireland (1997: 7–9). Rachel presents herself as a universal spokesperson. She claims authority over diverse religions, emphasizing their 'sameness' to justify her individual opinion as being valuable. Rachel assumes an omniscient, objective, god-like narrative position, using spiritual connotations to mask a lack of social, political and theological understanding. Her power of speech allows her to speak for and about others, painting a public image of the globe skewed so she is a benevolent authority. Balibar (2002: 4–5) states that:

> This is the case, in particular, with the idea of representing oneself and making oneself the spokesperson of the universal, given that speech is also a power relation, and that the unequal distribution of verbal skills cannot be corrected simply by acknowledging entitlement to [global] citizenship.

Rachel's claim about the 'sameness' of all allows her readers to assume her tourism is enacted on a level playing field. Simply stating that someone else is an equal does not change the fate of the other; it arbitrarily absolves the spokesperson from guilt.

Individual colonial narratives that use local knowledge and imagery as a scenic backdrop and justification for a consumer voyage of self-discovery are all too familiar in backpacker-tourist narrations. Backpacker voices alone do not explicitly reveal the powers and influence at play in the choice of their words or the circle they draw around 'multiple choice' letters or numbers in a limiting questionnaire. They do, however, understand the authority summoned when they are asked to communicate their tourist perspective to others. The subtext of Rachel's prose suggests that 'travel' provides the tourist with universal knowledge and global authorship. Political and economic statistics about poverty, mobility and access suggest Rachel is misleading herself and her readers. Rachel's political ignorance is evidence that Orientalist narrative techniques persist in globalizing times if, as Sardar (1999: 4) states, 'what is essential to the Orientalist vision is the desire not to know'. In this text, backpacker popular culture writes an image of otherness that sells squeaky-clean misinformation encouraging people to tour by omitting uncomfortable global political realities such as widespread poverty, exploitation, environmental damage, political and religious conflict, and the part tourism plays in a global stratum based on access to mobility (Urry, 2000).

Late capitalist, global media networks and their marriage with the tourism industry mean that independent tourism's benefits are part of globalization's dominant discourse. Unfair or uneasy consequences of backpacker travel are not discussed in backpacker popular culture, which is understandable given market demands. They should however be the focus of tourist study. Unfortunately this critical focus is not always heeded. Cultural-studies academic-cum-travel writer Berger exemplifies the diversity of perspectives used to propagate tourism's positive aspects. Berger filters the study of tourism through rose-coloured academic glasses made to fit his individual prescription. Following his initial tourism publication, *Deconstructing Travel* (2004) – where the intent to view multiple perspectives of tourism is suggested, if not delivered – Berger (2005) eschews critical reflexivity in favour of a celebration of Vietnam that reflects his generic shift from tourism academic to travel writer.

Vietnam Tourism (Berger, 2005) is an informative travel guide, peppered with a few generic 'cultural-studies' terms. Berger states:

> I hope that after reading this book you will not only have learned about the tourism industry in Vietnam but also, as the result of my use of ethnographic methods, that you will have a sense of what it is like to be a tourist there . . . I have interpreted a number of signs and icons in an attempt to capture what I have described as the 'genius' of Vietnam – the particular quality and character of life lived there as it is experienced by tourists.
>
> (Berger, 2005: 110)

Tourism discourse is disproportionately focused on the 'tourist experience' at the expense of the local. Local 'signs' and 'icons' are given more weight and attention in Berger's guide than local people and agency. Setting up expectations of a far-off land filled with spicy delights and a wealth of knowledge, Berger appears as an expert on tourism in Vietnam.

Berger tours with an academic gaze and written language that implies authority. He reverts to a generic travel-writing tradition that is disproportionately focused on the guest experience of tourism while the local experience is not given a first-person voice. Scholarly attempts at writing and promoting cultural difference such as Berger's are problematic, as Sardar (1999: 76) cites Robbins:

> Scholarly careers are made not just by representing those who cannot represent themselves but by keeping the unrepresented from representing themselves, substituting their own elite intellectual work for the voices of the oppressed even as they claim to represent these voices.

Berger sells the 'genius' of Vietnam yet fails to include Vietnamese voices in his book. His self-confessed intention to evoke an experience similar to being a tourist there thus maintains the omission of other perspectives. Like Rachel's claims to global 'equality' Berger's genius is assumed to exist simply because he says so. Sardar (1999: 53) states that in Orientalism 'there was no need for logic or integration because the object, the Orient, was not considered; it was constructed for present utility in the operation and advancement of Western thought'. Berger does not appoint a Vietnamese local to be the spokesperson for Vietnam tourism's 'genius', because his book is not really about Vietnam, it is about expanding tourism discourse and about his own cleverness. Berger commands Orientalist academic credit by defining and creating an exotic, smart and pleasurable Vietnamese culture.

If backpackers mirror Berger's quasi-academic, observational travel writer's styles then they are in danger of learning a sophisticated form of claiming authority for the self through the manipulation of images of culturally disparate others. Berger does not ask his readers to consider Vietnamese locals as the mouthpieces of his described 'genius'. They feature as metaphors in an academic hierarchy superimposed on to their nation. Local, national and individual Vietnamese perspectives are silenced through benevolent praise. Appearing an academic philanthropist, Berger paints a far clearer image of himself as an educated, open-minded lover of Vietnam's exotic and obvious differences, than he does of the multiple perspectives that might inform the tourism industry in Vietnam.

Backpacking and Terror: Transforming Political Others to Self Pleasures

Tourist identities from the worker to the traveller share a common influence, but it is not a universal humanity or equality. It is instead having life choices determined by a ruthless and unstable market. Tourism does not unite people, it stratifies them. Operating below the political radar, tourism *is* globalization's power. Smith (2005: 73) views:

> The tourism economy as a microcosm and reflection of the global economy in the information age in the late twenty-first century, as technology, information, and capital have converged to produce new and increased flows of information and knowledge.

This is why global leisure travel necessitates a further investigation into instances of terror, whether they are natural or political. Backpacker discourse's reaction to terror provides an insight into the maintenance of the global stratification of wealth, access and power. Cracks show in the multicoloured mural of other faces that backpacking celebrates, when terror attacks, increasing poverty, and anti-global lobbyists suggest that globalization is not an equivocal multicultural utopia.

The tourist industry is implicated in the problems as well as the benefits associated with market-driven globalization, and therefore it should be viewed as politically problematic. Smith (2005: 79) asks:

> With the World Trade Organization overseeing nearly 98 percent of global trade, and with a large percentage of this committed to the liberalization of trade in tourism services, we should expect tourism to increase in economic stature and financial power in the twenty-first century for developing economies. Should we, therefore, also expect tourism as a set of service industries to increase in stature as a symbol of free trade economies, a potential focus of criticism and protest by the anti-neo-liberal platform, or even attack by terrorist groups?

Given that tourism encourages trade liberalization, it works as a promotional tool for globalization. Consequently tourism's relationship with late capitalism and economic globalization is important when investigating terror attacks aimed at global targets. Tourist mobility has been a focus for global terrorist attacks. In politicized contexts it becomes more than a symbol or benefit of free trade; it is free trade policy and practice embodied. Backpacker markets initiate tourist trails in emergent, warring and poor destinations. Backpacker discourse needs to take responsibility for its global influence and recognize how destination choices and activities associated with independent tourist culture might be implicated in global misunderstandings, ideological differences and desperate situations that prompt tourist-focused terrorist violence and anger.

Terrorism has been re-packaged in backpacker discourse in a way that demonstrates the immense power the tourist market holds over political oppositions to the modality. The *Lonely Planet Bluelist . . . 06–07* (Wheeler, 2006) exemplifies a paradoxical rendering of terrorism in tourist media. Despite the apparent ideological separation between pleasure tourism and the politicized terrorist-ridden globalization, terrorism adds fuel to the independent traveller's desire to move off the beaten track and go to places where other tourists would not dare. Terrorism has been rewritten as a political justification for tourist movement and as a testament to the bravery and commitment of the independent tourist. Travel writer Don George (2006: 11) writes in the wake of global terror attacks that 'Travellers seem to have made peace with the truth that life is uncertain and instable wherever they may be, and seem to have recommitted themselves to traveling no matter what may happen'.

The Lonely Planet uses terrorism to 'set the scene' for a rewriting of the 'brave, fearless and adventurous' colonial explorer. The terrorist other reaffirms the traveller's power and determination in the face of adversity. George (p. 12) suggests that travel continues 'clearly in part a gritty defiance of the terrorists' goals of disrupting global commerce and communication and propagating intercultural distrust and fear'. Terrorism is rewritten into a narrative that maintains tourism is political 'in and of itself'. Such narratives deny backpacking's unbreakable alliance with the ruthless capitalist market that invented the travel genre.

Nearly 5 years after the terrorist attacks on the USA in 2001, tourist consumption is promoted in defiance of globalization's political, ideological and savage 'evil' other. The Lonely Planet (Wheeler, 2006: 4–5) – a global independent travel media publisher, founded and based in Australia – includes Nepal, Colombia, Indonesia, Israel and Yemen in its list of recommended 'places to go' in 2006 and 2007. All five destinations have travel advisory warnings placed on them by the Australian government in the recommended time period for travel. The website smartraveller.gov.au (http://smartraveller.gov.au/defer_all.html) advises 'against all travel' to Nepal and 'advises you to reconsider your need to travel' (http://smartraveller.gov.au/defer_all_non-essential.html) to Colombia, Indonesia, Israel and Yemen in April 2006. The Lonely Planet's encouragement to travel to places that are considered a danger to tourists confirms that backpacking dares to go places where mainstream tourists might not. Dangerous destinations are the unbeaten tracks in globalization. They are useful for backpacker consumers looking to appear as more adventurous and fearless than 'ordinary' tourists. Travel to foreign places where the threat of attack looms simulates the colonial explorer's conquering of savage landscapes and inhospitable natives.

Backpacker discourse's desire to isolate itself from the rest of the tourist market and to bravely go where no other travellers will dare is glaringly obvious in the positioning of Afghanistan in the *06–07 Bluelist*. The home of 11 September's publicly demonized instigator, Osama Bin Laden, is revered almost as the 'ultimate' backpacker destination in 2006. Afghanistan tops the Australian government's 'do not go' list (http://smartraveller.gov.au/defer_all.html) and is classified as having a high terrorist threat. The *Bluelist* (2006: 185) publication heeds this warning by mentioning late in the book that Afghanistan is an unsafe destination. Despite this 'warning', in the later pages however, Lonely Planet cofounder Tony Wheeler (2006) includes Afghanistan in his personal Bluelist for the coming 12 months. It is then rated as number three on a 'Tough Travel Destinations' (2006: 31) list with the blurb:

> Its people are friendly, its countryside is beautiful, it's blessed with an impressive history and rich and diverse culture, but . . . Afghanistan post-Taliban, is still a country to be avoided by the casual backpacker.

This blurb implies that, for adventurous backpackers like Tony Wheeler, Afghanistan is a fine place to travel to. It appears that the terror warnings, imminent danger and local people that violently oppose a tourist presence form an ideal destination for the flexing of backpacker muscle. Rather than being labelled as a place to be avoided, Afghanistan appears as the ultimate backpacker destination. It turns backpacking into an 'Xtreme' sport where 'terror-travel' joins 'base jumping' and 'cliff diving' as a travel experience offering an extra rush.

The Bush administration's global 'War on Terror' manipulates Orientalist understanding to explain what globalization is *not*. Because tourism is a part of economic and social globalization, terrorism, by implication, has also become a stand-in for what tourism is *not*. Sardar (1999: 116) states that 'Orientalism . . . is a rewriting through a disproportionate process of relationship in which one part, the Oriental, remains trapped, separate, unheard, though described to enable the freedom of the defining party'.

Terrorist bombings in Bali, Egypt, London, New York and Madrid threaten tourism and the capitalist ideology that promotes tourist mobility. Bali and Egypt in particular show that terrorism and tourism intersect with tragic and disastrous results. Practical instances where terrorists and tourists meet are appeased through mobility when the flow of tourists moves to 'safer' locations leaving the political ramifications of tourist-terror in other places in the pursuit of a pleasurable holiday. However, backpacker pursuits for exotic and unique experiences in an oversaturated tourist trail re-invent 'danger' as a niche market for the thrill-seeking traveller.

Conclusion

Tracking the Orientalist practice of defining and claiming to 'know' difference draws a more detailed map of the complex powers involved in the process of the narration of the global self. In what Bauman (2001) describes as 'the individualized society', the practice of naming and claiming a stake in others' differences reinstates the authority of the self. Individualism allows processes of global subordination to hide behind masks of 'subjective opinion'. Popular tourist discourses develop a popular pedagogy in everyday media that suggests tourists have expertise in other destinations, simply because they have toured there. A critical reading of backpacker Rachel's prose, Berger's Vietnam wisdom and the Lonely Planet *Bluelist* reveals repetitive narrations that render local, dissenting and immobile voices relatively invisible.

Summoning the seminal work of Said (1978) from the grave and mobilizing it through recent texts aimed at the backpacker market reaffirm the necessity of Orientalist critique in globalizing tourism theory. The 'scene of the other', a focus on who is left out and what is not said, is a vital step in tourist investigations that are looking to change the uneven distribution of power, agency and wealth that global tourism currently supports. Like many concepts and critical modalities, it appears that Orientalism has been liquefied and individualized in independent travel discourse, but the discursive and ideological patterns have changed little since *Orientalism* (Said, 1978) was released just shy of 30 years ago, in 1978.

The repetition of tourist-centric narrations in popular travel media aimed at independent tourists suggests that critical Orientalist theory has yet to make it out of the academy and into the travel section of the local bookstore. Given its relatively belated start as a focus for critical tourism theory, the BRG offers a necessary initial study to motivate a multifaceted critique of backpacker discourse because it solidifies self-focus among backpacker subcultures. However, tourism theory needs not only to 'catch up' with mobile touring cultures, but also to 'move on' by adopting a position on tourism that is reflexively subjective, remembering that tourism is not politically neutral. Backpacker research needs more critique to examine the intricate web of wealth, access and power that informs tourist interactions between pleasure and politics, global and local, self and other. An additional survey about backpacking by those who are familiar with the industry, but do not backpack, such as workers and locals, would complement the BRG's initial offering by providing a more balanced view of independent travel. Backpacker theory and practice need to realize and make visible repetitive omissions of non-tourist perspectives.

Many who are affected by tourism may not have the will, agency or literacy to fill in narrative gaps in backpacker discourse. This does not mean, however, that there are no moral or ideological 'holes' in the presentation and practice of backpacking. The ways that tourist others are construed or ignored visualize an imperial, Orientalist and colonialist legacy fuelling global leisure travel. Dismantling backpacker and tourist assumed 'truths' about the world searches for the 'scene of the other' to complement, inform and critique popular articulations of tourist-selves. The other side of the tourist coin, the 'local', the 'worker' and in some cases the 'terrorist', is given limited scope if any in the popular dissemination of tourism discourse. Balibar (2002: xiii) states that, 'The *other scene* of politics is also *the scene of the other*, where the visible – incomprehensible victims and enemies are located at the level of fantasy'.

Tourists are not the only identities involved in tourism; there is a less-often recognized infrastructure comprised of immobile locals and people at 'work' instead of 'leisure'. Voices of non-tourists are relatively invisible or imaginary in backpacker discourse. They appear as travel commodities rated on a scale of tourist satisfaction or as uncivilized, helpless or savage 'characters' that set the scene for a re-enactment of colonial narratives that place the traveller as hero/ protagonist. The tourist experience is rarely narrated with tourists in the background and local voices in the fore. Considering the way the 'scene of the other' is configured (or omitted) in backpacker theory and popular culture invites political discussions into a pleasurable realm. Leisure and pleasure have been allowed to shy away from politics for too long, given the histories of domination and power that inform leisure practices and discourses. Historical trajectories of power and marginalization are visualized when the other scene is given as much political weight as the backpacker 'scene of the self'.

References

Balibar, E. (2002) *Politics and the Other Scene.* Verso, London.

Bauman, Z. (2001) *The Individualized Society.* Polity Press, Cambridge, UK.

Berger, A.A. (2004) *Deconstructing Travel: Cultural Perspectives on Tourism.* AltaMira Press, Walnut Creek, California.

Berger, A.A. (2005) *Vietnam Tourism.* Haworth Hospitality Press, Birmingham, UK.

Bhabha, Homi K. (1990) The other question. In: Ferguson, R., Gever, M., Trinh Minh-ha and West, C. (eds) *Out There: Marginalization and Contemporary Cultures.* MIT Press, New York, pp. 71–80.

Cohen, E. (2004) Backpacking: diversity and change. In: Richards, G. and Wilson, J. (eds) *The Global Nomad: Backpacker Travel in Theory and Practice.* Channel View Publications, Clevedon, UK, pp. 43–59.

George, D. (2006) Defining moments in travel. In: Wheeler, T. (ed.) *Lonely Planet Blue List: 618 Things to Do and Places to Go, 06–07.* Lonely Planet Publications, Melbourne, Australia, pp. 10–13.

Hollinshead, K. (2004) Tourism and new sense. In: Hall, C.M. and Tucker, H. (eds) *Tourism and Postcolonialism.* Routledge, New York, pp. 25–42.

Kuhne, C. (2000) *On the Edge: Adventurous Escapades from Around the World.* Lonely Planet Publications, Footsgray, Melbourne, Australia.

Olsen, B. (1997) *World Stompers: a Guide to Travel Manifesto*, 3rd edn. CCC Publishing, San Francisco, California.

Richards, G. and Wilson, J. (eds) (2004a) *The Global Nomad: Backpacker Travel in Theory and Practice.* Channel View Publications, Clevedon, UK.

Richards, G. and Wilson, J. (2004b) Drifting towards the global nomad. In: Richards, G. and Wilson, J. (eds) *The Global Nomad: Backpacker Travel in Theory and Practice.* Channel View Publications, Clevedon, UK, pp. 3–13.

Richards, G and Wilson, J. (2004c) The global nomad: motivations and behavior of independent travellers worldwide. In: Richards, G. and Wilson, J. (eds) *The Global Nomad: Backpacker Travel in Theory and Practice.* Channel View Publications, Clevedon, UK, pp. 14–39.

Said, E. (1978) *Orientalism.* Random House, New York.

Sardar, Z. (1999) *Orientalism.* Open University Press, Buckingham, UK.

Smartraveller.gov.au Department of Foreign Affairs and Trade, Australian Government. Available at: http://smartraveller.gov.au/defer_all.html (accessed 28 April 2006) and also available at: http://smartraveller.gov.au/defer_all_non-essential.html (accessed 28 April 2006).

Smith, G. (2005) Tourism economy: the global landscape. In: Cartier, C. and Lew, A.A. (eds) *Seductions of Place: Geographical Perspectives on Globalization and Touristed Landscapes.* Routledge, New York, pp. 72–88.

Urry, J. (2000) *Sociology Beyond Societies; Mobilities for the Twenty-First Century.* Routledge, London.

Wheeler, T. (ed.) (2006) *Lonely Planet Bluelist: 618 Things to Do and Places to Go, 06–07.* Lonely Planet Publications, Melbourne, Australia.

9 Everyday Techno-social Devices in Everyday Travel Life: Digital Audio Devices in Solo Travelling Lifestyles

PETER M. BURNS AND MICHAEL O'REGAN

Introduction

The growing proliferation of digital information from place-bound desktops to pocket-sized portable digital technology has come to facilitate the mobility that characterizes modern society. Mobile technologies, from MP3 music players and mobile phones to PDAs, have made their users more networked, more connected, more secure and more mobile, freeing them and digital information from desktops, offices and homes, creating new relationships and meanings, and making information on the go indispensable to modern everyday existence.

> It is now a commonplace observation (to the point of weary cliché) that the explosive combination of tiny, inexpensive electronic devices, increasingly ubiquitous digital networking, and the world's rapidly growing stock of digital information is dramatically changing our daily lives.
>
> (Mitchell, 2002: 50)

While numerous studies have indicated mobile technologies, particularly mobile phones, are reconfiguring work, leisure, culture and the way social interactions take place, they have tended to ignore, downplay and avoid the importance of movable sound technologies, which are 'an immensely important part of everyday life' (O'Hara and Brown, 2006: 3). They are a rich part of an individual's life, now primarily mediated by technology from its conception, distribution, rendering, purchase and organization to how individuals choose to share, listen and interact with it. Since the advent of the Sony Walkman, on 1 July 1979, individuals have been quick to adopt and facilitate music on the go, changing the relationship between music and listener in quite fundamental ways. With the widespread adoption of the Internet, the digital MP3 audio format, online file sharing and digital technology in the late 1990s, the stage was set for a different type of movable sound technology.

During October 2001, Apple Inc. combined the existing technology of mini-drives with new software to create a digital audio device (MP3 player) called the iPod, which has since become an iconic digital music player brand (Bull, 2006b), selling over 110 million units in under 6 years and dominating the digital audio market for music listening on the go during home, transit, work and leisure time.

It is this use or crossover of personal technology with the travelscape which is at the core of this chapter. As a cultural artefact (Du Gay *et al.*, 1997) we examine the iPod from a socio-technical perspective in which neither social nor technical positions are privileged, utilizing the multidisciplinary approach of mobility studies – the 'social as mobility' (Urry, 2000: 2) – to examine how tourism and everyday life intersect in complex ways. This chapter investigates the effects of the iPod when merged with the mobility practised by budget travellers. Budget travel research itself often fails to capture the essence of 'everyday' traveller mobility, often seen as a temporary break from home and daily life routines with little focus on how budget travellers 'do' mobility with the help and support of mobile technologies, which for many extremely mobile groups (budget travellers, business people, academics) away from home for long periods of time take on a pivotal role in supporting that mobility. This chapter, then, follows the advice of Parrinello (2001: 214), who believes traveller mobility – 'historically made possible by technological developments and vastly increased by them' – should be analysed. Mobile computing and telecommunications technology's relationship with mobility holds the 'potential to transform everyday time and space', as well as change the rhythms of travel life including connections with others (Green, 2002: 281). According to Green (2002) '[s]ociologists are only just beginning to explore what the notion of "mobility" might mean when mediated through computing and communications technologies' (p. 281), potentially destabilizing existing cultural arrangements (Farnsworth and Austrin, 2005) and creating something of a cultural turn: a new form of culture in practice requiring fresh analysis and critique as social structures are 'produced and reproduced through mobility' (Nielsen, 2005: 53).

First, we shall look at the mobility of budget travellers and the mobility of objects. Secondly, we conceptually discuss the 'everyday' and, thirdly, we shall examine how the iPod allows its user to weave in and out of public space and virtual space (or cyberspace). Kohiyama (2005) and Graham (1998: 174) believe gateways to virtual places have been made omnipresent through iPods, laptops, mobile phones and places like Internet cafés, changing the way travellers experience place and even changing place in the process. Fourthly, we can begin to look at some of the consequences of travellers weaving in an out of these worlds. This is because, with the iPod, the public/private/virtual worlds intertwine, overlap, interact if not collide head on, causing new relationships, presences, absences, contexts and identities to change, emerge or be constrained (even if only temporarily). By examining how the iPod and mobilities blend together in the travelscape, we can examine the effects on a budget traveller's everyday activities, how they practise mobility, behaviour and management of everyday life and visualize the impact ubiquitous computing may have in the future.

From the Walkman to the iPod

Until the Sony Walkman's launch in July 1979, music had to be visited in a fixed place or brought on a ghetto blaster. The Walkman allowed its users to bring a fraction of their own music with them in portable, light devices, tapping into people's need for acoustic companionship (Bull, 2004b: 251), and it was a phenomenal success because it gave people what they wanted: their music – anytime and anywhere. If music was the factor that jump-started its success, then its legacy is the public 'solitary mobility' or 'headphone culture' that it generated and the start of mobile technology that was convenient, lightweight, wearable, portable and pocket-sized and wanted by many. While the Walkman was immensely successful, music changed again with the advent of a new file digital format called MP3 (Motion Picture Export Group-1 Audio Layer 3) in 1991. This triggered the shift from analogue to digital, impacting on patterns of music production, distribution and consumption (Boradkar, 2005). It is designed for mobility, easy storage, exchange and portability (Sterne, 2006: 345) while the CD was relatively immobile (Adey and Bevan, 2006: 49). The widespread take-up of the Internet and the introduction of MP3 computer software encoders and players helped MP3 playback and file sharing to flourish, replacing older methods of music sharing like mix-tapes (Voida *et al.*, 2006: 57). The usability of the Winamp Player (1997) for playback and Napster (1999) for illegal sharing of MP3s made it very easy for the average user to play, share and collect MP3s.

The introduction of the MP3 format also led the way for the introduction of the first MP3 player called the Diamond Rio in 1998. When launched by Diamond Multimedia, a lawsuit was brought against it by the Recording Industry Association of America (RIAA), which eventually failed, leading the way for the portable digital player market. In production terms, an iPod is simply the brand name for a portable digital audio music player released by Apple Inc. (formerly Apple Computer Inc.) in 2001 and is in generic form an MP3 player – a portable device that can store and play digital files, primarily audio – it is also a global object of mobility, having over 400 globally sourced parts (Linden *et al.*, 2007; Varian, 2007). Its parts, the finished product, its distribution and ultimately its use and user are all linked to the global 'space of flows' (Castells, 2004: 91). Its software, iTunes, was released in 2003 as a digital media player application, for organizing and playing digital files like music and video on personal computers and to interface with iPods. Since its release in 2001, the iPod remains the most popular MP3 player in the market – retaining over 80% of the market share of dedicated MP3 players sold, selling some 110 million (and counting) iPods worldwide. According to Madden (2006) 20% of American adults report ownership of an iPod or MP3 player. Research by Ofcom (the British communications industries regulator) suggests that household penetration of portable music players increased from 18% in December 2005 to 35% in March 2006 (Ofcom, 2007) while the International Federation of the Phonographic Industry (IFPI) (2007) state portable player sales totalled around 120 million units in 2006 and are expected to increase to 216 million units in 2007 (Bruno, 2007). For many, though, its success and popularity only began with the launch of the first iTunes store in April 2003, which allows iPod users to source music and other digital content. The first iTunes store was launched in the USA, allowing users (provided an Internet connection is present) to buy and download digital content like music, music videos, television shows, iPod games, podcasts and feature-length films for use on personal computers via the iTunes software application, which can then be transferred on to an iPod. Users can also upload content (such as CDs) for playback in a digital form for transfer to an iPod. Apple has partnered with the major record companies as well as movie and television companies to provide a vast amount of digital content. As of January 2007, the store has sold nearly 3 billion songs (1 billion in 2006 alone) and accounts for over 70% of worldwide online legal digital music sales. Since the launch of the American iTunes store in 2003, 21 other iTunes stores primarily based in developed world, industrialized countries have opened offering different content at different prices. This combination of the iPod and iTunes assemblage is manifested through its print, online and television advertisements, which simply end with the words 'iPod + iTunes', selling both mobility and a physical and virtual product. This is where online and offline marketing fuses into a single dialogue representing mobility and movement, reflecting traits in modern society – an association that has been so successful that many social commentators refer to today's generation of youth as the 'iPod generation', a generation that turns off 'faceless presenters' in favour of their own music, in their own way (Boradkar, 2005; Berry, 2006). These digital natives are used to participation and active control in their virtual lives, making the Internet and the iPod a very different medium from commercial radio and television, where 'corporations rather than people control the programming' (Boradkar, 2005).

The Mobility of Budget Independent Travellers and Techno-social Objects

Modern society is all about mobility, whether it be social mobility, mobile homes, mobile lives or multiple careers and money. The path towards individualization and mobility is in accordance with an increasing orientation towards post-material values of consumption and a diversification of lifestyles (Weber, 2004). Mobility, an inherent quality of globalization and of modernity, is characterized by movement and is arguably an integral part of modern travel. A particular category of mobility can be associated with the travel lives of budget travellers (backpackers, vagabonds, gap year travellers), falling within the realm of extreme mobility as they move from geographic location to geographic location with a constant high rate of change in their local environment highlighted by freedom of movement, capacity for risk and unpredictability. Even though extreme mobility is practised by many, much of it may be forced or coerced mobility (refugees, sex slaves), so that those who practise extreme mobility for leisure or business are a privileged minority (mobility for the minority). For many budget travellers 'there is an underlying drive for something not ordinary, a drive for mobility as an extraordinary experience' (D'Andrea, 2006: 106). Globalization has allowed them to overcome spatial barriers as they continuously move from place to place, travelling where they want in the world usually without restriction, doing what they want and covering great distances. MacCannell (1999: 1) and Urry (1997: 9) both note that acting as a tourist is one of the defining characteristics of being modern and tourism has a part in exporting that modernity worldwide.

The scale of contemporary travelling is immense, and can provide the context both for the environmental critique of 'hypermobility' and for the belief that travel has become central to contemporary socialites (Urry, 2002a: 257). There were 842 million international tourist arrivals in 2006, up from 766 million in 2004 while arrivals worldwide are expected to grow on average 4% through 2020 (UNWT0, 2007). In recent years, the gap year, mid-career travel and post-retirement travel have led to a growing number of independent travellers. According to research conducted between the United Nations World Tourism Organization (UNWTO) and the World Youth and Student Educational (WYSE) Travel Confederation, travellers between the ages of 16 and 24 accounted for more than 20% of international tourists during 2006 (Richards, 2007). While their form of travel has long been associated with leaving home, work, family, friends and/or life crises for months and years rather than days and weeks, this has now become an idea that many people aspire to, with mid-career and post-retirement budget independent travel growing increasingly popular. While numbers are an important indicator of mobility, budget travellers dwell in mobilities to varying degrees. Kakihara and Sørensen (2002: 1–2) argue that, while much debate on mobility is primarily concerned with human corporeal travel, the significance of mobility in modern society encompasses much broader aspects of human everyday activities. They point out that, apart from the geographical movement of the human body on foot, by car, train, aeroplane or other means of transportation, several other aspects of mobility in the modern society can be considered including the mobility of objects. The travel of objects is intertwined with human dwelling and travelling norms. Lury (1997: 83, original emphasis) believes 'objects move in relations of travelling-in-dwelling *and* relations of dwelling-in-travelling in the practices of global cosmopolitanism'. More conspicuously, this can be seen in the case of technological mobile devices, which indicates interplay between corporeal and object travel. It has been argued that we have 'entered a new nomadic age' (Makimoto and Manners, 1997: 2; cited in Urry, 2000: 28), believing '[o]ver the next decade, with digitalisation, most of the facilities of home and the office will be carried around on the body or at least in a small bag, making those that can afford such objects "geographically independent"' (Urry, 2000: 28). According to Urry (2002b: 6):

> Indeed I would suggest that the twenty first century will be the century of 'inhabited machines', machines inhabited by individuals or very small groups of individuals. It is through the inhabiting of such machines that humans will come to 'life'. Further, machines only function because they are so inhabited; they are machines only when one or more humans come to inhabit them. Such machines come to 'life' when they are humanly inhabited. These inhabited machines are miniaturised, privatised, digitised and mobilised. . . . Such machines are desired for their style, smallness, lightness and demonstrate a physical form often closely interwoven with the corporeal.

Mejias (1999, original emphasis) believes modernity perceives 'technologies as part of a factual reality that is not only beyond value considerations, but is in fact intrinsically *good*', considering not only the material but also its non-human agents, immobilities and immaterial dimensions. Du Gay *et al.* (1997) described the connections between the Walkman, launched in 1979, and the culture of late-modernity, believing it to be styled for a modern lifestyle – for movement, for mobility – 'is testimony to the high value which the culture of late-modernity places on mobility' (p. 24). Du Gay *et al.* (1997: 24) believed this mobility is 'both real and symbolic', fitting a world in which people are literally moving about more, created an age of consumers hungry for new initiatives in mobile technology (Buckley, 2001: 555).

> It is virtually an extension of the skin. It is fitted, moulded, like so much else in modern consumer culture, to the body itself. . . . It is designed for movement – for mobility, for people who are always out and about, for travelling light. It is part of the required equipment of the modern 'nomad'.
>
> Du Gay *et al.* (1997: 23–24)

In a society constantly on the move, books, newspapers and movable sound technologies (which are not as consumable or disposable as books and newspapers on journeys that last months, not weeks) are a constant companion for people. According to Kakihara and Sørensen (2002) these portable technologies will make people 'geographically independent', being 'free to live where they want and travel as much as they want', and thus they will be forced to consider whether they are settlers or true 'global nomads' (Kakihara and Sørensen, 2002). Everything from a traveller's total music collection to favourite web applications and digital pictures becomes portable including memories, extending the footprint of their homes and even reaffirming a sense of identity and perhaps a kind of virtual proximity with home. Sterne (2006: 339–340) believes while the 'iPod is a triumph of industrial design and consumer marketing . . . there is a subset of mp3 players purchased more out of the desire for a status symbol than for their utility, just as with cellphones before them, and e-mail addresses before that'. A study from Reppel *et al.* (2006: 249) found that an important aspect of the iPod is the generated feelings of pride and the good feelings that one gets from owning it, very much relating to the concept of 'impression management' – the process through which people try to control the impressions other people form of them by regulating and controlling information in social interaction and owning the latest technology may increase its user's interiority (personality, personal trait, substance and distinctiveness), thereby highlighting individuality.

In the rite-of-passage model that Victor Turner (1978) adopted from the Van Gennep book, *The Rites of Passage* (1960), in the 1970s, there are three stages to the 'rite-of-passage': separation; liminality; and incorporation – the liminal phase being the period between states during which people have left one place or state but haven't yet entered or joined the next. Turner noted that, in liminality, individuals did not belong to the society that they previously were a part of and they were not yet reincorporated into that society. This concept has long been associated with budget travellers including Graburn (1983), Jamieson (1996), Mason (2002), Cohen and Noy (2006) and O'Reilly (2006). Cohen (2003) believes the rite of passage is a useful heuristic device to interpret the dynamics and function of budget travelling, but points out several areas which mitigate its applicability, noting specifically the use of mobile phones and e-mail among budget travellers indicating that the transformation or reversal of 'everyday life' is not complete. Coleman and Eade (2004), who examined pilgrimage, have also criticized Turner's work due to his assertion that pilgrimage was, by its liminal nature, extraordinary and not part of everyday life.

Therefore, it is not safe to say that travellers automatically leave their home lives behind or that they overtly resist continuing their home, school or work routines or having their work and work lives blend/interfere in their performance as travellers during their travel experience. Many travellers are under greater obligation from family, friends and co-travellers to be 'reachable' and 'stay in touch' (Jansson, 2006), but, on the other hand, for a minority there may be a resistance to those objects and behaviours practised in their everyday lives, where new routines may be born. As Turner and Turner state '[t]he pilgrim undergoes a number of transformations, in which previous orderings of thought and behaviour are subject to revision and criticism and unprecedented modes of ordering relations between ideas and people become possible and desirable' (cited in Mason, 2002: 95). How can one differentiate between these two seemingly polarized perspectives regarding technology use during the travel experience? While the camera is a very different technology used rarely in capturing everyday existence (Kontogeorgopoulos, 2003), studies of budget travellers' use of cameras oscillate from limited use (Maoz, 2006) to perpetuation of iconic images (Jenkins, 2003) with limited reference to traveller performance. Early seminal work by Erik Cohen in the 1970s on 'drifters' shows that they are seen by many (O'Reilly, 2006) as representing an idealized or 'classical' style of budget travel. His drifter 'is an individualist, disdainful of ideologies . . . the drifter's escapism is hedonistic and often anarchist' (Cohen, 1973: 91–92). Research from Cohen and others, while still recognizing budget travel as a distinct type of contemporary tourism, also realizes they are not a homogeneous category (Noy and Cohen, 2005: 22) with many different forms of budget travel, which doesn't imply a structural determinism or typology but a continuum. So budget travellers move back and forth on a continuum between technology and non-technology use, a choice that 'becomes a vehicle for transmitting identity, by undertaking a particular form of travel, in a particular style' (Edensor, 2001: 74).

There have been many attempts to separate the conduct (rather than type) of tourists on this basis. Erik Cohen (1979) suggested that there are five different modes of touristic experience, ranging from superficial journeys in search of mere pleasure to profound journeys in search of meaning. These he calls the 'Recreational Mode', the 'Diversionary Mode', the 'Experiential Mode', the 'Experimental Mode' and the 'Existential Mode'. Cohen's drifter or idealized independent traveller (in experimental mode/existential mode) strived more than the ordinary tourist to reach places and people that are 'really' authentic, and 'would display considerable touristic angst that places or events that appear authentic are in fact staged' (Cohen, 2004: 46). Plog classified travellers as either psychocentric (to indicate those tourists who travelled short distances and sought out the familiar) or those he called allocentric (for people who travelled long distances to seek out different environments and cultures) (Plog, 1972; cited in Mason, 2002: 96). Shaffer (2004) proposes a distinction between 'culture back-packers' and 'leisure backpackers' while Urry distinguishes between two types of tourist gaze, the solitary 'romantic' gaze and the collective gaze (2003: 119). Jansson (2006), using Ateljevic's (2000) 'circuits of tourism' framework of social structuration, identifies certain lifestyle patterns among travellers and their use of technology, namely: the adventurer; the immersive; and the performative or tra-ditional traveller; each relating to technologies in different ways. The adventurer, according to Jansson, seeks new experiences in new environments (without seri-ous risk) primarily for the sake of personal challenge and arousal, and this may lead to a total rejection or total adoption of technology in order to put him or her self 'on the line' (Jansson, 2006). The immersive travellers share many features with those drifters or psychocentric travellers described by Plog and the cosmo-politan mobility portrayed by Lash and Urry (1994: 309). They identified features including 'extensive patterns of real and simulated mobility' and a:

> curiosity about all places, peoples and cultures and at least a rudimentary ability to map such places and cultures historically, geographically and anthropologically; an openness to other peoples and cultures and a willingness/ability to appreciate some elements of the language/culture of the place that is being visited; a willingness to take risks by virtue of moving outside the tourist environmental bubble. . .
>
> Lash and Urry (1994: 309)

According to Jansson (2006), the immersive type involves an ambition to be connected to local networks, trying not to reveal any expressions of the tourist gaze, and/or trigger the 'local gaze' (Maoz, 2006) by being 'on the same level', which may mean not utilizing or showing technology which would distort the 'authentic' texture of the interaction by presenting anti-materialistic, Western identities. This relates to the way that some budget travellers consider taking pictures of certain sites and locals as too 'touristy' (Maoz, 2006: 229). Finally, Jansson (2006) describes the performative (traditional) traveller who travels in a contextual mode emphasizing leisure activities and social events over cultural authenticity. He makes a distinction between performative travellers, who may use technology for enhancing the sense of liminal performativity for coordinating 'social activities within the tourist setting, and the desire to immediately share memorable moments and bodily performances with family and new and old friends', and traditional traveller use of technology. Such traditional use 'is not so much about producing social interaction and performance as it is about repro-ducing the classical pattern of touristic rituals' (Jansson, 2006) like taking photo-graphs at certain sites and situations and refusing to bring mobile phones, not wearing a watch, refusing to visit Western franchised restaurants like McDonald's or refusing to watch television.

From this analysis, while agreeing that budget travellers have much 'mobility and network capital', different travellers conduct, manage or perform mobility differently. To simplify the above, outward-looking, immersive or traditional budget travellers who avoid technology, its over use or its overt use, downplay their mobility capital or potential for mobility in various ways, through mobility choices and activities. By travelling on local (and probably slower) transport, eating local market food rather than patronizing tourist restaurants (global franchises where the food may have been sourced globally), staying with locals or within heterogeneous accommodation (Edensor, 2001), they incorporate a construction of identity through mobility performance and related mobility activity choice. In a transport choice metaphor, transport choice by budget travellers (given that access, cost and so on are not factors) is complex (Vance, 2004) as choice is not based on speed alone. Outward-looking travellers may choose the slower method as it may provide 'different experiences, performances and affordances . . . of moving, socialising and seeing' (Urry, 2004), with Kain and King (2004: 198) stating budget travellers may walk 'rather than taking taxis or local transport', providing a 'complex sensuous relationality' between the traveller and transport choice (Urry, 2004). Travellers have different experiences of a journey depending on their travel mode and activities. Movement itself can 'become a performance through which we make statements about ourselves and acquire status' (Pooley *et al.*, 2005: 15) as 'leisure and tourism consumption serves as an arena for social differentiation and the expression of identity' (Ateljevic and Doorne, 2003: 123). On the other hand, performative, inward-looking budget travellers (those who may be on short-term breaks, those in groups, those who value sharing their experiences locally/immediately taking full advantage of their 'mobility and network capital') may stay along the 'beaten tracks' or networks of mobility in familiar hostels, eat familiar food in familiar places (Starbucks, McDonald's), take 'backpacker' transport and tours, prefer the company of other like-minded budget travellers, and make full use of technology from digital cameras to phones and transport opportunities (aeroplanes) to speed up 'space–time compression'. Therefore, objects of mobility play an important role in traveller performance and identity.

From Everyday Lives to Everyday Travel Lives

Foth and Adkins (2005) state that place-based units such as 'home', 'work' and 'school' remain at the core of our understanding of everyday life, with much tourism theory from MacCannell (1999) to Urry (1990), Lengkeek (2001) and Suvantola (2002) contrasting tourism with home geographies and 'everydayness'. Tourist destinations are often seen as liminal spaces, as outlined by Turner (1974) and Shields (1991: 84); liminality according to Turner 'represents a liberation from the regimes of normative practices and performance codes of mundane life' where the routines and regulations of everyday life can be avoided (Rojek, 1993). Graburn (1989) believed tourism removes the individual from the ordinary everyday work and home life while Cohen (1979: 181) stated 'that tourism is essentially a temporary reversal of everyday activities – it is a no-work, no-care, no-thrift situation', where the budget traveller goes 'abroad to get away from his homeland' (Cohen, 1973: 91). Elsrud (1998: 324) believes '[m]any of the routines of everyday life at home are lost once the traveller starts moving' and 'new "traveller-routines" are created along the journey', but are routines also brought with travellers? In most of the everyday-life literature 'everydayness' is characterized by repetition, habitual practices, obligations and reproduction; a certain '[r]eflexivity refers to the mutual assumptions one carries into interaction that are built up and institutionalized over time' (Ling, 1997: 4). As Edensor (2005: 80–81) says: '[t]he ways in which we move through the city are generally part of that everyday practice through which unreflexive, routinized sequences of movement are performed' and '[s]ince these routines are repetitive, they tend to reinforce notions about what constitutes the common-sense and the unquestioned' strengthening 'affective and cognitive links' and consolidating 'a sense of shared natural habits and *doxa* to constitute a habitus, including acquired skills which minimise unnecessary reflection every time a decision is required'. The move from strict categorization between work, home and tourism has broken down or blurred these categories, and therefore tourism requires fresh analysis. The traveller's ability to use information and communications technology (ICT) and technology is taken as a given as their home societies see it as a prerequisite to living and working in the 'information society' and 'the indispensable grammar of modern life' (Selwyn, 2003: 99–100). It is assumed that technology is transforming all aspects of society including leisure as it is an 'inherently desirable and beneficial activity for all individuals' and 'to not use ICT is to choose not to be part of the information society – an irrational and ultimately disadvantageous position to adopt' (Selwyn, 2003: 106).

Our interpretation of technology use by budget travellers is based on a continuum of performances from use to non-use, relating to mobility as a performance. The iPod is not overtly visible, cumbersome or intrusive and so requires 'little thought or planning, it is just something that is done on a daily basis and the routine nature of such movment means that it disappears from view' (Pooley *et al.*, 2005: 35). It can slip easily into the rhythms of daily home and travel lives, constructed within their 'notions of mobility in their everyday lives and practice', which 'actively contribute to justifying and maintaining specific patterns of travel choice and behaviour' (Thomsen *et al.*, 2005: 2). For many travellers, then, '[t]he use of sound may be part of an everyday, habitual praxis of reflexive management of self and environment' (Edensor, 2003: 161; paraphrasing De Nora, 2000). Lie and Sørensen outline how technologies are integrated into the practices of everyday by individuals both adopting and adapting technologies, allowing individuals to make efforts 'to shape their lives through creative manipulation of artefacts, symbols and social systems in relation to their practical needs and competencies' (Lie and Sørenson, 1996: 9; cited in Michael, 2000: 9). Edensor (2001: 61) argues that 'tourists carry quotidian habits and responses with them: they are part of their baggage', reinforcing the notions of 'dwelling-in-travel' and 'travelling-in-dwelling' (Clifford, 1997) and the role of daily rituals, routines, habits, objects, (mobile) technologies and interactions. Berger (1984: 64) believes that the idea of a physically centred home has been transformed by extreme mobility to 'a far more mobile notion . . . a home which can be taken along whenever one decamps' (Rapport, 1997: 73). Edensor (2001: 61) states that '[t]he growing social and economic importance of leisure and a blurring between work and leisure in post-Fordist economies further obscures the distinction between tourism and the everyday' while 'tourist practices abound with their own habitual enactments, and tourism is never entirely separate from the habits of everyday life, since they are unreflexively embodied in the tourist'.

For many, there is little or no pre-travel consideration as to whether one should bring the iPod on an extended trip in comparison to the often more considered deliberations about using items like a mobile phone in order to guard against remote intervention and intrusion (Bohn *et al.*, 2004). In comparison, pre-iPod travellers during the days of the Walkman had to consider the weight of CDs and cassettes and the risk of losing their entire music collections to theft and loss. For Jamal and Hill (2002: 101–102) the travelscape is a stage where the iPod would be a prop, and if we were to:

> focus on all the elements of a staged production that impact on its authenticity, from the physical, objective props to the actors and directors who construct a performance, to the audience, which ultimately judges the performance, whether or not in terms of authenticity

travellers might feel little deliberation was required in bringing it. Pre-travel choices, then, to use mobile technology and especially miniaturized, portable devices that have fitted easily into home and work routines will very easily slip into travel lives, unlike bulkier and more visible items like laptops and camcorders, which cannot be secured easily while on the move and which cannot be kept permanently on your person. According to research by Bull (2006a: 132) iPod users disliked using mobile phones regularly, which he believes may relate to the:

> continuous nature of the iPod use through which the user constructs an auditory cocoon around them which in itself is often experienced as empowering as contrasted to the discontinuous nature of mobile phone use whereby the user is always potentially at the beck and call of others.

This reminds one of Nietzsche and his view that the letter is an unannounced visit and the postman an agent of rude surprises (cited in Hollingdale, 1977: 279). That is not to say that an iPod does not intervene in its user's everyday life. iPods also metaphorically drag individuals back to people, places and memories, expanding 'lived spaces of its users beyond their real locations' (Kellerman, 2006: 98) but not visibly, forcefully or intrusively.

If travellers bring those music-packed iPods and playlists they associate with home, work and in-between travel places, with these places referring to 'routine sets of practice, rather than fixed places' (Coleman and Eade, 2004: 5), are they presenting a musical identity and reliving old routines in new spaces, living within a chosen musical soundtrack that is out of sync with their present surroundings? Pearce (2000), Bull (2003, 2004a, b), Edensor (2003) and Sheller (2004a) all acknowledge the power of music to control space, create routine and conjure up past memories while mobile in automobiles as 'music possesses a host of cultural and individual associations' (Edensor, 2003: 163). Pearce (2000: 163) describes how listening to hours of contemporary and 'retro' music while driving long distances 'becomes an emotional palimpsest of past and future, in which events and feelings are recovered and, most importantly, rescripted from the present moment in time' as the drivers are suspended in motorways (similar to the suspension in those 'in-between' transit places in Western society). Music helps the travellers to explore 'various fantasies of home' (Pearce, 2000: 178). Boradkar (2005) states that the iPod affords the possibility of creating special 'soundtracks' to accompany routine activities from riding on a bus to working out in a gym, believing that playlists allow 'one-to-one correspondences between music and activity in terms of genre', signifying a practice that 'makes sense of the technology, the object, as well as the activity'. They are out of step, out of sync with the world around them, similar to the introduction of railway travel and how it altered visual perception '[a]s people became accustomed to train travel, traditional perception was replaced by "panoramic perception"' (Ross, 1995: 38): the kind of perception that prevails when the viewer sees objects and landscapes through the apparatus that moves him or her through the world (Larsen, 2001). Panoramic perception occurs when the viewer no longer belongs to the same space as the perceived object; as such, it pertains as much to the car driver as to the railway traveller. Like other mobility objects, the car or railway, the iPod user places himself or herself out of sync with the world, disjointed from the movement of those co-present, no longer in the same world as those they perceive.

The iPod and Everyday Travel Lives

Crary (1999: 1) points out that people do not require technology to exclude the immediate environment, highlighting that focus on anything from an opera performance to a computer screen allows us to exclude external stimuli, but the untethering of digital information and portable technologies has allowed individuals to exclude stimuli while on the move, expanding the times and places where/when these switches might be made (Bassett, 2003, 2005). According to Boradkar (2005) many aspects of mobile behaviour are heavily technologized, and this has made it easier to create private domains to withdraw into while being on display in the public realm, reshaping that public space, producing and reconfiguring human interaction (Farnsworth and Austrin, 2005), which in turn reconfigures 'the social rules around how such private and public boundaries are negotiated, along with the rituals and ceremonies around the use of these devices' (Farnsworth and Austrin, 2005: 16). Mobile technology and its interaction with humans, society and mobilities have the potential to produce new forms of behaviour, interaction and sociality. While travellers have always interacted with machines from transportation and automated teller machines (ATMs) to maps (which have their own embedded virtualizations), the use of mobile technologies, their continuous use as both a privatizing technology and a portal to virtual space, is new.

The 'ability to carry your auditory identity in the palm of your hand as you move from one place to another is a relatively recent event in the history of mobile sound technologies' (Bull, 2006a: 131) and Chambers (1994), Bull (2000) and Anderson and De Paula (2006) have looked at the effects of its introduction and use. Chambers (1994) suggested that, by bringing what was conventionally conceived of as a private act – private listening – into public spaces, the Walkman disturbed the boundaries between the private and public worlds (Du Gay et al., 1997: 142). Michael Bull's work is based on 'variants of urban theory as reference points' (Bull, 2006a: 133) and on the work of Georg Simmel (1949, 2004) and other urban studies theorists. Bull (2005: 352) emphasizes the struggle between the private and the public in a city full of strangers, crowds, noise, constant stimulation and awkward contact.

Simmel was perhaps the first sociologist to attempt to explain the significance and desire of urban citizens to maintain a sense of privacy, to create a mobile bubble, while on the move (Bull, 2005: 352). This was because he and many other urban theorists saw city life as primarily negative (Bull, 2006a: 133), providing a rationale as to why people may want to incorporate strategies into their lives in order to manage or resist being overwhelmed by the constant stimulation of the city, ease urban angst (Boradkar, 2005) and 'control or neutralise these negative experiences' (Bull, 2006a: 133). But, since the launch of the iPod, the ability of its users to weave in and out of public and private worlds has been a concern to social commentators (Du Gay et al., 1997; Bull, 2000). According to Bull (2004c) the search for public privacy has led to 'a discounting of the "public" realm', making public spaces conform to their notion of the 'domestic' or the 'intimate'; either literally or conceptually, its use is relational. Bull (2006a: 133) believes these relational experiences have three dimensions: the cognitive (how the user manages their moods and thoughts to music); the aesthetic (how they construct their relationship to the outside world); and the moral (how users relate to other people). Whether the description of iPod use is isolating or insulating, Hatton believes solitude may be a better word, as isolation is a state of nature imposed on the individual while solitude is out of choice (Hatton, 1998; cited in Chambers, 1994: 49).

Bull uses an auditory-based explanation to offer a typology of strategies that iPod users might use to exert 'control', many of them in direct response to the (urban) environment (Boradkar, 2005), but notes that users might switch strategies on any one journey (Bull, 2006a: 133). The strategies of control from Bull (2000, 2006a) are summarized below. iPod users can listen to their own music even in areas bereft of people or noise, and can also block external sound, creating their own auditory bubble to gain their own sense of space and deal with the close proximity of unknown others using music to 'aestheticize' their experience in filmic terms. Users can also eliminate any external stimuli, effectively placing themselves elsewhere. While Bassett (2005) would argue that the mobile phone is a prime example of how individuals can (potentially) disengage, we would argue that an iPod allows individuals far easier and quicker opportunities to exclude local stimuli, simply by slipping on a pair of headphones. Users can also use the device to allay feelings of isolation or loneliness and control unwanted thoughts and feelings and to control interaction with others. This goes back to Simmel's account of the urban experience and the ways in which people cope with the 'inflicted co-presence' of others by creating private spaces in public in order to avoid interaction and the gaze of others (Haddon, 2000). Users can also use the iPod as a method of regaining control over their time and, importantly, the iPod can represent a form of biographical travelling, allowing the user to reconstruct narrative memories at will. According to Boradkar (2005) iPods contain fragments of other spaces and places, giving us 'the ability to transport our cherished environments with us, no matter where we might be'.

Bull (2005: 353) concludes that 'a personalised soundworld through iPod use creates a form of accompanied solitude for its users in which they feel empowered, in control and self-sufficient'. This is not to say private listening is a good or bad thing. It has met an important need for people whose modern work and social lives require privatized listening and for many 'illustrates the ways in which experiences of technology can be as intense and moving as any experience of art' (Blythe and Wright, 2005). Yet solitary mobile technology such as the iPod represents an extraordinary contradiction in contemporary social life. On one level it is extremely social in the home (when its audio content is piped through external speakers or video through the television set) as well as allowing connectivity to globally sourced music; but at the same time it is anti-social insofar as face-to-face communication is hindered in the public/social spheres. In effect it causes 'absent presence', which can be loosely defined as people that are physically there, next to you, but, because of their technology, have no interaction with anyone else. So a paradox exists as spatial 'forms of association, integration and solidarity are both weakened and strengthened by technological and communicational extension' (Russell and Holmes, 1996).

> They are weakened because our life world no longer involves negotiating physical spaces with the same proximity that occurred before the rise of technological extension. They are strengthened in that we can simulate the properties of those spaces with ever-greater control.
>
> (Russell and Holmes, 1996)

By control we mean control over their immediate environment. Whether it is in a crowded bus, street, standing in line at the airport or standing in a queue, iPod users can feel that not everything, at least, is out of their control. These issues regarding the isolating effects of movable sound technologies and music are also of concern to those who study public spaces, the workplace and the travelscape. While mobile sound technologies may give people more personal freedom and control over their environment, they can also make them less connected to others. According to Voida (2005), Voida *et al.* (2005) and Haake (2006), using headphones (in a workplace study) can create frustration among non-listeners who wish to communicate and, while many respondents in the study believed that music induced positive mood and led to improved work performance (increased capability to deal with stressful situations), it also led to a decrease in social interaction. In the context of tourism, iPod use takes on moral dimensions concerning the level of commitment, engagement or immersion travellers are able to achieve in foreign cultures (Germann Molz, 2006).

The iPod does serve a need in diverse places where personal space is a bit compromised like the airport, the plane, the bus and/or queues but it is difficult to interrupt a traveller who is listening to an iPod (Bull, 2005, 2006a). While the same holds true of interrupting anyone involved in a telephone conversation, the act of writing a letter home or reading a book, the iPod is very different. According to Goffman (cited by Powell, 2004) from time to time the routine of 'public privacy' can be broken and people who were strangers can strike up conversations. Usually, these interactions occur when someone was placed in what Goffman calls an 'exposed position' – that is, when a physical, verbal or technological anomaly opens up the possibility for a social interaction. There are far fewer exposed positions while a person is listening to an iPod as they are more physically separated from other travellers by ear buds and music than if they were reading a book or writing a postcard. Now that MP3 players can connect wirelessly to the Internet (the current Sansa Connect MP3 player allows its users to see what their Yahoo Instant Messenger buddies are listening to) they can live *and* interact in virtual space. Jain and Lyons (2006: 125) states that '[t]he incorporation of mobile ICT into everyday social practices specifically provides a new trajectory for travel time use'. While they are physically present, their attention is focused on something 'not you' – you are in another place (absent presence). We know little of what an iPod wearer is listening to as it is only when their batteries run low or the user decides to take the headphones off that you have the opportunity to connect with them. Old headphones leaked music to those nearby while external stimuli leaked in, but today's modern noise-cancelling headphones are moulded to a user's ear; so we can only wonder at whether they are listening to a podcast, walking tour or music. Unlike books it is near impossible to catch a glimpse (with privacy screen protectors available) of an iPod screen to see what is been played. It doesn't provide the voyeur, the interested or the co-present the smallest hint or information about their playlists or songs and so they cannot extrapolate anything about their personalities, while an open book, a CD cover or a book cover lets those co-present, those we share a room with in a hostel or travel beside on a bus know a bit of who their travel companions are. But 'by his [sic] white wires, he is indicating he [sic] doesn't really want to know you' (Sullivan, 2005), hiding the personal technology in the accommodation safes when not in use or watching it recharge.

Isolation from the public travelscape and soundscape

Graham (2003: 155) believes social inequalities tend to be reinforced by unevenness in access to both electronic and physical forms of mobility. This is because the mobility of the iPod as an object has led to increased distinction between inclusion and exclusion, between insider and outsider and between traveller and host in the travelscape. The iPod provides its user with the ability to control space and with that control comes power as mobility and power are intertwined (Bauman, 2000). Graham (2003: 155–156) and Coleman and Eade (2004: 6) outlined the work of Massey (1993), who identified three main groups within this broad and uneven picture. First, she identified those who are 'hyper-mobile', who tend to be in control of the 'space–time compression' – dominant business leaders, media companies and affluent Western tourists. Secondly, she identified those who communicate and travel a great deal but aren't in control; and, thirdly, there are those who are on the receiving end or are excluded from these processes. Locals who can't afford the same physical and electronic mobility may be in this third category and coming into contact with travellers who are more mobile than them can lead to locals feeling degraded and humiliated. Graham (1997: 25) believes 'technologies of freedom' tend to be only available to already powerful social groups. Another reason, other than uneven access, may be the effect iPod use has in times of co-presence, which may affect relationship dynamics. Urry (2002b: 259) believes co-presence affords access to the eyes and eye contact enables the establishment of intimacy and trust, as well as insincerity and fear, power and control, but according to Bull (2005, 2006a) and Raybeck (cited in Taylor, 2005) the iPod is taking away this intimate eye contact. According to Raybeck, human beings need the kind of acknowledgement the iPod people are taking away. They engage in what Bull calls 'non-reciprocal looking' or 'civil inattention' as coined by Goffman. The user looks at others as if they were looking at objects with which they have no human involvement, as if they were not at all there, 'as objects not worthy of a glance, let alone close scrutiny' (Goffman, 1963). Sound 'looking' becomes both voyeuristic and omnipotent, whereby the viewing subject 'disappears' into an unobserved gaze, its users not imagining themselves in the shoes of those they observe (Bull, 2005: 350). Bull (2002: 88) says this 'looking' confers greater powers on the subject; as auditory looking substantially differs from non-auditory looking and in doing so escapes the reciprocal gaze (the local gaze). Whatever they are looking at, whether it is co-travellers in an airport, locals at a market or a beggar on the street, what their mind sees and consequently their mood is affected by is what they are listening to. They employ the iPod as a shield to manage their encounters with others and to establish a boundary between themselves and others. The iPod, in fact, may now be to people watching what sunglasses used to be (Kidd, 2005) in that you can stare, look away or meet other glances without detection or obligation, in virtual animosity destroying a degree of intimacy, equal status and trust. The iPod does not account for the unique cultural differences that may exist between everyday life and tourism. The iPod, while empowering, breeds 'a terror of direct experience' (Rosen, 2005: 71), allowing travellers to weave out of (potential) interaction and challenges that are posed by difficult or inconvenient expressions of culture. Whether they're conscious of it or not, travellers are erecting a defensive barrier against the new and alien by retreating into their own personal worlds. King and Spearitt (2001) ask why go to an island resort 'if fax, e-mail and mobile connections follow you about? Are patrons seeking escape, isolation and seclusion, or merely another setting in which to act out established or novel aspects of their lives?' (King and Spearitt, 2001: 250).

When travellers are using an iPod, they are not on the street sharing the communal experience of life. It makes them feel 'always at home' but this is in conflict with travellers' supposed inquisitiveness and their yearning to see, feel, touch and experience something new. When you block out public sound, you have the privilege of your own personal soundtrack, but you drown out all the travel destinations noise and character (Sacks, 2005). The 'acoustic experience of the streetscape has the ability to weave individuals into the fabric of everyday life' (Cranny-Francis, 2005: 73). Travel soundings include what may be considered sentimental – different languages, accents, the laughter of others, unfamiliar birds, background music, loud radios, hawkers (Flinn, 2005) – but they also include the ugliness one encounters when travelling – random exchanges with beggars, street children, overheard conversations, the hustle and bustle that makes a place. One of the more important aspects of travel is staying constantly engaged with your surroundings, physically, mentally and through omnipresent smells and sounds –'[t]he power of the acoustic sense is present even where there is an ominous silence' (Urry, 2000: 100–101). Georges Perec in his book *Espèces d'espaces* (1974), translated as *Species of Spaces and Other Pieces* (1997), attributes extreme importance to the everyday – the trivial, the insignificant, the things we generally do not notice, the thing that doesn't draw attention to itself, the banal, the background ordinary details of a life – and suggests that maybe people should reflect on the ordinary as extraordinary. John Frow's (1997: 91) analysis of Judith Adler's *Annals of Tourism* research article – 'The origins of sightseeing' (Adler, 1989; cited in Frow, 1997) – noted that the aristocratic traveller during the Renaissance period went abroad for discourse rather than for picturesque views or scenes. Travel was about 'learning foreign tongues, obtaining access to foreign courts, and conversing gracefully with eminent men, assimilating classical texts, appropriate to particular sites' (Adler, 1989: 3; cited in Frow, 1997) but the 16th and 17th centuries saw a shift towards an 'eye' approach, to experience a 'direct, unmediated, and personally verified experience' (Adler, 1989: 11; cited in Frow, 1997: 91). Now an iPod and its non-human agents can help its user learn foreign languages, contain e-books and travel information. While we do not counteract Urry (2002c) and his 'tourist gaze' metaphor, that the experience of looking at places is a key aspect of the tourist experience, whereby 'the view from the car, train or plane and the experience of passing through new places becomes of itself a leisure activity' (Pooley *et al.*, 2005: 17), the iPod and other devices will increasingly mediate all aspects of an experience – a development that is worrying given the importance of stimulating all five senses while travelling (Perkins and Thorns, 2001).

In-between places

According to Anderson and De Paula (2006), Bassoli and Martin (2006) and Bassoli *et al.* (2006) most ethnographic studies for businesses viewed transitional spaces and movements in Western society as 'non-places' or momentary space–time between activities increasingly associated with 'cocooning' products such as iPods. They examined the Tube in London, and found it was 'full of people staring: up at advertisements, down at shoes, off into space while listening to music'. Marc Augè (2002: 7) talks about this kind of experience as 'collectivity without festival and solitude without isolation' where people acknowledge the presence of others, then avoid them to show they are not a threat. But is such behaviour required in the travelscape, where the culture and context may be very different? These studies look at such periods as either 'dead time' or opportunities for economic productivity (Jara-Diaz, 2000; Mackie *et al.*, 2001) rather than looking at them for 'positive utility' (Lyons *et al.*, 2007), an 'aid to thought' (De Botton, 2003: 58) and an opportunity to network and interact. Are urban space, public transport, dead time and productive time objectively the same all over the world or does it depend on context? What is true for transit areas in the West may not be true in other contexts and cultures, some of which elude quantification and economic evaluation (Jain and Lyons, 2006). While it is not the primary role of this chapter to evaluate the unquantifiable aspects of travel life, interaction and authenticity remain of high value to budget travellers. If one were to take the transport example used earlier to describe the continuum between outward and inward travellers, which noted the importance of budget transport by outward-looking travellers, for them:

> getting *there* was as much a part of the experience of spiritual displacement as arrival at the destination. The tourist could . . . experience the changes in temperature, hear and smell sharply etched local sensations en route. Progress toward a destination was a series of arrivals and departures, each constituting itself as a distinct experience. Even the mode of conveyance . . . was integral to the succession of differences one felt each trip away from home.
> (MacCannell, 2001: 381–382; original emphasis)

This performance is reinforced by research from Anderson and De Paula (2006) that explored the in-between transitional moments on buses and commuter boats in Salvador, Bahia, Brazil and found these spaces engaged people and the environment in a moment of group solidarity and interactivity, viewing mobility as a collective rather than an individual phenomenon. Indeed, in a large number of recent movies with budget travel as a central theme, it is the interactions with strangers on public transport which have created pivotal moments in their narratives: the interactions on trains and buses in *Turistas* (2006), *Hostel* (2006) and *Eurotrip* (2004), while picking up strangers in hire vehicles during road journeys was pivotal in *Wolf Creek* (2005), *Gone* (2006) and *Big River* (2006). Larsen (2001: 81) believes the experience of mobility, being on the move, is part of the tourist experience itself: '[t]ouristic transportation, unlike coercive everyday mobility, is not *only* a trivial question of overcoming distance and reaching, it is also a way of being in, and experiencing various landscapes . . . through landscapes and cityscapes of visual "otherness"'. Yet, for many travellers (both inward and outward), long journeys necessitate mediation through the iPod, where playlists are used for certain situations, from gym workouts to journeys on public transport (Boradkar, 2005; Bull, 2006a), where many see mediation as nearly a prerequisite for long journeys in the travelscape as it temporally alters the perceived length of the journey. While those without iPods, confined to live in linear time, may react to that confinement by the use of books, etc., reading doesn't take out the user fully from the local context as much as the iPod. They are also being used to retrieve 'lost time' caused by unexpected disruptions to travel plans such as a delayed flight, a broken-down bus, similar to an office worker's attempt to remain in contact with head office when stranded after a missed flight (cf. Laurier, 2002).

Familiar strangers and budget traveller spaces

Personal space refers to the amount of physical space people need around them to feel comfortable and not be subject to invasion by others. It allows people of diverse cultural backgrounds to coexist in close quarters in their home or work environment, but are travellers losing out on the opportunity to find out something about the people around them (that person beside them on the bus, café, plane, street, bar, bus stop)? Rosen (2004: 26) believes that technology can disconnect people socially, ceding, in the process, much that was civil and civilized about the use of public space. While a controlling strategy at home and in the workplace, social interaction opportunities are damaged in the travelscape whether it is tourist–tourist, tourist–host, tourist–potential tourist or tourist–provider contact. None of these potential contacts are expected never to impinge upon the individual's right to withdraw from social space (Rosen, 2004).

> These devices are all used as a means to refuse to be 'in' the social space; they are technological cold shoulders that are worse than older forms of subordinate activity in that they impose visually and auditorily on others.
>
> (Rosen, 2004: 38)

Rosen believes society has allowed what should be subordinate activities in social space to become very dominant. It is far easier to feel secure, to feel connected, by slipping into private and virtual spaces, than talking to familiar strangers. While commitment to strangers leaves one vulnerable, Nietzsche suggests that we should not avoid such vulnerability or difficult experiences because they define what we are as individuals (cited in Ind, 2004: 170). While people don't normally strike up conversations with (familiar) strangers in the home environment, the need for collaborative networks, for 'thick co-present' (Urry, 2002a; Boden and Molotch, 2004) interaction is very much part of the travel experience. Richards and Wilson (2004b: 275) believe it is important to investigate how the budget traveller community might be sustained, believing it has a number of clearly structured means of maintaining itself, primarily through information circulation within the community (Cohen, 1973; Murphy, 2001). Through collaboration, sharing, gifting and word of mouth in unfamiliar environments as travellers move from location to location, they are open to creating ad hoc networks with co-travellers and locals. It is these interactions that are the building blocks that sustain and define the traveller network, the so-called 'imagined community' (Anderson, 1991) of travellers. There is ample evidence in budget traveller literature (Murphy, 2001) that indicates that social interaction and meeting others are an integral part of the experience. Binder (2004: 98–100) points out that meeting people is one of the main characteristics of travel and there are places from tours, travellers' bars to hostels that meet their compulsion to proximity (Boden and Molotch, 1994) in shared physical spaces even if this compulsion and their stay in such places are only temporary. Travellers flock to the same attractions, types of accommodation, restaurants, hotels, bars and nightclubs constituting a common and shared travelscape, allowing for the creation of social connections seeking opportunities to get into conversations with people co-present and directly participate in sustaining the community. The travelscapes are a guarantee to meet up with other people and it's easier to approach new people in the travelscape because of the common knowledge that everybody is eager to get to know people, to form groups, to share costs, risks and experiences and as an opportunity to socialize and meet new people and exchange information.

According to Wang (1999: 354, original emphasis) various contemporary cultural tribes search for the experiences of the emotional community:

> [t]hey also search for the authenticity of, and between, *themselves*. The toured objects or tourism can be just a means or medium by which tourists are called together, and then, an authentic inter-personal relationship between themselves is experienced subsequently.

Technology has brought an unqualified influence to the above-mentioned places and may not lead to focused interaction in the form of conversations. While the mobile technology (such as the mobile phone) has penetrated Western society and spaces of the everyday for the past two decades, it is new to budget travel culture and spaces. Kohiyama (2005) believes that given the ease of access to these virtual places people's understanding of 'place' will change as, during these times, 'local physical mobilities are dematerialized' (Germann Molz, 2006). The waiting e-mail, a person's favourite song, the incoming text and phone message – their private networks and virtual identity – take precedence over physical co-presence and interaction. Bassett (2003: 348) believes '[m]obile space tends to be prioritized over physical space, in the sense that it tends to be given more immediate attention', arguing virtual space is often prioritized over local space, and 'virtual interactions over physical ones', turning 'attention away from the sensory rich environment of the streets' and prioritizing 'the auditory at the expense of the embodied and visual world'. Manuel Castells has charted the development of the 'network society', in which flows of information, advertisements, capital and power are more influential than geographic spaces (cited in Savage *et al*., 2006: 148–149). According to Bassett (2003: 351) '[a]s we increasingly switch our attention from one place to another, each time at the expense of the last . . . our lives become fragmented'.

The iPod then can re-configure individuals' understanding and meanings they attribute to traveller spaces. Bull argues (2005: 351) iPod users choose the manner in which they attend to spaces, transforming space and time into their own personalized narrative. According to Holmes (2001: 7) headphone (Walkman) users can be agents of the 'reterritorialization' of space – 'in which the disembodied immersion provides the dominant space of attachment, making physical location less relevant or irrelevant', while Reybeck (cited in Taylor, 2005) believes the constant listening to music, spacing and lack of communication will exacerbate the tendency of individualism and insularity at the expense of community and sharing. This may lead to an inevitable decrease in collectivistic behaviours, values and group consciousness in traveller performance places like hostels. With the iPod and other devices, they are still mobile and immobile, both free and controlled and time rich and poor at the same time. Internet cafés fulfil similar roles to iPods, mobile technology and technosocial places, providing travellers with a sense of security, as lack of access to a communicative network in the travelscape may make travellers feel unsafe or at greater risk. They offer a respite, a temporary rootedness in a familiar anonymous place. Travellers may no longer need to rely on each other (Johnson and Bate, 2003: 107) where '[p]hysical closeness does not mean social closeness' (Wellman, 2001: 234). If iPods do disconnect users emotionally and physically, what effect has this on the places of 'informal co-presence' that create the opportunities for traveller–traveller interaction and the way travellers use performance spaces like hostel communal rooms?

Will budget travellers only go on those buses and trains, or stay in hostels where they can fulfil their potential mobility and the potential of the objects they carry? Wi-Fi may not just dictate power; it needs but also feeds into decisions about the security and connectivity of the places budget travellers stay in, the transport they take, the people they interact with. As well as adding higher costs to users and non-users alike, is it wise to follow the trend of electronic privatization seen in spaces of hypermobility like hotel lobbies, conference centres, airport lounges and railway stations? A hostel's communal area (the lobby) should remain a social gathering space as it both defines a hostel's unique character and facilitates intermittent moments of physical proximity and thick co-presence. The rush to facilitate the mobility of objects by installing Wi-Fi, power sockets, Internet telephony (VOIP) and webcams merely facilitates hypermobility and does not provide any incentive for communal living, interaction or sharing and in many ways may have the opposite effect as travellers seek increased portal time through desktop computers and their iPods. Co-present interaction 'requires participants to set aside not only a specific time but also a shared or shareable space, as well as generally constraining other activities at the same time or location' (Boden and Molotch, 2004: 103). By facilitating mobility in communal performance spaces, it reduces opportunities to interact and is an incentive to merely use communal areas as places of hypermobility (Internet cafés, railway stations) helping them to pass through on their way to somewhere else both physically and virtually, rather than seeing the hostel as a place to pause their extreme mobility, to gain respite from it, to linger. Facilitating technology in a place gives implicit or explicit approval to its use. The danger in this is that a travel community where cooperation and collaboration are so important will be increasingly interrupted by pervasive computing, personal portals and the techno-determinism of some travellers that many hostels seem determined to facilitate. Travellers who have incorporated hostels into their lifestyle for pause, dwelling, stability and interaction may find themselves subordinated by a system of (hyper)mobility, kept waiting unilaterally, delaying the kind of 'quality encounter' (Boden and Molotch, 2004: 103) that they have mentally and physically organized their lifestyle around. When people use technology like the iPod, it alters their behaviour but also the spaces in which they use it as well as the co-present who have to adapt to it, changing their reality in the process.

Are we treating other budget travellers – familiar strangers (Paulos and Goodman, 2004) – as we would people in our in-between places like buses, the trains, at home? Paulos and Goodman described these familiar strangers as 'individuals that we regularly observe but do not interact with' like budget travellers along the traveller 'networks of mobility' who are routinely observed without interaction. Paulos and Goodman (2004, original emphasis) claim that the relationship 'we have with these familiar strangers is indeed a *real* relationship in which both parties agree to mutually ignore each other, without any implications of hostility'. The travellers on the beaten tacks of mobility are a visual reminder of being on those well-beaten tracks. We can easily ignore them by deleting them from our camera viewfinder or with the use of an iPod, as they remind one that one is not really 'getting away' from home. This rise of 'networked individualism' in travel spaces, apparent in Western societies since the late 1970s (Wellman, 2001), where users of modern technology are less tied to local groups and increasingly part of more geographically scattered networks, is now apparent with the advent of mobile technology in the travelscape. While it can create linkages to other people, places and times, it can also diminish the importance of hostels and co-travellers in backpacker culture. Each person utilizing communication technologies becomes like a switchboard, connecting to each other as individuals, switching rapidly among personalized multiple sub-networks (or communities), which are easily formed and abandoned, consisting of both strong and weak social ties across different social strata. Because connections are to people (and to objects like the iPod) and not to places, the technology affords shifting of community ties from 'linking people-in-places to linking people at any place' (Wellman *et al.*, 2005: 431) because the technology-carrying traveller becomes the portal which can be utilized anywhere and is not associated with any one place.

Both theoretical and empirical work (Foth and Adkins, 2005) suggests that networking technologies rarely focus on identifications between people based solely on co-location in tourist space (and can actually work against it). Physical closeness or co-presence does not mean social closeness, in a space where virtual sharing and participation (Cunningham and Murphy, 2003) is highly valued. The Walkman itself at one time had a 'hot-line switch' to mute the device when somebody wanted to speak to the headphone-wearing user. However, this was quickly dropped (Du Gay *et al.*, 1997: 59) as Akio Morita, the head of Sony, soon recognized Walkman users saw the device as very personal and it seems very few attempts have been made by manufacturers to reintroduce sociability to devices. What of the many extremely mobile travellers, many of whom travel alone but who temporarily pause their extreme mobility in hostels in the belief that these places are socially important as places of informal co-presence? People share rooms, toilets, tables, bedrooms and tasks, yet personal computing devices, by their very nature, claim territory and diminish the chance of unmediated social interaction or sharing. So the iPod user in the dormitory or the laptop owner with headphones in communal areas is cut off from social interaction. Even though those co-present are relative strangers with weak ties, they are operationally strong as they exchange important travel information among themselves. Many 'outward-looking' budget travellers become more alienated from hostels that have facilitated mobile-networked and computing devices for a minority who want them, and these facilities push up prices and reduce face-to-face interaction, making such hostels less attractive for informal co-presence. The greater facilitation and use (and their obligation to use them by others) of devices among 'inward-looking' travellers may create new ways of connection for the nomadic elite in these newly developing hypermobile places, in order to integrate and participate in their personal networks and virtual identities and maybe in a networked 'imagined community' of travellers. The use and exchange of an e-mail address are nearly obligatory among budget travellers (Cohen, 2004:

53), with many e-mail addresses set up specifically for the trip; however, they can be easily discarded and messages ignored, attention being switched to new and more personal devices like mobile phones or a social networking address on Wayn, MySpace or Linkedin, giving personal access to aspects of an individual's home, work and everyday life.

'Out of place' issues

Like the advent of any new technology whether it be the train, car (Larsen, 2001), the original transistor radio, the Walkman, the iPod or the mobile phone, there were always early negative reactions to its use in public space. When the Walkman was initially launched, there were many 'out of place' criticisms about its 'usefulness' and 'anti-social, atomizing effects' and that its presence in the public domain somehow offended the 'social order' and people's ideas of what was appropriate/inappropriate in certain settings (Du Gay *et al.*, 1997: 89, 115–116). Scholars have noted that the introduction of any new technology in society raises different kinds of debates about the nature of its impact on social interactions and public sociability. This reaction draws on the anthropology of Mary Douglas, who argued that this private listening in public spaces was 'out of place', that is, objects, actions or ideas which appear in the 'wrong' context (Eriksen, 2004). In the 1950s, people lamented that the transistor radio would spell the end of families gathered around the radio (Soojung-Kim Pang, 2005), while there was early criticism of the Walkman because consumers could not envisage the benefit it might bring (Hackley, 2005: 71). This anxiety is centuries old, much of it centred on concerns about the consequences of isolation (Soojung-Kim Pang, 2005). For example, scholars like Putnam (2000) have raised concerns about the decline of traditional face-to-face interactions, the loss of interest in taking part in social activities or inconsiderate behaviour, privatization of public space, increased possibility of control and individual empowerment but loss of serendipitous encounters. In his book *Bowling Alone: the Collapse and Revival of American Community* (2000), Putnam argued that in the USA individualized entertainment has gained the upper hand over shared communal activities since the 1970s.

Negative reaction to the headphone and the mobile phone for work, household use and leisure has diminished somewhat over time, as they have become a more accepted feature of everyday life – largely by dint of the weight of numbers of people using them – but negative commentary is beginning to be directed at their use in the travel environment (Bergvik, 2004). For example, a British adventure holiday company, called Adventure Company, became the first travel group in 2005 to ban tourists from carrying mobile telephones after customers complained that 'intrusive' ringtones and the 'endless chatter' that followed were ruining once-in-a-lifetime trips to places like Petra in Jordan, Machu Picchu in Peru and the Taj Mahal in India (Harrison, 2005). Howker (2004) advises budget travellers to leave these devices at home. Boradkar (2005) believes that, as an object designed primarily for personal, mobile use, the iPod can be critiqued in terms of the relationship between the individual and society, with commentators still remarking on how headphone culture is affecting social behaviour. Even today the:

> [W]alkman is still not accorded a secure home in the world, that it continues to occupy an ambivalent position between public and private, can be evidenced by simply gauging one's own reaction when someone close to you in a public place puts on those little headphones.
>
> (Du Gay *et al.*, 1997: 118)

Recent discussion regarding the use of mobile phones on aeroplanes (and mobile phones in public areas) reinforces the notion that 'out of place' issues will never be totally discounted from any discussion on techno-social devices (Ling, 1997, 2002; Harper, 2003; Jansson, 2006), especially for the hard core of travellers who resist technological use. This is especially true for those travellers mentioned above who believe home and work should be kept at arm's length, whether it be refusing to carry technology (especially mobile phones) or answer e-mail messages, believing 'the illusion of demediation offers the false promise of communion with authenticity and an escape from the very mediation that the semiotics of tourism unveils' (Strain, 2003: 4). They believe that stripping themselves of their Western cultural baggage can lead to authentic experiences and interactions.

The virtualization of objects

The iPod's usefulness demands more and more connection time to the virtual. According to Farnsworth and Austrin (2005: 14) 'humans and their objects become, in effect, a hybrid entity themselves – an entity connected to, and connecting up, other communities and worlds'. Their connection to the virtual, mediated via technology, both facilitates traveller mobility and helps them manage it at the same time. According to Richards and Wilson (2004a: 22) young travellers tend to be information-intensive, consulting a wide range of information sources before departure. While independent travellers can also get information from information brokers like travel agencies, tourism offices, tour organizers, pamphlets and brochures, independent travellers distrust these sources as they are from authoritative figures within the tourism industry. These sources are also promotional rather than factual and are not necessarily objective and unbiased. According to Noy and Cohen (2005: 2) '[d]ue to the backpackers' suspicion of formal tourist material, a marked feature of this system is a heightened pattern of the informal communication and narration among the travelers', but their growing numbers make them a target for commercialization and commodification, testified by the increase in magazines, television shows, websites and dedicated information provided for them. This exploitation or control is not in the Foucaldian sense but a more 'pervasive and intrusive society of control' (Galloway, 2004: 401) or 'societies of control' as formulated by Deleuze (1992), who saw a shift away from disciplinary societies.

De Nora (2006: 19–34) in her work introduced some of the key ways in which music 'gets into' our daily lives and argues that music is a key resource in the formation of a social reality. But what of the other content that makes up a traveller's MP3 player? The tourist industry naturally takes advantage of budget traveller mobility and the mobile technology that is worn close to their body and as many budget travellers have integrated iPods into the rhythm of their lives they may prefer podcasts over the overt obtrusiveness of bulky and overtly 'touristy' guidebooks. There are websites that offer content for iPods from tourist boards, museums and travel companies. There are virtual online companies and user-generated content by co-travellers including companies such as Audible, iJourneys, Walki-Talki, iAudioGuide, IPREPpress, which all offer travel guidebooks, self-guided tours and books for download. Lonely Planet and Rough Guide have audio-video guides to popular destinations as well as language phrasebooks. The Greek Culture Ministry in 2007 launched a handheld gadget for visitors to rent at 15 sites that offers high-resolution video, detailed diagrams of sites such as ancient temples, position indicators and imagery along with stereo sound. In Tokyo's Ginza shopping district 12,000 embedded computer chips send directions, store guides and historical titbits via headphones to portable media players. These virtual intrusions are welcomed by most travellers as the podcasts are usually free or low cost and could be what Parrinello (2001: 205) might consider prostheses that extend the abilities of the tourist's body and mind and contribute to an increasingly artificial environment, which 'interfere with the deep structure of the everyday lifeworld and modify paradigms of seeing, even interpretive models of the world' (p. 212).

Many tourist boards, museums and tourist attractions offer podcasts and this will continue as people more fully utilize mobile technologies in the travelscape. While the Internet has always been seen as authority free without boundaries, there is increased commercialization of information as handset makers, tourist boards, content providers like Google and commercial bodies become the new gatekeepers of information. A major problem for those budget independent travellers who rely too heavily on technology, believing it to be free of authority and political interference, is that they also rely on the corporations who build these products and services (with Apple very carefully maintaining a powerful brand). Stevenson (2002: 187) asks who will control the information? While there may be a virtual community, where is the local (or tacit) knowledge in these communities, when the traveller is sourcing for local music online instead of listening out for the sounds of the city, the radio from that country or browsing in record stores? For those travellers who buy music online, they have no access to ethnic music on iTunes and have neither immaterial nor material musical souvenirs to remind them (and others at home) that they were ever there (Ateljevic and Doorne, 2003: 134). The iPod and its content do not reflect their time on the ground (unless used for photo storage). If a product's immaterial dimensions demand a virtual life, when information is rendered, distributed and consumed as digital music is, will it too become encrypted, copyrighted and controlled by the network rather than the individual? Will online digital, convenient 'word of mouth' supersede the offline word of mouth – an important building block in budget travel communities? Will information be so personalized, so immediate as to become non-shareable, 'reinforcing the overarching post-Fordist regime of reflexive accumulation, customization and market segmentation' (Jansson, 2006)?

What are the spatial consequences of utilizing virtual remote intervention in the practices of everyday leisure travel? Caroline Basset (2005) explored the use of the mobile phone and the 'new spatial economy it has created as a result of the dynamics between physical and virtual space, between old and new space'. She contrasted the differences in the practice of walking as described by de Certeau (1984), in his book *The Practice of Everyday Life*, as a spatializing, narrativizing practice with walking today with portable technologies which embed you in the global as much as they do in the immediate locality. One would also have to question de Certeau's view (Tonkiss, 2005: 127) that the ordinary individual is not merely a consumer of urban space on some occasions. De Certeau believes people do not 'simply rehearse an established spatial script, nor are the meanings of the city given by material forms and their instructions for use' (Tonkiss, 2005: 127–128), but today with the iPod and the multitude of walking tours, travel guides and travel videos (one's own personal tour guide) that tell travellers where to look, what to see, where to turn and what to think and with the tourist industry exploiting GPS systems, the amount of instruction given to travellers on the move will increase. (Some guidebooks are already adding GPS coordinates to their pages.) According to Tonkiss, for de Certeau, 'the practice of walking in the city is a matter of telling one's own spatial stories, drawing on a mobile and private language of the streets' (Tonkiss, 2005: 128), and 'involves danger, exile, discover and transformation' (Kellerman, 2006: 89), but following the iPod is no different from following a guided tour or a set of 'painted footsteps around approved sites of interest' such as the famous Boston Freedom Trail. Many audio trails or podcasts may be selective in their content, trivialize local problems, lack local consultation, sanitize unwholesome conditions, glamorize unpleasant situations and may marginalize issues of race, gender and social class (Ball *et al.*, 2005), commodifying the places themselves (their people, history, culture). For budget travellers, an escape from 'representations' of the place, from the tourist industry trying to impose where to go and what to see and do is important, as '[n]ot everything shows up on the map . . . the chance encounters and cross-cutting paths . . . the tricky and momentary ways in which people make space' (Tonkiss, 2005: 128). Aren't the search for sites, the misdirection and mishaps associated with walking in an unfamiliar environment as much a part of travel as getting to the site itself?

The iPod assemblage, a virtual portal embedded with restrictive rules of use, impacts upon social reality, asking the question as to whether information gathered virtually is applied to interacting and sharing locally. Are travellers detaching themselves 'from the world while imagining that they are actually more integrated in it' through persuasive technologies like the iPod and information provided by 'professionals and specialists' like tourist boards and online companies which allow for virtual simulated experiences (Mejias, 1999)? They are confusing the consumption of virtual information produced by unknown others with 'being in the world', creating a 'false sense of integration to reality, while in fact further alienating him/her from it' (Mejias, 1999). While camera or camcorder lenses may be similar, their use is momentary and doesn't remotely intervene upon a traveller's relations to touristic spaces, co-travellers and locals. According to Mejias (1999) unconditional surrender to virtuality will result in 'unsustainable communicational realities, the sterile elimination of masses of Third World peoples condensed into a few images on the screen', and perpetuate social divisions by giving the elite the means to distance themselves from the 'ugliness' of reality.

Similar to the effect of musical privacy, connection to the virtual world which is becoming more pervasive can be both isolating and empowering at the same time. With mobile Internet, MP3 capabilities and GPS facilities becoming more standard on phones, potentially travellers will be able to continuously isolate themselves in virtual worlds while participating in the real world of travel. This is related to Umberto Eco (1986) and his notion of 'hyperreality' – a faith in fakes – where podcasts take on the role of locals, local celebrities or past citizens, but are scripted and rehearsed. In a world of digital natives growing up within a digital culture, where virtual friends are as real as those in a physical sense, it is no surprise that individuals will happily accept virtual mediation. According to Fjellman, modern technology can make the inauthentic look more authentic (Fjellman, 1992; cited in Wang, 1999: 357). As McCrone *et al.* (1995: 46) put it:

> Authenticity and originality are, above all, matters of technique . . . What is interesting to postmodernists about heritage is that reality depends on how convincing the presentation is, how well the 'staged authenticity' works . . . The more 'authentic' the representation, the more 'real' it is.
>
> (McCrone *et al.*, 1995; cited in Wang, 1999: 357)

For postmodernists, gone is the 'authenticity of the original' (Wang, 1999: 358), replaced by podcasts, answers and script 'designated in advance' (Smart, 1992: 124). According to Smart (1992: 124) '[s]uch a situation does not allow for contemplation' and 'media communications and images no longer inform as much as test and control'. Baudrillard (1983: 120, quoted in Smart, 1992: 124) comments that 'objects and information result already from a selection, a montage, from a point of view'. Technology facilitates traveller mobility and helps travellers to manage it, but Mejias (2007) wonders what happens when technology goes from 'mediating our interactions with what is physically far to mediating our interactions with our immediate surroundings'. There is no technology currently available to facilitate new forms of engaging the local, but the technologies mentioned above (and GPS, local search and mapping) show there is much technology for travellers to mediate their local interactions. According to Mejias (2007) this 'introduces a form of epistemological exclusivity that discriminates against that which is not part of the network, whether it is because it can't be part of the network, it doesn't want to, or we don't want it to', resulting in a form of hyerlocality that filters out certain elements of our environment, making them irrelevant. From trusting them to store our most precious songs, copies of our most precious documents like one's passport and travel photos, to waking us up in the morning, with our interaction with the local, travellers are delegating more and more to non-human actors. Bassett (2003, 2005) believes technology offers us more freedom and simultaneously exerts more control over us at the same time. As Mejias (2007) points out, the whole point of delegation is that we no longer have to worry about the process, entrusting technology with the details, but 'if we forget to the point that we can no longer reverse the process of delegation, we end up *surrendering* agency to technology instead of delegating it' (Mejias, 2007). By 'setting parameters for the user's actions' (Woolgar, 1991: 61), the behaviour of the traveller is configured by the designer of the technology and the user is disciplined by the technology itself.

Conclusion

> Accessible technology alters the way in which individuals conduct their everyday lives. It has extensive implications for the cultures and societies in which it is used; it changes the nature of communication, and affects identities and relationships. It affects the development of social structures and economic activities, and has considerable bearing on its users' perceptions of themselves and their world.
> (Cultural anthropologist Sadie Plant, 2001: 23 writing about the mobile phone)

The mobility that characterizes budget travel has led to a quick adoption of technologies which are increasingly mobile, pervasive and ubiquitous (and which designers embody with mobility and which represent mobility itself) – so 'people can indeed be said to dwell in various mobilities' (Urry, 2000: 157). The iPod helps travellers manage and facilitate their mobility, allowing them to bring 'home, work and in-between places' with them, and allows them to weave in and out of both private and virtual space, redefining the relationship between everyday life and tourism. The places (portals) where individuals can and are increasingly likely to switch from public to private/virtual space are growing as is the length of time they are prepared to do so. This is due to the decreasing cost and size of these devices and the nature of the technological convergence. These objects of mobility are now part of modern life, and, like the mobile phone and car before, are now part of thinking about how to organize one's everyday work and home life. The iPod is a machine of private virtual journey, representing a 'mobilized virtual embodied gaze' (paraphrasing Friedberg's (1993) view of cinematic spectatorship). Solo budget travellers are consuming 'scapes, spaces and strangers on their terms, through the blended geographies created by the iPod – both a privatizing and a virtualized world, related but very different from the temporary tourist visual gaze created by cameras and camcorders. One outcome of such mediated interaction is a 'disembedding' of people from their traditional relations and environments and a 're-embedding' into different social formations (Jensen, 2002: 2), increasing the similarities between behaviours that are 'home' and 'away' (Urry, 2002c: 161) and between organizing one's everyday home and work lives and organizing one's travel life, which may be contextually different but behaviourally similar, requiring a 'mobility burden' for those maintaining home and work routines.

Many devices are now being marketed solely on their ability to access virtual space and personalized portals (like one's Flickr or social networking homepage), promoting an 'illusion of control' where the notions of what is real and what is virtual become blurred. This has a knock-on effect on traveller performance, traveller behaviour, identity and practice, transforming 'what we think of as near and far, present and absent' (Urry, 2002b: 8). Mattel, a large toy company, introduced a Barbie-inspired handheld MP3 music device in 2007 to connect with Barbiegirls.com, creating a global online virtual world exclusively for girls to interact within. Similarly, services like kyte.com allow users to send their mobile phone photos and videos directly to their own 'online channels' and respond instantly to live 'audience' participants – an interactive real-time travel diary, documenting their daily experiences, living a virtual life that other offline travellers/locals can't see. Castells (2004: 87) writes about '[m]oving physically while keeping the networking connection to everything we do in a new realm of the human adventure, on which we know little'. According to Holmes (2001: 5) '[s]uch spaces are valued for their convenience and global familiarity'. Access to virtual space is marketed on the basis of convenience, reducing virtual spaces to those virtual spaces authorized by the network (mobile phone companies, Apple). Jansson (2006) explains that, while, on the one hand, travel may be reinforced by the ability to share one's travel experiences immediately while on the go (via uploading sounds, pictures, stories), on the other hand, the distinction between tourism and everyday life becomes further blurred, diminishing the experience, the 'rite of passage concept' and the value of the experience to both the travellers and the significant others in their everyday life, who may receive daily montages and snapshots of the traveller's life in *their* everyday home and work life. This highlights the significance of Urry's gaze in everyday life, but expands it to a more embodied perspective: the blurring of the distinctiveness of everyday life and travel life through the 'hyper-mediation and hyper-consumption of liminality' (Jansson, 2006), where 'everyday looking' is the same as 'travel life looking'.

Not only are they weaving out of public and private worlds, virtual space and real space, but also 'different contexts, identities, and relationships' (Sheller, 2004b: 41), whether it is using technology to be elsewhere (absent presence), using it to communicate with significant others or maintaining ties with virtual communities that they share an interest with (personal networking/personal community). Moreover, not only are they able to do this in spaces like Internet cafés and hostels, but also 'on the go'. Unlike the 'dumb' hardware that characterized the Walkman, today's iPod reaffirms the 'reality' of the virtual (Fletcher, 1998) in showing us how ubiquitous everyday pervasive computing will become part of travel culture and some of the virtual/physical and public/private issues and dilemmas that arise from that use. Boradkar (2005) claims the virtual (along with the real) will continue to claim territory by its very existence as they both reach out, expanding their territory. They are collapsing, blending and conflicting with each other and the occurrences, times and spaces when it happens are increasing. There is merit in Boradkar's (2005) description of the iPod as an assemblage with multiple dimensions, 'real and virtual, enveloping but permeable, territorialized but moving, and entirely soaked in sound'. The iPod and mobile technology will continue to mediate between the traveller and the travelscape, between the public and the private and the physical and the virtual. According to Soojung-Kim Pang (2006, quoted in Wolverton and Boudreau, 2006) '[t]hat will have an effect on the way people relate to their pasts, and the way media serves as a source for shaping their identities'.

How travellers present their identity is their prerogative, and some technologies actually facilitate greater understandings of reality as well as offering a kind of 'ontological security' (Holmes, 2001: 5). However, does the use of an iPod do travellers a disservice to themselves, the traveller spaces that facilitate its use and the manufacturers who fail to take into account the concept of culture in their products? Will GPS systems on their phones and convergent devices become their new 'point of reference' over that of place, the guidebook, the hostel and other travellers? Technology has given travellers a universe entirely for themselves – where the chances of meeting a new stranger, hearing a local music station or a piece of music they haven't chosen and heard before have diminished. This is not to say the travel community and tourism itself will collapse once pervasive computing becomes ubiquitous. While the differences between the near and there, between home and away are blurring, tourism is 'an interest and curiously in the world beyond our own immediate lives and circles' (Franklin, 2003: 11), pointing to its survival. The iPod points to a travelscape where the individual's control over the content, style and timing of what they consume is becoming increasingly absolute, which may in turn loosen the bonds between travellers, and travellers and place. One of the most important dystopian fictions was written by E.M. Forster in 1909, called 'The machine stops', which envisions a society of people living in isolated rooms, the world brought to them through visual and audio technologies. Forster explores the ensuing horror of the body and of the contact with other bodies and cautions against putting too much power into our machines and allowing feelings of technological empowerment to mask human weakness. Beyond a certain point, this isn't good for a community, including the travelling community, which requires gifting, sharing and participation in order to survive. Ateljevic and Doorne (2003: 138) believe 'the act of gifting . . . assimilated into the life worlds of consumers . . . [is] fundamental to identity-formation and to the creation of self images, yet it was also a contradictory expression of consumer values and life philosophies'. One just has to realize that much of the thrill of travel comes in leaving home behind and making oneself vulnerable to the chaos of life overseas without over controlling your space, time and interactions. Rosen (2005: 52) says 'by giving us the illusion of perfect control, these technologies risk making us incapable of ever being surprised', creating or supplying a structured personalized soundtrack instead of building up new memories in the travelscape, which has a soundtrack of its very own.

As expanded upon earlier, technology use is not spread evenly among travellers. Castells' (2004: 85) networked society is 'characterized by the opposing development of individuation and communalism'. By individuation he means 'the projects, interests, and representation of the individual' and by communalism he is 'referring to the enclosure of meaning in a shared identity, based on a system of values and beliefs'. Of course, society exists in the interface between individuals and identities, and while some travellers will adopt the network fully, other travellers may decide to live off the grid and step outside the network. Will non-ownership be an increasingly popular option to reaffirm a status of distinction (Bourdieu, 1984) within budget travellers' lifestyles or will technology become so ubiquitous and miniaturized that travellers may not even know if they are carrying it? For others technology use may be a way to increase cultural capital. Genevieve Bell, the 'resident anthropologist' at Intel, believes from preliminary research that budget travellers frequently look for a respite from technology (Goodin, 2007). However, Holmes (2001: 8–9) asks whether travellers distinguish themselves with their own status systems, their global elite status:

> consuming spaces that provide mobility are among the most prized items of global status – being on the Internet, being able to recount impressive travel stories,

obtaining the newest communication device, phone or PDA . . . are, for many, new avenues for collecting cultural capital.

Budget travellers like to think of themselves as independent travellers – independent from tourist infrastructure, from tourists and from undue interference from commercial tourist information. However, once they allow for fully pervasive devices, they are travelling from within a world created for a privileged minority where they may never get lost, never meet people outside their virtual and personal networks, creating a travel community not generated by participation, gifting, sharing and word of mouth but defined by whether their devices can talk to each other, and who can afford and use such electronic mobility. While our discussion of budget travel shows that portability and convenience are highly rated in the home, work and transit environments, maybe among colleagues of equal status, it is not obvious as to whether budget traveller culture will value more convergent devices if they are intrusive or allow for an invasion of privacy. It is obvious that travellers will need to judge for themselves the balance between privacy and surveillance, between control and resistance, between collective and individual travel, between push and pull information and whether specific uses of technology increase or decrease their understanding of the world around them. But this cannot be done unless technology designers and the information gatekeepers adhere to their different cultural needs.

Independent travellers have traditionally gelled long enough to create ad hoc networks to share travel costs, travel information, to share risk and find temporary travel companions. However, manufacturers who have designed devices for the home, work and transit spaces, rather than for specific (sub)cultures like budget travellers, have not understood how tacit and soft assets within the imagined community can be 'elicited, connected, networked and harnessed to become "smart" assets' in the service of both themselves, inter-cultural exchange and for social and economic benefit to tourism-attracting areas (Foth and Adkins, 2005). Graham (1997: 22) believes technological development is 'designed, applied and shaped within specific political, social, economic and cultural contexts'. Organizational innovation makes new technologies culturally emblematic (Lash and Urry, 1994: 252–253). They illustrate how the early railway company did not realize the leisure potential of their business. As it is, devices like the iPod are changing travel behaviour and social relations in very unpredictable ways. The ability of travellers to shape the iPod to help them create community or give them a handle or connection to an unfamiliar location is very limited, with the balance of power (content ownership) controlled by the manufacturers and new information gatekeepers like Apple. Such gatekeepers manage the amount of mobility that a user can access, as well as being a taste purveyor, music journalist and record company combined, and with other gatekeepers such as handset makers, the tourist industry, mobile operators, copyright owners and content aggregators (like Yahoo and Google) control access to virtual space. There has been some recent movement on this: Cellular Abroad launched a National Geographic-branded Talk Abroad phone in 2007 which allows free incoming calls in 65 counties using a UK-based phone number, while Nokia has been looking at how phones are specifically shared and used in Africa.

'Today, it is the individual who must conform to the needs of technology. It is time to make technology conform to the needs of people' (Norman, 1998: 261; cited in Galloway, 2004: 387), replacing a situation, as Woolgar (1991) describes, where designers are seeking to 'configure the user' (in terms of defining the characteristics of the user and how they may respond).

This chapter has shown that access to too much 'mobility and network capital' facilitates and encourages some travellers to bring home with them rather than, paraphrasing De Botton (2003: 59), providing them with opportunities to escape their habits of mind. Until recently, everyday life and tourism were seen as very different 'scapes, but, as this chapter has shown, everyday lives and tourism interact and collide, with objects of mobility playing an important part. Bringing 'home' or 'work' strategies for certain spaces, places and situations to the travelscape performed through technology brings to mind Alain De Botton's view of travel companions, which could be equally expressed about a traveller's iPod. He said:

> Our responses to the world are crucially moulded by the whom we are with, we temper our curiosity to fit in with the expectations of others. They may have a particular vision of who we are and hence subtly prevent certain sides of us from emerging . . . Being closely observed by a companion can inhibit us from observing others . . .
>
> (De Botton, 2003: 252)

References

Adey, P. and Bevan, P. (2006) Between the physical and the virtual: connected mobility? In: Sheller, M. and Urry, J. (eds) *Mobile Technologies of the City*. Routledge, London, pp. 44–60.

Anderson, B. (1991) *Imagined Communities: Reflections on the Origin and Spread of Nationalism*. Verso, London.

Anderson, K. and De Paula, R. (2006) We we we all the way home: the 'we' affect in transitional spaces. The Second Ethnographic Praxis in Industry Conference (EPIC). Intel Corporation Conference Center, Portland, Oregon, 24–26 September.

Ateljevic, I. (2000) Circuits of tourism: stepping beyond the 'production/consumption' dichotomy. *Tourism Geographies* 2(4), 369–388.

Ateljevic, I. and Doorne, S. (2003) Culture, economy and tourism commodities: social relations of production and consumption. *Tourist Studies* 3(2), 123–141.

Augè, M. (2002) *In the Metro*. University of Minnesota Press, Minneapolis, Minnesota.

Ball, M., Day, K., Liverganr, E. and Tivers, J. (2005) Wapping: the 'stage' for an audio trail. Paper presented to the Critical Tourism Research Conference: Tourism and Performance: Scripts, Stages and Stories, Sheffield, July 2005. Available at: http://www.wappingaudio.org/pdf/wapping_audio_paper.pdf (accessed 11 January 2007).

Bassett, C. (2003) How many movements? In: Bull, M. and Beck, L. (eds) *Auditory Culture Reader*. Berg, Oxford, UK, pp. 343–354.

Bassett, C. (2005) How many movements? *Open, Cahier on Art and the Public Domain* (online journal), pp. 38–48. Available at: http://www.skor.nl/article-2854-en.html (accessed 1 June 2006).

Bassoli, A. and Martin, K. (2006) Exploring in-between-ness: the experience of riding the London tube. Paper for the workshop Exurban Noir, Eighth International

Conference of Ubiquitous Computing. Available at: http://www.inbetweeness.org/Bassoli-Martin-ExploringInbetweenness-ExurbanNoir2006.pdf (accessed 11 January 2007).

Bassoli, A., Brewer, J. and Martin, K. (2006) Undersound: music and mobility under the city. Poster at the Eighth International Conference of Ubiquitous Computing. Available at: http://www.inbetweeness.org/BrewerBassoliMartin-undersound.pdf (accessed 11 January 2007).

Bauman, Z. (2000) *Liquid Modernity*. Polity Press, Cambridge, UK.

Berger, J. (1984) *And Our Faces, My Heart, Brief as Photos*. Writers and Readers Publishing Cooperative, London.

Bergvik, S. (2004) Disturbing Cell Phone Behaviour – a Psychological Perspective. Implications for Mobile Technology in Tourism. Kjeller: Telenor Research and Development Report R 29/2004. Available at: http://moveweb.no/pub/R%2029%202004%20Disturbing%20cell%20phones.pdf (accessed 31 December 2004).

Berry, R. (2006) Will the iPod kill the radio star? Profiling podcasting as radio. *Convergence* 12(2), 143–162.

Binder, J. (2004) The whole point of backpacking: anthropological perspectives on the characteristics of backpacking. In: Wilson, J. and Richards, G. (eds) *The Global Nomad: Backpacker Travel in Theory and Practice*. Channel View Publications, Clevedon, UK, pp. 92–108.

Blythe, M. and Wright, P. (2005) Bridget Jones' iPod: relating macro and micro theories of user experience through pastiche scenarios. In: *Proceedings from Home-Oriented Information Technologies* (HOIT 2005), Springer, New York, pp. 291–302.

Boden, D. and Molotch, H. (1994) The compulsion to proximity. In: Friedland, R. and Boden, D. (eds) *Nowhere. Space, Time and Modernity*. University of California Press, Berkeley, California, pp. 257–286.

Boden, D. and Molotch, H. (2004) Cyberspace meets the compulsion of proximity. In: Graham, S. (ed.) *The Cybercities Reader*. Routledge, New York, pp. 101–105.

Bohn, J., Coroama, V., Langheinrich, M., Mattern, F. and Rohs, M. (2004) Living in a world of smart everyday objects – social, economic and ethical implications. *Journal of Human and Ecological Risk Assessment* 10(5), 763–786.

Boradkar, P. (2005) 10,000 Songs in your pocket: the iPod as environment. In: Kronenberg, R. (ed.) *Transportable Environments 3*. Spon Press, Oxford, pp. 21–29. Available at: criticalcorps.caed.asu.edu/people/10000_Songs_in_Pocket.pdf (accessed 11 January 2006).

Bourdieu, P. (1984) *Distinction. A Social Critique of the Judgement of Taste*. Routledge, London.

Bruno, A. (2007) Digital music no environmental cure. (Previously published by *Billboard* magazine, Denver). Available at: http://uk.reuters.com/article/musicNews/idUKN1928923720070621 (accessed 19 June 2007).

Buckley, S. (2001) *Encyclopedia of Contemporary Japanese Culture*. Routledge, London.

Bull, M. (2000) *Sounding Out the City: Personal Stereos and the Management of Everyday Life*. Berg, Oxford, UK.

Bull, M. (2002) The seduction of sound in consumer culture: investigating Walkman desires. *Journal of Consumer Culture* 2(1), 81–101.

Bull, M. (2003) Soundscapes of the car: a critical ethnography of automobile. In: Bull, M. and Back, L. (eds) *The Auditory Culture Reader*. Berg, Oxford, UK, pp. 357–380.

Bull, M. (2004a) Sound connections: an aural epistemology of proximity and distance in urban culture. *Society and Space* 22(1), 103–116.

Bull, M. (2004b) Automobility and the power of sound theory. *Culture and Society* 21(4/5), 243–259.

Bull, M. (2004c) The intimate sounds of urban experience: an auditory epistemology of everyday mobility. The Global and the Local in Mobile Communication: Places, Images, People, Connections. Hungarian Academy of Sciences, Budapest, Hungary, 10–12 June.

Bull, M. (2005) No dead air! The iPod and the culture of mobile listening. *Leisure Studies* 24(4), 343–355.

Bull, M. (2006a) Investigating the culture of mobile listening: from Walkman to iPod. In: O'Hara, K. and Brown, B. (eds) *Consuming Music Together: Social and Collaborative Aspects of Music Consumption Technologies*. Springer, Dordrecht, The Netherlands, pp. 131–150.

Bull, M. (2006b) Iconic designs: the Apple iPod. *The Senses and Society* 1(1), 105–108.

Castells, M. (2004) Space of flows, space of places: materials for a theory of urbanism in the information age. In: Graham, S. (ed.) *The Cybercities Reader*. Routledge, London, pp. 82–93.

Chambers, I. (1994) The aural walk. In: Chambers, I. (ed.) *Migrancy, Culture, Identity*. Routledge, London, pp. 49–53.

Clifford, J. (1997) *Routes*. Harvard University Press, Cambridge, Massachusetts.

Cohen, E. (1973) Nomads from affluence: notes on the phenomenon of drifter-tourism. *International Journal of Comparative Sociology* 14(1–2), 89–103.

Cohen, E. (1979) A phenomenology of tourist experiences. *Sociology* 13(2), 179–201.

Cohen, E. (2003) Backpacking: diversity and change. *Journal of Tourism and Cultural Change* 1(2), 95–110.

Cohen, E. (2004) Backpacking: diversity and change. In: Wilson, J. and Richards, G. (eds) *The Global Nomad: Backpacker Travel in Theory and Practice*. Channel View Publications, Clevedon, UK, pp. 43–59.

Cohen, E. and Noy, C. (2006) Introduction: backpacking as a rite of passage in Israel. In: Cohen, E. and Noy, C. (eds) *Israeli Backpackers: a View from Afar*. State University of New York Press, Albany, New York, pp. 1–44.

Coleman, S. and Eade, J. (2004) Introduction: reframing pilgrimage. In: Coleman, S. and Eade, J. (eds) *Reframing Pilgrimage: Cultures in Motion*. Routledge, London, pp. 1–25.

Cranny-Francis, A. (2005) *Multimedia: Texts and Contexts*. Sage, London.

Crary, J. (1999) *Suspensions of Perception: Attention, Spectacle and Modern Culture*. MIT Press, London.

Cunningham, J. and Murphy, P. (2003) *Organizing for Community Controlled Development, Renewing Civil Society*. Sage Publications, London.

D'Andrea, A. (2006) Neo-nomadism: a theory of post-identitarian mobility in the global age. *Mobilities* 1(1), 95–119.

De Botton, A. (2003) *The Art of Travel*. Penguin, London.

De Certeau, M. (1984) *The Practice of Everyday Life*. University of California Press, London.

Deleuze, G. (1992) *Postscript on the Societies of Control*. MIT Press, Cambridge, Massachusetts. Available at: http://www.spunk.org/texts/misc/sp000962.txt (accessed 10 March 2007).

De Nora, T. (2000) *Music and Everyday Life*. Cambridge University Press, Cambridge.

De Nora, T. (2006) Music and emotion in real time. In: O'Hara, K. and Brown, B. (eds) *Consuming Music Together: Social and Collaborative Aspects of Music Consumption Technologies*. Springer, Dordrecht, The Netherlands, pp. 19–34.

Du Gay, P., Hall, S., Janes, L., Negus, K. and MacKay, H. (1997) *Doing Cultural Studies: the Story of the Sony Walkman*. Sage, London.

Eco, U. (1986) *Travels in Hyperreality*. Pan in association with Secker and Warburg, London.

Edensor, T. (2001) Performing tourism, staging tourism – (re)producing tourist space and practice. *Tourist Studies* 1, 59–81.

Edensor, T. (2003) Defamiliarizing the mundane roadscape. *Space and Culture* 6(2), 151–168.

Edensor, T. (2005) *Industrial Ruins: Aesthetics, Materiality and Memory*. Berg, Oxford, UK.

Elsrud, T. (1998) Time creation in travelling: the taking and making of time among women backpackers. *Time and Society* 7(2), 309–334.

Eriksen, T.H. (2004) *What is Anthropology?* Pluto Press, London.

Farnsworth, J. and Austrin, T. (2005) Assembling portable talk and mobile worlds: sound technologies and mobile social networks. *Convergence* 11(2), 14–22.

Fletcher, G. (1998) All that is virtual bleeds into reality. In: *Proceedings of the Australian Sociological Association*, Queensland University of Technology, Brisbane. Available at: http://www.spaceless.com/papers/1.htm (accessed 12 March 2007).

Flinn, J. (2005) Time to come out of your pod. *San Francisco Chronicle* 29 May. Available at: http://sfgate.com/cgi-bin/article.cgi?file = /chronicle/archive/2005/05/29/TRG1QCSL6M1.DTL (accessed 28 November 2005).

Forster, E.M. (1909) The machine stops. In: Forster, E.M. (ed.) *Oxford and Cambridge Review*. Reprinted in *The New Collected Short Stories* (1985). Sidgwick and Jackson, London.

Foth, M. and Adkins, B. (2005) A research design to build effective partnerships between city planners, developers, government and urban neighbourhood communities. *The Journal of Community Informatics* 2(2), 116–133.

Franklin, A. (2003) *Tourism: an Introduction*. Sage, London.

Friedberg, A. (1993) *Window Shopping: Cinema and the Postmodern*. University of California Press, Berkeley, California.

Frow, J. (1997) *Time and Commodity Culture: Essays on Cultural Theory and Postmodernity*. Oxford University Press, Oxford, UK.

Galloway, A. (2004) Intimations of everyday life. *Cultural Studies* 18(2/3), 384–408.

Germann Molz, J. (2006) Travels in blended geographies: technologies, mobilities and 'new' tourist destinations. Paper presented to Mobilities, Technologies, and Travel workshop, Roskilde University, Roskilde, Denmark, 20 April.

Goffman, E. (1963) *Behavior in Public Places: Notes on the Social Organization of Gatherings*. Free Press, Collier-Macmillan, New York.

Goodin, D. (2007) Intel admits tech can be tedious. *The Register* 24 March. Available at: http://www.theregister.co.uk/2007/03/24/intel_anthropologist/ (accessed 24 March 2007).

Graburn, N. (1983) The anthropology of tourism. *Annals of Tourism Research* 10, 9–13.

Graburn, N. (1989) Tourism: the sacred journey. In: Smith, V. (ed.) *Hosts and Guests: the Anthropology of Tourism*, 2nd edn. University of Pennsylvania Press, Philadelphia, Pennsylvania, pp. 21–36.

Graham, S. (1997) Telecommunications and the future of cities: debunking the myths. *Cities* 14(1), 21–29.

Graham, S. (1998) The end of geography or the explosion of place? Conceptualizing space, place and information technology. *Progress in Human Geography* 22(2), 165–185.

Graham, S. (ed.) (2003) *The Cybercities Reader*. Routledge, London.

Green, N. (2002) On the move: technology, mobility, and the mediation of social time and space. *The Information Society* 18(4), 281–292.

Haake, A.B. (2006) Music listening practices in workplace settings in the UK: an exploratory survey of office-based settings. In: *Proceedings of the Ninth International Conference on Music Perception and Cognition*. Alma Mater Studiorum University of

Bologna, Bologna, Italy, 22–26 August. Available at: http://www.shef.ac.uk/content/1/c6/05/52/50/ICMPC9%20ABH%20.doc (accessed 15 April 2006).

Hackley, C. (2005) *Understanding Advertising: Communicating Brands*. Sage, London.

Haddon, L. (2000) The social consequences of mobile telephony: framing questions. Paper presented at the seminar Sosiale Konsekvenser av Mobiltelefoni, organized by Telenor, Oslo, Norway, 16 June.

Harper, R. (2003) Are mobiles good or bad for society? In: Nyiri, K. (ed.) *Mobile Communication: Social and Political Effects*. Passagen Verlag, Vienna, pp. 185–214.

Harrison, D. (2005) Banned: mobile phones that get a bad reception in unspoilt places. *Daily Telegraph* 2 October. Available at: http://www.telegraph.co.uk/news/main. jhtml?xml = /news/2005/10/02/nmob02.xml&sSheet = /news/2005/10/02/ixhome.html (accessed 2 October 2005).

Hollingdale, R.J. (1977) *A Nietzsche Reader*. Penguin, London.

Holmes, D. (2001) Virtual globalization – an introduction. In: Holmes, D. (ed.) *Virtual Globalization: Virtual Spaces/Tourist Spaces*. Routledge, London, pp. 1–53.

Howker, E. (2004) Backpackers told to forget the iPod. *Daily Telegraph* 26 April. Available at: http://www.telegraph.co.uk/news/main.jhtml?xml=/news/2004/04/26/nback26.xml (accessed 15 April 2006).

Ind, N. (2004) *Living the Brand: How to Transform Every Member of Your Organization Into a Brand Champion*. Kogan Page, London.

International Federation of the Phonographic Industry (IFPI) (2007) Digital Music Report. Available at: http://www.ifpi.org/content/library/digital-music-report-2007.pdf (accessed 10 March 2007).

Jain, J. and Lyons, G. (2006) Connecting dispersed communities on the move. In: Marshall, S., Taylor, W. and Yu, X. (eds) *Encyclopedia of Developing Regional Communities with Information and Communication Technology*. Idea Group Reference, Hershey, Pennsylvania, pp. 124–129.

Jamal, T. and Hill, S. (2002) The home and the world: (post)touristic spaces of (in)authenticity? In: Dann, G. (ed.) *The Tourist as a Metaphor of the Social World*. CAB International, Wallingford, UK, pp. 77–108.

Jamieson, T. (1996) Been there – done that: identity and the overseas experience of young Pakeha New Zealanders. MA thesis in Social Anthropology, Massey University, Palmerston North, New Zealand.

Jansson, A. (2006) Specialized spaces. Touristic communication in the age of hyper-space biased media. Working paper no. 137–06. Centre for Cultural Research, University of Aarhus, Denmark. Available at: ahttp://www.hum.au.dk/ ckulturf/pages/publications/ aj/specialized_spaces.pdf (accessed 20 February 2007).

Jara-Diaz, S.R. (2000) Allocation and valuation of travel time savings. In: Hensher, D. and Button, K. (eds) *Handbooks in Transport, Vol. 1: Transport Modelling*. Pergamon Press, Oxford, UK, pp. 303–319.

Jenkins, O.H. (2003) Photography and travel brochures: the circle of representation. *Tourism Geographies* 5(3), 305–328.

Jensen, K.B. (2002) Introduction: the state of convergence in media and communication research. In: Jensen, K.B. (ed.) *The Quantitative Research Process. A Handbook of Media and Communication Research: Qualitative and Quantitative Methodologies*. Routledge, London, pp. 1–14.

Johnson, R.E. and Bate, J.D. (2003) *The Power of Strategy Innovation: a New Way of Linking Creativity and Strategic Planning*. AMACOM Div American Management Association, New York.

Kain, D. and King, B. (2004) Destination-based product selections by international backpackers in Australia. In: Wilson, J. and Richards, G. (eds) *The Global Nomad:*

Backpacker Travel in Theory and Practice. Channel View Publications, Clevedon, UK, pp. 196–216.

Kakihara, M. and Sørensen, C. (2002) Mobility: an extended perspective. Paper 15(2). In: Sprague Jr, R. (ed.) *Proceedings of the 35th Hawaii International Conference on System Sciences* (HICSS-35). Big Island, Hawaii, 7–10 January. Institute of Electrical and Electronics Engineers (IEEE) Computer Society, Los Alamitos, California.

Kellerman, A. (2006) *Personal Mobilities*. Routledge, New York.

Kidd, K. (2005) It's all in your head. *The Toronto Star* 9 October. Available at: http://www.thestar.com (accessed 1 March 2006).

King, B. and Spearitt, P. (2001) Resort curtilages: the creation of physical and psychological tourism spaces. In: Holmes, D. (ed.) *Virtual Globalization: Virtual Spaces/Tourist Spaces*. Routledge, London, pp. 245–261.

Kohiyama, K. (2005) Mobile communication and place. *Vodafone Receiver* 13. Available at: http://www.vodafone.com/flash/receiver/13/articles/pdf/13_06.pdf (accessed 24 February 2006).

Kontogeorgopoulos, N. (2003) Tourists, travellers, and the quest for cultural authenticity in southern Thailand. *Tourist Studies* 3(2), 171–203.

Larsen, J. (2001) Tourism mobilities and the travel glance: experiences of being on the move. *Scandinavian Journal of Hospitality and Tourism* 1, 80–98.

Lash, S. and Urry, J. (1994) *Economies of Signs and Space*. Sage, London.

Laurier, E. (2002) The region as a socio-technical accomplishment. In: Brown, B., Green, N. and Harper, R. (eds) *Wireless World: Social and Interactional Aspects of the Mobile Age*. Springer, Berlin, pp. 46–61.

Lengkeek, J. (2001) Leisure experience and imagination: rethinking Cohen's modes of tourism experience. *International Sociology* 16(2), 173–184.

Linden, G., Kraemer, K.L. and Dedrick, J. (2007) Who Captures Value in a Global Innovation System? The case of Apple's iPod' Personal Computing Industry Center (PCIC). University of California. Available at: http://pcic.merage.uci.edu/papers/2007/AppleiPod.pdf (accessed 30 June 2007).

Ling, R. (1997) One can talk about common manners! The use of mobile telephones in inappropriate situations. In: Haddon, L. (ed.) *Themes in Mobile Telephony*. Final Report of the COST 248 Home and Work group, Chunchon, South Korea.

Ling, R. (2002) The social juxtaposition of mobile telephone conversations and public spaces. Social consequences of mobile telephones. Paper presented at The Social and Cultural Impact/Meaning of Mobile Communication, School of Communication, Hallym University, Chunchon, Korea, 13–15 July.

Lury, C. (1997) The objects of travel. In: Rojek, C. and Urry, J. (eds) *Touring Cultures*. Routledge, London, pp. 75–95.

Lyons, G., Jain, J. and Holley, D. (2007) The use of travel time by rail passengers in Great Britain. *Transportation Research A* 41, 107–120.

MacCannell, D. (1999) *The Tourist*. University of California Press, Berkeley, California.

MacCannell, D. (2001) Remarks on the commodification of cultures. In: Smith, V.L. and Brent, M. (eds) *Hosts and Guests Revisited: Tourism Issues of the 21st Century*. Cognizant Communication Corp, New York, pp. 380–390.

Mackie, P.J., Jara-Diaz, S.R. and Fowkes, A. (2001) The value of travel time savings in evaluation. *Transportation Research* 37E, 91–106.

Madden, M. (2006) Pew Internet Project Data Memo. Pew Research Center. Available at: http://www.pewinternet.org/pdfs/PIP_Podcasting.pdf (accessed 21 July 2006).

Maoz, D. (2006) The mutual gaze. *Annals of Tourism Research* 33(1), 221–239.

Mason, P. (2002) The big OE: New Zealanders' overseas experience in the UK. In: Williams, A. and Hall, C.M. (eds) *Tourism and Migration*. Kluwer Publications, New York, pp. 87–101.

Massey, D. (1993) Power-geometry and a progressive sense of place. In: Bird, J., Curtis, B., Putnam, T., Robertson, G. and Tickner, L. (eds) *Mapping the Futures: Local Cultures, Global Change*. Routledge, London, pp. 59–69.

Mejias, U. (1999) Sustainable communicational realities in the age of virtuality. *Critical Studies in Media Communication* 18(2), 211–228.

Mejias, U. (2007) Networked participation: wisdom of crowds or stupidity of masses? Floating Points 4 Conference on Participatory Media. Emerson College, Boston, Massachusetts, 28 February.

Michael, M. (2000) *Reconnecting Culture, Technology and Nature: from Society to Heterogeneity*. Routledge, London.

Mitchell, W. (2002) E-bodies, e-building, e-cities. In: Leach, N. (ed.) *Designing for a Digital World*. Wiley-Academy, Chichester, UK, pp. 50–56.

Murphy, L. (2001) Exploring social interactions of backpackers. *Annals of Tourism Research* 28(1), 50–67.

Nielsen, L.D. (2005) Reflexive mobility – a critical and action oriented perspective on transport research. In: Thomsen, T.U., Nielsen, L.D. and Gudmundsson, H. (eds) *Social Perspectives on Mobility*. Ashgate, Aldershot, UK, pp. 47–66.

Noy, C. and Cohen, E. (2005) Introduction: backpacking as a rite of passage in Israel. In: Noy, C. and Cohen, E. (eds) *Israeli Backpackers and their Society: a View from Afar*. State University of New York Press, Albany, New York, pp. 1–44.

Ofcom (2007) Overview – the Year in Communications. Available at: http://www.ofcom.org.uk/research/cm/cm06/overview06/year/ (accessed 30 March 2007).

O'Hara, K. and Brown, B. (2006) Consuming music together: introduction and overview. In: O'Hara, K. and Brown, B. (eds) *Consuming Music Together: Social and Collaborative Aspects of Music Consumption Technologies*. Springer, Dordrecht, The Netherlands, pp. 3–18.

O'Reilly, C.C. (2006) From drifter to gap year tourist: mainstream backpacker travel. *Annals of Tourism Research* 33(4), 998–1017.

Parrinello, G.L. (2001) The technological body in tourism, research and praxis. *International Sociology* 16, 205–219.

Paulos, E. and Goodman, E. (2004) The familiar stranger: anxiety, comfort, and play in public places. In: *Proceedings of Special Interest Group on Computer–Human Interaction Conference on Human Factors in Computing Systems* 6(1), 223–230. Available at: berkeley.intel-research.net/paulos/pubs/papers/Familiar%20Stranger%20(CHI%202004).pdf (accessed 14 February 2007).

Pearce, L. (2000) Driving north/driving south: reflections upon the spatial/temporal co-ordinates of 'home'. In: Pearce, L. (ed.) *Devolving Identities: Feminist Readings in Home and Belonging*. Ashgate, Aldershot, UK, pp. 162–178.

Perec, G. (1997) *Species of Spaces and Other Pieces*. (Edited and translated by J. Sturrock). Penguin Books, London.

Perkins, H.C. and Thorns, D.C. (2001) Gazing or performing? Reflections on Urry's tourist gaze in the context of contemporary experience in the Antipodes. *International Sociology* 16(2), 185–204.

Plant, S. (2001) On the Mobile. The Effect of Mobile Telephones on Social and Individual Life. Motorola Report. Available at: www.motorola.com/mot/doc/0/234_MotDoc.pdf (accessed 20 February 2007).

Pooley, C., Turnbull, J. and Adams, M. (2005) *A Mobile Century? Changes in Everyday Mobility in Britain in the Twentieth Century*. Ashgate, Aldershot, UK.

Powell, A. (2004) Space, place, reality and virtuality in urban internet cafés. In: *Proceedings of the Second Annual Canadian Association of Cultural Studies Conference*. The Canadian Association of Culture Studies, McMaster University, Hamilton,

Ontario, Canada, 13–15 February. Available at: http://www.culturalstudies.ca/ proceedings04/pdfs/powell.pdf (accessed 15 June 2006).

Putnam, R.D. (2000) *Bowling Alone: the Collapse and Revival of American Community.* Simon and Schuster, New York.

Rapport, N. (1997) *Transcendent Individual: Towards a Literary and Liberal Anthropology.* Routledge, London.

Reppel, A., Szmigin, I. and Gruber, T. (2006) The iPod phenomenon: identifying a market leader's secrets through qualitative marketing research. *Journal of Product and Brand Management* 15(4), 239–249.

Richards, G. (2007) New Horizons II – the Young Independent Traveller. World Youth and Student Educational (WYSE) Travel Confederation. Available at: http://www. aboutwysetc.org/Docs/New_HorizonsII.pdf (accessed 30 August 2007).

Richards, G. and Wilson, J. (2004a) The global nomad: motivations and behaviour of independent travellers worldwide. In: Wilson, J. and Richards, G. (eds) *The Global Nomad: Backpacker Travel in Theory and Practice.* Channel View Publications, Clevedon, UK, pp. 14–42.

Richards, G. and Wilson, J. (2004b) Widening perspectives in backpacker research. In: Wilson, J. and Richards, G. (eds) *The Global Nomad: Backpacker Travel in Theory and Practice.* Channel View Publications, Clevedon, UK, pp. 253–279.

Rojek, C. (1993) *Ways of Escape: Modern Transformations in Leisure and Travel.* Macmillan, Basingstoke, UK.

Rosen, C. (2004) Our cell phones, ourselves. *The New Atlantis* 6 (Summer), 26–45. Available at: http://www.thenewatlantis.com/archive/6/TNA06-CRosen.pdf (accessed 5 July 2005).

Rosen, C. (2005) The age of egocasting. *The New Atlantis* 7 (Fall 2004/Winter 2005), 51–72. Available at: http://www.thenewatlantis.com/archive/7/TNA07-Rosen.pdf (accessed 17 January 2006).

Ross, K. (1995) *Fast Cars, Clean Bodies: Decolonization and the Reordering of French Culture.* MIT Press, Cambridge, Massachusetts.

Russell, G. and Holmes, D. (1996) Electronic nomads? Implications of trends in adolescents' use of communication and information technology. *Australian Journal of Educational Technology* 12(2), 130–144. Available at: http://www.ascilite.org.au/ajet/ ajet12/russell.html (accessed 2 November 2005).

Sacks, D. (2005) Act II: the iPod effect. *Fast Company* 8 April. Available at: http:// blog.fastcompany.com/archives/2005/04/08/act_ii_the_ipod_effect.html (accessed 5 December 2005).

Savage, S., Collins-Mayo, S., Mayo, B. and Cray, G. (2006) *Making Sense of Generation Y.* Church House Publishing, London.

Selwyn, N. (2003) Apart from technology: understanding people's non-use of information and communication technologies in everyday life. *Technology in Society* 25(1), 99–116.

Shaffer, T.S. (2004) Performing backpacking: constructing 'authenticity' every step of the way. *Text and Performance Quarterly* 24(2), 139–160.

Sheller, M. (2004a) Automotive emotions: feeling the car. *Theory, Culture, Society* 21(4–5), 221–242.

Sheller, M. (2004b) Mobile publics: beyond the network perspective. *Environment and Planning D: Society and Space* 22, 39–52.

Shields, R. (1991) *Places on the Margins: Alternative Geographies of Modernity.* Routledge, London.

Simmel, G. (1949) The sociology of sociability. (Translated by E.C. Hughes). Originally from *Soziologie der Geselligkeit*, his speech to first meeting of the German Sociol Society, 1911. *American Journal of Sociology* 55(3), 254–261.

Simmel, G. (2004) *The Philosophy of Money*. Routledge, London.

Smart, B. (1992) *Modern Conditions, Postmodern Controversies*. Routledge, London.

Soojung-Kim Pang, A. (2005) From iPod to ourpod: will it become a more social machine? *Mercury News* 7 October. Available at: http://www.mercurynews.com/mld/mercurynews/news/local/12848273.htm (accessed 25 November 2005).

Sterne, J. (2006) The death and life of digital audio. *Interdisciplinary Science Reviews* 31(4), 338–348.

Stevenson, N. (2002) *Understanding Media Cultures*, 2nd edn. Sage Publications, London.

Strain, E. (2003) *Public Places, Private Journeys: Ethnography, Entertainment and the Tourist Gaze*. Rutgers University Press, New Brunswick, New Jersey.

Sullivan, A. (2005) Society is dead, we have retreated into the iWorld. *The Times* 20 February. Available at: http://www.timesonline.co.uk/article/0,,2088-1491500_1,00.html (accessed 25 September 2005).

Suvantola, J. (2002) *Tourist's Experience of Place*. Ashgate, Aldershot, UK.

Taylor, K. (2005) iPods set off iMania. *Detroit News* 31 January. Available at: http://www.detnews.com/2005/lifestyle/0501/31/C01- 74555.htm (accessed 16 November 2005).

Thomsen, T.U., Nielsen. L.D. and Gudmundsson, H. (eds) (2005) *Social Perspectives on Mobility*. Ashgate, Aldershot, UK.

Tonkiss, F. (2005) *Space, the City and Social Theory: Social Relations and Urban Forms*. Blackwell Publishing, Oxford, UK.

Turner, V. (1974) *Dramas, Fields and Metaphors*. Cornell University Press, Ithaca, New York.

Turner, V. (1978) *Image and Pilgrimage in Christian Culture: Anthropological Perspectives*. Columbia University Press, New York.

United Nations World Tourism Organization (UNWTO) (2007) *UNWTO World Tourism Barometer* 5(1), January. Available at: http://www.unwto.org (accessed 11 February 2007).

Urry, J. (1990) *The Tourist Gaze*. Sage, London.

Urry, J. (1997) *The Tourist Gaze: Leisure and Travel in Contemporary Societies*. Sage, London.

Urry, J. (2000) *Sociology Beyond Societies: Mobilities for the Twenty First Century*. Routledge, London.

Urry, J. (2002a) Mobility and proximity. *Sociology* 36(2), 255–274.

Urry, J. (2002b) Mobility and Connections. Department of Sociology, Lancaster University, UK. Available at: http://www.ville-en-mouvement.com/telechargement/040602/mobility.pdf (accessed 28 August 2006).

Urry, J. (2002c) *The Tourist Gaze*, 2nd edn. Sage, London.

Urry, J. (2003) The 'consumption' of tourism. In: Clarke, D.B., Doel, M.A. and Housiaux, K.M.L. (eds) *The Consumption Read*. Routledge, London, pp. 117–121.

Urry, J. (2004) The new mobilities paradigm. In: Bonß, W., Kesselring, S. and Vogl, G. (eds) *Mobility and the Cosmopolitan Perspective*. Workshop at the Munich Reflexive Modernization Research Centre (SFB 536), 29–30 January. Available at: http//www.cosmobilities.net (accessed 28 June 2005).

Vance, P. (2004) Backpacker transport choice: a conceptual framework applied to New Zealand. In: Wilson, J. and Richards, G. (eds) *The Global Nomad: Backpacker Travel in Theory and Practice*. Channel View Publications, Clevedon, UK, pp. 237–250.

Van Gennep, A. (1960) *The Rites of Passage*. Routledge, London.

Varian, H.R. (2007) An iPod has global value. Ask the (many) countries that make it. *New York Times* 28 June. Available at: http://www.nytimes.com/2007/06/

28/business/worldbusiness/28scene.html?ref=worldbusiness (accessed 28 June 2005).

Voida, A. (2005) Digital music in the workplace. Georgia Institute of Technology Press Release 4 April. Available at: http://www.cc.gatech.edu/news/digitalmusic.html (accessed 11 January 2005).

Voida, A., Grinter, R.E., Ducheneaut, N., Edwards, W.K. and Newman, M.W (2005) Listening. In: *Practices Surrounding iTunes Music Sharing. Proceedings of the Special Interest Group on Computer–Human Interaction (SIGCHI) Conference on Human Factors in Computing Systems (Computer–Human Interaction (CHI) 2005)*, Portland, Oregon, 2–7 April.

Voida, A., Grinter, R.E. and Ducheneaut, N. (2006) Social practices around iTunes. In: O'Hara, K. and Brown, B. (eds) *Consuming Music Together: Social and Collaborative Aspects of Music Consumption Technologies*. Springer, Dordrecht, The Netherlands, pp. 57–83.

Wang, N. (1999) Rethinking authenticity in tourism experience. *Annals of Tourism Research* 26(2), 349–370.

Weber, H. (2004) Portable audio equipment of the 80 s in urban and domestic spaces: Walkmans and Ghetto Blasters as mobile listening tools. Working paper, winter 2004, based on the talk 'Portable pleasures: audio equipment of the 80s in urban and domestic spaces' presented in the Panel: The Electronic Eighties: Domesticating, Gendering and Consuming, 1975–1990 at the Annual Meeting of the Society for the History of Technology (SHOT), Amsterdam, 7–10 October.

Wellman, B. (2001) Physical place and cyberplace: the rise of personalized networking. *International Journal of Urban and Regional Research* 25(2), 227–252.

Wellman, B., Miyata, K. and Boase, J. (2005) The wired – and wireless – Japanese webphones, PCs and social networks. In: Pedersen, P.E. (ed.) *Mobile Communications: Re-negotiation of the Social Sphere*. Springer, London, pp. 427–450.

Wolverton, T. and Boudreau, J. (2006) In 5 years, iPod has become a pop icon. *Mercury News* 24 October. Available at: http://www.findarticles.com/p/articles/mi_kmtmn/ is_200610/ai_n16951929 (accessed 24 October 2006).

Woolgar, S. (1991) Configuring the user: the case of usability trials. In: Law, J. (ed.) *A Sociology of Monsters. Essays on Power, Technology and Domination*. Routledge, London, pp. 57–102.

10 Environmental Discourses in the Aviation Industry: the Reproduction of Mobility

PAUL PEETERS AND STEFAN GÖSSLING

Introduction

Tourism mobility in the industrialized countries has changed substantially in the past decade, with a general trend towards more frequent, but shorter trips, and trips to more distant locations. Within Europe, this development is characterized by the emergence of low-fare airlines offering, for example, a wide variety of city breaks. Globally, an increasing number of people travel to distant or peripheral destinations, often for short periods of time. These developments are facilitated by air travel, which, since the early 1960s, has turned from a luxury form of mobility for the wealthy few into a contemporary form of hypermobility (Adams, 2005). Hypermobility – mobility patterns that involve movements that are frequent in time and often long distance in space – is a characteristic of industrialized societies (Khisty and Zeitler, 2001) that has emerged with the growing network of airports facilitating global travel between any two places, perceived cheap fares for air travel (particularly in contrast to other means of transport), better education, higher incomes and more leisure time (including opportunities to leave work for longer periods of time) (Hall, 2005). Changing global mobility patterns can be seen as resulting in the transformation of social identities towards cosmopolitan ones (Urry, 1995; Gössling, 2002b; Hall, 2005). This cosmopolitanizing of parts of contemporary society is based on physical movement, with no signs being evident that the revolution of communication technologies will slow down or reverse the trend towards cosmopolitan, hypermobile travellers (Lassen, 2006).

More generally, air travel now serves a wide range of functions: business travellers may increasingly rely on air connections, even to cover short distances, and a growing number of people may commute by air between their places of residence and work on a daily basis. Trends also bear witness to the inclusion of new societal groups in air travel, such as children regularly flying on their own to visit friends and relatives, elderly people commuting to warmer and drier climates for health care, and, probably most importantly in terms of volume, the movement of long-distance leisure travellers. Clearly, movement is now a norm (Hall, 2005) and 'for many people leisure mobility is now routine' (Gössling and Hall, 2006: 5). Global air travel growth rates have been in the order of 5–6%/ year in the period 1970–2000; air transport volume is now five times as large as it was in 1970. Globally, some 42% of all international tourist arrivals are now by air (WTO, 2005). Airbus (2004) suggests that air travel will continue to grow rapidly, with average annual growth rates of 5.3% up to 2023. Boeing (2005) predicts a growth rate of 4.8% until 2024, taking into account strong competition, more airline entrants, lower fares and improved networks. Simultaneously, it is anticipated that governments will continue to deregulate air travel markets. Consequently, air travel will continue to be one of the key factors in international long-haul tourism development, outpacing growth rates for surface transport. Within the European Union (EU), the growth of air travel will mean that average distances covered by each tourist are predicted to increase from about 1150 km in 2000 to about 1600–1700 km by 2020 (Peeters et al., 2004).

Mobility growth has always been viewed as an indicator of progress and economic growth. However, during the past 15 years, concerns have been raised that air travel has increasingly significant environmental consequences (Schumann, 1990, 2003; Penner et al., 1999; Sausen et al., 2005). For example, in an average trip involving air transport, 60–95% of its contribution to global warming will be caused by the flight (Gössling et al., 2005; Peeters and Schouten, 2006). Air travel also deserves special attention because most emissions are released at 10–12 km height in the upper troposphere and lower stratosphere, where they have a larger impact on ozone, cloudiness and radiative forcing than they do at the Earth's surface (Penner et al., 1999). Aircraft emissions thus need to be weighted with a factor of two to four to compare their radiative forcing potential with that of carbon dioxide (CO_2) emissions (Sausen et al., 2005; note that due to differences in relative concentrations and lifetimes of emissions, their radiative forcing contribution needs to be calculated for a given year, in this case 2000). For rail, road and sea-based transport modes the radiative forcing factor is near to one (Peeters et al., 2007). Hence, tourism based on air travel is the most environmentally harmful form of tourism with respect to climate change (Gössling et al., 2005). These insights have only recently been incorporated in tourism research, indicating that a broadening of perspective is necessary in order to move from the consideration of the local environmental consequences of tourism to the consideration of its global environmental consequences (Høyer, 2000; Gössling, 2002a).

European outbound tourism illustrates the role of aviation in terms of tourist movements and corresponding emissions. The share of tourism trips by citizens of the EU based on air transport was less than 20% in Europe in 2000 (Fig. 10.1, including all current 25 European member states). However, these trips accounted for more than half the distances travelled and almost 80% of the greenhouse gas (GHG) emissions released through tourism-related transport. By 2020, the share of outbound tourism trips based on air travel is predicted to increase to 30%, accounting for almost 90% of all emissions resulting from international tourist travel (Peeters et al., 2007).

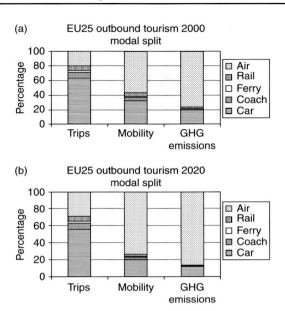

Fig. 10.1. Modal split of number of trips, distances (pkm) and greenhouse gas (GHG) emissions of EU25 outbound tourism transport in 2000 (a) and 2020 (b) (Source: calculation based on Peeters *et al.*, 2004).

The strong growth in air travel and its impact on climate change raise the question of the environmental awareness of air travellers. Knowledge of environmental problems associated with air travel seems low in industrialized societies, even though there are, as yet, few studies to confirm this hypothesis. For example, Gössling *et al.* (2006) conducted a study among international leisure tourists (n = 252) in Zanzibar, Tanzania in order to understand the tourist's perception of tourism-related environmental problems. Results indicated that tourists were largely unaware of the consequences of air travel, while their perception was dominated by local, visible, 'immediate' and comprehensible environmental problems, such as plastic bags deposited along roads. Only 17% of the tourists interviewed mentioned problems associated with air travel, and even fewer had a more profound understanding of the issue, that is, were able to describe the interaction of GHG emissions and climate change. These results need to be seen in the light of the fact that 68% of the respondents reported having university degrees.

Similar results were obtained by a study of international tourists (n = 201) visiting New Zealand and delegates visiting the Council for Australian University Tourism and Hospitality Education Conference (n = 33) in February 2003 (Becken, 2004). About 50% of the tourists believed that a relationship exists between climate change and tourism, in the sense that climate change will affect tourism, but only 12% believed that tourism contributes to climate change. Likewise, almost all of the conference delegates (97%) believed that climate change was an issue for tourism, but only 9% believed that tourism contributes to climate change.

A third study shows that environmental awareness of Dutch tourists declined between 1998 and 2004 (Maas, 2005). In 1998, 68% (n = 2176; representative of the Dutch population) said that they took the environment into consideration at least 'to some extent' when going on vacation. This figure had fallen to 61% (n = 2603) in 2004. Respondents were also asked which pro-environmental measures they took. The broad majority of answers fell into the category 're-move rubbish' (49%), followed by 'leave everything tidy' (17%) and 'drive less/ slower with my car or use public transport' (15%). However, only four of 2603 respondents mentioned 'less/no flying'. All case studies thus indicate that the public awareness of environmental problems connected to flying is low.

Methodology

Various groups in society, including governments, companies and organizations of various kinds, are active in providing information on sustainability. This infor-mation is often discursive in the sense that it presents only part of the aspects of relevance for a balanced understanding of an issue. Clearly, there is no single 'truth' or 'reality', and we thus seek to understand how 'realities' and 'truths' are created in the context of aviation and its environmental performance. We focus on the language and interpretations of the aviation industry, aircraft manufactur-ers and its organizations. This includes both written and spoken forms of lan-guage, as well as language form and function (Burman and Parker, 1993; Pritchard and Jaworski, 2005). The study is delimited by the choice of airlines, aircraft manufacturers and associated international organizations, including British Airways (BA), Lufthansa, Scandinavian Airlines, Airbus, Boeing, Interna-tional Air Transport Association (IATA), International Civil Aviation Organisation (ICAO), Association of European Airlines (AEA), Air Transport Action Group (ATAG), Airports Council International (ACI) Europe, Collaborative Forum of Air Transport Stakeholders, Advisory Council for Aeronautics Research in Europe (ACARE) and the World Tourism Organization (UNWTO). In order to identify discourses, information available in various in-flight magazines, journals, brochures and magazines printed and distributed by airlines and aviation organi-zations, as well as the homepages of airlines and aviation organizations was ana-lysed with a focus on information on the environmental performance of aircraft as well as other environmental issues. Information was collected until no further statements could be found. Research was carried out during 2005. In total, some 40 statements were identified, which seem to comprise and represent the totality of arguments forwarded in the context of air traffic's environmental performance and sustainability. Based on comparative analysis of these statements, four major lines of argument have been identified:

1. Air travel is energy efficient. Globally, it accounts only for marginal emis-sions of CO_2.
2. Air travel is economically and socially too important to be restricted.
3. Environmental impacts exist, but technology will solve the problem.
4. Air travel is treated 'unfairly' in comparison to other means of transport.

The four lines of argument are then compared to material and data available in scientific publications and similar sources of information, in order to understand whether the statements provided by the industry match with scientific insights. Unspecific statements were not considered, including for instance 'protecting our planet is a serious responsibility, and Airbus is aware that reducing environmental impact at the source is a key factor' (Airbus, 2004: 32) or 'environmental responsibility is a pillar of our industry, along with safety and security' (Bisignani, 2005). Obviously, these statements represent discourses as well, as they claim environmental responsibility and promise action, but they are difficult to compare to more specific scientific data. Finally, we discuss how these discourses reproduce contemporary mobility patterns.

Analysis

Argument 1: Air travel is energy efficient. Globally, it accounts only for marginal emissions of CO_2

The two most frequently encountered arguments in the context of the aviation industry's environmental performance are: (i) air travel is 'energy efficient'; and (ii) the contribution of aviation to global emissions of GHGs is negligible in comparison to other sources.

> It [the Airbus A380] will be the first aircraft to crack the 3 l/100 seat-km barrier. Astonishingly, at a typical occupancy rate of 70% this translates into 4 l/100 passenger-km; about the same as a small car with an average load of 1.25 passengers. It also means that the A380 will be some 12% more fuel-efficient per seat than the 747–400, enabling it to save 53 tonnes of fuel, and a corresponding volume of emissions, for every 1000 passengers flown on a 13-h flight. The A380 is truly a 'Green Giant'!
>
> (Bickerstaff, 2005)

> At US$40 per barrel (Brent) fuel is 18% of our total cost. The fuel bill last year was US$63 billion. Even a 10% improvement in fuel efficiency would deliver 2% to our bottom line. The case for investment in more fuel-efficient aircraft is compelling.
>
> (Bisignani, 2005)

The statements are intended to show that relative energy use by aircraft is low, while economic pressures force airlines to further reduce fuel use. Furthermore, technological progress has already led to substantial reductions in fuel use. However, a critical analysis shows that the statement does represent a discourse, as facts are simplified or appear to be incorrect for at least four reasons.

First, comparison is made with small cars in order to show that energy use is low. However, cars can generally not be seen as environmentally friendly, and particularly not at a low occupancy rate of 1.25 passengers/car. Furthermore, in order to compare aircraft to cars, comparison should rather be made with long-distance car occupancy rates, which are higher at about 2 persons/car. Low occupancy rates are particularly found among commuters on short distances (Peeters et al., 2004: Annex VII). Using this more adequate occupancy rate of 2 for comparison, the A380 uses an estimated 60% more fuel per passenger km than the small car used for comparison by Airbus.

Second, comparison with surface-bound means of transport fails to consider that the contribution to global warming by aircraft is significantly higher per unit of fossil fuel burnt, as emissions released at cruise altitude cause additional radiative forcing (Penner et al., 1999; Schumann, 2003).

Third, the presentation of data on relative fuel use should be accompanied by data on fuel use per trip, as people travelling by aircraft usually cover larger distances. To illustrate this: the average fuel use per passenger for a 11,000 km one-way flight corresponds to a Dutch citizen's annual average consumption of fuel used for travel by car. Airlines seem to frequently use relative measures for comparison, such as emissions per seat km, which obscures the fact that total fuel use is high when distance is taken into account.

Finally, the Airbus A380 is an example of an aircraft not reaching highest fuel efficiency. This is because the wingspan of the A380 is limited by the maximum wingspan that can be accommodated by airports (the so-called 80 m box, see de Barros and Wirasinghe, 1997). Therefore the wingspan is less than would be the optimum for such a large and heavy aircraft. It has been estimated that the loss of fuel efficiency is 11% compared to an optimized wingspan of 90.2 m (Dalhuijsen and Slingerland, 2004). This optimal wing design would also lead to 2.4% lower operating costs. However, the costs and implications of modifying many airports to accommodate larger than 80 m spans may be prohibitive. An option to overcome this problem is folding wingtips. Dalhuijsen and Slingerland (2004) show that a folding wing design would result in savings of 10.9% fuel corresponding to 2.1% of the costs. Despite this, the A380 has a non-optimal wingspan of roughly 80 m, which shows that new aircraft are not constructed with a total focus on efficiency.

In conclusion, the figures presented by the industry do not adequately represent air travel's environmental performance, efficiency and sustainability. Similar inadequacies can be found in the statement that GHG emissions by aviation are negligible in comparison to emissions from other sources.

> Today's level of air traffic has a 3.5% share of the man-made greenhouse effect. Industry, power stations and road traffic all have double-digit shares. Even higher is the difference between man-made and natural emission sources, such as volcanic eruptions.
>
> (Lufthansa, 2005)

The figure of 3.5% is widely used, and can, for example, be found in reports of ACI Europe (2005) and Airbus (2004: 38). Obviously, the figure is presented to underline that air transport is not a significant contributor to climate change. The origin of the figure is the International Panel of Climate Change's (IPCC) Third Assessment Report (IPCC, 2001). The figure refers to the overall contribution of subsonic aircraft to radiative forcing as compared to all radiative forcing by anthropogenic activities. Even though the Third Assessment Report is the most recent one published by the IPCC (the Fourth Assessment Report is due in 2007), the figure refers to 1992 and is thus outdated given the over-proportionally strong growth in the aviation sector. Since 1992, total emissions of air transport have increased by 50%, while GHG emissions in the EU have slightly decreased (Gugele *et al.*, 2002). The 2005 contribution of aviation to all anthropogenic radiative forcing is rather in the order of 3.4–6.6% (own calculation; the range being a result of the consideration of radiative forcing; Sausen *et al.*, 2005). Within Europe, GHG emissions of tourism-related aviation account already for 7% of all emissions (in 2000) and are predicted to grow to 15% by 2020 (Peeters *et al.*, 2004) and a (theoretical) 100% by 2050, if a sustainable path of GHG emissions from all other sectors is followed (Bows *et al.*, 2006).

The share of 5.1% (average of range) needs to be seen in the light of the fact that only a minor proportion of the world population participates in air travel. For international air travel, this is 4.6% (all international arrivals by air divided by the world population; based on WTO (2005)). The share of individuals participating in international flights is in reality lower, as many tourists make several trips per year (Gössling *et al.*, 2006). Given the high number of frequent flyers, we estimate that less than 3% of the world's population participates in air travel (international and domestic). Given the current growth rate of aviation emissions, which is in the order of 3.5%/year, the goal to reduce global GHG emissions by 42% by 2050 (Åkerman, 2005: 114) will become difficult to achieve. Under a 'no limits to growth for aviation' scenario, aviation would, as the only sector with continued strong growth in emissions, account for 40% of global total emissions by 2050 (calculation based on Åkerman (2005: 114)). In order to stay within a 'safe rate of climate change' (Graßl *et al.*, 2003), no other economic sector would have room to grow in emissions, not even by moderate rates of 3–4%/year. The contribution of air travel to climate change is thus relevant both in relative and in absolute terms.

Finally, the statement that 'even higher is the difference between man-made and natural emission sources, such as volcanic eruptions' indicates that action to mitigate the anthropogenic greenhouse effect is negligible in the face of the 'natural greenhouse effect'. Clearly, anthropogenic emissions might tip the balance of the climate system, and 'the difference between man-made and natural emission sources' is thus irrelevant. Consequently, comments such as this could thus be interpreted as attempts to render discussions on mitigation irrelevant. In conclusion, the statements presented by the industry on its efficiency and aviation's overall contribution to climate change seem to trivialize the environmental impact, representing a discourse that there are no physical limits to mobility, that is, that the cultural construction of hypermobile lifestyles does not need to be embedded in physical considerations.

Argument 2: Air travel is economically and socially too important to be restricted

Environmental considerations are likely to lead to restrictions in air travel. A second line of argumentation frequently encountered thus highlights the indispensability of aviation for global and national economies and its importance for global cultural and social exchange:

Air transport is the backbone of global tourism – the number one employer in the world. [. . .] remember the facts: air transport employs 4 million people and generates US$400 billion in output. Indirectly it creates a further 24 million jobs with nearly US$1.4 trillion in output. This is 4.5% of global GNP.

(Bisignani, 2005)

Similar statements are made by other aviation organizations, for example the Collaborative Forum of Air Transport Stakeholders (2003) or Air Transport Action Group (ATAG, 2005b). Clearly, all tourism depends on transport. However, the economic role of air transport seems often exaggerated. For instance, a survey on European tourism transport revealed that only 5% of all trips by EU citizens are intercontinental and thus necessarily based on air travel. However, the broad majority (75%) of all EU tourism trips (domestic and international) are not based on air travel (Peeters et al., 2004).

In terms of direct and indirect employment, air traffic is certainly of importance. However, the number of jobs in the aviation sector needs to be seen in comparison to jobs in other traffic sectors. For example, the 4 million direct air transport jobs worldwide (Bisignani, 2005: 3) can be compared to 6.9 million direct jobs created by railways worldwide, producing 2000 billion passenger km and 7000 billion t km (UIC, 2003), compared to 3300 billion passenger km and 150 billion t km by air (Pulles et al., 2002). Moreover, it seems likely that the growth in aviation partly entails losses in other traffic sectors (e.g. ferries, railways). Turnover in the aviation sector also needs to be seen from an alternative spending point of view. Clearly, tourists might spend a share of their money on other modes of transport or other consumption goods, should there be no opportunities to spend it on air travel (cf. Alfredsson, 2002).

More generally, it is transport that generates multipliers, not necessarily air transport. Therefore it seems likely that multiplier effects would also occur in other transport sectors. Statements also seek to underline the importance of air transport by making connections to the turnover generated in other sectors: 'aviation is directly linked to the tourism industry in Europe, generating receipts of 700 million Euro per day' (Collaborative Forum of Air Transport Stakeholders, 2003). Note as well that air transport creates jobs and economic growth, but economic turnover comes at a high price for the environment. As economic growth is mostly accumulated in countries with heavy air operations, while global warming will mostly affect poor developing countries (IPCC, 2001), it is also questionable whether the global distribution of benefits and costs is even or just.

Accounts of economic performance are generally difficult to validate. For example, Airports Council International (ACI Europe, 2004) states that: 'a study for the UK Government and the air transport industry estimated that restricting the growth of UK air passenger demand (with 25 million passengers in 2015) could result in a 2.5% reduction in overall UK GDP by 2015, equivalent to £30 billion a year (at 1998 prices)'. Our analysis of the references given by ACI Europe – Oxford Economic Forecasting (OEF, 1999: 46) – shows, however, that the cited losses of £30 billion are not occurring in 1 year, but represent the projected accumulated losses over the period 1998–2015. Hence, expected annual losses correspond to a fraction of the amount cited by ACI Europe. Industry reports such as this one seem not always to be crosschecked, which is problematic, as economic figures usually have great weight in influencing governmental decision making and public opinion. Note that an alternative view of the economic performance of air travel has recently been published by Friends of the Earth UK (2005), showing that spending abroad by UK residents resulted in net losses for the UK economy of £15 billion in 2004.

Discourses on the economic importance of air transport also include the development of 'poor' regions: 'if ministers were sincere about helping developing countries, they would be asking themselves how they could encourage, not discourage, travel and tourism to these regions' (Ulrich Schulte-Strathaus, Director of the Association of European Airlines; cited in T&E, 2005). Various tour operators, the WTO and IATA present similar arguments.

While it is clear that tourism is an important pillar of national economies in many developing countries, particularly small-island developing states, the argument is nevertheless simplified. Tourism in poor developing countries is often to the benefit of foreign investors, who are usually from countries in transition or industrialized countries, with a high concomitant backflow of money (Gössling, 2003). Within developing countries, the distribution of benefits can be skewed, with the majority of benefits being captured by a few well-established actors. Hence, it needs to be questioned whether increases in national GDP through tourism adequately reflect its benefits for local, 'poor' population groups or development processes in general.

Statements also refer frequently to the importance of cultural exchange and 'world peace'. It is undisputed that air transport facilitates cultural exchange, as well as the exchange of knowledge and ideas. However, there is also evidence that not all cross-cultural contacts will have 'positive' results. For the broad majority of mass leisure tourists, for instance, contacts with locals are likely to remain superficial in character and to reinforce stereotypes rather than to create insights in other cultures (Pearce, 2005; van Egmond, 2006: 89). There is, thus, reason for caution about all-too-optimistic views on the cultural dimension of air travel.

Argument 3: Environmental impacts exist, but technology will solve the problem

The third line of argument is one of technological achievement. Here, environmental impacts are usually acknowledged, but it is simultaneously pointed out that technological improvements have already contributed to major efficiency gains, while future technology will solve the remaining problems.

> Building on its impressive environmental record, which includes a 70% reduction in [. . .] emissions at source during the past 40 years, the aviation industry reaffirmed its commitment to [. . .] further develop and use new technologies and operational procedures aimed at minimising noise, fuel consumption and emissions [. . .].
> (ATAG, 2005a; Collaborative Forum of Air Transport Stakeholders, 2003)

> Research programmes typically aim to achieve a 50% fuel- and CO2-reduction per passenger-kilometre by 2020, relative to 2000.
> (ATAG, 2005b)

The figure of a '70% reduction in emissions during the past 40 years' is based on the IPCC special report on aviation (Penner *et al.*, 1999: 298, Fig. 9-3), which compares the least efficient long-haul jet airliner that ever flew, the De Havilland DH106 Comet 4, with the most fuel-efficient commercial aircraft currently operating, the Boeing 777, and is, thus, not representing the environmental performance of the world aircraft fleet. Furthermore, the figure ignores that the last generation of long-haul propeller aircraft (e.g. Lockheed Super Constellations L-1049, L-1049 H and L-1649 and the DC 7C, see Fig. 10.2) had a fuel efficiency equalling that of jets developed between 1980 and 1990 (Peeters *et al.*, 2005).

The statement also suggests that there will be further gains in efficiency in the future. However, contrary to the common presentation of constant annual increases in efficiency (Penner *et al.*, 1999; Lee, 2003), historic data for the development of both piston-engined airliners after the Second World War and jet-engined airliners show that annual gains appear to decrease over time (see Fig. 10.2). Peeters *et al.* (2005) show that further efficiency gains between 2000 and 2040 are likely to be in the order of 20–26%, which is substantially lower than the most conservative IPCC scenario at 43% (Penner *et al.*, 1999). The performance of the new Airbus A380 fits neatly in the regression, while the goal of 50% more efficient aircraft by 2020 (e.g. ATAG, 2005b) appears unrealistic.

Clearly, the statements ignore that relative efficiency gains have decreased over time, and that the projections given by the industry are optimistic. Note, however, that, even with technological achievements, absolute growth in fuel use by aircraft is in the order of 3%/year (Airbus, 2004), with an overall increase from 54.3 megatons (Mt) in 1976 to 101.4 Mt in 1992 and a projected use of 266 Mt by 2015 (Penner *et al.*, 1999: 303).

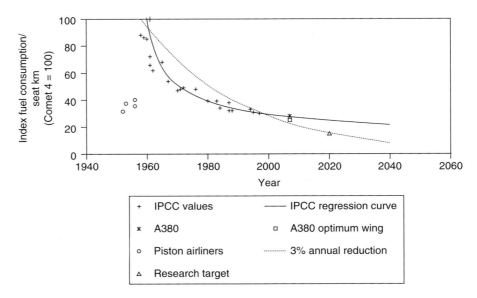

Fig. 10.2. Long-haul aircraft fuel efficiency gains since 1950 as an index (100) of De Havilland DH106 Comet 4 (Source: based on Peeters *et al.*, 2005).

Obstacles to making aviation sustainable have also been discussed by Åkerman (2005), who analysed different targets for GHG emissions in the air transportation sector. The results of two scenarios show that fuel consumption per passenger km would have to be reduced by 80–90% to make the sector sustainable, which cannot be achieved by current aircraft flying at high cruise speeds and altitudes. Alternative fuels are sometimes presented as a future solution to the problem. For example, hydrogen is frequently mentioned in alternative fuel contexts, even though the industry itself is not seriously engaged in developing this kind of technology. Note, for example, that Airbus does not consider hydrogen as a significant aviation fuel in the next 30–40 years (Bickerstaff, 2005). Even if hydrogen-based aircraft existed, it is not clear where the vast amounts of sustainable energy needed for producing hydrogen would come from.

Argument 4: Air travel is 'treated unfairly' in comparison to other means of transport

> In France the government makes a net profit of 67 Euros for every 1,000 passenger kilometres travelled by air. But it pays 78 Euros for the same distance by train. Airlines pay when we park, fly, land or take-off.
>
> (Bisignani, 2005)

'Unfair treatment' of aviation is a recurrent theme in statements released by the industry and its organizations, even though air traffic is, in contrast to other means of transport, certainly favoured, not disadvantaged. For instance, there is no tax on aviation fuels, while there are various taxes on fuel for private transport – and usually, though not always, public transport as well.[1] Likewise, there is a value added tax (VAT) on most international rail and coach tickets, while international aviation is exempted from VAT. It is true that airlines and their customers face charges for 'parking, landing, and take-off', but these are charged by the airport authorities to cover the costs of maintaining and operating the airport. These cannot be compared to taxes. Furthermore, as a result of the ongoing trend of privatizing railways in Europe, many railways do pay explicitly for the use of infrastructure. The Dutch railways, for example, pay over €100 million/year (van Goeverden and Peeters, 2005: 107). The comparison of air transport with rail transport is also inadequate, as, for instance, the European high-speed rail system is profitable. Railway transport systems are, however, accumulating losses on short distances and particularly in rural areas. Government subsidies in these areas are necessary to maintain public transport systems, a state responsibility. Air traffic itself is often subsidized. For instance, governments in many countries have invested substantial amounts of money in national airlines. In other cases, governments have financially supported airlines when they faced bankruptcy; there are numerous examples after 11 September 2001. Ayral (2005) concludes that governments in the EU and the USA 'have always given the airline industry special treatment to shield it from foreign competition [. . .] ranging from price controls and restrictions on market access to tax breaks, discriminatory treatment and straightforward subsidies'. Low-fare carriers such as

Ryanair have received substantial subsidies to serve local, peripheral airports (DFS, 2004: 8). An example is the case of subsidies given by the Walloon Region and Brussels South Charleroi Airport to Ryanair. The European Commission decided in February 2004 that these subsidies were illegal (European Commission, 2004). Subsidies included, for example, a ground-handling fee of €1.00 per passenger, which is 90% less than the European average, a conditional subsidy of €160,000 for each new route opened, €770,000 for recruiting/training pilots and crews for these new routes, and €250,000 for staff accommodation at the opening of the airport as a Ryanair base. Secondary airports generally seem to receive substantial subsidies (cf. Cranfield University, 2002).

The aviation industry often seeks financial comparison with railways, but never makes reference to transport by private car, which is heavily taxed, including fuel excise duty, vehicle purchase tax, vehicle excise duty and VAT (e.g. Swedish Environmental Protection Agency, 2000). In the 15 member states of the EU (members as of April 2004) the tax on petrol and diesel often exceeds the cost of the fuel. Nevertheless, it is clear that the internalization of environmental costs remains insufficient for all transport modes.

Concluding Remarks

The analysis of statements by the aviation industry and its organizations on environmental performance and sustainability shows that these seek to create a positive image of aviation. Statements analysed often use 'scientific' language, presenting indisputable 'facts', coupled with enthusiasm about technological progress. Comparisons are selected carefully, for instance pointing out that aviation is not more environmentally harmful than cars (not trains), that fuel is 'saved' (not used), etc. As the 'facts' presented by the aviation industry only partially match scientific insights, they can be understood as discourses. Consequently, the apparent lack of public awareness of the environmental impacts of aviation might be founded in the fact that the aviation industry puts itself in a good light environmentally.

Four major lines of argument were discussed, representing the main discourses surrounding the environmental harmfulness of aviation. All these arguments seek to create an understanding of the necessity of unrestricted growth of aviation in the public and political debate, based on misrepresentation of the scientific evidence. To some extent, the industry even takes the position of a victim of deliberate government policies hampering its development. This analysis has found little evidence that this position can be supported. However, aviation is supported by most governments, which believe in its economic and social importance, and express optimism that sustainability can be achieved (for the UK, see Sustainable Aviation, 2005). The current situation in the aviation sector can thus be compared to that of the automobile in the mid-1970s, where the use of the car was justified by some societal groups – the 'automobile apologists' and 'social engineers' – over environmental concerns for reasons of free choice and social equity (Taebel and Cornehls, 1977). Indeed, the rhetoric structures underlying and fostering hypermobile, unsustainable lifestyles seemingly have not changed much since the mid-1970s. If anything, they continue to exist in more subtle forms, to also include the aviation sector. Contemporary society thus seems to reproduce unsustainable mobility patterns through discourses on 'environmental harmlessness', 'technology advancement' and 'social or economic benefits'. The power of these discourses, created and maintained by the aviation industry and its organizations, is such that alternative messages have very limited scope to be heard. Even the more recent acknowledgement of the environmental harmfulness of air travel by the EU (European Commission, 2006) or some airlines (i.e. the Scandinavian Airline (SAS) and BA) is for several reasons not as yet a sign of a changing social understanding of mobility. First, it remains to be seen whether environmental problems associated with air travel will be acknowledged by wider parts of society or whether they will be 'neutralized' by the notion of technological advancement. To use the analogy of the car: there has arguably been limited progress in spreading the message of environmental harmfulness of automobility since the mid-1970s, and aviation has only just entered its boom-and-bust cycle of expansion. Second, even if environmental harmfulness is acknowledged by different levels in society (government, industry, public), it remains questionable whether this will affect mobility patterns, with respect to both governmental command-and-control measures and voluntary action. To the contrary, current trends manifested in both travel statistics and development plans by the aviation industry show that per capita average travel distances continue to increase, while the new frontier of expansion is now space (e.g. http://www.spacefuture.com/ and http://www.virgingalactic.com/).

As Khisty and Zeitler (2001: 602) remark: 'Indeed, the automobile-industrial complex, through advertising, lobbying and other influences on public discourse, helps to sustain an "auto culture", cleverly masking its problematic and costly features.' As this chapter has shown, much the same can be said about the discourses created and sustained by the aviation industry. 'Aviation culture' might be characterized by a number of differences to 'auto culture', though, namely its inclusion of a comparably small part of humanity, its greater environmental harmfulness, and its more limited options to solve environmental problems technically. Sheller and Urry (2006: 209) remind us of how the car 'reconfigures urban life, with novel ways of dwelling, travelling, and socialising in, and through, an automobilised time–space'. If anything, this must be as true for aviation. Aviation as no other means of transport changes perceptions of distance, space and time, creating cosmopolitan identities and generating new global social networks. The importance of this transformation lies in the magnitude of the step from automobile to airborne societies, which, in any of its cultural and physical dimensions, must be seen as more fundamental than any earlier change of mobility patterns in human history.

While as yet only parts of society regularly make use of aircraft (e.g. Lassen, 2006), the inclusion of new groups, such as children, health-migrants or commuters, will unavoidably aggregate environmental problems. The societal trends towards the use of aircraft currently observed might also be increasingly irreversible, because of the symbolic power associated with this transport mode in terms of a 'right of mobility', as well as very real need to travel arising in globalized social and economic networks. These findings underline the current dichotomy between Kyoto- and post-Kyoto-reduction needs and the reproduction of mobility through discourses created and maintained by the aviation industry.

Acknowledgements

The chapter is based on an article published in 2007 under the title, 'It does not harm the environment!', an analysis of industry discourses on tourism, air travel and the environment, in the *Journal of Sustainable Tourism* 15(4), pp. 402–417.

We should like to express our gratitude to Susanne Becken, John Broderick, Alexander de Haan and Jo Guiver for their comments on an earlier version of this chapter. The views expressed are entirely our own.

Note

[1]Tax laws for energy products and fuels are a complex matter within the EU. A range of reduced fuel tax rates exists for surface public passenger transport within the 25 EU member states, with rail transport and electric trains, trams and trolleybuses receiving especially favourable treatment. See http://europa.eu.int/scadplus/leg/en/lvb/l27019.htm for more information.

References

Adams, J. (2005) Hypermobility: a challenge to governance. In: Lyall, C. and Tait, J. (eds) *New Modes of Governance: Developing an Integrated Policy Approach to Science, Technology, Risk and the Environment.* Ashgate, Aldershot, UK.

Airbus (2004) *The Airbus Way – Environment.* Environment, Health and Safety (Ehs) Report. Airbus Environmental Affairs, Blagnac, France.

Airports Council International (ACI) Europe (2004) *ACI Europe Comments on the Nera Study to Assess the Effects of Different Slot Allocation Schemes.* ACI Europe, Brussels.

Airports Council International (ACI) Europe (2005) *Strategy on Climate Change.* ACI Europe, Brussels.

Air Transport Action Group (ATAG) (2005a) Air Transport Industry Calls for Collaborative Environmental Action. Press release. Available at: www.environment.aero (accessed 11 May 2005).

Air Transport Action Group (ATAG) (2005b) *Aviation and Environment Summit Discussion Paper.* Air Transport Action Group, Geneva.

Åkerman, J. (2005) Sustainable air transport – on track in 2050. *Transportation Research – D* 10, 111–126.

Alfredsson, E. (2002) *Green Consumption, Energy Use and Carbon Dioxide Emissions.* Department of Geography, Umeå University, Umeå, Sweden.

Ayral, M. (2005) The EU Wants Free Skies over the North Atlantic. Available at: http://www.europeanaffairs.org/archive/2003_fall/2003_fall_92.php4 (accessed 11 May 2005).

Becken, S. (2004) How tourists and tourism experts perceive climate change and carbon-offsetting schemes. *Journal of Sustainable Tourism* 12, 332–345.

Bickerstaff, C. (2005) Aircraft technological developments. AERONET III Workshop on Air Transportation Systems, Stockholm.

Bisignani, G. (2005) Aviation and the Environment. Speech at the First Aviation and the Environment Summit, 17–18 March. Available at: http://www.iata.org/pressroom/speeches/2005-03-17-01 (accessed 11 May 2005).

Boeing (2005) *Current Market Outlook 2005*. Boeing Commercial Airplanes (Marketing), Seattle, Washington.

Bows, A., Anderson, K. and Upham, P. (2006) *Contraction and Convergence: UK Carbon Emissions and the Implications for UK Air Traffic*. Technical Report 40. Tyndall Centre, Manchester, UK.

Burman, E. and Parker, I. (1993) *Discourse Analytic Research: Repertoires and Readings of Texts in Action*. Routledge, London.

Collaborative Forum of Air Transport Stakeholders (2003) *Fast Facts. The Air Transport Industry in Europe Has United to Present Its Key Facts and Figures*. Collaborative Forum of Air Transport Stakeholders, Brussels.

Cranfield University (2002) *Study on Competition Between Airports and the Application of State Aid Rules. Final Report*. Volume 1. Air Transport Group, School of Engineering, Cranfield University, Cranfield, UK.

Dalhuijsen, J.L. and Slingerland, R. (2004) Preliminary wing optimization for very large transport aircraft with wingspan constraints. 42nd American Institute of Aeronautics and Astronautics (AIAA) Aerospace Sciences Meeting and Exhibit, Reno, Nevada, 5–8 January.

de Barros, A.G. and Wirasinghe, S.C. (1997) New aircraft characteristics related to airport planning. First Air Transport Research Group (ATRG) Conference. Vancouver, Canada, 25–27 June.

Deutsche Flug Sicherung (DFS) (2004) *Air Transport in Germany*. Mobility Report 2004. DFS, Langen, Hessen, Germany.

European Commission (2004) Commission decision of 12 February 2004 concerning advantages granted by the Walloon region and Brussels South Charleroi Airport to the airline Ryanair in connection with its establishment at Charleroi (Notified in Number C(2004) 516). *Official Journal of the European Union* 47, 1–62.

European Commission (2006) Aviation and Climate Change. Available at: http://ec.europa.eu/environment/climat/aviation_en.htm (accessed 22 November 2006).

Friends of the Earth UK (2005) Why Airport Expansion is Bad for Regional Economies. Available at: http://www.foe.co.uk/resource/briefings/regional_tourism_deficit.pdf (accessed 11 May 2006).

Gössling, S. (2002a) Global environmental consequences of tourism. *Global Environmental Change part A* 12, 283–302.

Gössling, S. (2002b) Human-environmental relation with tourism. *Annals of Tourism Research* 29, 539–556.

Gössling, S. (ed.) (2003) *Tourism and Development in Tropical Islands: Political Ecology Perspectives*. Edward Elgar Publishing Limited, Cheltenham, UK.

Gössling, S. and Hall, C.M. (2006) An introduction to tourism and global environmental change. In: Gössling, S. and Hall, C.M. (eds) *Tourism and Global Environmental Change. Ecological, Social, Economic and Political Interrelationships*. Routledge, London, pp. 1–33.

Gössling, S., Peeters, P.M., Ceron, J.-P., Dubois, G., Patterson, T. and Richardson, R.B. (2005) The eco-efficiency of tourism. *Ecological Economics* 54, 417–434.

Gössling, S., Bredberg, M., Randow, A., Svensson, P. and Swedlin, E. (2006) Tourist perceptions of climate change: a study of international tourists in Zanzibar. *Current Issues in Tourism* 9(4–5), 419–435.

Graßl, H., Kokott, J., Kulessa, M., Luther, J., Nuscheler, F., Sauerborn, R., Schellnhuber, H.-J., Schubert, R. and Schulze, E.-D. (2003) *Climate Protection Strategies for the 21st Century: Kyoto and Beyond*. Special Report. WBGU (German Advisory Council on Global Change), Berlin.

Gugele, B., Ritter, M. and Marecková, K. (2002) *Greenhouse Gas Emission Trends in Europe, 1990–2000*. 7/2002 European Environmental Agency, Luxembourg.

Hall, C.M. (2005) *Tourism: Rethinking the Social Science of Mobility*. Pearson Education Limited, London.

Høyer, K.G. (2000) Sustainable tourism or sustainable mobility? The Norwegian case. *Journal of Sustainable Tourism* 8, 147–160.

International Panel on Climate Change (IPCC) (2001) *Climate Change 2001: Synthesis Report. Summary for Policymakers*. International Panel on Climate Change, Cambridge.

Khisty, C.J. and Zeitler, U. (2001) Is hypermobility a challenge for transport ethics and systemicity? *Systemic Practice and Action Research* 14, 597–613.

Lassen, C. (2006) Aeromobility and work. *Environment and Planning A* 38, 301–312.

Lee, J. (2003) The potential offered by aircraft and engine technologies. In: Upham, P., Magham, J., Raper, D. and Callum, T. (eds) *Towards Sustainable Aviation*. Earthscan Publications Ltd, London, pp. 162–178.

Lufthansa (2005) Global Aspects. Air Traffic's Impacts on the Earth's Climate. Available at: http://konzern.lufthansa.com/en/html/ueber_uns/balance/umwelt_sozialthemen/ emissionen/globaleaspekte/index.html (accessed 11 May 2005).

Maas, B. (2005) *Duurzaam Toerisme Anwb*. Omnibuspanel 2004, Meting 2 (Sustainable Tourism Anwb). Algemene Nederlandse Wielrijdersbond (ANWB), Den Haag.

Oxford Economic Forecasting (OEF) (1999) *The Contribution of the Aviation Industry to the UK Economy. Final Report*. OEF, London.

Pearce, P.L. (2005) *Tourist Behaviour. Themes and Conceptual Schemes*. Channel View Press, Clevedon, UK.

Peeters, P. and Schouten, F. (2006) Reducing the ecological footprint of inbound tourism and transport to Amsterdam. *Journal of Sustainable Tourism* 14, 157–171.

Peeters, P.M., van Egmond, T. and Visser, N. (2004) *European Tourism, Transport and Environment. Final Version*. NHTV Centre for Sustainable Tourism and Transport, Breda, The Netherlands.

Peeters, P.M., Middel, J. and Hoolhorst, A. (2005) *Fuel Efficiency of Commercial Aircraft. An Overview of Historical and Future Trends*. NLR-CR-2005- 269. Peeters Advies/Nationaal Lucht- en Ruimtevaardlaboratorium (NLR) (National Aerospace Laboratory), Amsterdam.

Peeters, P.M., Szimba, E. and Duijnisveld, M. (2007) Major environmental impacts of European tourist transport. *Journal of Transport Geography* 15, 83–93.

Penner, J.E., Lister, D.H., Griggs, D.J., Dokken, D.J. and McFarland, M. (eds) (1999) *Aviation and the Global Atmosphere: a Special Report of IPCC Working Groups I and Iii*. Cambridge University Press, Cambridge.

Pritchard, A. and Jaworski, A. (2005) Introduction. Discourses, communication and tourism dialogues. In: Pritchard, A. and Jaworski, A. (eds) *Discourse, Communication and Tourism*. Channel View Press, Clevedon, UK, pp. 1–16.

Pulles, J.W., Baarse, G., Hancox, R., Middel, J. and van Velthoven, P.F.J. (2002) *Aviation Emissions and Evaluation of Reduction Options. Aero Main Report*. Ministerie van Verkeer & Waterstaat (Transport and Water Management), Den Haag, the Netherlands.

Sausen, R., Isaksen, I., Grewe, V., Hauglustaine, D., Lee, D.S., Myhre, G., Köhler, M.O., Pitari, G., Schumann, U., Stordal, F. and Zerefos, C. (2005) Aviation radiative forcing in 2000: an update on IPCC (1999). *Meteorologische Zeitschrift* 14, 555–561.

Schumann, U. (1990) *Air Traffic and the Environment*. Springer, Hamburg, Germany.

Schumann, U. (2003) Aviation, atmosphere and climate – what has been learned. In: Sausen, R., Fichter, C. and Amanatidis, G. (eds) *Proceedings of the Aac-Conference*, 30 June–3 July. European Commission, Friedrichshafen, Germany, pp. 349–355.

Sheller, M. and Urry, J. (2006) The new mobilities paradigm. *Environment and Planning A* 38, 207–226.

Sustainable Aviation (2005) A Strategy Towards Sustainable Development of UK Aviation. Available at: http://www.sustainableaviation.co.uk/doc/summarydocument.pdf (accessed 19 August 2005).

Swedish Environmental Protection Agency (2000) *EU – Fuel and Vehicle Tax Policy*. 5084. Swedish Environmental Protection Agency, Stockholm.

Taebel, D.A. and Cornehls, J.V. (1977) *The Political Economy of Urban Transportation*. Kennikat Press, Port Washington, New York.

T&E (2005) Ministers said to be open to tax on aviation fuel. *T&E Bulletin. News from the European Federation for Transport and Environment (T&E)* 2.

UIC (2003) *Railway Statistics 2002. Synopsis*. International Union of Railways (UIC), Paris.

Urry, J. (1995) *Consuming Places*. Routledge, London.

van Egmond, T. (2006) *Understanding the Tourist Phenomenon. An Analysis of 'West–South' Tourism*. Wageningen University, Wageningen, The Netherlands.

van Goeverden, C.D. and Peeters, P.M. (2005) Financially independent public transport; its impacts on the public transport system in the Netherlands. *European Journal of Transport and Infrastructure Research* 5, 97–114.

World Tourism Organization (WTO) (2005) *Tourism Market Trends. World Overview and Tourism Topics*, 2004 edn. WTO, Madrid, Spain.

11 Business Relations in the Design of Package Tours in a Changing Environment: the Case of Tourism from Germany to Jordan

Sabine Dörry

Introduction

The academic tourism discourse about the phenomenon of mobility from a sociological perspective centrally broaches the issue of physical mobility of individual travellers and their varying influences. Due to this dominant demand-side oriented research, social relations of economic players on the supply side are often neglected. In 1991, Britton (1991: 456) stated that at that point:

> treatments of the economic mechanisms and organisation of the tourism system in the geographic literature cease. The geography texts on tourism offer little more than a cursory and superficial analysis of how the tourism industry is structured and regulated by the classic imperatives and laws governing capitalist accumulation.

Up to now, research focus has only marginally been directed towards the supply-side structure and coordination patterns of the tourism industry (Ioannides and Debbage, 1998). This criticism can also be applied to the influence of the demand on the supply side, or, in other words, the relations between suppliers within the tourist production system because producers and therefore suppliers need to react to changes on the demand side. In response to these changes, socio-economic relations are highly affected in the first instance by strategic decisions of the firm with access to the final consumer markets. Gereffi's (1994, 1996) global value chain (GVC)[1] approach provides a fruitful analytical framework on the mesoscopic level for investigating both the influence of the demand side on the supply side and the effect of changes in the demand side on socio-economic relations. This will be applied in the context of this chapter.

Tourist flows within the scope of package-tour tourism are usually handled by two central agents: the tour operator (TO) in the source market, in the present case situated in Germany, and the incoming agency (IA) in the destination, in this case in Jordan. TOs act as independent companies offering their services under their own name and carrying the whole responsibility towards their customers. In contrast, IAs are responsible for ground handling in the destination itself which comprises preparatory tasks (e.g. supply of required hotel rooms) as well as operational tasks during the tourists' stay (e.g. organization of local transfer and handling of potential complaints). IAs are able to realize economies of scale by bundling demand from different TOs to achieve lower prices. German standardized package-tour holidays to the southern sunny beach destinations have experienced an increase in the leisure segment during the last decade (1994: 25%; 2004: 31.5%; FUR, 2005) and remain an important pillar of the German TO's range of products, especially to rather exotic countries.

The Jordanian incoming market is highly professionalized due to a long tourist tradition as well as long-lasting experiences with different TOs from a wide range of miscellaneous countries. The competition among the agencies has drastically increased as a result of a lot of spin-offs and start-ups, especially within the last few years when the sector largely suffered from a wide absence of (Western) tourists. Comparing different Jordan travel packages of German TOs, one can observe that the average Jordan travel product offered to German customers is rather standardized and differs mainly, if at all, in regard to the standard of the chosen facilities (e.g. local transport, accommodation) and therefore in the price of the package tour. Presently, the situation on the German travel market can be referred to as a combined price and quality competition. TOs occupy an important 'doubly strategic position between all the principal suppliers and between suppliers and customers' as Britton (1991: 457) appositely points out.

Both players, TO and IA, are central to the 'production' process of a package tour. TOs need to cooperate with their selected local partners in Jordan as this results in a reduction of the TO's transaction costs. Unlike IAs, TOs possess exclusive access to the final consumer market. Therefore, it is assumed that TOs, in their decision making towards defining a package-tour design and the service quality in Jordan, might regulate the IA's action. This strategic disequilibrium could be intensified in case of a sudden drop of tourist numbers to Jordan.

TOs often promote travel destinations, for example with the aid of their travel catalogues, which emphasize traditional clichés such as camels, desert and Bedouins in the case of Jordan. Generally they promote themselves as a company, so the customer's choice in favour of a certain destination is not as important to the TO as long as it benefits the business. Therefore, in order to promote the destination to stimulate travelling, particular national tourist boards need to campaign, as is the case of Egypt or Dubai, two current success stories.

Germany is one of the most established tourist source markets for Jordan, with a long travel tradition. In 2004, Germany was the second largest Western European source market (about 28,000 tourists), only exceeded by the UK (about 54,100 tourist arrivals) (Ministry of Tourism, 2005), although the number of tourists visiting Jordan is comparatively small compared to those visiting other destinations like Spain, where German tourist arrivals reached more than 10 million in 2003, or Egypt with more than 900,000 German tourist arrivals in 2004 (Auswärtiges Amt, Deutschland, 2005). For these comparatively small numbers, Jordan cannot be recognized as a mass market but as a niche market, mostly for culturally and religiously motivated German tourists. In fact, this is indicated by the absence of giant travel companies like Thomas Cook or TUI. Indeed, at present only their subsidiaries as well as independent small and medium-sized travel companies offer package tours from Germany to Jordan.[2] So far, within the scope of the aforementioned project, I have empirically analysed 25 German small and medium-sized TOs working in the Jordanian market.

More and more, socio-political events determine the individual's attitude towards travelling (Bachleitner, 2004). For Jordan as a leisure destination, a whole bundle of exogenous shock moments have been responsible for a sudden absence of Western, especially German, tourists during the last 3 years. Essentially, Jordan's difficult geopolitical location within the politically unstable region of the Middle East and its shared borders with the conflict parties Palestine and Israel as well as the war in Iraq have not added to a secure feeling for potential German tourists travelling to Jordan. In Germany, reports in the daily mass media (e.g. newspapers, television and the Internet) about these events contributed to this widely recognized uncertainty regarding Jordan as a famous tourist destination. In addition, the catastrophe of 9/11 obviously played an important role for postponing planned trips to Jordan. Therefore, the dynamic, global and complex tourist system is indeed sensitive to external events. However, as Bachleitner observes, it seems to be stable in the long run (Bachleitner, 2004). Nevertheless, German tourists are highly susceptible to any security risk. Despite the occurrence of global crises, income receipts from tourism still accounted for 8–9% of Jordan's GDP in 2003 (Barham, 2004).

Tourism markets are to a large extent nationally defined in spite of the argument in favour of an international equalization through the 'proliferation of images and symbols', which consolidate judgements of taste and the distinction between different societies (Lash and Urry, 1994: 256). Travellers from different countries require varying travel standards due to differing expectations and travel habits, even for example in the context of a perceived present-day 'common' European culture. If IAs want to develop new markets they can only benefit from synergies to a certain extent and still have to invest in each single market.[3] Urry (2002a: 271) claims that the 'intersecting mobilities and diverse proximities are topics' for a forthcoming sociology. For the analysis of social business exchange relations in tourism, Leslie and Reimer (1999: 410) suggest connecting the consumption with the production side in order 'to encourage a politics of consumption through the "thickening" of producer–consumer connection'. According to Gereffi (1994) this can best be done by defining a product-specific input–output design. In the case of the leisure tourism industry a suitable and product-based research scope might be the package tour. This chapter will look at causes on the consumption side and, in regard to that, discuss some central consequences for a focused relationship on the production side between TO and IA.

Global Value Chain Approach and Tourism

The causalities of economic relations within the scope of today's increasing global integration can be demonstrated with the aid of Gereffi's (1994, 1996) GVC approach. It connects contemporary events on a macroscopic level dynamically with the organizational structures of firms on a microscopic scale (Gereffi, 1995) framed by a spatial dimension. Basically, the concept starts from a perspective of dependency between industrialized and developing economies. It is assumed that the local production of goods (and services) in a developing country is highly dependent from being embedded into a GVC which is 'governed' by powerful firms in industrialized countries. These firms are able to organize the production chain according to their concepts of tremendous purchasing power as well as their exclusive access to the final consumer market (a so-called buyer-driven chain). Governance in this context has been characterized as an 'authority and power relationship between firms that determines how financial, material, and human resources are allocated and flow within a chain' (Gereffi, 1995: 96). As a result, upgrading opportunities for 'suppliers' in developing countries are either in the interest of the purchasing firm or they are simply blocked. However, this process of upgrading is not the subject of the analysis in this chapter.

Up to now, the attempt of Clancy (1998) to connect the specific concept of GVC with tourism with a focus on the production side seems to be considered by only very few researchers (see for instance Mosedale, 2006). However, Clancy's rather restricted view on the two largest touristic subsectors, hotels and airlines, within the so-called sun, sand and sea mass-tourism sector lacks a product-specific connection. Hence, the interaction of the multitude of touristic sub-sectors such as handicraft, tour guides, etc. on a product-specific base, like the package tour, still remains unreflected.

Since the GVC concept will be used for analysis in the present case, this chapter will discuss two aspects which have so far largely been neglected by the GVC scholars: (i) the characteristics of the final consumer market; and (ii) the perspective of small and medium-sized enterprises (SMEs). Although it is argued that package-tour tourism can be clearly seen as a buyer-driven commodity chain and the German market shows the highest firm concentration in TOs in Europe (TUI, Thomas Cook and REWE as the major companies), there is not just one lead firm governing this cross-country business relationship. The approach at hand therefore sees less the power of a large firm as the main driver of this particular kind of value chain but rather specific rules and conventions between cooperating firms of fairly equal size and capacity. Hence governance in this specific case is characterized by:

> more symmetrical [power balance between the firms], given that both contribute key competence. There is a great deal of explicit coordination in relational global value chains, but it is achieved through a close dialogue between more or less equal partners.
>
> (Gereffi *et al.*, 2005: 88)

In contrast to previous approaches in tourism research, the GVC concept mainly deals with the supply side and starts from a product-specific view which is indicated by an input–output structure. In tourism as a service industry, the production process is considered as a multi-parallel activity rather than a sequential one (Fig. 11.1). Both TO and IA are in strategic bundling positions organizing different activities of different suppliers. Whereas TOs hold a double strategic position, coordinating the access to the final consumer market on the one hand and designing the travel product as a whole on the other, IAs in contrast are 'only' responsible for the smooth handling of the travel arrangements within a specific destination context as an integral part of the product.

German travellers purchase the package tour and later fly to Jordan to spend their time pursuing various leisure activities in the destination. Despite the trend for independent travel and e-purchase, it is assumed that the main share of cultural round trips, especially to destinations that differ from the source country in language, cultural history or background, will still be handled through package tours in the near future. In tourism as a service sector, consumers are actively involved in the production process, contrary to the large number of case studies within GVC research that have hitherto been carried out that focus on the industry sector. Since tourists simultaneously consume the provided services as they are produced, they are aware of what is referred to in managerial literature as the 'line of visibility' (Fig. 11.1). Territoriality, the spatial feature and another of Gereffi's four analytical levels, indicates that different business units are located in different countries (Fig. 11.1). In the present case, socio-economic players are situated either in the touristic incoming or outgoing country and are economically connected to each other, despite being separated by great geographical distances.

The analytical sections of the approach can be divided into a level of configuration, comprising *input–output structure* and *territoriality*, and a level of coordination, including the inner-chain *governance* and the *institutional* level, which includes the impacts on the GVC in Fig. 11.1 among others. Both conditions of coordination influence one another rather than being separated from each other. In contrast to Gereffi's concept, I will not deal with large transnationally operating

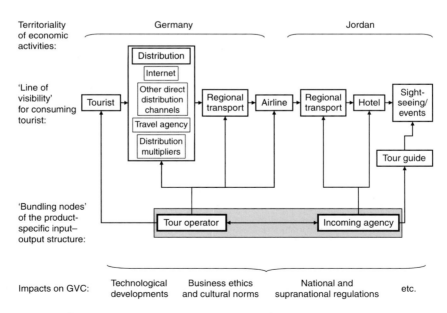

Fig. 11.1. Configuration of a global value chain (GVC) for a package tour.

companies in the present case but rather with SMEs. I will also rather neglect the institutional level, although I consider it utterly important, since it influences the extent and efficiency of the performed governance. Instead, I want to 'zoom' into the 'chain' and put the spotlight on what I have identified as one of the most important parts of the supply side, in order to look at the relationship between the TO and IA and how they collaborate with each other (Fig. 11.1). Gereffi (1995: 113) defines governance as the 'inter-firm relationships and institutional mechanisms through which non-market co-ordination of activities in the chain is achieved'. Thus, what mechanisms does the TO use to ensure that the upfront services that will be performed by the IA located in Jordan and communicated to the final consumer are of high quality and in scale? Surprisingly in the first instance, it is apparent that there is a great deal of heterogeneity in the mechanisms applied and these will be introduced and discussed in the next-but-one section. Additionally, it could be expected that if the number of German travellers to Jordan dropped significantly there might be no need to keep up the relationship with the local business partners. The question about the strategic consequences of this global–local business connection arises from nearly 3 years of disruption of German leisure travels to Jordan due to the aforementioned external shocks.

And the Consumers' Perspective?

Urry (2002b: 161), speaking of the 'end of tourism', refers more generally to an increasing homogeneity of the world's sites caused by the accelerating 'economy of signs'. This seems to be traceable, but in terms of touristic outgoing markets one can still speak of heterogeneous, if not rather 'closed' national markets, which are also handled by nationally operating TOs. Lash and Urry (1994: 254) state that '[t]he absence of sociology of travel illustrates the salience of these various priorities within the "academy"'. Research contributions in tourism sociology so far have concentrated on social travel conditions and development or issues about the importance of mobility and proximity (Lash and Urry, 1994; Schimany, 1999; Urry, 2002a). Others have mainly focused on motives and motivations of tourists as well as the effects of travelling on travellers, on hosting countries and on tourism employees (Vester, 1999). Recently, sociological interest has increased, particularly caused by perpetually changing and risk-susceptible tourists (Bachleitner, 2004). Only lately, scientists have multi-disciplinarily begun 'to rethink the implications of consumption for economics and politics' (Leslie and Reimer, 1999: 401). Yet a systemic theoretical approach is still unavailable.

Within the scope of the GVC debate, the concept was criticized for two aspects in particular: its emphasis on the production side and its insufficient reflection of consumer characteristics and patterns in the well-funded (Western) main sales market (Leslie and Reimer, 1999: 407). So far, the final consumer market for the previously analysed transnational companies in different industrial sectors has been assumed to simply be existent. However, small and medium-sized TOs have to permanently define and defend their niche markets. In today's polarizing markets, this argument also seems to apply increasingly to the final markets of large corporate groups. Original buyer groups of the past decades progressively abscond with the mainstream for the benefit of segmentation towards prestigious, expensive premium brands or towards good value products. Lash and Urry (1994: 273) add that the demand of today's consumers in the era of so-called 'post-Cookism'[4] has advanced to more flexible and individualized (package) tours. The increasingly polarized and segmented markets also exercise a sustainable impact on the 'production' of package tours. Today's consumer demand supports the development of more flexible and individualized package tours; the last decade indicated a shift towards product modularization. Whereas TOs first and foremost promote themselves, they also use popular regional images to promote destinations and to basically sell an illusion to the tourist by packaging these tours.

Not only in this specific context is information a vital part of the lately emerging and highly heterogeneous phenomenon '"new mobilities" paradigm' (Sheller and Urry, 2006: 208), constituted by a number of 'different social, geographical, and virtual elements' (Kesselring, 2006: 270). Various production and consumption sites in today's globalized world are connected from information receivers through unequally weighted information flows, some of them deployed highly strategically. In tourism, information flows, as one specific element of the 'new mobilities' paradigm, play a fundamental role, which eventually results in shaping a destination's image from the consumer's perspective, and his or her own security rating (e.g. after an external shock event affecting Jordan), and therefore its demand. Information permanently circulates between different firms, internal and external to the GVC at hand, between such firms and customers, between customers, between destinations, firms and customers, etc., which Sheller and Urry (2006: 212) refer to as 'many-to-many communications'. Heavyweight daily media reports as well as promotion campaigns of TOs or the national tourist boards are likely to influence, although to a differing extent, tourist travellers in their decision-making process in favour of or against a holiday destination.

Final consumers can be grouped into price-oriented or quality and service-oriented customers. Considering these different target groups any company's decision is either made in favour of standardized or sophisticated commodities and services. In turn, the categorization of a characteristic firm policy is either evident in a policy of market development or of market backup (Rudolph, 2001). This seems to be significant in the context of shifting consumer preferences, which consequently influence the downstream 'production' units as well as the marketing activities of the 'gate keeping' TO. Thus, in principle, a GVC can only be read from the final product and its consumers (Schamp, 2004). The spatial proximity between the consumer and the firm occupying these highly profitable, knowledge-intensive and marketing-oriented core segments sustains the firm's access monopoly to the final consumer market within the product-specific value chain. Hartwick (1998: 427) points out that '[i]mages are usually added to commodities at, or near, organizational centres [. . .] where the producers of sign value share the cultural norms of consumers'.

Strategic Mobility: Changing Business Relationships in a Changing Environment

Based on structured, in-depth personal interviews, empirical work has so far been carried out with 25 German TOs, between May 2004 and May 2005. These include some TO brands of the big companies, but mostly independent medium-sized and small TOs of regular Jordan packages as well as some occasional providers. The in-depth interviews were subsequently transcribed for the purpose of qualitative analysis as well as interpretation and predominantly take over the TO's perspective.

In reaction to the outbreak of the second Intifada in September 2000 and the ensuing sharp decline in tourism from Germany to Jordan, most of the investigated TOs took Jordan off their destination programme. Facing declining demand, Jordanian IAs tried to spread their risk and expanded to more resistant tourist source markets such as Eastern Europe, Russia or China. However, developing new source markets remains to be highly time and cost intensive (sunk costs) due to expenditures regarding research on the current market situation, tourist requirements or own promotional actions aiming at the local TOs, as long as local TO markets are actually established. To keep the business up, some IAs took part in price dumping. This indeed may have strengthened the price competitiveness for the TOs in their markets and might have led to lower consumer prices. Still, it seems to be futile if tourists will postpone their journey to Jordan for the benefit of other destinations despite these advantageous travel packages.

Tour operators' perspective: heterogeneous ways of cooperation and control

Before a business relationship can be set up, a TO needs to make sure that its local partner internalizes the specific requirements of the TO as well as those of German tourists. This can be realized in a number of different ways like searching different quotations of IAs, business travels of the TO product managers, meetings at trade fairs or visits by the IA in Germany. Though modes of contact initiation between both players are manifold, it seems that personal contacts, networks and recommendations are profound and essential.

TOs are fully liable to their customers for failings of the IA in the destination. To avoid opportunistic action of the IA, a TO needs to establish effective control mechanisms. In contrast to integrated TO structures, specialized small and medium-sized TOs have to apply pressure in alternative ways. Its success depends on several factors. Due to their comparatively low fault tolerance, SMEs have developed special management practices to control that kind of business relationship with their fairly equal but still dependent incoming business partners. Examples of these management practices range from modes of controlling the package production upfront, like different payment modes, to modes of control upon completion of the traveller's journey, such as a variety of feedback instruments.

A TO calculation of the number of tourists per group is based on economic principles. It is used to differentiate themselves from competitors. Some TOs work with travel catalogues, some do not. The former usually offer trips on a regular basis, whereas the latter offer the destination to customers in a more sporadic way. The minimum number of travellers per group with catalogue-TOs lies between 12 and 15. In contrast, specialized trekking providers undertake journeys starting with only four people. Often, homogeneous groups (people knowing each other before the journey, e.g. sports clubs, Christian communities) bring a turnout in excess of 20 people. Again, the aforementioned heterogeneity becomes apparent among German TOs offering Jordan as a destination.

Overall, empirical data suggest a large heterogeneity regarding the structures of cooperation mechanisms, often depending not least on the resources of the TO. Despite Jordan's minor importance as a holiday destination based on numbers of tourist arrivals, cooperation between TO and IA seems to be determined by factors of economic strength, which means frequency and regularity of trips as well as the realized numbers of guests.

Most IAs are driven by the expectations of follow-up business from the TO. In this connection Sayer (2000: 9) points out that: 'Cooperation occurs among firms in similar or related lines of business not simply because they trust one another but because they recognize that it is sometimes in their self-interest to do so.' However, there is in any case an immediate exit-alternative of collaboration because written contracts between both parties are not common practice. In the sense of Hirschman's (1970: 82) theory of exit, voice and loyalty, one may argue that in general a TO's voice is backed up by the IA's threat of the TO's exit. Moreover, this threat, to use Sayer's (2000: 9) words, 'may even be used to develop a long-term relationship'. This leads to another, supporting explanation of the two parties collaborating this closely. Large travel giants such as TUI have the power to define the needs and wishes of their customers. Because of their smaller demand and therefore weaker purchasing power, SMEs are not able to do so. Neither can they dictate prices to the extent of large travel companies. Rather, small and medium-sized TOs operating on niche markets need specialized, often even custom-made services and packages to compete in their market. Experience as well as repeatedly fulfilled expectations might lead to a successful business exchange over a long period of time. In this case, both players might establish interpersonal networks building on mutual trust and being socially embedded. For TOs it is important to rely on trustworthy incoming partners, in order to not constantly having to search for a new, unacquainted business partner. Again, sunk costs as well as low customer complaint rates due to an IA's high service quality orientation are economic arguments for sticking to a rather stable relationship from a TO's point of view.

A number of TOs even maintain relatively stable relationships with more than one local partner. Among other reasons, TOs justified this by: (i) *strategic considerations* during the high season, which enables the TO to deal more easily with expected bottlenecks of service providers, such as hotels in the destination; and (ii) *aspects of competition*, through which TOs try to encourage competition between IAs in order to succeed in their own TO market, offering competitive products in terms of quality and price in the long run.

Embedded modes of control and sanction seem to be important for the present cooperation between TO and IA due to its partly non-existent legal coverage. Pressure exerted on the IA can be roughly subdivided into *ex ante* mechanisms regarding service procurement and modes working *ex post* upon completion of the journey.

First, looking at the phase of service procurement, data suggest that TOs with comparatively high purchasing power severely negotiate final prices with their local partners, as one interview partner expressed:

> I take the prices I don't agree with and do not calculate with them but with lower prices. Afterwards, I re-negotiate the contract with the IA [. . .]. We carry the risk of sales and marketing, so we expect good prices.
>
> (Interview 2, translated)

Considering this statement, one can argue that IAs have clear reasons to accept such dictated conditions. Some economically strong TOs might inherit image functions associated with a certain reputation that IAs can rely on during their customer acquisition process. On the other hand, TOs have exclusive *access* to the final consumer market, operating in the highest capitalist accumulation functions such as marketing, branding, sales or distribution. The economic criterion 'buying power' is pivotal to a successful accomplishment of cooperation in favour of the TO. Mostly 'weaker' TOs did affirm a less insistent way of purchasing services as the following example shows:

> The IA has a very good buying power in Jordan; we would have no chance to get these good prices.
>
> (Interview 8, translated)

Secondly, financially strong TOs with large legal departments partly and pre-liminarily insure against secondary service providers like hotels. Product managers of TOs regularly travel to the destinations to make inspections, albeit that these inspections have no legal meaning. On the one hand, they become acquainted with 'their' products while they check for example the quality of hotels or transport facilities. In very few cases TOs were not in a position, financially and in terms of staff, to undertake such inspection visits. Hence, without destination-specific knowledge the product definition power for the package tour is to a large degree dislocated from the TO and instead the responsibility for product definition lies with the local partners.

Similar to the thus far outlined heterogeneity of cooperation mechanisms, payment modes between both players vary as well. Some TOs pay for the package fully or partly in advance, whereas other TOs are invoiced for the whole travel package after tourists return from the journey. In case of justified complaints against an IA, TOs have varied chances regarding financial compensation from the IA depending on the mode of payment. For example, TOs who did not (fully) pay in advance are able financially to balance the complaint instantly by withholding the outstanding share of payment, while TOs who paid in full in advance apparently cannot realize this. In this case, data suggest TOs differ in their views between those who have hardly any chance of getting financial compensation from the IA and those who smoothly enforce it. The latter explain it with 'trust'. It is assumed that trust in this case is based on the TO's economic strength in Jordan. Noticeably, in long-term relations *ex post* payments were more accepted than in short-term relationships. IAs, dependent on the volume of business from TOs, might act more opportunely in case of sporadic business where the cost value ratio is inferior to that of constant relationships.

So far, short-term external impacts on the business relations between TOs and IAs have been discussed. The process of space–time compression (Harvey, 1990; Lash and Urry, 1994) can be traced back to enhanced information and communication technologies. Customer expectations have changed as they ask for flexible tour packages and reduced time response. Taking up new technologies like the Internet or computer reservation systems has transformed business relations between TOs and IAs, who now handle customer demand by minimizing responding time and flexibly creating customized tour packages, etc. According to Flaschka's (1998) assumption, TOs might become redundant due to the fast-changing technology and the possibilities for individuals to book each travel service without resorting to an intermediary such as a TO. He argues that this development would give rise to a radical change of the industry's established structure. However, especially with respect to widely non-familiar holiday destinations like Jordan with German tourists, where the language and culture are quite different, this assumed development on the supply-side's structure seems thus far to be questionable. Hence the configuration of the business relationship between TOs and IAs described above is still applicable.

Final option exit?

Data imply that there is no homogeneous regulatory procedure regarding legal coverage between the two firms. Surprisingly, often written legal contracts between them are rather uncommon. However, subsidiaries of integrated firms do place a legal contract with their business partners but interviews have shown that no TO ever sued their local business partners. Instead, formal legal contracts have a deterrent effect. Verbal contracts, common with the independent small and medium-sized TOs, enable both business partners to save costs due to time savings as a result of a low level of bureaucracy and being appropriately flexible to change business partners in case of one side's low performance. In general, the exit of one partner is relatively simple, as there is no legal contract between both players. As mentioned above, taking legal action is neither target-oriented to both agents, nor reasonable. Therefore, the fastest and cheapest alternative is to withdraw from their cooperation. Serious service failings, non-competitive prices as well as dishonesty regarding changes in the destination are the most common reasons causing a TO's *exit* of the partnership. One may argue that a TO's *voice* is backed up by the IA's threat of the TO's exit. Data also suggest that in most cases the voice option is chosen over an exit strategy. Hirschman (1970: 125) notes, 'conditions are seldom favourable for the emergence of any stable and optimal mix of exit and voice', but each firm has to find its own mix of exit and voice via trial and error, which underlines the large heterogeneity. As suggested above, TOs try to set up stable relations with their local partners due to high transaction costs as well as sunk costs in case of searching for new local partners. TOs, being interested in serving Jordan as a long-term destination, are assumed to invest time in communicating their expectations to their local partners and making emphatically sure the IA understands exactly. Informal contacts such as e-mailing, telephone calls, visits, fair trade shows, etc. contribute to keeping up the contact between individuals in charge of TO and IA. Exits seldom occur, for example during a continuous absence of German tourist arrivals as happened between the years 2000 and 2003. Of course, to stay in business both players, TO and IA, will try to avoid becoming too strongly dependent on the other side by diversifying risk strategies, regarding, that is, their customers (IA) or their destinations (TO). However, the high investment in the form of sunk costs when establishing a new market explains a relatively low number of TOs ceasing the relationship within a time period of more than 1 year. After this dry spell, in most cases, business partners have not changed and business between the German TO and Jordanian IA is flourishing again today.

Conclusions

Long-lasting, dependent relationships between both players might be in peril in times of tourism absence, especially for the local IA. The chapter further explored the question of the implications of tourism travel performance for two selected small and medium-sized economic players, TOs and IAs. Sudden external changes as well as long-term changes were debated. With the help of the systemic GVC approach, I referred to one important aspect of the local–global collaboration between different organizational package-tour business units as well as to their sensitivity to external shocks in terms of a sudden drop of tourist arrivals. Since leisure travel can be seen as luxury goods, IAs are dependent on their partners in the outgoing country because of their strategic position along the value chain. Moreover, comparatively small destinations like Jordan as well as its tourism industry are highly vulnerable due to the flexibility of TOs to change their offered destinations. TOs did not invest in real estate and therefore experience no need to ensure the occupancy of hotels.

Three findings were essential in this chapter. First, it was possible to show that the global–local business connections between the German small and medium-sized TO and the Jordanian IA within a changing external political environment of the destination mainly remained stable and would not be given up for the benefit of short-term price advantages.

Secondly, it was indicated that the stability of these relationships largely depends on the realized economic strength of a TO in a specific destination. The majority of the thus-far interviewed German small and medium-sized TOs tend to build long-lasting relationships, despite the increasing price-competition in the TO's market. Sayer's (2000: 9) summary can be transferred to the discussed relationship: 'The more firms need each other the more they are likely to develop trust relations beyond a base level of generalized probity to a level where they put considerable trust in each other.' Hirschman (1970: 82) adds that 'chances for voice to function effectively as a recuperation mechanism are appreciably strengthened if voice is backed up by the threat of exit'. Recapitulating, social structures with their various characteristics such as trust, mutual understanding or shared values and behaviour between business partners are in this case a key basis for the economic interaction between both TO and IA.

Thirdly, it has been shown that there exists a large heterogeneity between the TO's ability to actually perform according to their strategic chain position. In general, TOs are able to control important value chain interfaces between the demand and the supply side as well as between different suppliers due to their strategic position. However, not all interviewed TOs benefit from this strategic advantage. External, accompanying determinants, such as the significance of the destination for a TO and therefore the frequency and number of performed package tours, play a crucial role for their destination-specific economic strength.

In this chapter, mobility was predominantly discussed in terms of 'mobility of adjustment' in reaction to strategic economic challenges caused by changing environmental settings. From a socio-economic point of view, the focus lay on two central players on the supply side in the tourism industry. No occasion legitimates speaking about the 'end of tourism' within the context setting of this chapter. Although the regional political environment of the destination of Jordan is presently rather unstable, there are many reasons to disprove its 'end of tourism'. Jordan has some unique selling points like the rock-carved rose-red city of Petra as well as important religious sites, which will facilitate tourist flows to Jordan from all over the world.

Acknowledgement

This chapter has benefited from an ongoing research project funded by the German Research Council (DFG).

Notes

[1]Bair (2005) provides a comprehensive debate about the background and development of the GVC research school, its intentions and the development of varying approaches reflected in different terms such as global value chains or global production networks.

[2]An exception is TUI's one package tour in wellness tourism to the Dead Sea, which still only generates a small business number to Jordan and will therefore only be included in this analysis in a minor way (as of spring 2005).

[3]Exceptions might include culturally similar markets, for example the Germanophone markets like Germany, Austria, partly Switzerland, etc., where the language barrier is not applicable.

[4]Derived from the 'inventor' of mass tourism, Thomas Cook, 'post-Cookism' means to overcome Fordist consumption.

References

Auswärtiges Amt, Deutschland (2005) Länder- und Reiseinformationen Ägypten. Available at: http://www.auswaertiges-amt.de/diplo/de/Laenderinformationen/Aegypten/Bilateral.html#t2 (accessed 10 October 2006).

Bachleitner, R. (2004) Tourismussoziologie oder zur Soziologie des Reisens. *Sociologia Internationalis* 42(2), 243–263.

Bair, J. (2005) Global capitalism and commodity chains: looking back, going forward. *Competition and Change* 9(2), 153–180.

Barham, N. (2004) Tourismus in Jordanien. In: Meyer, G. (ed.) *Die arabische Welt im Spiegel der Kulturgeographie.* ZEFAW, Mainz, Germany.

Britton, S. (1991) Tourism, capital, and place: towards a critical geography of tourism. *Environment and Planning D: Society and Space* 9(4), 451–478.

Clancy, M. (1998) Commodity chains, services and development: theory and preliminary evidence from the tourism industry. *Review of International Political Economy* 5(1), 122–148.

Flaschka, M. (1998) *The Intelligent Travel Company. Enhancing the Intelligence of Travel Companies through Management Systems.* Haupt, Bern, Switzerland.

Forschungsgemeinschaft Urlaub und Reisen e.V. (FUR) (2005) *RA Reiseanalyse Aktuell 2005.* FUR, Hamburg, Germany.

Gereffi, G. (1994) The international economy and economic development. In: Smelser, N.J. and Swedberg, R. (eds) *Handbook of Economic Sociology.* Princeton University Press, Princeton, New Jersey, pp. 206–233.

Gereffi, G. (1995) Global production systems and third world development. In: Stallings, B. (ed.) *Global Change, Regional Response. The New International Context of Development.* Cambridge University Press, Cambridge, UK.

Gereffi, G. (1996) Global commodity chains: new forms of coordination and control among nations and firms in international industries. *Competition and Change* 1(4), 427–439.

Gereffi, G., Humphrey, J. and Sturgeon, T. (2005) The governance of global value chains. *Review of International Political Economy* 12(1), 78–104.

Hartwick, E. (1998) Geographies of consumption: a commodity-chain approach. *Environment and Planning D: Society and Space* 16(4), 423–437.

Harvey, D. (1990) *The Condition of Postmodernity.* Blackwell, Oxford, UK.

Hirschman, A.O. (1970) *Exit, Voice, and Loyalty: Responses to Decline in Firms, Organizations, and States.* Harvard University Press, Cambridge, Massachusetts.

Ioannides, D. and Debbage, K.G. (eds) (1998) *The Economic Geography of the Tourist Industry.* Routledge, London.

Kesselring, S. (2006) Pioneering mobilities: new patterns of movement and mobility in a mobile world. *Environment and Planning A* 38(2), 269–279.

Lash, S. and Urry, J. (1994) *Economies of Signs and Space.* Sage, London.

Leslie, D. and Reimer, S. (1999) Spatializing commodity chains. *Progress in Human Geography* 23(3), 401–420.

Ministry of Tourism (2005) Tourists by Nationality 2004. Ministry of Tourism, Information Statistics Dept., Amman, Jordan. Available at: http://www.tourism.jo/GuestBook/Statistics.asp (accessed 17 December 2007).

Mosedale, J. (2006) Tourism commodity chains: market entry and its effects on St Lucia. *Current Issues in Tourism* 9(4 and 5), 436–458.

Rudolph, H. (2001) Der Lebensmitteleinzelhandel als Treiber weltregionaler Warenketten. In: Rudolph, H. (ed.) *Aldi oder Arkaden? – Unternehmen und Arbeit im europäischen Einzelhandel.* Ed. Sigma, Berlin, pp. 81–102.

Sayer, A. (2000) Markets, Embeddedness and Trust: Problems of Polysemy an Idealism. Sociology Department, Lancaster University, Lancaster, UK. Available at: http://www.lancs.ac.uk/fss/sociology/papers/sayer-markets-embeddedness-and-trust.pdf (accessed 2 June 2005).

Schamp, E.W. (2004) Lokale Verankerung und Globale Vernetzung – Neue Konzepte in der Wirtschaftsgeographie. Paper presented at the Thursday Evening Lecture at SFB 560, Bayreuth, Germany, 22 January.

Schimany, P. (1999) Tourismussoziologie zwischen Begrenzung und Entgrenzung. Eine vorläufige Zwischenbilanz. In: Bachleitner, R. and Schimany, P. (eds) *Grenzenlose Gesellschaft – Grenzenloser Tourismus? Neue Ergebnisse der Tourismussoziologie.* Profilverlag, München, pp. 7–24.

Sheller, M. and Urry, J. (2006) The new mobilities paradigm. *Environment and Planning A* 38(2), 207–226.

Urry, J. (2002a) Mobility and proximity. *Sociology* 36(2), 255–274.

Urry, J. (2002b) *The Tourist Gaze.* Sage, London.

Vester, H.-G. (1999) *Tourismustheorie. Soziologische Wegweiser zum Verständnis Touristischer Phänomene.* Profilverlag, München, Germany.

Index